CONTEMPORARY STYLISTICS

Also available from Continuum

Geoffrey Sampson and Diana McCarthy: *Corpus Linguistics*

M. A. K. Halliday and Jonathan J. Webster: *Linguistic Studies of Text and Discourse*

CONTEMPORARY STYLISTICS

Edited by
Marina Lambrou and Peter Stockwell

continuum

Continuum

The Tower Building
11 York Road
London SE1 7NX

80 Maiden Lane, Suite 704
New York
NY 10038

First published in 2007
Paperback edition 2010

British Library Cataloguing-in-Publication Data
A catalogue record for this book is available from the British Library.

ISBN: 978–14411–8384–2 (paperback)

Library of Congress Cataloging-in-Publication Data
A catalog record for this book is available from the Library of Congress.

Typeset by YHT Ltd, London
Printed and bound by Antony Rowe

Contents

Acknowledgements   viii

Notes on Contributors   ix

Introduction: The State of Contemporary Stylistics –
Marina Lambrou and Peter Stockwell   1

PART A – STYLISTICS OF PROSE   5

Chapter 1   Woolf's Experiments with Consciousness in
             Fiction – *Violeta Sotirova*
             Introduced by Lesley Jeffries   7

Chapter 2   A Corpus Stylistic Perspective on Dickens' *Great
             Expectations* – *Michaela Mahlberg*
             Introduced by Michael McCarthy   19

Chapter 3   The Stylistics of True Crime: Mapping the Minds of
             Serial Killers – *Christiana Gregoriou*
             Introduced by Urszula Clark   32

Chapter 4   'Do you want to hear about it?' Exploring Possible
             Worlds in Michael Joyce's Hyperfiction, *afternoon, a
             story* – *Alice Bell*
             Introduced by Brian McHale   43

Chapter 5   The Effects of Free Indirect Discourse: Empathy
             Revisited – *Joe Bray*
             Introduced by Geoff Hall   56

Chapter 6   The Stylistics of Cappuccino Fiction: A Socio-cognitive
             Perspective – *Rocio Montoro*
             Introduced by Imelda Whelehan   68

Chapter 7   Attribution Theory: Action and Emotion in Dickens and
             Pynchon – *Alan Palmer*
             Introduced by Elena Semino   81

Chapter 8   *Bridget Jones's Diary* and Feminist Narratology – *Ruth Page*
               Introduced by Sara Mills   93

Chapter 9   Schema Poetics and Crossover Fiction – *Clare Walsh*
               Introduced by John McRae   106

Chapter 10   Deixis, Cognition and the Construction of Viewpoint –
               Dan McIntyre
               Introduced by Paul Simpson   118

PART B – STYLISTICS OF POETRY   131

Chapter 11   'And everyone and I stopped breathing': Familiarity and
               Ambiguity in the Text World of 'The day lady died' –
               Joanna Gavins
               Introduced by Catherine Emmott   133

Chapter 12   'Progress is a comfortable disease': Cognition in a Stylistic
               Analysis of e.e. cummings – *Michael Burke*
               Introduced by Peter Stockwell   144

Chapter 13   Megametaphorical Mappings and the Landscapes of
               Canadian Poetry – *Ernestine Lahey*
               Introduced by Peter Verdonk   156

Chapter 14   Perception and the Lyric: The Emerging Mind of the
               Poem – *Sharon Lattig*
               Introduced by Alan Durant   168

Chapter 15   Stylistics and Language Teaching: Deviant Collocation in
               Literature as a Tool for Vocabulary Expansion –
               Dany Badran
               Introduced by Ron Carter   180

PART C – STYLISTICS OF DIALOGUE AND DRAMA   193

Chapter 16   Oral Accounts of Personal Experiences: When is a
               Narrative a Recount? – *Marina Lambrou*
               Introduced by David Herman   195

Chapter 17   'Never a truer word said in jest': A Pragmastylistic
               Analysis of Impoliteness as Banter in *Henry IV, Part I* –
               Derek Bousfield
               Introduced by Billy Clark   209

Chapter 18   The Cognitive Rhetoric of Arthur Miller's *The Crucible* –
             Craig Hamilton
             Introduced by Peter Crisp   221

Chapter 19   The Stylistics of Drama: *The Reign of King Edward III* –
             Beatrix Busse
             Introduced by Monika Fludernik   232

Chapter 20   Computer-assisted Literary Stylistics: The State of the
             Field – *Dawn Archer*
             Introduced by Jonathan Culpeper   244

References   257
Index   285

Acknowledgements

The authors and editors would like to thank the following for allowing reproduction of their copyright work:

Alan Moore, Eddie Campbell and Chris Staros from Top Shelf Productions for
    the panels of *From Hell*, www.topshelfcomix.com
The estate of e.e. cummings and Norton publishers for 'the hours rise up putting
    off stars' from *Tulips & Chimneys* (1923).
The Doors Music Company (administered by Wixen Music Publishing, Inc.) for
    lyrics of 'Awake' from the album *An American Prayer* (released 1978).

Every effort has been made to contact other copyright holders. If any material has
been missed, we will be pleased to make a correction at the earliest opportunity.

Notes on Contributors

Dawn Archer is a Reader in Corpus Linguistics at the University of Central Lancashire. Her research interests are in (historical) pragmatics, stylistics and corpus linguistics (particularly, the development of pragmatic annotation schemes). Her publications include *Questions and Answers in the English Courtroom (1640-1760)* (2005) and *What's in a Word-list? Investigating word frequency and keyword extraction* (ed.) (2009).

Dany Badran is Assistant Professor at the Lebanese American University in Beirut. He has research interests in modality, language and politics, rhetoric and stylistics in general. He took his doctorate, 'Ideology through modality in discourse analysis' (2003) at the University of Nottingham.

Alice Bell is a lecturer at Sheffield Hallam University. Her main research interests are narrative theory, digital literature, stylistics and Possible Worlds Theory. She is author of *The Possible Worlds of Hypertext Fiction* (Palgrave Macmillan, forthcoming 2010).

Derek Bousfield is a lecturer in English Language and Linguistics at the University of Central Lancashire, UK. His main research interests are in pragmatics, stylistics, aspects of context, and linguistic approaches to impoliteness, conflict management and conflict resolution. He is the author of *Impoliteness in Interaction*, and co-editor of *Impoliteness in Language* (with Miriam Locher); *Stylistics and Social Cognition* (with Lesley Jeffries and Dan McIntyre); and a special edition of the *Journal of Politeness Research* entitled in 'Impoliteness: Eclecticism and Diaspora' (with Jonathan Culpeper).

Joe Bray lectures at the University of Sheffield, where he works on literary stylistics. He is the author of *The Epistolary Novel: Representations of Consciousness* (Routledge, 2003), *The Female Reader in the Late Eighteenth-Century Novel* (Routledge, 2008) and he co-edited *Ma(r)king the Text: The Presentation of Meaning on the Literary Page* (Ashgate, 2000).

Michael Burke is a senior lecturer at the Roosevelt Academy, a college of Utrecht University in Middleburg, Netherlands. His research interests are classical rhetoric, cognitive stylistics, critical discourse analysis and argumentation analysis. He co-edited *Contextualized Stylistics* (with Tony Bex and Peter Stockwell, Rodopi, 2000).

Beatrix Busse is an assistant professor at the University of Berne. Her research interests include the history of English, stylistics, (historical) pragmatics, Shakespeare studies, corpus linguistics, narratology, cognitive linguistics and e-learning and e-teaching. She is the author of *Vocative Constructions in the Language of Shakespeare* (John Benjamins, 2006).

Ron Carter is Professor of Modern English Language at the University of Nottingham. He is a fellow of the Royal Society of Arts, a fellow of the Academy for Social Sciences, a member of the ESRC Virtual College and Chair of the British Association for Applied Linguistics. He has written and edited more than 50 books in the fields of literary linguistics, language and education, applied linguistics and the teaching of English.

Billy Clark works at Middlesex University, where his research interests centre mainly on linguistic meaning (semantics and pragmatics). He is currently working on intonational meaning, pragmatic stylistics and the inferential processes involved in writing. He was Section Editor and contributor for the section on 'Foundations of linguistics' in the ten-volume *Elsevier Encyclopedia of Language and Linguistics*, edited by Keith Brown in 2006. He is currently preparing a textbook on 'Relevance Theory' for Cambridge University Press.

Urszula Clark is a senior lecturer in English at Aston University. Her research interests include language and identity, stylistics, particularly popular fiction, theories of discourse, sociohistorical dialectology, language and education, and discourse analysis. Her publications include *Studying Language: English in Action* (Palgrave, 2006) and *War Words: Language, History and the Disciplining of English* (Elsevier, 2001).

Peter Crisp is a senior lecturer in English at the Chinese University in Hong Kong. His major research interests are in metaphor in poetry and literature, the identification of metaphorical language, cognitive poetics, literary stylistics, the acquisition of second languages, metaphorical competence by Chinese learners of English and the cross-linguistic/cultural study of metaphor in English and Chinese.

Jonathan Culpeper is a lecturer at Lancaster University. His main research interests are centred in historical pragmatics, cognitive linguistics and corpus stylistics. His publications include *Language and Characterisation: People in Plays and Other Texts* (Longman, 2001), *Studying Drama: From Text to Context* (with Mick Short and Peter Verdonk, Routledge, 1998), and he is currently writing *Early Modern English Dialogues: Spoken Interaction as Writing* (with Prof. Merja Kytö, for Cambridge University Press).

Alan Durant is Professor of Communication at Middlesex University Business School, London, where his current research is into the adjudication of contested meanings in media law. His publications include the co-authored *Ways of Reading: Advanced Reading Skills for Students of Literature* (Routledge, 2006), *How to Write Essays and Dissertations* (Pearson, 2005), *The Linguistics of Writing: Arguments between*

Language and Literature (Manchester University Press, 1987) and *Literary Studies in Action* (Routledge, 1990).

Catherine Emmott is a senior lecturer at the University of Glasgow. She is Assistant Editor of *Language and Literature*, the international journal of the *Poetics and Linguistics Association* (PALA). Her main research interests are in the mental processing of text, discourse anaphora and stylistics. Her publications include *Narrative Comprehension: A Discourse Perspective* (Oxford University Press, 1997).

Monika Fludernik is Professor of English Literature at Albert Ludwigs University in Freiburg. She is on the editorial board of *Language and Literature* and *Style* journals. Her publications include *Towards a 'Natural' Narratology* (Routledge, 1996) and *The Fictions of Language and the Languages of Fiction* (Routledge, 1993).

Joanna Gavins is a lecturer at the University of Sheffield. Her research is in the interface of literary and linguistic study with particular interests in the area of cognitive poetics, specifically Text World Theory. She is Co-editor, with Gerard Steen, of *Cognitive Poetics in Practice* (Routledge, 2002) and her most recent book was *Text World Theory: An Introduction* (Edinburgh University Press, 2007).

Christiana Gregoriou is a lecturer at the University of Leeds. She teaches on the language and literature interface, and in cognitive poetics. She has recently published *Deviance in Contemporary Crime Fiction* (Palgrave, 2007).

Geoff Hall is a senior lecturer at the University of Swansea. His research interests are in applied linguistics and literary stylistics. Recent publications include *Literature in Language Education* (Palgrave Macmillan, 2005). He is Assistant Editor of the journal *Language and Literature*.

Craig Hamilton is Senior Lecturer at the University of Haute Alsace. He has written widely on his primary research areas of cognitive poetics, cognitive rhetoric and cognitive linguistic approaches to modern literature. He took his PhD in mind, body and metaphor in W. H. Auden from the University of Maryland.

David Herman is a professor at Ohio State University where he is also Director of Project Narrative. His main research interests are interdisciplinary narrative theory; discourse analysis; conversational and multimodal storytelling; cognitive science and narrative; twentieth-century studies; modern and postmodern narrative; critical theory and linguistic and cognitive approaches to literature. His publications include *Story Logic* (University of Nebraska Press, 2002) and the *Routledge Encyclopedia of Narrative Theory* (co-edited with Manfred Jahn and Marie-Laure Ryan, Routledge, 2005).

Lesley Jeffries is Professor of English Language at the University of Huddersfield. She has recently completed *Textual Construction of the Female Body: A Critical Discourse Approach* (Palgrave Macmillan, 2007) and is working on the application of discourse analysis to conflict situations and the resolution of conflict. She edits a language textbook series for Palgrave, and is currently the Chair of the Poetics and Linguistics Association (PALA).

Ernestine Lahey is a lecturer at Roosevelt Academy, Middleburg, Netherlands. Her research interests include cognitive poetics, Text World Theory, English-Canadian literature and literary landscapes. Her doctoral thesis was entitled, 'Text-world landscapes and English-Canadian national identity in the poetry of Al Purdy, Milton Acorn and Alden Nowlan'.

Marina Lambrou is a senior lecturer in English Language and Communication at Kingston University, London. Her main areas of interests include non literary stylistics, narrative theory, particularly oral narratives, spoken and written discourse, language in the media including the mediation of personal narratives, and sociolinguistics. She is the co-author of *Language and Media* (with Alan Durant, Routledge, 2009)

Sharon Lattig teaches American literature at the University of Connecticut, Stamford. At present, she is co-editing the volume *Prospect and Retrospect* with David Hoover (Rodopi, 2007). A poet, Sharon holds an M.F.A. in creative writing from the City College of New York and is the Poetry Series Curator at the Dactyl Foundation for the Arts and Humanities.

Michael McCarthy is Emeritus Professor of Applied Linguistics, University of Nottingham; Adjunct Professor of Applied Linguistics, Penn State University, USA; and Adjunct Professor of Applied Linguistics, University of Limerick, Ireland. He is a Fellow of the Royal Society of Arts, and the author of many influential books in applied linguistics.

Brian McHale is a professor of English at the Ohio State University. He is the author of *Postmodernist Fiction* (Methuen, 1987), *Constructing Postmodernism* (1992) and *The Obligation towards the Difficult Whole* (2004), and is Co-editor with Randall Stevenson of *The Edinburgh Companion to Twentieth-Century Literatures in English* (2006).

Dan McIntyre is Senior Lecturer in English Language at the University of Huddersfield. His current research interests include corpus stylistics and the stylistics of film. He is the author of *Point of View in Plays* (John Benjamins, 2006), *History of English* (Routledge, 2008) and co-editor of *Stylistics and Social Cognition* (Rodopi, 2007). He is the series editor of *Advances in Stylistics* (Continuum) and co-series editor of *Perspectives on the English Language* series (Palgrave, with Lesley Jeffries).

John McRae is Special Professor at the University of Nottingham, and Visiting Professor at the University of Avignon. He has published several books in language pedagogy, stylistics and international Englishes, including *The Routledge History of Literature in English* (2001), *Language, Literature and the Learner* (Longman, 1996), both with Ron Carter, and (with Ed Vethamani) *Now Read On: A Course in Multicultural Reading* (Routledge, 1999).

Michaela Mahlberg is a lecturer at the University of Liverpool. She has worked at the Universities of Bari, Birmingham, Saarbrücken, and Liverpool Hope University College. She is the author of *English General Nouns: A Corpus Theoretical*

Approach (John Benjamins, 2005), Editor of the *International Journal of Corpus Linguistics* (John Benjamins) and Co-editor of the series *Corpus and Discourse* (Continuum).

Sara Mills is Research Professor in Linguistics at Sheffield Hallam University. Her publications include *Discourses of Difference* (Routledge, 1991), *Feminist Stylistics* (Routledge 1996), *Discourse* (Routledge 1998) and *Gender and Politeness* (2003). She is also co-editor of *Gender and Language*, the new journal of the International Gender and Language Association (IGALA).

Rocio Montoro is a lecturer at the University of Huddersfield. She is interested in the stylistic analysis of cappuccino fiction, the interface of literature and film and the applicability of cognitive models of analysis to media, literary and cinematic discourses. She is writing a book on *The Poetics of Cappuccino Fiction.*

Ruth Page is a senior lecturer at the University of Central England. Her research interests lie in narrative analysis and language and gender studies. She has published various works which focus on feminist narratology, including *Literary and Linguistic Approaches to Feminist Narratology* (Palgrave, 2006).

Alan Palmer is an independent scholar living in London. His book *Fictional Minds* (University of Nebraska Press, 2004) has won the Modern Language Association Prize for Independent Scholars and also the Perkins Prize (awarded by the Society for the Study of Narrative Literature). He is an honorary research fellow at Lancaster University.

Elena Semino teaches and researches at Lancaster University. Her interests are in stylistics, corpus linguistics and cognitive linguistics (especially cognitive metaphor theory). Her publications include *Corpus Stylistics: Speech, Writing and Thought Presentation in a Corpus of English Narratives* (with Mick Short, Routledge, 2004) and *Cognitive Stylistics: Language and Cognition in Text Analysis* (with Jonathan Culpeper, John Benjamins, 2002)

Paul Simpson is Professor of English Language in the School of English at Queen's University Belfast. He is best known for his books and articles in stylistics and critical linguistics, including *Language, Ideology and Point of View* (Routledge, 1993), *Language through Literature* (Routledge, 1997) and *Stylistics* (Routledge, 2004). He is the co-editor of *Language, Discourse and Literature* (Unwin Hyman, 1989) and is Editor of the journal *Language and Literature.*

Violeta Sotirova is a lecturer at the University of Nottingham. Her research interests are in the field of stylistics, narrative theory, discourse analysis and history of the novel. Her doctorate, 'Dialogism in free indirect style', was completed at the University of Manchester (2003).

Peter Stockwell is Professor of Literary Linguistics at the University of Nottingham. His most recent books include *Texture: A Cognitive Aesthetics of Reading* (Edinburgh UP, 2009), several volumes and editions in sociolinguistics (with Routledge), *Language in Theory* (with Mark Robson, Routledge, 2004), *Cognitive*

Poetics (Routledge, 2002), *The Poetics of Science Fiction* (Longman, 2000), the co-edited *Language and Literature Reader* (Routledge, 2008), and *Contextualized Stylistics* (Rodopi, 2000), He is the Editor of the *Routledge English Language Introductions* series.

Peter Verdonk is Emeritus Professor of Stylistics in the University of Amsterdam. His main interests lie in rhetoric, literary criticism, discourse analysis, narratology and cognitive poetics. His books include *Twentieth-Century Poetry* (1993), *Twentieth-Century Fiction* (with Jean Jacques Weber, 1995), *Exploring the Language of Drama* (with Jonathan Culpeper and Mick Short, 1998) and *Stylistics* (Oxford University Press, 2002).

Clare Walsh is a senior lecturer at the University of Bedfordshire. She has published in the field of language and gender as well as a number of articles on the poetics of young adult fiction. Her book *Gender and Discourse: Language and Power in Politics, the Church and Other Organisations* was published by Longman in 2001. She is currently working on a book on the poetics of young adult and crossover fiction.

Imelda Whelehan is Professor of English and Women's Studies at De Montfort University, Leicester. Her research is in the fields of women's writing, feminism and literary adaptations. Her publications include *Modern Feminist Thought* (New York University Press, 1995), *Helen Fielding's Bridget Jones' Diary: A Reader's Guide* (Continuum, 2002) and *The Feminist Bestseller* (Palgrave Macmillan, 2005). She has recently co-edited *The Cambridge Companion to Literature on Screen* (Cambridge University Press).

Introduction: The State of Contemporary Stylistics

Marina Lambrou and Peter Stockwell

Contemporary Stylistics presents the current state of the integrated study of language and literature. From its emergence as an interdisciplinary blend of literary criticism, linguistics, psychology, cognitive science, social studies and philosophy, *stylistics* is now a mature and vibrant single discipline, with a confident new generation of researchers engaged in the proper study of literature. This book collects some of these new voices together for the first time, and presents their latest work in a form that is accessible and placed into context. The book includes specific introductions to each piece of work by an established figure in stylistics. Taken together, the book offers a comprehensive showcase for the range of approaches and practices which form modern stylistics: from cognitive poetics to corpus linguistics, from explorations of mind style and spoken discourse in narrative to the workings of viewpoint in lyric poetry, from word meanings to the meanings and emotions of literary worlds, and more.

In identifying the new generation of stylisticians, we were faced with an embarrassment of riches: stylistics is practised in its broadest terms across the world, across all the fields of literary scholarship, genre, culture and period, and is increasingly used as the core discipline for further interdisciplinary encounters with literary historiography, critical theory, second language and cultural pedagogy and other forms of literary and language study. More stylisticians are being trained and are holding important academic posts than ever before. More students and graduate researchers are being enthused by the energy and rigour of stylistics than ever before. In order to keep the book under control, we set ourselves a limit in determining a profile for our contributors: each had to be in the first few years of their full academic career; each had to have a proven research record in terms of published articles and conference paper output; more trickily for us, in each contributor we had to see the sort of passion and sharp analytical intelligence that convinced us that here was a person who would be significant in the field in the future.

In literary studies in general, stylistics offers rational and progressive continuity where there is elsewhere so much self-generated crisis. In this book, we also wanted to demonstrate these features of the discipline. An appreciation of earlier work makes it possible for this generation, and indeed subsequent generations of stylisticians, to make further advances through new research. Our new stylisticians have enough self-confidence to respect previous work and develop it, without being threatened by past success or afraid to challenge perceived deficiencies in order to progress the discipline. We gave our contributors an almost free licence to produce a chapter from their own latest research with just a few suggestions as a guide: we asked them to apply or critique an existing model for stylistic analysis; present a new tool, model or method for analysis; review or discuss the current state, thinking or advances in stylistics; provide a comparative stylistic analysis or discussion across texts or a comparison in the historical sense of literary analysis. As the central focus, all the chapters present accessible, practical, stylistic analysis of a particular text that is also challenging and original. Taken altogether, the book covers an extraordinarily broad range of literary genres and texts.

In order to pay proper attention to the traditions, roots and richness of stylistics, we asked several key figures in the field to introduce each chapter. It is a mark of the collegiality of the discipline of stylistics that almost everyone we asked enthusiastically agreed to support this project. We gave our eminent writers a narrower brief: they had to pick out the key features of the chapter, and highlight where the writer was doing something significant or particularly interesting. We asked them to contextualize the chapter in relation to the field. We also asked them to mention any points with which they took issue, or did not agree, and of course said that they could point to possible further directions for work. In short, we wanted to enact the start of the sort of dialogue that has been the hallmark of work in stylistics ever since its inception.

Stylistics is usually drawn with its origins in classical rhetoric, though its modern incarnation stems most directly from the practical criticism and structuralism of the middle of the twentieth century. Stylistics has long outgrown this recent rebirth, and though it was never as formalist as its detractors liked to think, the field went on to gather to itself new analytical tools in pragmatics, text linguistics, discourse analysis, sociolinguistics, computational corpus linguistics and cognitive linguistics. As each innovation in the source disciplines became available for literary investigations, so the stylistic exploration reached out with infectious excitement away from short, simple and linguistically deviant texts to address longer, more complex and richer literature and literary contexts and readings. What is particularly noteworthy in the work which came back to us for this book is the return to the earlier sorts of texts equipped with the analytical capacities of the present. Just under half of the chapters in the book explore aspects of prose fiction, employing techniques which were simply not available to early stylisticians. The range of literary texts covered is also broad: from the most experimental hyperfiction to the most canonical, from the frothiest of popular fiction to the most serious high art, across the history of the novel to writing for young adults, stylistics has always had a demonstrably practical democratic instinct while retaining an aesthetic and social scientific sense of literary value.

We did not intend to divide the book into the three traditional modes of writing: prose, poetry and drama, but the chapters simply fell out that way. Two things surprised us: firstly, the innovations that the cognitive poetic branch of stylistics is bringing to the exploration of poetry, which reinvigorates this substantial body of work in stylistics; secondly, the renewed interest in drama and dialogue. Early stylistics struggled with poor tools to analyse the rich setting and context of drama and performance. Now, several different analytical techniques are being triangulated on script and dialogue, with productive effects.

One early idea we had for the organisation of the book was to section it by the sub-disciplines of stylistics, which also reflected the specific expertise of each of our authors, but we quickly had to abandon that when it became apparent what a rich diversity of tools the contemporary stylistician has available. Numerous linguistic models of syntax, transitivity, deixis, modality, lexical choice, pragmatics, corpus linguistics, world-building and management, and many other aspects of language have been used by our contributors in this book. Equally, stylisticians are not fossilised or frightened by historical periods or the traditional literary divisions, so arranging the book by literary genre, theme or period was also not viable. It is a quality of the stylistician that is immediately apparent to students that the analytical techniques we use – rigorous, thorough, transparent, articulate, and open to betterment – are adaptable across a range of literary works. This is not to say that stylistics renders the singularity of literary texts as a reduced set of 'features', 'patterns' and other universals: the best contemporary stylistics is as interested in the appreciation of the particular piece of literary art in hand as in the shared conventions of language that configure it. However, stylistic analysis can make a contribution not only to literary criticism, but also in varying ways to linguistics, psychology, cognitive science, corpus analysis and the philosophy of language.

Moreover, stylistics has always been an *applied* discipline. Stylisticians have traditionally spent far less time pondering methodology compared with the practical matter of getting on with the analytical and exploratory work. This is not to say that stylisticians have ignored the methodological and critical theoretical dimensions of our practices, but by and large stylistics is an artisanal pursuit. It is noticeable that there is little anxiety about this in evidence amongst our contributors. In general, they are alive to the critical and theoretical positions they have adopted, but they do not make a fuss about the matter. Detractors might see this as naivety or complacency; we see it as confident self-assurance, and a sign that the discipline has come of age.

There are two views of what stylistics is for, what its functions are, and what it can achieve. All stylisticians would agree that the discipline accounts for the workings of literary texts. That is a matter of describing as systematically and openly as possible the nature of the textual evidence which accompanies a particular reading of the text. Stylistics can always do this, and it works 100% of the time with all texts and all readings. This basic outcome of stylistics provides a descriptive account of textual mechanics and the reading process which is made available in a common currency of register, in order to allow other stylisticians to compare their own account, verify or take issue with the analysis. The procedure is neither objective (since it involves analytical judgements and selections in context) nor purely subjective, since the models for analysis are conventionally shared and validated in a range of other disciplines. Stylistics offers an intersubjective analysis that can be shared, compared and evaluated on the basis of explicit criteria. One happy consequence of this fact is that engaging with stylistic analyses often enriches the reading experience: the stylistician-reader gathers together perspectives from others and can make imaginative leaps into different viewpoints and feelings about a literary work.

Some stylisticians also believe that stylistics has a further power beyond this central and permanent descriptive advantage. While stylistic frameworks cannot in general really be predictive of certain readings, they are certainly often *productive* of new ways of seeing the literary work. These moments of insight are what create the spark of engagement in many students of literature as they come to demystify the meaning of the text in an interpretation that is fresh rather than subjectively theirs alone. It is not so much that the linguistic approach has generated a reading by itself, as the fact that the systematic effort towards pattern-description encourages the recognition of a reading that the stylistician might have come to eventually, or that others might reasonably have come to, or which might be seen as appropriate in the future. In other words, stylistics can sometimes (or even, can *often*) produce the sort of startling, pleasurable and perspective-changing moments in reading that literary criticism traditionally stumbles over clumsily and inarticulately. Both of these views of stylistics are represented in this book.

Contemporary stylistics is in bouncing and dynamic health. We hope this collection of twenty new chapters by contemporary scholars in the field will encourage you to read more stylistics, engage more with its theory and practice, learn more about how verbal art and language work, roll your sleeves up and start doing some stylistics.

PART A

Stylistics of Prose

1

Woolf's Experiments with Consciousness in Fiction

Violeta Sotirova

Sotirova's chapter is a refreshing new take on Virginia Woolf's extraordinary style and draws upon conventional stylistics, cognitive poetics and literary theory to produce an explanation not just of how Woolf presents her characters to us, but also of how readers may relate to them, and even of what it means to be human at all.

Stylistics has a strong history of modelling the range of speech and thought presentation in literary and non-literary texts (see, for example, Leech and Short 1981; Semino *et al.* 1997 and Sotirova 2004). Woolf and other modernist writers have been cited as taking narrative telling in new directions by their use of Free Indirect Style, particularly the switching of implicit narrators in third-person narratives. Here, Sotirova takes the descriptive apparatus of stylistics and explains how the presentation of a range of consciousnesses in Woolf's *To the Lighthouse* is not simply passing the narrative 'turn' to different characters, but demonstrates something more profound about how human beings are thought by psychologists to communicate directly through empathetic cognitive understanding and not just through a behaviourist analysis of the likely motivations and impulses behind outward actions and words.

Sotirova demonstrates clearly that Woolf was suggesting that an ability to read minds is not exceptional but an everyday phenomenon. This tendency, particularly to hold imagined conversations between one's own mind and another's, is explained by Sotirova as a kind of Bakhtinian dialogism which is fundamental to human thought processes and characterizes the 'inner voice' phenomenon which Faulks recently explores in his novel about the nature and origins of human consciousness:

> consciousness enables us to make conjectures in which someone called 'I' can be seen in a hypothetical situation of a story.

> (Faulks 2006: 454)

In addition to drawing upon cultural theory and conventional stylistics, Sotirova places her analysis of Woolf's internal dialogic style into the context of current cognitive poetics (see for example, Stockwell 2002) by examining the reader's place in being the privileged observer of the interplay of minds between Woolf's characters. This, then is a subtler view of what it is to be human, where those familiar with each other's reactions and states of mind do not need to engage in Austen-like dialogue constantly, and where the almost constant representation of the story through one or another character's mind's eye means that there is not, in fact, room for an omniscient narrator in the text. The reader takes up this role without the intermediary of the implicit narrator, and achieves the illusion of an even more direct access to not just the thoughts of fictional characters, but to their ability to mind-read.

Lesley Jeffries

Theories of Consciousness

Writing consciousness in narrative means capturing the minutest details of a fictional mind and presenting them so that they retain the quality of ver-isimilitude with what we experience in our own minds. One central aspect of this experience is the dialogical orientedness of our thoughts, sensations and perceptions. This has prompted narratologists to describe the presentation of consciousness in terms evocative of Vigotsky's (1986) description of the formation of inner speech in children. For him speech is primarily social in nature and only later does it get internalized by the child as inner speech which still retains its addressivity. Cohn talks about the characters in the novel of consciousness as 'thoughtful characters' engaged in 'self-communion' (1978: v). Radzikhovskii, following Vigotsky, states that 'every mental function or mental process was originally formed in the consciousness of an individual, in the context of that individual's dialogue with other people' (1991: 12). He makes an even bolder assertion that 'the most interesting description of dialogic consciousness, one that elucidates latent dialogic phenomena, is to be found not in the scientific literature, but in literature itself …' (Radzikhovskii 1991: 12). Alluding specifically to Dostoevsky, Radzikhovskii follows in the tradition of Bakhtin's pioneering work on dialogicity in novelistic discourse. The dialogic relationship between the subject and the other has deeper philosophical significance than just a latent ability for communication:

> I am conscious of myself and become myself only while revealing myself to another, through another, and with the help of another. The most important acts constituting self-consciousness are determined by a relationship towards another consciousness (towards a *thou*). Separation, dissociation, and enclosure within the self as the main reason for the loss of one's self.
>
> (Bakhtin 1984: 287)

Even self-consciousness, on this analysis, is predicated on an orientedness towards another consciousness. The self-other relationship is thus posited as primary even in the emergence of subjectivity. This dialogic relationship is a complex dialectical process in which the self is constituted 'with one's own and with others' eyes simultaneously' and emerges in the process of 'a meeting and interaction between the others' and one's own eyes, an intersection of world views (one's own and the other's), an intersection of two consciousnesses' (1984: 289). And it is no surprise that in this process of relating to the other, in this 'questioning, provoking, answering, agreeing, objecting activity', i.e. in this 'dialogic activity' (1984: 285), language should occupy a central place. For Bakhtin existence itself is defined as communication:

> The very being of man (both external and internal) is the *deepest communion. To be* means to *communicate.* [...] To be means to be for another, and through the other, for oneself. A person has no internal sovereign territory, he is wholly and always on the boundary; looking inside himself, he looks *into the eyes of another* or *with the eyes of another.*
>
> (Bakhtin 1984: 287)

This sense of relatedness pervades Bakhtin's entire existential philosophy and his theory of novelistic discourse. Sadly, though, as Palmer observes, this dialogical dimension has been neglected by narrative theory because it 'has been concerned for too long primarily with the privacy of consciousness' (2004: 11). Palmer's plea 'that an emphasis on the social nature of thought might form an informative and suggestive perspective on fictional minds' (Palmer 2004: 11) can be answered in part by his own programmatic statement that:

> A postclassical perspective on the construction of fictional minds should be concerned with this complex relationship between the inaccessibility to others of a character's thought and the extent to which the same thought is publicly available to others in the story world. This relationship is very clearly shown when a character is anticipating, speculating on, reconstructing, misunderstanding, evaluating, reacting to, and acting upon the thought of another.
>
> (Palmer 2004: 174)

Drawing attention to the possibility for other characters and for readers to be able to have glimpses into a character's mind is important because it shatters the old myth that our thoughts and minds are impenetrable to other people. As Palmer (2002: 6, 2004: 87–129) points out, we do infer a great deal about the thoughts and states of others just by observing their behaviour. In narrative, through the presentation of these outward cues, readers, who are external observers of the narrative world, and characters who are internal participants in the story world, can reconstruct the mind of another with varying degrees of accuracy. This focus on a character's responses to another's thoughts and states and the possibility for group thoughts and experiences to occur, what Palmer calls 'intermental thought' (2004: 218–29), are dimensions of narrative study that can enhance our understanding of the dialogical construction of narratives.

This reconstruction of others' minds can be pushed to its limits by multiple embedded perceptions of others' actions, states and thoughts. One such challenging example from Woolf's *Mrs Dalloway* prompts Zunshine to go as far as to say that 'certain aspects of Woolf's prose do place extraordinarily high demands on our mind-reading ability and that this could account, at least in part, for the fact that many readers feel challenged by that novel' (2003: 278). Both Zunshine (2003) and Palmer (2004) work on the assumption widely accepted by cognitive theorists that we can reconstruct the content of other people's thoughts and feelings through a so-called process of 'mind-reading' (Dennett 1987; Gallese and Goldman 1998). This process is based on 'our ability to explain people's behaviour in terms of their thoughts, feelings, beliefs, and desires' (Zunshine 2003: 271). But is such a reconstruction based solely on the experiences or knowledge we have of how behaviour can be linked with inner states? The idea of a process of mind-reading, if correct, relies too much on inferences that we make based on outward cues. The dialogical fabric of novels that Bakhtin discusses presupposes a dialogical orientedness towards the other that permeates each and every level of existence, that even underlies the formation of subjectivity. Zunshine draws attention to the fact that such mind-reading is a lot more complex than simply being able to ascribe motives and states to outward behaviour (2003: 273). If it were not so, she explains, then people with autism would be able to learn eventually how to interpret behaviour and how to respond to it adequately. The overwhelming evidence, on the contrary, points to the fact 'that we do not just "learn" how to communicate with people and read their emotions [...] but that we also have evolved cognitive architecture that makes this particular kind of learning possible' (Zunshine 2003: 273).

Bakhtin's starting point, as we know, was novelistic texts themselves and his abstract philosophy of language and the self was built on his analyses of the presentation of fictional consciousness. Perhaps Zunshine's (2003: 278) confession that she 'ha[s] come to be "afraid" of *Mrs Dalloway* – and, indeed, other novels' because of the realization that 'any initial inquiry into the ways fiction teases our theory of mind immediately raises more questions about theory of mind than we are currently able to answer' should, in fact, prompt us to look more closely at how consciousness is written in literary texts, regardless of whether the empirically tested explanation of cognitive psychology is available as yet. Since Woolf's fiction is known for its intricate portrayals of consciousness and since one narratologist specifically refers to her as a challenging example of how consciousness works, in my analysis I will focus on examples taken from her writing.

The Writing of Consciousness

I begin with an example from another novel by Woolf – *To the Lighthouse*, published in 1927. Extract A below shows Mrs Ramsay and Mr Ramsay conducting a silent dialogue, captured by Woolf in a series of alternate snippets of the two characters' perceptions of each other:

Extract A

1 And what then? For she felt that he was still looking at her, but that his look
2 had changed. He wanted something – wanted the thing she always found so
3 difficult to give him; wanted her to tell him that she loved him. And that, no,
4 she could not do. He found talking so much easier than she did. He could say
5 things – she never could. So naturally it was always he that said the things, and
6 then for some reason he would mind this suddenly, and would reproach her. A
7 heartless woman he called her; she never told him that she loved him. But it
8 was not so – it was not so. It was only that she never could say what she felt. Was
9 there no crumb on his coat? Nothing she could do for him? Getting up she
10 stood at the window with the reddish-brown stocking in her hands partly to
11 turn away from him, partly because she did not mind looking now, with him
12 watching, at the Lighthouse. For she knew that he had turned his head as she
13 turned; he was watching her. She knew that he was thinking, You are more
14 beautiful than ever. And she felt very beautiful. Will you not tell me just for
15 once that you love me? He was thinking that, for what with Minta and his book,
16 and its being the end of the day and their having quarrelled about going to the
17 Lighthouse. But she could not do it; she could not say it. Then, knowing that
18 he was watching her, instead of saying anything she turned, holding her
19 stocking, and looked at him. And as she looked at him she began to smile, for
20 though she had not said a word, he knew, of course he knew, that she loved
21 him. He could not deny it. And smiling she looked out of the window and said
22 (thinking to herself, Nothing on earth can equal this happiness) –
23   'Yes, you were right. It's going to be wet tomorrow.'
24   She had not said it, but he knew it. And she looked at him smiling. For she
25 had triumphed again.

(Woolf 1977: 133)

The whole passage alternates between Mr Ramsay's thoughts and Mrs Ramsay's responses. What is not entirely clear is whether we remain within Mrs Ramsay's consciousness throughout or whether shifts to Mr Ramsay's mind also occur. If we follow the principle of 'interpretative obstination' or 'syntactic inertia', in other words if we accept that unless strongly prompted to reshape an interpretation, a reader will keep an established interpretation within sentence boundaries, and even across sentences and within paragraphs (Mey 1998: 33), it is more likely that readers would interpret the whole as stemming from Mrs Ramsay's viewpoint and all of the thoughts and feelings attributed to Mr Ramsay as her reconstruction. This is so because the passage opens with Mrs Ramsay's direct question (*And what then?* – line 1), as if in continuation to the spoken dialogue the two characters were conducting, and what follows is a sentence in which her feelings are transcribed (*For she felt that he was still looking at her, but that his look had changed* – lines 1–2). This orientation of the perspective as anchored with Mrs Ramsay would probably continue throughout the passage unless a strong signal for shifting the perspective occurs. What is striking, though, even if this analysis of the viewpoint is correct, is the precision with which Mrs Ramsay can sense her husband's thoughts, to the very fine detail of their temporal unfolding. Woolf's handling of time has been seen as one of the major achievements of her prose which can be studied on a par with philosophical writings of the same period (Banfield 2003). Perhaps the temporal unfolding of consciousness that Woolf manages to capture is one of the finest illustrations of what she meant when she wrote in her essay 'Modern Fiction':

> Let us record the atoms as they fall upon the mind in the order in which they fall, let us trace the pattern, however disconnected and incoherent in appearance, which each sight or incidence scores upon the consciousness. Let us not take it for granted that life exists more fully in what is commonly thought big than in what is commonly thought small
>
> (in McNeillie 1994: 161)

Mrs Ramsay's sharpened sensitivity towards what her husband is thinking allows her to trace the movement of his thoughts, and alongside to conduct a silent dialogue with him. This dialogue begins to unfold from the very start of the passage and it links their two experiences to each other in a similar way to utterances in a spoken exchange. The prominence of sentence-initial connectives (*and, for* – line 1; *and* – line 3; *so* – line 5; *but* – line 7; *for* – line 12; *and* – line 14; *but* – line 17; *and* – line 19; *and* – line 21; *and, for* – line 24), the use of pronominal deixis (*And that, no, she could not do* – lines 3–4; *But she could not do it; she could not say it* – line 17, etc.) and substitution (*But it was not so – it was not so* – lines 7–8) dialogically link their two perspectives, albeit that one is perhaps embedded within the other. This interpretation of the whole episode as stemming from Mrs Ramsay's consciousness is perhaps challenged most strongly at the point of Mr Ramsay's interior monologue (*Will you not tell me just for once that you love me?* – lines 14–15). It is at this point that we may feel that a transition to his consciousness has occurred. If his thought here is embedded into Mrs Ramsay's experience of the situation, the direct mode of presenting it is rather unsettling. The sentence that follows (*He was thinking that, for what with Minta and his book, and its being the end of the day and their having quarrelled about going to the Lighthouse* – lines 15–17) is also very strongly experiential with the use of the progressive aspect; its choppy syntax and the detail of his other experiences during that day suggest a very intimate knowledge of the precise movements of his mind. That is why a shift to his consciousness at this point is plausible. And again the return to Mrs Ramsay's response, linked pragmatically and semantically to Mr Ramsay's demand with the discourse marker *but* (line 17), juxtaposes their thoughts as if they were engaged in real conversation where the shared context allows for the heavy use of substitution and deixis (*do, it* – line 17). It is also possible that readers experience a perspectival shift half-way through another sentence: *for though she had not said a word, he knew, of course he knew, that she loved him* (lines 19–21) is not explicitly embedded in Mrs Ramsay's experience in the same way as *she knew that he was thinking* ... (line 13) is. Again the connective *for* links the two experiences as if the characters share exact knowledge of what the other is feeling.

Woolf's experiments with writing consciousness go further when the minds of two characters clearly demarcated as two distinct viewpoints are involved in dialogue:

Extract B

1   He felt extremely, even physically, uncomfortable. He wanted somebody to
2   give him a chance of asserting himself. He wanted it so urgently that he fid-
3   geted in his chair, looked at this person, then at that person, tried to break into
4   their talk, opened his mouth and shut it again. They were talking about the
5   fishing industry. Why did no one ask him his opinion? What did they know
6   about the fishing industry?
7   Lily Briscoe knew all that. Sitting opposite him could she not see, as in an X-
8   ray photograph, the ribs and thigh bones of the young man's desire to impress
9   himself lying dark in the mist of his flesh – that thick mist which convention
10   had laid over his burning desire to break into the conversation? But, she
11   thought, screwing up her Chinese eyes, and remembering how he sneered at
12   women, 'can't paint, can't write', why should I help him to relieve himself?

(Woolf 1977: 98–9)

The first part of this episode (lines 1–6) is a transcription of William Bankes' internal state, with the subjective experience enhanced through the use of mental verbs (*felt, wanted* – lines 1, 2), intensifiers (*extremely* – line 1), evaluative adjectives (*uncomfortable* – line 1) and the past progressive (*were talking* – line 4). The whole experience is presented from the character's viewpoint and it ends with two questions that he poses to himself in free indirect thought: *Why did no one ask him his opinion? What did they know about the fishing industry?* (lines 5–6). The transition to a new paragraph that follows marks a transition to a new viewpoint – Lily Briscoe's. But rather than being given Lily's response to the external situation that causes William Bankes so much anxiety, we witness her almost direct knowledge of his state. The anaphoric use of the demonstrative *all that* (line 7) refers to the whole experience of William Bankes, spelt out in the previous passage entirely from his own viewpoint. The first part of the second sentence in this second paragraph (lines 7–8) gives us an explanation from Lily's viewpoint why she is so aware of William Bankes' state: she is sitting opposite him, she can see the outward signals of his urge to assert himself. But funnily enough it is not the outward signals that lead her to infer his state through a process of 'mind-reading', but an even more improbable explanation that she can see through him as in an X-ray photograph (lines 7–8). The sense of a dialogue between these two characters is intensified through the exact repetition at the point of transition to Lily's viewpoint: *know* (line 5) – *knew* (line 7) and through the use of the con-textually bound discourse deictic *that* (line 7). Had we been given the same information through a full noun phrase, not dependent on the previous discourse for the disambiguation of its reference, and had we been led to read what goes on in Lily's mind without the repetition of the verb, the two viewpoints would have remained separate and self-contained. As it is, they are linked to each other through discourse ties that suggest this silent interaction between the characters.

Similar interactive devices are used on another occasion, when Lily is reflecting on Mrs Ramsay's behaviour.

Extract C

1   As usual, Lily thought. There was always something that had to be done at that
2   precise moment, something that Mrs Ramsay had decided for reasons of her
3   own to do instantly, it might be with everyone standing about making jokes, as
4   now, not being able to decide whether they were going into the smoking-room,
5   into the drawing-room, up to the attics. [...] Where, Lily wondered, was she
6   going so quickly?
7   Not that she did in fact run or hurry; she went indeed rather slowly. She felt
8   rather inclined just for a moment to stand still after all that chatter, and pick
9   out one particular thing; the thing that mattered; to detach it; separate it off;
10   clean it of all the emotions and odds and ends of things, and so hold it before
11   her.

(Woolf 1977: 120–1)

A similar interactive juxtaposition of viewpoints occurs in this extract as well at the paragraph break (line 6). While we are clearly inside Lily's mind from the beginning of the episode, signalled with the parenthetical *Lily thought* (line 1) and confirmed at the end of the paragraph with another parenthetical, *Lily wondered* (line 5), the shift to the new paragraph also marks a shift to Mrs Ramsay's consciousness. Perhaps it is in the second sentence of this new paragraph, *She felt rather inclined ...* (lines 7–8), that the reader, initially unsettled by the viewpoint shift, settles for an interpretation of the new paragraph as Mrs Ramsay's own experience. In a similar way to Extract B, the first sentence stemming from Mrs Ramsay's consciousness is almost conversationally orientated towards the final question Lily poses to herself:

> *Where, Lily wondered, was she going so quickly?* (lines 5–6)
> *Not that she did in fact run or hurry; she went indeed rather slowly.* (line 7)

Mrs Ramsay's thoughts and experience of her own movement come as a response to Lily's slight irritation that she had left them so quickly. The two adverbials, *in fact* and *indeed* (line 7), counter Lily's evaluation of Mrs Ramsay's movement away from the guests, their adversative, argumentative force intertwining the two viewpoints as if in spoken dialogue. The semantic content *per se*, the fact that both characters are thinking of how quickly Mrs Ramsay has gone, the symmetry of the lexical choices: *was she going so quickly* (lines 5–6) – *run or hurry* (line 7), *going* (line 6)

– *stand still* (line 8), *so quickly* (line 6) – *rather slowly* (line 7), *was going* (lines 5–6) – *went* (line 7), create this sense of permeability between the characters' minds.

And finally, we can venture even further in our understanding of dialogicity and the interactive human consciousness through exploring how not just two, but several minds are intersubjectively linked in a shared experience. The following passage illustrates cutting across several perspectives in successive clauses and uniting the consciousness of several characters who respond identically to an external event.

Extract D

1   Perhaps the others were saying something interesting? What were they saying?
2   That the fishing season was bad; that the men were emigrating. They were
3   talking about wages and unemployment. The young man was abusing the
4   government. William Bankes, thinking what a relief it was to catch on to
5   something of this sort when private life was disagreeable, heard him say
6   something about 'one of the most scandalous acts of the present government'.
7   Lily was listening; Mrs Ramsey was listening; they were all listening. But already
8   bored, Lily felt that something was lacking; Mr Bankes felt that something was
9   lacking. Pulling her shawl round her, Mrs Ramsay felt that something was
10 lacking. All of them bending themselves to listen thought, 'Pray heaven that
11 the inside of my mind may not be exposed,' for each thought, 'The others are
12 feeling this. They are outraged and indignant with the government about the
13 fishermen. Whereas I feel nothing at all.' But perhaps, thought Mr Bankes, as
14 he looked at Mr Tansley, here is the man. One was always waiting for the man.
15 There was always a chance. At any moment the leader might arise; the man of
16 genius, in politics as in anything else.

(Woolf 1977: 102)

There is perhaps an extraordinary coincidence of emotion and inner response to something that is happening in the narrative world which are shared by several characters at the same time. What is also significant in the passage is the mode of presentation. Through a number of linguistic cues we are invited to read each sentence as stemming from the viewpoint of a character and not as external narratorial report.

The passage begins with William Bankes' questions presented in free indirect thought (line 1). After the paragraph break (line 2) the elided main clause links the next two clauses to this character's viewpoint – the dialogue he is having with himself continues with the answer to the question he was posing to himself. After the direct quotation (line 6) embedded in William Bankes' thoughts, a new subject of the sentence moves us out of his consciousness. This time the experiencing self is Lily: *Lily was listening* (line 7). The parallelism that follows in the next two clauses (*Mrs Ramsey was listening; they were all listening* – line 7), reinforced by exact repetition, aligns Lily with Mrs Ramsay, and with all of the other characters in a shared experience of the same event – *they were all listening*.

While these three clauses can be read as a continuation of William Bankes' viewpoint (the act of listening is perhaps visible to an external observer), what follows is Lily's private feeling (*But already bored, Lily felt that something was lacking* – lines 7–8). And again all three of the characters are curiously united in sharing the same feeling: *that something was lacking.* The group perspective that follows (lines 8–10) is spelt out in direct thought to a rather comic effect: everyone is pretending that they are listening intently while at the same time feeling bored of the topic, and at the same time feeling guilty of not getting engaged with problems of such social magnitude that are being discussed.

By cutting across three perspectives in successive clauses and doing this twice, Woolf manages to suggest that the minds of these characters are permeable to the others' experiences and responses. But what is perhaps slightly disturbing is that this shared experience is not described by an external narratorial figure who has access to the minds of the characters, but rather the unison in their responses is suggested through direct glimpses into each individual consciousness which seems extraordinarily aligned with the experience of the others. This presentation of simultaneous identical reactions of several characters through directly cutting across their perspectives gives the reader a slightly unsettling sensation of some kind of a collective consciousness that unites the minds of all of these characters, at the same time as they remain separate, each suffering the embarrassment of being the only one who is not feeling engaged with the social plight of fishermen. In this passage, then, paradoxically, a kind of undoing of the shared subliminal experience is suggested through the directly spelt out thought that all of the protagonists have of being the only one who is feeling bored. But rather than take this as an ultimate sign of Woolf's scepticism of the possibility of consciousness being interactive, I prefer to interpret this passage as creating the opposite effect. The irony here lies not so much in the fact that ultimately consciousness is impenetrable and experience is enclosed within the isolated self, but rather in the fact that everybody is finely attuned to the experience of the others without at the same time being aware of it. What Woolf is undoing, in fact, is the false belief in the impermeable walls surrounding individual consciousness.

Experiments with Consciousness: Fiction or Reality?

If in all of the examples considered so far we assume the presence of a narratorial figure who controls the narrative and who reports what is going on in each character's consciousness, then the challenge to our expectations of realism is lessened. At least, we can say that the narrator is omniscient and glides freely from one character's mind to another. But the use of interactive devices that link two minds in a manner evocative of conversational exchanges does pose a challenge to our assumptions about the impenetrability of individual consciousness. It is difficult to conceive of two minds being engaged in such dialogical exchanges when the words are not spoken aloud. Each shift to a new consciousness that occurs in the extracts discussed takes us by surprise, especially since the transition to a new consciousness is carried out with the heavy use of interactive devices that presuppose knowledge of the other's inner discourse. It is precisely this dialogical juxtaposition of viewpoints which are discoursally bound together in a manner similar to spoken interaction that unsettles our sense of reality.

Woolf's fiction and her practice of writing consciousness are experimental. One of the experiments to which most of her novels are dedicated is to explore the 'silent moments' in which what matters is not what people say but what they don't say, 'their musings and reflections on the complexities of the inner self and human relationship', and most challengingly the 'silent communications between the characters, which in Woolf often meant the truer understanding between people than that achieved through speech' (Da Silva 1990: 196–7). But perhaps all there is to the examples that I have assembled here is to say that they stretch the boundaries of our imagination and our knowledge of how consciousness works. On the mind-reading analysis that both Palmer (2004) and Zunshine (2003) allude to, these experimental dialogues between characters' minds would be inexplicable. One character's immediate experience cannot be followed by an absolutely adequate response in another character's mind: even the presence of outward cues, such as behaviour, gesture, facial expression, etc. cannot account for this. But we can begin to understand our own readiness to naturalize such examples if we consider again some more recent proposals about the inherent dialogicity of consciousness.

A social psychologist, Bråten, challenges the idea that our ability to interpret another's emotions and moreover our ability to share them is something that we learn through a process of ascription of feelings to observable behaviour:

> In the shared cultural lifeworld of *experienced* participants, intersubjective understanding may be considered to be mediated by acquired internal representations in the form of a generalised, evoked, simulated, or imagined other. But such an internal working model, or 'theory of mind', formed on the basis of previous face-to-face interaction experiences, can hardly be attributed to the neo-nate. Even if it were, this would not account for the immediate and affective quality of mutual attunement that infant-adult dyads and infant-infant dyads sometimes appear to exhibit.
>
> (Bråten 1992: 79)

Bråten refers to empirical data gathered in existing studies (Field 1990; Murray and Trevarthen 1985) which show that already 'at birth, or soon after, being especially alert during the first 24 hours, infants appear ready to enter into an engagement of feeling with another' (Bråten 1992: 79). The evidence that children, almost as soon as they are born, can show awareness and readiness of engagement with another, as well as the ability of children as young as 26 weeks to respond with empathy to another, would suggest that there is an inherent ability in each of us for 'prosocial behaviour, and probably related to that, the ability to take [...], to feel the other's perspective' (Bråten 1992: 91).

A contemporary philosopher, Hutto (2002), also takes issue with the 'mind-reading' theory and argues that children do not learn to interpret others' inner states and emotions through learning to link behavioural responses to emotional states. The so far prevailing belief that a child first acquires a sense of self and a sense of other as distinct, and only then learns to interpret how different emotions can manifest themselves in behaviour is challenged by Hutto as inadequate. Rather, Hutto (2002: 41) believes that there is an intersubjective dimension even to the first and most fundamental activity of concept learning. What this means is that 'the connection between ourselves and others derives from the fact that their expressive behaviour has dramatic effects on us' (Hutto 2002: 41). He points out that children, even in the process of acquiring knowledge about the world, do this in dialogue with another person. Only half of this process is concerned with the acquisition of a concept; the other half is devoted to mutual understanding of what the other means, sharing of attention focus and cross-checking. This intersubjective orientedness which we all experience very early in life then shapes our ability to experience with the other. Thus, we can be affected physically by the experience of pain in another, and the physical basis for this is what cognitive scientists call mirror neurons – neurons responsible for a particular emotional reaction that fire in the brain when we observe another experiencing it. For Hutto, 'we are naturally calibrated in such a way that we can share experiences with others and respond, with feeling, to their circumstances', a predisposition which, if it requires any acquisition, is acquired as early as the acquisition of various language items (Hutto 2002: 49).

This analysis, then, along with the empirical observations of social psychologists, undermines the belief in 'a strong first/third person divide upon which the conceptual problem of other minds rests' (Hutto 2002: 49). If it is the case that we learn about the world, and more specifically about psychological concepts, simultaneously as we develop our sense of self and other, then a naturally occurring sense of empathy and shared responses is perhaps the explanation for what Modernist writers, such as Woolf, do in their exploration of the interrelations between individual consciousnesses. Fictional works, such as Woolf's, which push the boundaries of individual consciousness to their limit and experiment with portraying characters' minds as engaged in a constant dialogue with one another, are perhaps closer to our own experiences of sharing emotions and responding to the other's emotions, even when these are not overtly articulated, than would appear at first. It is precisely because intersubjectivity is the foundation of our lives that we can read Woolf's portrayal of fictional consciousness with ease, our engagement as readers adding yet another layer of dialogue.

2

A Corpus Stylistic Perspective on Dickens' *Great Expectations*

Michaela Mahlberg

The advantages of using corpora for the stylistician are many, and their avail-
ability and use in recent years has increased, thanks to resources such as Project
Gutenberg (2003–06), and the ease of use of analytical software such as *Wordsmith
Tools* (Scott 2004). With texts stored as a corpus, scholars can access frequency
lists and concordances from the works of an author or group of authors. These in
turn can be compared statistically with texts by other authors, or with larger
benchmark corpora, in ways that offer the promise of isolating authorial 'fin-
gerprints'. Indeed, computerized concordances of the works of famous authors
have been around for many decades, and, if anything, stylisticians have underused
them to a surprising extent. Fiction has been concordanced aplenty: at least eight
concordances of works by Conrad were published between 1979 and 1985, thanks
to scholars such as Bender and Higdon, while others focusing on writers such as
Gerard Manley Hopkins and T. S. Eliot have brought the advantages of concordances to poetry and plays. Mahlberg gives us further such references in this
chapter.

Mahlberg indicates two useful ways of using corpus analysis of literary texts: to test
out existing theories of stylistics, and to call to account the interpretations literary
critics make of texts by offering the power of quantified data. But she is wise to
sound a note of caution as to what automated analysis can deliver. What corpus
linguists can offer is, as Mahlberg says, never the total sum of linguistic features
that characterize a style. Corpus linguists are at best offering a contribution to
that sum.

Of particular value in Mahlberg's chapter is the analysis of clusters (in this case,
five-word clusters generated by the *Wordsmith Tools* software). Concordances alone
often cannot deliver the same clarity which automatically generated cluster lists
can achieve; if there is too much data, even with intelligent sorting and random-
izing, recurring strings of words can easily be missed. It is also wise to take a figure
such as five for the extent of clusters: six- and seven-word clusters are generally
extremely rare and thus yield little in the way of patterning. On the other hand,
two- and three-word cluster lists necessarily include the occurrences of parts of

longer clusters. One can always work back from five to smaller extents, as Mahl-berg does.

What Mahlberg's analysis gives us is essentially a picture of Dickens' love of irrealis in his use of expressions enabling the contemplation of worlds which were not but which might have been, most notably, constructions based on *as if* … (on the relationship between irrealis, negation and modality, see Hidalgo Downing 2000: 83). The quantitative evidence shines a convincing light onto a key feature of Dickens' techniques of characterization, and lends support to claims made by other scholars working through more traditional literary exegesis. As a meth-odology, Mahlberg's chapter suggests that cluster analysis has much to offer, highlighting, as it does, the preferred lexico-grammatical configurations that authors unconsciously select, and which readers process, over and over again.

Michael McCarthy

Introduction

Corpora are collections of computer-readable texts that often contain several million words. Corpora provide data for the study of linguistic phenomena, and corpus software helps to search, quantify and display the data. Although com-puter technology plays an important role in corpus linguistics, it is the task of the linguist to find the appropriate tools for the questions that he/she wants to investigate. The study of literature may not seem to be an obvious field for the application of corpus linguistic tools. In particular when the focus is on a single text, the usefulness of tools designed to deal with huge amounts of data is more difficult to see. However, corpus linguistics is not only about computer-assisted methodologies; the interpretation of the data is equally important. With the analysis of local textual functions in Charles Dickens' *Great Expectations*, this chapter exemplifies how corpus stylistic methodologies and descriptive categories can contribute to the characterization of the style of a text. I begin with an overview of different approaches to the use of corpora for stylistic analysis. I then briefly introduce the methodological context for the present study, before I deal with five-word clusters as pointers to local textual functions, investigate *as if* patterns and finally focus on the theme of 'seeing is not knowing'.

Corpus Data and the Study of Literature

In her discussion of electronic explorations of literary texts, Adolphs (2006: 65ff.) distinguishes between 'intra-textual' and 'inter-textual' analysis. The former is 'the manipulation of a text or text collections in a way that might reveal further information about the data' (Adolphs 2006: 65), whereas the latter focuses on 'the comparison of individual lexical items and phrases in literary texts with those that occur in other, possibly non-literary, corpora' (Adolphs 2006: 66). This dis-tinction relates to different linguistic norms and to how the deviation from lin-guistic norms foregrounds elements in a literary text. Deviation can be understood as both abnormal irregularity and regularity (Leech 1985: 46). The type of deviation varies with the type of norm. Leech distinguishes between 'primary' deviation, the deviation from norms of the language as a whole (Leech 1985: 45), 'secondary' deviation, the deviation from norms of literary composition, for instance norms of author or genre (Leech 1985: 48), and 'tertiary deviation', also called 'internal' deviation, which relates to norms within a particular text (Leech 1985: 49).

Different sets of corpora can be taken to represent different types of norm. To gain insights into the norms of one particular text, an electronic version of the text constitutes the corpus. An example of a corpus stylistic study of this kind is Starcke's (2006) analysis of the phraseology in Jane Austen's *Persuasion*. A study dealing with a collection of works by one author is, for instance, Tabata's (2002) stylometric analysis of a Dickens corpus. Tabata (2002) identifies a contrast between Dickens' serial fictions and his sketches, and he investigates the variation of Dickens' style over time. Hori (2004) also works with a Dickens corpus to study collocations that characterize Dickens' style. In order to assess to what extent specific collocations are typical of Dickens, Hori (2004) draws on additional data from other eighteenth and nineteenth-century fiction, thus adding information on the genre. For the description of norms of the language as a whole more general reference corpora are needed. In his analysis of *Heart of Darkness*, Stubbs (2005) not only compares Conrad's novel with other fiction but also with data from the *British National Corpus*. It is important to stress, however, that comparative corpus data can only provide relative norms. Even for very large general-reference corpora representativeness is not an absolute term (see further Mahlberg 2005b).

On the one hand, corpora can add detail to stylistic analyses by providing quantitative information or pointing to features that may be easily overlooked. On the other hand, corpora can help to test and develop existing approaches in stylistics. Semino and Short (2004) show how a corpus approach leads to further development of the Leech and Short (1981) model of speech and thought representation. Additionally, stylistics can employ descriptive tools that originated in the field of corpus linguistics. Adolphs and Carter (2002) study an extract from Virginia Woolf's *To the Lighthouse*. They identify semantic prosodies for lexical items in the extract with the help of reference data from large corpora. Semantic prosodies are elements of evaluative and pragmatic meaning that are often subtle and difficult to identify on the basis of intuition alone. The concept is part of fundamental work in corpus linguistics to describe the phraseology of lexical items (see Sinclair 2004). As Adolphs and Carter (2002) show, it can also provide an additional layer in the analysis of point of view.

The present chapter presents a corpus stylistic perspective that builds on the concept of 'local textual functions'. These describe repeated patterns of lexical items in relation to their textual functions. The functions are local since they do not claim to be applicable to the English language in general but to a specific set of lexical items and/or to a specific (set of) text(s); therefore the description of such functions has to be flexible and works to some extent with *ad hoc* categories (see Mahlberg 2005a, and 2007 a, b). The concept of local textual functions relates to the following definition of style: 'A style X is the sum of linguistic features associated with texts or textual samples defined by some set of contextual parameters' (Leech 1985: 39). The contextual parameters for local textual functions are given through the corpus or corpora on which their identification is based. However, it is not claimed that a set of local textual functions can be regarded as the 'sum' of linguistic features that characterizes a style. Rather, local textual functions are viewed as contributing to this sum.

Data and Methodology for the Study of *Great Expectations*

When a specific lexical item is given, the investigation of its local textual functions in the novel starts with the analysis of concordance data to identify the patterns and functions of the item, which relate to themes and characters in the novel. To select lexical items for closer analysis there are different options. Literary insights and arguments from literary criticism can suggest items for a concordance analysis. Another option is to start with frequency information on words in the text and pick those whose frequencies appear noteworthy, as identified, for instance, with the help of the KeyWords Tool in *WordSmith* (Scott 2004; see also Scott and Tribble 2006). The preferred option is a combination of corpus methodologies, previous corpus stylistic work and literary criticism.

The analysis of *Great Expectations* in the present chapter is part of work in a wider corpus stylistic context that aims to explore corpus approaches to identify and describe stylistically relevant features of texts. The corpora that are used are a Dickens corpus and a corpus of nineteenth-century fiction from authors other than Dickens (from now on referred to as 19C); the corpora contain about 4.5 million words each, and the texts are taken from *Project Gutenberg* (2003–06) (see Mahlberg 2007 a). On the basis of findings from these corpora it is suggested that five-word clusters can serve as pointers to local textual functions in Dickens, and a set of functional categories has been developed to describe them (see Mahlberg 2007 a, b). The present chapter applies these categories to *Great Expectations* and explores them in more detail with regard to themes of the novel. *Great Expectations* is a retrospective first-person narration. The narrator Pip had lived his life with the dreams of his 'great expectations', but eventually learns that his mysterious benefactor is not the rich spinster Miss Havisham, but Abel Magwitch, the escaped convict who confronted Pip in the marshes when he was a child.

The analysis begins with an overview of the different types of five-word clusters, i.e. repeated sequences of five words, in the novel. The clusters were retrieved with the software *WordSmith Tools* (Scott 2004); only clusters that occur five times or more are taken into account. After the initial overview, the analysis focuses on more flexible patterns around the core *as if.* The identification of the patterns is based on the repetition of surface features, thus frequency information plays a role. However, the numbers are fairly small and only taken to point towards tendencies. Exact statistical measures are not employed in the present study. The focus is on a qualitative analysis. The analysis also tries to relate features that are thrown up by the corpus analysis to arguments in Dickens criticism. Within the limited space of the present chapter the discussion necessarily has to focus on selected examples.

Starting with Five-word Clusters

Table 2.1 lists the 21 different five-word clusters that occur five times and more in *Great Expectations*.

Table 2.1 Five-word clusters in *Great Expectations* that occur five times and more

	Cluster	Freq.	Type
1	AS IF HE HAD BEEN	7	AI
2	IT APPEARED TO ME THAT	7	S
3	AS IF IT WERE A	6	AI
4	DEAR OLD PIP OLD CHAP	6	L
5	HIS HANDS IN HIS POCKETS	6	BP
6	ALL RIGHT JOHN ALL RIGHT	5	L
7	AT THE THREE JOLLY BARGEMEN	5	L
8	BAD SIDE OF HUMAN NATURE	5	L
9	DEAR BOY AND PIP'S COMRADE	5	L
10	THE LEG OF THE TABLE	5	L
11	THE OLD GREEN COPPER ROPE-WALK	5	L
12	I FELT THAT I WAS	5	S
13	IN THE SAME MOMENT I	5	S
14	THE SAME MOMENT I SAW	5	S
15	AT THE END OF THE	5	TP
16	AT THE SIDE OF THE	5	TP
17	BY THE LIGHT OF THE	5	TP
18	AS IF I WERE A	5	AI
19	AS IF IT HAD BEEN	5	AI
20	HIS HEAD ON ONE SIDE	5	BP
21	AS A MATTER OF COURSE	5	O

(L = Labels, S = Speech, BP = Body parts, AI = *as if,* TP = Time and place, O = Other)

The five categories that have been developed to classify five-word clusters in Dickens (see Mahlberg 2007 a) are label clusters, speech clusters, *as if* clusters, time and place clusters and body part clusters. 'Labels' are clusters that are or contain names of people or places. Examples of this type are *the Old Green Copper Rope-Walk, at the Three Jolly Bargemen, all right John all right, dear boy and Pip's comrade, dear old Pip old chap.* For the last three of them, the label not only refers to the person whose name is mentioned, but the cluster also 'labels' the person who uses it. The Aged Parent in Wemmick's household typically uses *all right John all right* when he talks to Wemmick, *dear boy and Pip's comrade* is used by Magwitch to address Pip and Herbert, and *dear old Pip old chap* is associated with Joe, but not always spoken by Joe. When Pip is ill, he is nursed by Joe. Joe is the husband of Pip's sister with whom he lived when he was a child, and Pip observes that Joe falls 'into the old tone' and calls Pip 'by the old names, the dear "old Pip, old chap"' (Chapter 57). Another label that does not contain a name is *bad side of human nature*, but again it is associated with a particular character. It relates to the way in which Pip talks to Biddy (Chapters 19, 35). The remaining label is *the leg of the table*. This cluster is classified as label, as it occurs only in Chapter 4, where it characterizes Pip's behaviour. Pip has stolen food and drink for the convict from his sister's kitchen. During the Christmas dinner he is now scared of being found out. His anxiety is reflected by the way in which he clutches the leg of the table, so the cluster occurs repeatedly throughout the chapter, as in 'I held tight to *the leg of the table* under the cloth, with both hands, and awaited my fate' (Chapter 4).

The group 'Time and place' collects the clusters *at the end of the, at the side of the* and *by the light of the* which are parts of longer expressions referring to time (*at the end of the week*) or place (*at the side of the churchyard*). 'Body part' clusters contain nouns such *hands* or *head* that refer to parts of the body. They are used in descriptions such as 'Herbert crossed his feet, looked at the fire *with his head on one side*, and . . .' (Chapter 30) (for a more detailed discussion of functions of body part clusters see Mahlberg 2007 a, c). 'As if' clusters are defined by the presence of *as if* in the five-word sequence, and 'speech' clusters have to contain a first or second person pronoun. The speech clusters 13 and 14 in Table 2.1 are in fact part of the same six-word cluster. What is noticeable about the speech clusters is that all belong to Pip as the *I*-narrator, who describes what he sees and notices and how he feels (*it appeared to me that, I felt that I was, in the same moment I, the same moment I saw*).

Within the space of the present chapter, the overview of cluster types has to remain brief. The important point is that the five categories cover almost all the clusters in Table 2.1 (except *as a matter of course*). Table 2.2 shows that all five categories that were developed on the basis of the norms of author are applicable to one particular text. Links to Dickens criticism are also apparent. It is often pointed out that Dickens uses language to 'individualize' characters (see also

Table 2.2 Frequencies of cluster types

Cluster type	Freq.
Label (L)	7
Speech (S)	4
as if (AI)	4
Time and place (TP)	3
Body parts (BP)	2
Other (O)	1
Sum	21

Quirk 1961), and a term that overlaps with labels (although only to some degree) refers to 'tags' for characters (Newsom 1999: 543). The remainder of this chapter deals with the question of how the general functional categories that are applied to five-word clusters function in one specific text. The five functional groups can relate in different ways to the themes of a particular text. A study of *Bleak House,* for instance, shows that more than half of the five-word clusters in the novel are labels signalling relationships between characters (see Mahlberg 2007 b). This function is also visible in *Great Expectations,* but to a lesser degree. To investigate specific local textual functions in *Great Expectations* the following section starts with *as if* clusters and then focuses on more flexible *as if* patterns that illustrate links to a major theme of the novel.

Local Textual Functions of *as if*

Some of the functions of *as if* clusters are similar to what Brook (1970) calls the 'fanciful as if'. Brook points out that 'Dickens was fond of one particular type of comparison, which might be called the fanciful "as if"' (1970: 33). Typically there is 'some improbable but amusing explanation of the appearance or behaviour of one of the characters in a novel' (Brook 1970: 33). One of Brook's examples is Mr Merdle in *Little Dorrit* who is described as 'suddenly getting up, as if he had been waiting in the interval for his legs and they had just come' (1970: 34). The frequency of *as if* in the Dickens corpus compared with the frequency in 19C supports the claim that Dickens makes particular use of *as if:* in about 4.5 million words of Dickens texts we find 4,220 occurrences of *as if,* whereas 19C only contains 2,471 in about the same number of words. What does not seem to receive equal attention from critics is the occurrence of *as if* as part of longer sequences. A key cluster comparison with *WordSmith Tools* (Scott 2004) points to the fact that the frequency difference of *as if he were a* in Dickens compared to 19C (45 vs. 7 occurrences) is more significant than the difference for *as if he had been* (90 vs. 49 occurrences), so *as if he were a* is more key to Dickens than *as if he had been.* For the former cluster the comparison mostly involves noun phrases, including examples such as *as if he were a great bottle, a hackney-coach, a mechanical toy.* Examples of this type are quoted by critics to illustrate Dickens' tendency to describe people as though they were objects. The cluster *as if he had been* can also be followed by noun phrases, but this is not the only option as examples such as *as if he had been in the coals* or *as if he had been summoned from the grave* show. The differences in frequency are also linked to functional differences.

Exact repetitions of sequences of words are not very common and the numbers for a single novel are very small. This makes it easy to look at all clusters in detail, and the five functional groups can provide an overview. However, a larger number of examples would reveal more detailed information on patterns. The evidential basis of the description of local textual functions can be increased when more flexible patterns are investigated. Therefore the following analysis looks at the two-word cluster *as if.* To come to *as if* by actually starting with two-word clusters would have been more complex because of the variety and high frequency of two-word clusters. *Great Expectations* contains 266 examples of *as if*. Compared with the other texts in the Dickens corpus, *Great Expectations* has the highest normalized frequency for *as if*: 1.43 per 1,000 words. Table 2.3 provides details on the distribution across the texts in the corpus.

Table 2.3 Distribution of *as if* in the Dickens corpus

	Text	Words in text	Hits	Hits per 1,000
1	*Great Expectations*	186,274	266	1.43
2	*The Haunted Man*	33,752	48	1.42
3	*Our Mutual Friend*	325,424	392	1.20
4	*Dombey and Son*	359,409	413	1.15
5	*The Battle of Life*	30,012	34	1.13
6	*The Mystery of Edwin Drood*	93,845	105	1.12
7	*David Copperfield*	359,374	393	1.09
8	*A Christmas Carol*	28,541	30	1.05
9	*Little Dorrit*	337,739	348	1.03
10	*The Chimes*	30,582	31	1.01
11	*Martin Chuzzlewit*	336,952	336	1.00
12	*The Uncommercial Traveller*	142,407	137	0.96
13	*The Haunted Man*	104,187	93	0.89
14	*The Cricket on the Heath*	31,451	28	0.89
15	*A Tale of Two Cities*	135,925	121	0.89
16	*Bleak House*	353,774	311	0.88
17	*The Old Curiosity Shop*	216,186	183	0.85
18	*Oliver Twist*	157,208	126	0.80
19	*Barnaby Rudge*	253,499	188	0.74
20	*Sketches by Boz*	248,573	184	0.74
21	*Nicholas Nickleby*	322,586	235	0.73
22	*The Pickwick Papers*	299,561	180	0.60
23	*American Notes*	103,552	38	0.37

Obvious examples for the functions of *as if* are those illustrating improbable explanations of the fanciful *as if* type as in:

> The two ghastly casts on the shelf were not far from him, and their expression was *as if* they were making a stupid apoplectic attempt to attend to the conversation.
>
> (Chapter 36)

This example illustrates a case of what is referred to as 'animism' (Brook 1970: 35) whereby inanimate objects receive human attributes and powers. Such examples become more relevant to a specific novel, i.e. more local, when a specific pattern is sustained throughout the text. The above casts belong to the odd objects that Pip notices in the office of the lawyer Jaggers:

> and there were some odd objects about, [...] such as an old rusty pistol, [...] and *two dreadful casts* on a shelf, of faces peculiarly swollen, and twitchy about the nose.
>
> (Chapter 20)

In Chapter 24 Pip learns from Wemmick that the casts are likenesses of famous clients, and they catch Pip's attention repeatedly, for him they are 'inseparable [...] from the official proceedings' (Chapter 51). Below is another example:

> As I stood idle by Mr. Jaggers's fire, its rising and falling flame made the two casts on the shelf look *as if* they were playing a diabolical game at bo-peep with me; while the pair of coarse fat office candles that dimly lighted Mr. Jaggers as he wrote in a corner, were decorated with dirty winding-sheets, *as if* in remembrance of a host of hanged clients.
>
> (Chapter 48)

The second *as if* in the example refers to the *remembrance of a host of hanged clients* and further adds to the dark atmosphere that Pip experiences in Jaggers' office and that is also reflected in the adjectives that describe the casts as *dreadful,* or *ghastly.* In addition to the description of an atmosphere, the core *as if* functions in patterns of characterisation. The following example stresses that Jaggers is a very cool person: 'he washed his clients off, as if he were a surgeon or a dentist' (Chapter 26).

A closer look at the pronouns that follow *as if* reveals further information. The most frequent pronoun to follow *as if* is *he.* Table 2.4 provides an overview of the characters to which *he* refers; *as if he* occurs 78 times, two of these examples appear in speech and are not included in Table 2.4.

The frequencies in Table 2.4 are initial pointers to functions. There are also cases of characterization with *as if* that do not need a pronoun, as shown by the following example telling us that Wemmick is a different man when he is at work, where he appears unconscious of his life at home: 'he looked as unconscious of his Walworth property *as if* the Castle and the drawbridge [...] had all been blown into space together by the last discharge of the Stinger' (Chapter 25).

The repetitions listed in Table 2.4 can point to different examples of *as if* that relate to the same character. As we see the world of the novel through Pip's eyes, his subjectivity tells us as much about Pip's feelings as about the characters that he describes. The following two examples illustrate differences in Pip's feelings towards Joe. When Joe tells Pip about his relationship with Pip's sister, Pip feels very close to him. Pip interprets the way Joe looks at him as showing that he knows what he is thinking:

Table 2.4 Characters referred to by *as if he*

Character	'as if he' frequency
Joe	18
Magwitch	15
Jaggers	8
Pumblechook	6
Orlick	6
Wemmick	6
Wopsle	3
Stranger (in chapter 10)	3
Herbert/pale young gentleman	3
Mike, client of Jaggers	2
Mr Pocket	1
Clerk of Jaggers	1
Man in pub	1
Coachman	1
Startop	1
Waiter in Blue Boar	1
Sum	76

'[...] Now, Pip;' Joe looked firmly at me, *as if* he knew I was not going to agree with him; 'your sister is a fine figure of a woman.'

(Chapter 7)

This description fits into the picture created in Chapter 7, where Pip comes to the conclusion that he 'was looking up to Joe in my heart' (Chapter 7). In contrast, when Pip feels embarrassed by Joe the *as if* introduces a different type of comparison. In Chapter 13 Joe and Pip go to see Miss Havisham at Satis House, where Joe feels uncomfortable and behaves in a clumsy way. Pip is embarrassed and feels distant from the Joe he sees; he compares him in a very unfavourable way to an extraordinary bird, the comparison is also supported by *unlike* and *like*:

I could hardly have imagined dear old Joe looking so *unlike* himself or so *like* some extraordinary bird; standing, as he did, speechless, with his tuft of feathers ruffled, and his mouth open, *as if* he wanted a worm.

(Chapter 13)

Pip's view of the world is also crucial for his illusion about his 'great expectations'. As Brooks (1984: 130) puts it 'Pip has in fact misread the plot of his life', which affects the way in which he narrates his story and the clues that the reader receives.

In Chapter 39, Magwitch, the convict of Pip's childhood, comes to see Pip in

London. The scene builds up to the 'central moment of recognition' (Brooks 1984: 128), where it becomes clear to Pip who the strange visitor is. Here the *as if* underlines that the story is told retrospectively. It gives a clue as to the identity of the stranger before Pip explicitly says that he recognizes Magwitch. It is due to Magwitch that Pip came to London to become a gentleman, so he has indeed some part in Pip's life: 'He looked about him with the strangest air – an air of wondering pleasure, *as if* he had some part in the things he admired' (Chapter 39).

Clues to the plot that are given with the help of *as if* can also be more subtle. The following two examples refer to Orlick, who used to work in Joe's forge. In the first example Orlick is jealous of Pip who has just got a half-holiday.

> Orlick plunged at the furnace, drew out a red-hot bar, made at me with it *as if* he were going to run it through my body, whisked it round my head, laid it on the anvil, hammered it out – *as if* it were I, I thought, and the sparks were my spurting blood – and finally said, when he had hammered himself hot and the iron cold [...]
>
> (Chapter 15)

The frightening picture that Pip draws of Orlick with the help of two *as if* constructions is paralleled later in the novel in Chapter 53, where Orlick comes to take revenge on him for spoiling his chances with Biddy. Instead of an iron bar, Orlick now aims a gun at Pip: 'he [...] took up a gun with a brass-bound stock. "Do you know this?" said he, making *as if* he would take aim at me' (Chapter 53). Orlick is now even more hostile towards Pip, as he works for Compeyson, the enemy of Magwitch.

'Seeing is not knowing'

In his discussion of Dickens' use of language, Quirk (1961: 23) points out how lexical signals can be used to sustain the equivocation with which the story in *Great Expectations* is told to the reader. He describes the repetition of *I saw in this* in Chapter 38, when Pip thinks about the role Miss Havisham plays in his life. Quirk notes that Pip's 'experience leads him (and the reader) to believe that what he sees is correct [...]: to Pip seeing is knowing, and the book's theme is to show that seeing is *not* knowing' (1961: 23). Quirk (1961: 23) further points out that had Dickens used another verb such as *know* instead of *see* the reader would have been explicitly misled, whereas a verb such as *conclude* as in *I concluded from this* would have made Pip's misconception too obvious.

The theme of 'seeing is not knowing' is linked to functions of *as if*. A concordance analysis of *as if he/she* shows that the way in which Pip draws conclusions about people's behaviour is associated with at least four patterns (P1–P4).

P1: Appearance

Pip observes how people look and appear. Words and phrases that occur in the context of *as if*, are, for instance, *looked* (line 1), *with an air of* (line 2), *manner* (line 3) or *expression* (lines 4 and 5).

```
1    ient looked scared, but bewildered too, as if he were unconscious what he had d
2     ed Joe, with an air of legal formality, as if he were making his will, ''Miss A
3      orgot it!'' At a change in his manner as if he were even going to embrace me,
4    assumed a knitted and intent expression as if she had been reading for a week,
5      remarked a new expression on her face, as if she were afraid of me. ''I want
```

P2: Looking at

In the second pattern, Pip describes how people 'look at' someone or something. Their eyes and the way they focus on something provide Pip with clues as to what they think or mean. Words in this pattern are, for instance, *look at, glance at, peep down, eye* and *watch.*

```
1      whisker and looking dejectedly at me, as if he thought it really might have b
2     nd, and glancing at my untasted supper as if he thought of the time when we
3      s, Joe peeped down at me over his leg, as if he were mentally casting me and
4    echanical nicety, and eyeing my anatomy as if he were minutely choosing his
5     ;to drink. She watched his countenance as if she were particularly wishful to b
6      ay it?'' Miss Havisham glanced at him as if she understood what he really was
```

P3: Speech

The speech pattern shows how Pip interprets the tone in which people say something. A signal of this pattern is *in a tone of* (line 1), but also adverbs that accompany a speech verb *triumphantly demanded* (line 2), or a speech verb on its own with *as if* following its subject (line 3).

```
1    ph,'' in a tone of the deepest reproach, as if he were the most callous of
2     ence,'' and then triumphantly demanded, as if he had done for me, ''Now! How muc
3     rd bless the boy!'' exclaimed my sister, as if she didn't quite mean that, but r
```

P4: Body Language and Non-verbal Sounds

The final pattern shows how Pip reads body language (*nodded*) and interprets non-verbal sounds (*coughed, with a sigh, gave a cry*).

```
1    air, and nodded at her and at the fire, as if he had known all about it
2      ing to Joseph.'' The waiter coughed, as if he modestly invited me to get over
3    r me, Pip,'' said Estella, with a sigh, as if she were tired; ''I am to write to
4      m in arm. At first Biddy gave a cry, as if she thought it was my apparition,
```

The four patterns illustrate how Pip interprets what he sees. The *as if* helps to underline the subjectivity of his observations. It is important to note that the description of these patterns is qualitative. Frequency information is only taken into account in the sense that the repetition of similar examples makes a pattern visible. The interpretation of the patterns then focuses on their relationship to other factors in the novel. The five-word clusters above show that the speech clusters are associated with the *I*-narrator Pip and with what he feels and sees. With only a few exceptions, the *as if* clusters are also used by Pip in the telling of his story and not in the speech of characters. Thus, we have different types of linguistic features that point to a mysterious plot. Different functions of *as if* reveal how Pip tells his story. With the help of *as if*, the reader can gain insights into Pip's feelings, the *as if* shows that Pip tells his story retrospectively and *as if* constructions indicate links between situations that occur in different chapters. However, it is important to stress that the *as if* patterns are not the only linguistic options that provide insights into Pip's point of view. The four-word cluster *with an air of* can function in a way similar to *as if*:

> This reply seemed agreeable to Mr. Jaggers, who said, 'I thought so!' and blew his nose *with an air of* satisfaction.
>
> (Chapter 36)

Conclusions

The advantage of a corpus approach to a novel is that patterns can be traced systematically throughout the text. However, the application of corpus methodology is not an automated process. Although associations between form and meaning are made visible with the help of corpus tools, there is no one-to-one relationship between form and meaning. Five-word clusters are ultimately only pointers to textual functions and functions of *as if* patterns may be fulfilled by a number of other linguistic units, too. Within the scope of the present chapter only a limited number of examples could be discussed in detail and more patterns have to be investigated to broaden the evidential base. However, it can be argued that corpus methodology opens additional perspectives on a text that can support and complement a more intuition-based analysis. The possibility to identify repetitions systematically and compare similar examples can help the identification of patterns and relationships between parts of the text that, in turn, relate to themes and characters. Lexical features in the text are interpreted in terms of their local textual functions. In this sense they contribute to the description of the style of the text.

The Stylistics of True Crime: Mapping the Minds of Serial Killers

Christiana Gregoriou

This chapter undertakes an investigation into the representation of true crime, and in particular, the way in which the serial killer is linguistically conceptualized in a collection of interviewer informed narratives: *Talking with Serial Killers: The Most Evil People in the World Tell Their Own Stories* by Christopher Berry-Dee (2003). This focus is chosen because in serial killer narratives, the author claims, the distinction between fact and fiction is a difficult one to make, since there is more than one crime involved, generating multiple storylines and often motiveless murders, which feed into fictional literature.

The chapter is mainly concerned with the application of an increasingly important theoretical and analytical framework in stylistics, that of *mind style*. Mind style is currently the term given to identifying how a fictional character's world view is represented in a narrative, through the identification and grouping of linguistic features such as transitivity, emotive lexis and figurative language. Mind style has normally been applied to a single character's viewpoint, where a fiction writer limits omniscience to that character's world view. In this chapter, Gregoriou investigates how figurative language expressions in the book, and particularly metaphor, give access to criminal mind styles and its representations of deviant consciousness. It does this by grouping them into thematic sections that reflect narrative structure, and underpin ideological positioning. The term *criminal mind style* then, rather than describing a single fictional character, is used as a generic one, focusing upon representation of the criminal mind outside of their own consciousness as given by the author, Christopher Berry-Dee. This can be done because the interviews conducted with the serial killers are mediated through his narrative, and it is his representation of the serial killers, rather than the accounts they give themselves, with which the analysis of criminal mind style is concerned. Although Gregoriou attempts to identify both a criminal's world view, and also how the narrator reacts or engages with it, a point for discussion here is how far the chapter has been successful in this dual undertaking, and whether or not it is more concerned with the mind style of the author than those of the serial killers he represents.

The narrative structure identified is a chronological one, taken from early childhood through to fully fledged adult monsterhood. Through her analysis,

Gregoriou shows how the discourse used by others to describe serial killers contributes to mystifying them, presenting them as 'other' and, in some cases, literally alien. Analysis of metaphor particularly shows how killers are often conceptualized as devils, monsters or vampires, because, unlike in the case of single murders, there is so often so little justification of why they act as they do. Since 'ordinary' people do not behave in this way, they must, according to the discourse, be monstrous, and their reason for killing embedded in some other or outside source, such as Satanism or extraterrestrial presence. In this way, Gregoriou's analysis shows how Berry Dee's *Talking with Serial Killers* serves to help alienate such killers and reinforce our schematic expectations.

Urszula Clark

Introduction

With 'reality TV' and other such docusoaps (a type of television documentary series following people in a particular location or occupation over a period of time) filling prime-time television slots across the globe, *reality* appears to altogether feature as a rather fashionable contemporary theme. It is no wonder that viewers as well as readers are currently fascinated by the dramatization of actual events, involving real people and real dramas. And the dramatization of actual *criminal* events holds a special fascination for all kinds of audience. As Tithecott (1997: 130) argues, 'the pleasure of horror, that which was deemed appropriate only in a recognizable world of fiction, is now something one can experience (without fear of condemnation) on television framed as reality'. Real crime guarantees readers and viewers; it ensures an audience, especially where a greater sense of fluidity between the 'real' and the 'unreal' comes into place. In other words, such American tabloid-style crime TV documentaries as CBS's *Real Patrol* and *Top Cops*, NBC's *Law and Order* and *Prime Suspect* and Fox's *Code 3* and *America's Most Wanted* more often than not transcend the barrier between the 'real' and the 'fictional', fictionalizing elements of real criminal stories for greater entertaining effect. As Tithecott put it, 'reality hasn't been real for a long time' (1997: 118).

This chapter is concerned with the linguistic nature of the true crime genre, one of the fastest growing genres at the moment. I here concentrate on the written as opposed to the televised real crime genre. In particular, I consider the way in which the 'serial killer' mind is linguistically conceptualized in *Talking with Serial Killers: The Most Evil People in the World Tell Their Own Stories*, a collection of interview-informed narratives, put together by the investigative criminologist Christopher Berry-Dee (2003). On its own cover, the *true crime* book promises to be 'more horrifying than Hannibal', in that 'every word is true'. According to the book's own blurb, here,

not only does [Berry-Dee] describe the circumstances of his meeting with some of the world's most evil men and women, [but] he reproduces, verbatim, their own words as they describe their crimes and discuss their remorse – or alarming lack of it.

The book claims to be unique in that the author discusses in detail horrific crimes through the eyes of the perpetrators themselves, while it further promises to be required reading for anyone interested in the workings of the criminal mind. Interestingly, the book has proved such a true-time classic that it prompted the production of Berry-Dee's (2005) sequel, *Talking with Serial Killers 2.*

I start by defining crime fiction, the serial-killer narrative and the true crime genre, briefly tracing their evolution and growing popularity, whilst sketching some of the links between the three. I then introduce the theoretical and ana-lytical feature I apply to the book at hand, namely *mind style*, which bears links with *figurative language* usage. Having traced the various figurative linguistic expressions that allow access to the book's criminal mind style(s) (not restricting myself to those limited excerpts where the book allows direct access to the criminals' consciousness), I group them into thematic sections that reflect the book's narrative structure, underpinning ideological positioning, and inter-pretative effects.

Crime Fiction, the Serial Killer Narrative and the True Crime Genre: Evolution and Growing Popularity

I use the term *crime fiction* to refer to those stories to do with the detection of (most usually) a murderer. Furthermore, the definition I adopt for crime-fiction narratives coincides with that definition Priestman (1998: 5) adopted when defining the *detective thriller*, a hybrid form between the *detective whodunnit* and the *thriller*. To clarify, the whodunnit is primarily concerned with unravelling past events which either involve a crime or seem to do so, while the action in the thriller is primarily in the present tense of the narrative. In other words, crime novels are often concerned with a past event of murder that gets to be resolved, while a present action of events is followed. Such fiction is most often concerned with the *search* for truth, motive, not to mention the identity of the killer him/herself. Postmodern crime fiction has given rise to such literary experiments as Paul Auster's *The New York Trilogy* (1988), which is instead concerned with the *lack* of truth, that is, the posing, as opposed to the answering, of such questions.

Equally concerned with this 'lack' of truth are *serial-killer narratives*, which make it hard for detectives to rely on traditional motivations for murder (such as greed, jealousy and ambition) that would lead them to the murderers. Rather than one crime or murder dominating the story, the serial-killer narrative features several seemingly unrelated and unmotivated murders, committed by one or more individuals over an extended period of time. And, as Binyan (1989: 105) notes, multiple crimes generate multiple storylines. Swales (2000: xiii) argues that seriality has come to be fashionable not only because it brings an urgency to the chasing and capturing of the murderer at hand, but also in that it brings out the issue of there being a pattern, one whose justification remains withheld up until the story's end.

This late 1980s and 1990s fascination with serial killers was undoubtedly sparked off by a number of notorious real-life instances (Bertens and D'haen 2001: 8). Note that no easy distinction between the fact and fiction of serial murder can be drawn, seeing that 'the fictional and non-fictional texts feed off each other in such a way that they become indistinguishable from each other in the public imagination' (D'Cruz 1994: 328). Similarly, Newitz (1995: 39) argues that serial-killer narratives span both fictional and non-fictional genres, because fictional representations of serial killers are often based on biographies of actual killers.

There are deep similarities between the cultural and fictional representation of *true crime*. Tabloids, TV documentaries and books concerned with true crime all make use of similar figurative language and strongly emotive lexis, allowing the readers insight into a certainly flawed, yet believable representation of the criminal perspective. In other words, though far from accurate, such depiction of criminality correlates closely with the way in which people *understand* criminality. We could even argue that these serial killers' linguistic and social behaviour is compatible with a widely shared 'group schema' for criminality (for schema theory, see Cook 1994; Short 1996: 227; Stockwell 2002). Interestingly, Tithecott (1997: 20) notices that the language of good and evil transcends the barrier between 'serious' and 'tabloid' journalism. Also, Nellis (2002: 442) notes that true crime representations overall reveal an emphasis on celebrity and non-repentance. In other words, criminals are often glamorized, celebrated and even worshipped in such contexts, as very special human beings, worthy of scientific study. In addition, when given a voice, such killers are not afraid to admit that they lack remorse. For instance, when Michael Bruce Ross, one of the serial killers in Berry-Dee's book, was asked about his feelings towards his victims, he characteristically said that he merely 'used' and 'abused' them, treating them like 'so much garbage' (2005: 117).

Analysing True Crime Narratives through Mind Style

Simpson (2000: 2) notes that, in America alone, especially since the early to mid-1960s, literally dozens of fiction and non-fiction accounts of serial murder have attracted enough public and critical attention to warrant serious academic study, including feminist investigations of serial murder (see, for instance, Caputi 1987; Cameron and Fraser 1987) and various social-construction approaches (see Jenkins 1994; Tithecott 1997; Seltzer 1998). Here and elsewhere (see Gregoriou 2002, 2003a, 2003b and 2007), I approach the subject of serial murder narratives from a uniquely linguistic perspective, to explore the criminal portrayal further.

In particular, I use the notion of *mind style*, developed by Fowler (1977: 76), to refer to 'cumulatively, consistent structural options, agreeing in cutting the presented world to one pattern or another', giving rise to 'an impression of a world-view', to talk about instances of realisation of narrative viewpoint that *deviate* from a commonsense version of reality (for more on mind style see Leech and Short 1981; Bockting 1994; Semino and Swindlehurst 1996; Gregoriou 2003b). Hence, mind style is a useful notion to consider in an analysis of extracts to do with *access to* and the *representation of* socially deviant consciousness, such as that of criminals. Normally, the notion of mind style is employed where the fiction writer, though not compelled to take on a single character's viewpoint, voluntarily 'limits' his omniscience to those things which belong to a criminal's world view, though I here use *criminal mind style* to also talk about the representation of the criminals' mind outside their consciousness. The sorts of linguistic phenomena used to present deviant mental selves include primarily choices in transitivity (see Leech and Short 1981: 189) and metaphorical patterns (see Semino and Swindlehurst 1996). I see *metaphor, simile* and *irony* as basic aspects of *figurative language,* like many cognitive stylisticians (see Gibbs 1994) and linguists (see Leech 1969), and hence consider these features in particular in connection to the portrayal of the serial-killer mind. Besides, current metaphor theory holds that even the most conventional figurative language connects into our pattern of thinking (see Lakoff and Johnson 1980). Hence, the more we recontextualize, reuse and share such figurative language across various cultural and fictional textual chains, the more the criminal discourse is naturalized and comes to connect to our way of thinking about criminality itself. What is more, such study of the mental functioning and mental representation of criminal personas can also help illuminate our understanding of actual criminal minds.

As Semino notes, 'when dealing with lengthy and complex texts such as literary narratives, analysts have to strike a difficult balance between exhaustively capturing the potential richness of the text and producing analyses that are reasonably economical and comprehensible' (2006: 70). I compartmentalize my analysis of *Talking with Serial Killers* in terms of thematic sections, which I hope will capture the narrative structure as well as the major themes of the true crime book. I argue that the discourse used to describe our extreme criminals helps to mystify them whilst presenting them as 'others', setting them apart from ourselves, and hence alienating them further.

'Talking with Serial Killers'

'Seeking the truth of the serial killer, we find it in the discourse with which we seek it.'

(Tithecott 1997: 106)

Talking with Serial Killers tells the separate and interview-informed stories of a number of real-life criminals, namely Harvey Louis Carignan, Arthur John Shawcross, John Martin Scripps, Michael Bruce Ross, Ronald Joseph 'Butch' DeFeo Jr, Aileen Carol Wuornos, Kenneth Allen McDuff, Douglas Daniel Clark and Carol Mary Bundy and, finally, Henry Lee Lucas. Each of these narratives details the killer's childhood, upbringing and criminal activities.

The Early Childhood

The widespread belief that childhood trauma can explain adult deviance (Simpson 2000: xiii) is evident in the book at hand. In 'like so many serial killers, Harvey was an illegitimate child who never knew his genetic father' (Berry-Dee 2003: 11), an unnecessary link is established between parental neglect and serial killing. Similarly, in 'there is little doubt, though, that his mother and other female relations, including his aunts and grandmother, treated him with contempt [...] Revenge – more particularly, revenge against women – played an important part in his motivation' (Berry-Dee 2003: 29), the apparent mistreatment by female figures Carignan endured comes to be linked to his later criminal behaviour towards women. Also, 'we know he was bullied, before the worm finally turned and he became a bully and sadist himself. The roots of evil had already been planted' (Berry-Dee 2003: 75), links Shawcross's high-school bullying to a rather vampiric reaction (see Gregoriou 2007, for the VAMPIRE criminal archetype). The metaphors of EVIL IS A ROOT and HUMAN BEING IS A PLANT are here evoked; people experience growth, yet evil takes the form of seeds which, once planted, affect the nature and behaviour of the adult the child grows into. The same sort of metaphor is evoked in reference to Wuornos's antisocial behaviour, which was 'implanted by the family surroundings in which she was reared' (Berry-Dee 2003: 229).

Interestingly, once we identify a link between an abnormal or traumatic childhood background and serial killers, the link is made to look causal. As Tithecott (1977: 43) notes, however, we forget the majority of those serial killers who have suffered no abuse or neglect, or those who indeed have suffered from these, and yet do not go on to commit horrific crimes as adults as a result. Yet a traumatic childhood is not enough to account for our serial killers' criminal behaviour, and it is not uncommon for the blame for their actions to be assigned to a whole range of sources other than the killer him/herself.

The Blame Game

One common source for the blame is the victims. In 'older men with sex on their minds, maybe in the image of her grandfather, crossed her path' (Berry-Dee 2003: 232), the victims are placed in the agent position of the relevant clause, leaving the killer Wuornos appear as an almost innocent bystander in these apparently very dangerous men's path. Similarly, in 'she finally made me so mad that I hit her [...] Then I noticed I had my knife in my hand and she had been cut [...] [I]t had to happen' (Berry-Dee 2003: 319), Lucas takes no responsibility or agency over his criminal actions. He instead blames the victim for having made him mad, while the agentless passive in 'she had been cut' is used to redeem himself of blame as well as place himself in the position of a victim of circumstances beyond his control.

But when victims do not prove suitable causes for the killing sprees, external forces and nature itself often have to do so. In the story of the Aileen Wuornos shootings, the bullets are personified, striking arms, entering and penetrating bodies, slamming into torsos, 'passing through' and 'coming to rest' (Berry-Dee 2003: 202) in organs, causing fatal wounds. Similarly, in describing DeFeo's shooting of his sister Allison, the bullet smashes and enters the victim's body, before exiting, hitting the wall and bouncing on the floor to rest (Berry-Dee 2003: 171). Like a human being, the bullet acquires agency when entering into the room-like body and, in turn, removes responsibility from the perpetrator altogether.

In 'at first, he stated that he was ordered by God to murder them because they all had AIDS [...] Then Arthur argued that he was suffering from a rare genetic disorder, and this was why he turned to serial homicide' (Berry-Dee 2003: 65–6), God and genetic disorders are identified as the sources responsible for Arthur Shawcross's criminal behaviour. In 'there is also evidence suggesting that people with the genetic and chemical disorders ascribed to Shawcross can metamorphose into extremely dangerous individuals who thrive during the hours of darkness' (Berry-Dee 2003: 80), a modalized and hence very tentative connection between faulty genes and criminal tendencies is established (see Gregoriou 2007, for the MONSTER criminal archetype). Here, the criminal is metaphorically conceptualized as a type of werewolf, who inadvertently goes out in search of prey at night-time.

If the criminals are captured and then released to kill again, the system is blamed, as is the overcrowding of the entire US penal system:

> What was the real reason for the release of such a dangerous man as Shawcross? [...] Overcrowding is a serious problem [... and] policy dictates that if there is the slightest chance that an inmate is 'reformed', then the authorities want him out of prison as soon as possible.
>
> (Berry-Dee 2003: 49)

The 'Emerging Criminal Self': Metaphors of Criminality

'In the figure of the serial killer, whether presented in fictional or "tabloid" "true crime" fashion, we see a similar human monster, textually coded as generically supernatural but, in part, vampiric' (Simpson 2000: 4). According to the same source, such metaphors are, in part, designed for arriving at an intuitive explanation of the human ability to murder other humans for symbolic reasons having nothing to do with literal survival. In other words, killers are most often conceptualized as devils, vampires or monsters merely because we lack a good justification as to why they act the way they do. Thinking of killing in terms of Satanism and extraterrestrial presence on earth is the only logical explanation we see in a world bearing purposeless crimes. Meehan (1994) even paradoxically concludes that calling a human murderer a monster eases the fear surrounding the crimes. Despite such alienation, Simpson (2000: 11) notes that the tragic personal background humanizes the coded monster making it capable of earning the audience's sympathy.

Talking with Serial Killers employs a huge range of such dehumanizing metaphors and similes to portray the emerging criminal self. Lucas is out on a mission, 'presumably with the Devil sitting on his shoulder' (Berry-Dee 2003: 327), while Carignan is referred to as 'the fuckin' Devil.... [T]hey should have driven a stake through his heart' (Berry-Dee 2003: 9), who 'smashed [his victims'] skulls to an unrecognisable pulp using demoniacal and inhuman force' (p. 29) and 'turned into something from Hell. His fury came out of nowhere, like he was suddenly switched on with evil' (p. 13). Carignan's fury is here anthropomorphized, he himself is demonized, and evil is conceptualized as a light being switched on. This correlation between light and darkness as basic human experiences is also evident in 'there was a darker side that surfaced when he was alone' (pp. 14–15), which additionally and rather unusually evokes the correlation between upwards orientation and some sort of release into criminality. In 'you'll get to interview Harvey, or something living inside his head. You'll get to interview him, and Evil will get to interview you' (pp. 22–3), evil is personified and located inside a human's head, capable of interacting with others. It is not uncommon for killers to use the MONSTER metaphor themselves to externalize the blame: 'That's where the monster inside of me came out' (p.34). Similarly, on p.151, thoughts of killing are conceptualized by the killer Ross as a tune he cannot get rid of, and which then gets personified into an obnoxious and intruding room-mate, 'butting' into his life and having effect and taking responsibility over his criminal actions.

Another common metaphor is CRIMINAL IS A HUNTER or ANIMAL, where the killers are conceptualized as a powerful hunting species, often in need of feeding to survive. In such contexts, the acts of the serial killer are 'figured as continuous with the craving of food, as one of the more recent and extreme examples of man fulfilling his ever-changing needs' (Tithecott 1997: 63). Such metaphors and similes are evident in 'Arthur [...] possesses a certain kind of animal cunning, and has the instinct to smell a rat a mile away' (Berry-Dee 2003: 70), in '*I am like a predator, able to hunt and to wantonly destroy at any given time*' (p.83), and in 'Wuornos haunted those places like a deadly spider sitting at the centre of its web' (p.225), and have the effect of naturalizing and even normalizing the serial killer's acts (Tithecott 1997: 151).

KILLERS ARE FAULTY MACHINES is yet another common metaphor. Such metaphors help justify our impression of the killers as unfeeling, preprogrammed and automatic, while they take responsibility away from the perpetrators, often therefore assigning it onto the writer or maker of the relevant computer program (in other words, either nature or God himself). For instance, in 'paedophiliac behaviour leading to rape and homicide was pre-programmed into him like a faulty computer chip' (Berry-Dee 2003: 80), the human body is conceptualized through the simile as a badly formatted computer, preprogrammed into criminality. Killers are conceptualized as 'wrongly "wired-up"' (p.154), their hypothalamus's switch being jammed (p.155), and the so-called electromechanical switching systems being 'inherently flawed' (p.156):

For basic functions, it might even work quite well for some of the time, but it will break down when more complicated calculations are required of it. This seems to illustrate what happened to Michael Ross.

(Berry-Dee 2003: 156)

According to Tithecott (1997: 98), our construction of mechanized monsters can indicate our humanity's 'naturalness' or its future in a technological age, as well as force us into questioning what kind of a culture is in fact capable of generating and using such 'machines' in the first place.

The Abnormalities of the Formative Years

The serial killer narratives often make mention of early behavioural problems, establishing connections between the killers' early harmless social abnormalities and their later criminality. For instance, 'very early in his formative years, Harvey developed a facial twitch and suffered from bed-wetting until he was 13 years old' (Berry-Dee 2003: 11), while Shawcross 'developed a characteristic blink, which he still has today. He also started to make a noise like a bleating lamb, and often lapsed into baby talk' (p.37), and spoke 'in a childish, duck-like, high-pitched voice' (p.39). The fact that we are told about these strange blinking, twitching and babbling idiosyncrasies makes them relevant and hence linked to the subject's later criminal behaviour, though there is no evidence to actually establish there being a link between the two. And it is not uncommon for such non-threatening early social abnormalities to be accompanied by a physically abnormal appearance.

The Monstrous Appearance

Carignan's 'massive-frame' is described as 'ape-like' and 'Neanderthal-like', his 'piercing blue' and 'dangerous eyes' (Berry-Dee 2003: 23) staring into his interviewer's face. Though Carignan is, at first, described as a 'gentle, even understanding giant of a man', he is also said to be like 'some alien creature, an insidious force even', probing into Berry-Dee's mind, 'using long, squirming tentacles of enquiring thought, exploring, touching, sensing with taste and smell' (p.23). Carignan's features are here personified, made to look scary in themselves, establishing an unnecessary link between his perhaps unusual physical appearance and criminal behaviour. Even more terrifying, though, are our Average-Joe looking killers, not because their appearance is extraordinary, but precisely because it is so ordinary. Ross, for instance, is described as a 'stereotypical "All-American" homespun boy [...], very much the boy next door; the type a father might approve of his daughter dating' (p.118).

The Psychological Evaluation

The serial-killer narratives often lapse into descriptions of each criminal's medical and psychological evaluation, profiling the criminal personalities into supposed types. Such discourse is diffused with 'impressive-sounding but almost uselessly vague psychological jargon' (Simpson 2000: 81), and it helps frame the criminal personas, concealing contradictions and merging distinctions. In discussing the behaviour of Carol Bundy, Berry-Dee describes her as a hedonist killer, a category he in turn divides into two types: the lust killers who kill for sexual enjoyment and the thrill killers who kill for the excitement of a novel experience (see Gregoriou 2007, for the SPOILT CHILD criminal archetype, which encapsulates both sub-types). Bundy is said to fit both categories extremely well (Berry-Dee 2003: 308). Similarly, Shawcross was 'assessed as "an immature adolescent with a schizoid personality who decompensated [disintegrated or broke down] in ego functioning under the influence of unemployment stress, employment stress, rejection by wife"' (p.43). Interestingly, Berry-Dee notes that 'Shawcross's prison psychiatric records show a hotchpotch of so-called professional interpretations laced with educated and uneducated guesswork with just the one inconsistency; that he might, or might not, murder again' (p.74), drawing on the metaphor of PSYCHOLOGICAL RECORDS ARE FABRIC to ironically express their uselessness.

The Victims

The victims are often depersonalized and dehumanized such as in 'he had a fixation with young flesh' (Berry-Dee 2003: 15) and in 'he threw her, like a sack of potatoes, into the trunk of his car' (p.247). Here, the victims are conceptualized as things to be consumed or eaten. Reducing the actual people into objects or food to be consumed inscribes them with 'victimhood', which could be thought of as a 'second death' (Tithecott 1997: 107). Also, in describing June Scott, one of Shawcross's victims, Berry-Dee interestingly refers to her as a non-hooker and a non-drug addict, but a mere 'lost and lonely soul' (Berry-Dee 2003: 55), which itself implies that prostitutes and drug addicts are in fact deserving victims.

Irony

The serial-killer narratives employ plenty of irony. For instance, Shawcross is said to have 'repaid' (Berry-Dee 2003: 42) his firm for giving him a job by setting fire to the place. When, three days later, he set fire to a milk bottling plant, this time 'our community-minded' Arthur is said to have at least been 'considerate enough to telephone the fire brigade, then stand back admiring the red vehicles as his handiwork reduced the building to ashes' (p.43). Further down, the lives of Shawcross's victims are said to have been 'sacrificed to bureaucracy' (p.50). Similarly, while Scripps was in prison, he is said to have been trained in butchery skills, enabling him to later slaughter and dismember humans. Ironically, he is also described as 'sitting down to a plate of fillet steak' (p.95) after his butchering of a human being.

Conclusion

In this chapter, the way in which the serial killer mind is linguistically conceptualized in Berry-Dee's *Talking with Serial Killers* was explored. The serial-killer narratives were defined as those centred round multiple and often motiveless murders, generating multiple storylines and bringing out urgency to the capturing of the perpetrators. The true-crime narratives feed from and into fictional literature, and reinforce and preserve the audience's schematic expectations to do with the nature and justification of the criminal mind. In an analysis of Berry-Dee's true and interview-based storylines, the term criminal mind style was used to group features which give an impression of a deviant world view and representation of the criminal perspective, affecting our way of thinking about criminality itself. Such features included interesting uses of transitivity patterns, figurative language and emotive lexis. The analysis of the various storylines was compartmentalised into thematic sections detailing the criminal's upbringing, criminal activities and interviews with the author.

The narratives often establish unnecessary links between parental neglect and abuse, early non-dangerous idiosyncratic abnormalities, an abnormal physical appearance and genetic disorders on the one hand, and serial homicide on the other. Interesting transitivity patterns are employed where the killers tell their own stories, removing responsibility from themselves, and placing it either on chance, nature, God, the now animated and personified weapons or the victims themselves. Both in the context of factual and fictional representations of crime, our serial killers are metaphorically constructed as extraterrestrials, vampires, werewolf-like monsters and devils, not to mention animals and faulty machines. Psychological jargon is also often employed and discussed ironically to express its uselessness. At the same time, the victims are dehumanized, conceptualized as food to be consumed and even placed in some sort of pecking order. Finally, irony is often employed as yet another feature also evident in fictional representations of crime. As Tithecott (1997: 179) put it, '[the serial killer myth] is a myth in which victims are represented in contrast to the glamour, mystery, and power of those who brought their lives to an end'. Overall, such narratives help to alienate our killers and reinforce such myths, serving to explain our society's anxieties, fantasies and preoccupations.

'Do you want to hear about it?' Exploring Possible Worlds in Michael Joyce's Hyperfiction, *afternoon, a story*

Alice Bell

'Do you want to hear about it?' somebody, presumably the narrator, asks somebody else, presumably the reader, in the first lexia of the best-known of all hypertext fictions, Michael Joyce's *afternoon, a story*. The question invites us to engage with the insoluble puzzle of Joyce's story, but it also, in the same economical gesture, calls our attention to the boundary that separates the world where we reside from the world of Joyce's text. Another such ontological split, but one level down, occurs later on in a different lexia, when we learn that part of the text that we might have assumed was narrated *about* Peter by someone else, is actually authored *by* Peter and read by his therapist. With that gesture, as economical as the first one, the fictional world of *afternoon* splits, or perhaps 'calves', like a glacier, and we become aware of the text's ontological multiplicity. We become aware, in other words, that apart from posing an epistemological puzzle (What happened that afternoon?), *afternoon* also challenges us to determine 'how much of [its] world is textual reality and how much is textual fiction'.

These are among the complexities that Alice Bell illuminates by applying the tools and insights of Possible Worlds Theory to Joyce's seminal hyperfiction. Bell's analysis cuts more than one way – perhaps as many as three ways, in fact. On the one hand, of course, it cuts hermeneutically, making available to us aspects of meaning in Joyce's text that up till now had remained invisible, or at any rate hard to see clearly. Second, her analysis aligns Bell decisively with the 'second wave' of hypertext theorists. 'First-wave' theorists, including George Landow, Janet Murray, J. Yellowlees Douglas, were preoccupied with sharpening the distinctions between hypertext and print media, and with legitimizing hypertext intellectually by associating it with post-structuralist theory. Moreover, they were prone to exaggerate the 'liberatory' effects of hypertext for the reader. 'Second-wave' theorists, beginning perhaps with Espen Aarseth, and including Raine Koskimaa, Dave Ciccoricco and now Alice Bell, among others, display appropriate scepticism towards the more utopian claims of first-wave theory, are less impressed by poststructuralism, and seem generally more at home with digital media – less like explorers dispatched from the print-based world to scout out the alien digital terrain, more like native informants. (Marie-Laure Ryan, perhaps alone among hypertext theorists, has managed to surf both waves.)

Finally, Bell's analysis demonstrates the usefulness of Possible Worlds Theory in elucidating a particular text, and in capturing the poetics of the genre to which it belongs. This was not a foregone conclusion, for the applicability of Possible Worlds Theory to poetics and interpretation has long remained an open question. Originating as it does in analytical philosophy, Possible Worlds Theory has been regarded (for instance by Ruth Ronen) as too 'philosophical' to provide the kind of fine-toothed instruments needed to engage with the particularities of actual fictional texts. Indeed, literary applications of Possible Worlds Theory have been few, and half-hearted. Typically, Possible Worlds are invoked as a general framework, only to be ignored once 'properly' literary description and interpretation get under way. (Among such half-hearted applications I include my own application of Possible Worlds Theory to postmodernist fiction.) Bell's analysis suggests that, far from being too 'philosophical', Possible Worlds Theory might simply have been waiting for the emergence of an object to which its tools were ideally suited. That object is hypertext fiction – or so Bell persuades us.

Brian McHale

Introduction

This chapter provides an analysis of Michael Joyce's (1987) hyperfiction, *afternoon, a story* using Possible Worlds Theory. Hyperfictions are novels written in hypertext and read from a computer screen. Each section of text within a hyperfiction, equivalent to a page in a book, is displayed within a separate window. These chunks are referred to as 'nodes' and have titles rather than being numbered. While the reader may access the next default page in a near-linear fashion, by clicking on the 'Next' button or pressing the 'Enter' key, specific words and sentences are also hyperlinked to provide non-linear access to other nodes. In some instances, the text asks a question, requiring a 'yes' or 'no' response, with each answer leading to a different part of the text. *afternoon* exploits hypertext capabilities such that a number of different possible paths exist within the text, describing different events or presenting different versions of those events.

Approaches to Hyperfiction

Hypertext theory has accompanied hyperfiction from its earliest conception (e.g. Aarseth 1994; Landow 1994, 1997; Landow and Delany 1991; Bolter 2001); many hyperfiction authors, including Joyce, are also prominent theoretical figures. However, much of the early hypertext theory does have theoretical and methodological limitations. Hyperfiction is situated relative to print, with the role of the hyperfiction reader sometimes elevated to disproportionate levels. In addition, perhaps because of the esoteric status of the hypertext form and structure, reading path descriptions are sometimes favoured over critical analyses (see Koskimaa 2000; Miles 2003; Bell 2006; Ciccoricco 2007; Ensslin 2007 for more detailed discussion).

However, despite such potential shortcomings, two very relevant themes are addressed: the reader's exploratory role and the multiple reading paths. What is important to point out here is that the different choices granted to the reader represent different possibilities in the ontological domain to which they belong. In addition, because readers experience different courses of events, or different versions of events, depending upon the path taken, hyperfictions also offer different possibilities in the ontological domain within the text. While these two processes are distinct, they do happen simultaneously and are intrinsically linked, exposing the divide between the world in the text and the world in which the reader resides. Readers can influence the world in the text, but only from a position *external* to it. Thus their interactive role actually draws attention to their part in the fiction making process. The different possibilities within the text further foreground its artificiality because the reader is always aware that what they are reading can be replaced by an alternative – it is merely a temporary construction.

The analysis here will verify these theoretical conjectures by providing examples of how and where such displacement operates in *afternoon*. In addition to the multiple paths and ensuing concurrent narratives that are enabled by the hypertext structure *outside* of the text, stylistic analysis also shows how worlds are built *within* the novels. What is often underemphasized in hypertext theory is that the ontological landscapes of hyperfiction are built both narratalogically *and* linguistically.

Hyperfiction and Ontology

Clearly hyperfiction is not the only type of fiction which foregrounds its ontological status. An overarching preoccupation with worlds and fictional ontology is theoretically consistent with other genres such as Hutcheon's (1988, 1989) 'historiographic metafiction', Waugh's (1984) 'metafiction' and McHale's (1987, 1992) 'postmodernist fiction'. Indeed, McHale emphasizes that 'the dominant of postmodernist fiction is *ontological*' (McHale 1987: 10) and argues that typical questions about postmodernist fiction

> bear either on the ontology of the literary text itself or on the ontology of the world which it projects, for instance: What is a world?, What kinds of world are there, how are they constituted? [...] What happens when [...] boundaries between worlds are violated?

> (McHale 1987: 10)

McHale's questions are relevant because they offer a potential framework from which to work. However, the point here is not to group hyperfiction under a pre-established term, such as 'postmodern'. Neither is it to suggest that hyper-fiction is unique in its ontological preoccupation. Rather, the aim is to demon-strate how one particular hyperfiction novel links questions concerning reality and truth with its own thematic concerns.

McHale's approach is therefore tangential with regard to his particular subject matter. Importantly, however, like Ashline (1995), Hutcheon (1988: 147, 152), Punday (1997) and Ryan (1992, 1998), he engages with and endorses Possible Worlds Theory as an appropriate analytical framework for fiction which fore-grounds its ontological status (see McHale 1987: 33–6; 1992: 45, 252 for brief discussions).

Possible Worlds Theory

Possible Worlds Theory in literary studies (e.g. Pavel 1986; Doležel 1989, 1998a; Ryan 1991; Ronen 1994) appropriates the concepts of ontology, reference and modality from possible-worlds logic (e.g. Hintikka 1967; Kripke 1972; Lewis 1973; Plantinga 1974; Rescher 1975), applying the metaphor of a 'world' to fictional texts. It is particularly relevant for hyperfiction because it offers an appropriate means of dissecting a fictional universe into its constituent ontological domains whilst also providing accompanying terminology. A tendency towards a very high level of abstraction has been noted (see Werth 1999: 80; Semino 2003: 87). However, in a complex fictional universe, this provides a very useful analytical foundation and Possible Worlds Theory is extremely proficient at simplifying intricate ontological configurations.

Crucially, the application of Possible Worlds Theory differs from other approaches, such as Text World Theory (e.g. Werth 1999; Hidalgo Downing 2000; Gavins 2005, 2007), which also apply the metaphor of 'world' to fictional domains. The focus of Possible Worlds Theory is on the ontological landscapes within fictional texts, rather than the associated cognitive processes which build those domains in the minds of readers. This might imply that the reader is relegated, if not neglected, in this analysis. However, limiting their involvement does not mean that the role of the hyperfiction reader is unacknowledged. Nor does it seek to discredit other analyses, which would focus more specifically on the choices and cognitive processes of the reader. It is rather that the emphasis here is placed primarily on the possibilities in the text and the ensuing ontolo-gical structures and not necessarily the reader's cognition of those structures. Consequently, the term 'reader' is used here in the most universal and idealized sense, as opposed to a particular cognitive sense.

Possible Worlds Theory has been imported into literary studies and casually invoked, sometimes without an explanation or elaboration of why it is useful or *how* it is to be used. This is perhaps why the field currently lacks conceptual and terminological coherence and consistency (see Ronen 1994: 60 and Bell 2006 for such charges). It is precisely for this reason that it is important to outline the modal universe and accompanying terminology that will be adopted for the purpose of this analysis.

With influence from possible worlds logic and Ryan's (1991) literary adaptation, the 'Actual World' describes the centre of our ontological universe; 'Possible Worlds' represent alternatives to the Actual World and are indefinite in number. In the fictional universe, the 'Textual Actual World' is an autonomous world described by any particular fictional text and 'Textual Possible Worlds' are alternatives to that respective Textual Actual World.

By examining the interplay between worlds in *afternoon*, the success of Possible Worlds Theory for hyperfiction will be demonstrated. More specifically, the analysis will reveal how the novel is deliberately vague in its presentation of 'facts' and while this is evidenced and understood in terms of ontology, it will also be shown to be of central hermeneutic significance.

afternoon as Story

afternoon is set in modern-day America and centres around four main characters. Peter is the central protagonist. He has an ex-wife, Lisa, and a son, Andrew. Peter works with Werther, who is romantically involved with Peter's confidante, Lolly. Lolly also advises Nausicaa, who is probably Peter's lover. There are many uncertainties in the text, including the fact that Werther and Nausicaa may be having an affair, as might Peter and Lolly. As this short synopsis demonstrates, the characters' lives are deeply intertwined and the circumstances surrounding them are equally complex. The text pivots around a number of separate events, of which the most influential is a car accident, in which Lisa and Andrew may have been involved. Readers are never quite sure what has happened because different reading paths reveal different outcomes. The accident is, however, crucial to the thematic concerns of the novel because it is used to explore each character's search for or denial of the truth.

Most discussions of *afternoon* do note structural idiosyncrasies and narrative contradictions, particularly relating to the pivotal car accident in which Andrew may or may not have been killed (e.g. Douglas 1992, 1994; Gaggi 1997: 123–6; Murray 1997: 57–8; Walker 1999; Bolter 2001: 124–8). However, in addition to what are obviously very important narrative events, Peter's role is also entirely significant because he performs two integral narratological functions. Primarily and most obviously, he is the main protagonist, with events largely revolving around him. In addition, however, he is also utilized as a tool for challenging the text's ontological landscape and, as such, as a mechanism for thwarting any pursuit of definitive conclusions.

Entering the Textual Actual World of *afternoon*

While *afternoon* houses 539 nodes, 951 links which comprise many different paths, there is actually only one entrance to the hyperfiction. The entrance node is entitled 'begin' and it contains the following text:

I try to recall winter. 'As if it were yesterday?' she says, but I do not signify one way or another.

By five the sun sets and the afternoon freeze melts again across the blacktop into crystal octopi and palms of ice – rivers and continents beset by fear, and we walk out to the car, the snow moaning beneath our boots and the oaks exploding in series along the fenceline of the horizon, the shrapnel settling like relics, the echoing off far ice. This was the essence of wood these fragments say. And this darkness is air.

'Poetry' she says, without emotion, one way or another.

Do you want to hear about it?

{begin}

(The node titles are referenced within this chapter using curly brackets.) Primarily, the node describes an interchange between two people, using first-person narration. A winter scene is described and finally, a question is asked. More specifically, the first sentence suggests that the narrator is describing a generic 'winter'; the absence of a definite or indefinite article implying eternal qualities. However, the following paragraph then adopts a style which draws us more closely towards the entities described. Here, there is consistent use of the definite article, as in 'the sun', 'the car' and 'the shrapnel', implying that this winter is somewhat recognisable to the reader. Similarly, the consistent use of personal pronouns throughout and the associated absence of preliminary proper names provide a very familiar feel to the address; the lack of specificity presumes that the reader knows the referent. Consequently, it suggests that this is a private and intimate scene on which we are intruding, albeit with permission.

However, in contrast to the apparent familiarity invoked by the articles and pronouns, an elusive atmosphere is also apparent. This is largely because the entrance to the text is highly poetic and the resulting Textual Actual World is somewhat opaque. The central paragraph constitutes one complex sentence, largely comprised of metaphorical language. The climate, the light and the natural surroundings frame this scene figuratively and metaphors, such as 'crystal octopi' and 'palms of ice', are abundant throughout. Similarly, the natural phenomena are personified with negative qualities: rivers and continents are 'beset by fear' and the snow is 'moaning'. This winter is quite a dangerous place and violent images such as 'exploding', 'thundering' and 'shrapnel' confirm an intimidating, confrontational and antagonistic presence. Nouns such as 'relics', 'ice' and 'darkness' likewise construct tomb-like images, incrementally constructing a scene tainted with decay. Primarily, the emotive descriptions might imply a romantic mood within a somewhat clichéd winter setting. However, the moans, explosions, echoes and thunder also suggest an emptiness that is more than just literal and therefore might extend to the atmosphere between the two figures.

The central paragraph, thus, offers a predominantly symbolic description, offering little in terms of literal description. The metaphors drawing on domains of violence and fear might, at first, imply a potentially volatile relationship. However, while the description offers a small glimpse of their world, there is very little deictic detail here. The female speaker's words are uttered 'without emotion' and this evaluative reporting clause makes it difficult to determine whether the comment is complimentary or ironic. Similarly, neither the narrator nor the speaker is named; the speech reported with a personal pronoun, 'she', signifying the gender of the speaker only. The exact time and location is also lacking. Rather than being given information from which the reader can start to build a definitive Textual Actual World, this mass of indistinct imagery makes the scene increasingly imprecise. However, while the indeterminacy is certainly provoking, it is not particularly unusual. Up until the final line, the opening establishes an ontological dichotomy between the Actual World and the Textual Actual World, which is common in many other fictional texts.

However, despite a comforting familiarity, the direct second person address in the final line of the {begin} node, 'Do you want to hear about it?', significantly affects this landscape. The lack of speech marks in the text suggests that the narrator is asking the reader a question, rather than it constituting speech between the two characters. This is important for two reasons, which operate at two different ontological levels. In the Actual World, it highlights the position of the reader relative to the Textual Actual World. In the Textual Actual World, it affords significant information about the narrator.

Occlusion from the Textual Actual World

Starting with the Actual World, the direct address alerts us to the artificial status of the text with self-reflexivity primarily initiated linguistically. There is an evident stylistic shift at the third paragraph from the figurative descriptions of the landscape and atmosphere to a literal statement, ' "Poetry" she says, without emotion, one way or another'. In addition, there is a notable change from the uninterrupted declaratives of the first three paragraphs to a single interrogative: 'Do you want to hear about it?' Its positioning in a separate paragraph also visually disconnects the interjection from the rest of the text.

In terms of its pragmatic function, the address is particularly significant because it highlights the structural peculiarity of the text by signalling a possible split or fork in the text, foregrounding the multilinearity of the narrative in the Actual World and also the many possibilities in the Textual Actual World. The reader can hear about this part or opt for another. Overall, the contrast in both style and function foregrounds the role of the narrator, reminding us that this is a prefabricated *account* of a world. The reader can influence the text, but from an outsider's position, ontologically disconnected from the Textual Actual World. As such, an ontological incongruity between the reader, in their world, and the narrator, in his, begins to be made much more apparent.

However, while readers are alienated from the Textual Actual World in terms of their relative position to it, they are actually ultimately invited to visit. By explicitly inviting the reader from the Actual World into the Textual Actual World, the ontological boundaries between these domains also become less divisive. Instead of there being a clear distinction between the worlds, what ensues is what McHale calls a 'semipermeable membrane' (McHale 1987: 34), where each world seems to be accessible to the other. While readers inevitably have access to the Textual Actual World, a second person address from the text playfully implies that this domain also has access to the Actual World. While this is not logically possible, the effect is enough to draw attention to the ontological game in which readers normally passively partake. Thus, rather than the semipermeable membrane erasing or concealing the frontier between the Textual Actual World and the Actual World, it instead 'foregrounds ontological boundaries and ontological structure' (McHale 1987: 35), so that the reader becomes much more conscious of the distinction between the two domains. While the boundary between the worlds in *afternoon* is not solely created by this direct question, the address works as a way of deliberately accentuating it. It is precisely because this boundary is so prominent that it is unsettling when fictional entities appear to cross or permeate it.

Controlling the Textual Actual World

Interestingly, by referring to his own capacity to open up this world, it is the narrator himself, in this case, Peter, who is responsible for ejecting the reader from this domain. However, despite the occlusion from the Textual Actual World by the self-reflexive address, Peter asks the reader to respond to his question in order that he/she can continue through the text. Somewhat ironically, however, the vagueness with which the Textual Actual World is presented in {begin} actually impairs our ability to make such decisions. Peter asks whether we, as readers, want to hear about 'it', but because this is at the beginning of the text, we do not have adequate details to know what 'it' is and we must make a decision based on very little information. Readers may feel temporarily empowered in their ability to make a choice, but it is only because the narrator has permitted such a choice that they have any influential role. Further, any degree of power that readers might feel granted by the choice is immediately superseded by incapacity because they have no way of knowing whether Peter accepts their response. They are ultimately powerless, primarily because of their lack of knowledge about the Textual Actual World and its rules, but more specifically because of the narrator and his agenda.

Ontologically, it is the invitation from Peter which actually marks the occlusion from the Textual Actual World. However, hermeneutically, the invitation is important in terms of what it also reveals about him. In taking on the role of guardian of the text, he implies that he holds control of the narrative and may divulge information only if he wishes; he certainly presents himself as omniscient and omnipotent in {begin}. However, much of the rest of the text suggests that Peter is anything but self-assured. In fact, his reluctance to confront his own world resonates throughout the entire novel, forming one of the central themes. Crucially, however, because of the many different paths, the different versions of events and the resultant indeterminacy, the text continually forces us to revise both our view of Peter and also our understanding of the ontological structure of the novel itself. It exploits the fact that readers cannot find the truth, juxtaposing their behaviour with that of Peter's. That is, while readers may search for answers within the text, Peter frequently thwarts that investigation. Most obviously, Peter delays determining the details of the car accident – 'part of me does not yet want to know' {I would have asked} – or simply opts to numb his consciousness: 'I do not call the hospital. I take a pill' {I call}.

Peter's explicit apathy signals his denial to address reality. However, the novel also offers much more subtle means of obstruction, utilising the ontological multiplicity that the hypertext form facilitates. In both individual nodes and also lengthier sequences, other characters take control of the narration, often contributing their version of events. This not only challenges Peter's omnipotence, but also undermines any seeming omniscience that he may have. In a node entitled {ex-wife}, for example, the observer appears to be someone other than Peter:

> She'd prefer that little be said about her. Consider her name. [...]
> 'Lisa ...' Her mother's friends would say. 'Sounds a little French doesn't it?'
> [...] When they had a child they named him Andrew because it seemed timeless and unlikely to be popular.
>
> {ex-wife}

This node details the naming of Peter's ex-wife, Lisa, and the impact this has on the naming of their child, Andrew. Significantly, the pronoun used in the final paragraph suggests that this narrator is not the same as that used in {begin}. While the characters are those discussed in the opening, the use of 'they' to refer to Lisa and her then husband Peter suggests a distance between the narrator and the subjects of that narration. This, at least, gives a sense that the narrator is not Peter. The narration moves from first to third person, thus effecting a more detached view than is evident in the {begin} node, for example. Thus, an additional narrator appears to be introduced and the ontological landscape established in nodes such as {begin} is changed. Peter, Lisa and Andrew exist in the same ontological domain: the Textual Actual World. However, this domain now contains multiple perspectives. Peter sometimes assumes the role of first person narrator in the Textual Actual World. However, in the {ex-wife} node, the narration is adopted by an unknown third person.

While another entity has been added to the Textual Actual World, this is not particularly disturbing to the ontological landscape. The text has changed from having one narrator to two, but the ontological dichotomy still remains intact. The frequency of multiple viewpoints and narrative contradictions within this hypertext may mean that changes in perspectives do not challenge the reader particularly. However, it is precisely such expectations that the text exploits, encouraging us to draw conclusions about the ontological landscape before then subverting and unsettling them.

Multiple Worlds?

Like many other nodes in *afternoon*, explanatory information about {ex-wife} lies in a node which is structurally unconnected, so that clarification is found in a different reading path or is located by exploring the text in an experimental non-linear fashion. This fragmentation encourages, if not enforces, exploratory reading behaviour. More importantly for the purpose of this analysis, however, it also requires an analytical approach, such as Possible Worlds Theory, which can comprehend the text's multidimensionality.

The node entitled {gift of hearing} clarifies what the {ex-wife} narration change signifies:

> ' "She'd prefer that little be said about her" indeed! [...] For all your sup-posed variations, you've written nothing but the same old patterns: the wooden wife, the receptive whore, the all accepting female mind!
> [...] No, you have no right to such a term, not even in passing, not even as part of some supposed narrativistic point of view [...] I mean what could you possibly know of women's friendships, of women's fears, of women's minds?'
> {gift of hearing}

Apart from the evident citation in the first sentence, signalled by embedded quotation marks, this node largely comprises direct speech only. It is apostrophic – a critical rebuke from one person directly to another with speech marks also indicating that the exchange is verbal. Crucially, however, the opening sentence is exactly the same as the opening sentence of the {ex-wife} node: 'She'd prefer that little be said about her'. Again, this feature works in two independent ontological domains.

In the Actual World, it can act as a trigger to remind readers of the {ex-wife} node. Even if they cannot remember the exact context, they may well remember the sentence, if not acknowledge that they have encountered it before. Nodes such as {ex-wife}, which constitutes one of many such examples in *afternoon*, give a dream-like sense to the text and an accompanying *déjà vu* feel to readers' experience.

In the second context of the quotation – the Textual Actual World – the speaker confirms that this text may have come from elsewhere because it is dis-played using double quotation marks. The node title, {gift of hearing}, further implies an association with surveillance, as if an overheard conversation. Thus, even if readers have not encountered the {ex-wife} node directly, graphological features signify that this text is taken from elsewhere. The speaker's own com-ments upon the 'writing' and the 'narrativistic point of view' also suggest that they are talking about a written account, particularly some kind of fabricated or fic-tional narrative. Each textual detail combines to suggest that the speaker has heard or, more accurately, read the depiction of Lisa and Peter given elsewhere.

This incident is highly significant because it challenges the status of the {ex-wife} node, while simultaneously raising questions about the ontological position of the speaker in {gift of hearing}. Readers do not know how or why the speaker has access to {ex-wife} and consequently the status and function of that node is ambiguous. The ontology is disrupted because readers encounter a crossing of world boundaries. It appears as if someone else – another textual entity – has been reading the same text and therefore someone else has access to the Textual Actual World narrated by Peter. In nodes such as {begin} and {ex-wife}, the ontological landscape is comprised of the Actual World and the Textual Actual World – it is dichotomous. However, the {gift of hearing} mutates this ontological landscape because the narrator here does not belong to the same ontological domain as the narrator in {ex-wife} and, implicitly, {begin}.

In the Actual World, this temporarily causes a feeling of disruption and ontological ambiguity because the extra narrator is somewhat nomadic – readers cannot place them in relation to the rest of the text. However, resolution is imminently achieved:

> 'Fuck this! – I say – I don't need this ...' I stop this short. It is what she wishes me to do.
>
> {salt washed}

In this accompanying node it is revealed that the conversation in {ex-wife} actually forms part of a meeting between Peter and a female confidante. Ontologically situating this node, Peter is restored as first-person narrator. Working backwards therefore, his confidante is the critic in {gift of hearing} and Peter is the narrator of his own take in {ex-wife}. What appear to be two different perspectives in the same Textual Actual World – Peter as first person narrator and an unnamed distanced third-person narrator – have actually become one. That is, sometimes Peter is first and sometimes Peter is third person narrator. However, when Peter uses third person, other characters have access to this narration.

Worlds within Worlds

The {gift of hearing} node thus illustrates that the {ex-wife} node is actually a separate text which posits an additional ontological domain. Therefore, we have two Textual Actual Worlds: one in which we read directly about Peter's Actual World and one in which Peter's Actual World is fictionalized by him to become his own authored text – another Textual Actual World. The reason that this is disorientating and confusing, if only temporarily, is that an extra ontological level is introduced into what was initially thought to be a dichotomous ontological relationship. The {ex-wife} node appeared to be an alternative perspective in the same Textual Actual World, but this is shifted by the {gift of hearing} and {salt-washed} sequence. Moving the {ex-wife} node into an ontological domain quite separate to its initial position means that rather than it forming part of the Textual Actual World, it actually comprises a Textual Actual World *within* a Textual Actual World.

McHale uses the metaphor of 'Chinese box worlds' to describe the recursive stacking of Textual Actual Worlds (McHale 1987: 112) and argues that this 'intensif[ies] ontological instability, titillating and horrifying the reader' (McHale 1987: 116). The effect in *afternoon* is certainly unsettling because, in response to such a shift, readers must reconsider where the characters and the worlds sit in relation to each other. This creates a feeling of uneasiness because their original relationship to the text is disturbed. Implicitly trusting that the text was depicting the Textual Actual World, readers have been deceived. The disorientation does lessen when a stable ontology can be established. However, they will inevitably feel suspicious, and perhaps unsure, because the evidence suggests that the Textual Actual World is no longer stable – it is susceptible to shifts.

Significantly, the narrative's thematic concerns remain unaffected by ontological shifts. That is, if readers encounter {gift of hearing} and {salt washed} but not the {ex-wife} node, they will still learn that Peter has to articulate his past as a written story, rather than providing an oral account. It does not matter exactly what was contained in Peter's narrative because the significance lies in the fact that the counselling session revolves around a story; Peter can only confront his life by fictionalizing it. Without seeing the primary source – Peter's written account in {ex-wife} – the significance of the change in narration from third to first person will be missed and the ontological significance of the quotation will also not be perceived. In fact, the ontological trickery will be entirely removed from readers because they will not experience the required renegotiation. However, hermeneutically, Peter's procrastination is significant in both cases.

In the analysis given above, ontological reconciliation is reached by situating the {ex-wife} node as a world within a world. Nevertheless, the ontological ambiguity that such shifts create means that the authenticity of the different narratives within the *entire* text is called into question. After such an encounter, readers cannot be sure how much of the rest of the text is the Textual Actual World in which Peter resides and how much is the Textual Actual World of his own construction. That is, how much of the world is textual reality and how much is textual fiction. Thus, in addition to the epistemological barriers enforced by the text's vastly complex structure, we are also inhibited by the gatekeeper himself. Peter cannot confront his own reality and, as such, in our pursuit of the story in *afternoon*, it is ultimately the narrator and not just the narrative that refuses to distinguish between what is actual and what is merely possible.

Conclusion

In *afternoon* the structural capacity of the medium is directly linked to or exploited by the thematic concerns of the novel itself. The text is not just multilinear for the sake of being multilinear. Rather, multilinearity is linked to Peter's inability to confront his own world. Thus, a preoccupation with actuality, possibility, potentiality and choice pervades the text both structurally and thematically.

Methodologically, as the analysis of four nodes here demonstrates, Possible Worlds Theory is an appropriate tool for hyperfiction. Principally, it provides the terminological and conceptual apparatus required to negotiate multilinearity and resulting fickle ontological landscapes. Importantly, however, the analysis above also demonstrates that Possible Worlds Theory relies on stylistic analysis in order to substantiate ontological configurations. The examination of both structural *and* linguistic world builders is imperative in any analysis, irrespective of the specifics of the medium or the thematic preoccupation of the message itself.

The Effects of Free Indirect Discourse: Empathy Revisited

Joe Bray

The label Free Indirect Discourse (FID) conveniently elides the much discussed stylistic phenomena of free indirect speech (FIS) and free indirect thought (FIT). For some it is a ducking of the analyst's responsibilities to make fine but important distinctions, while for others it acknowledges the final fuzziness of the distinctions when tested against actual occurrences. An additional reason for preferring the more inclusive term, however, to which I return, may be that it takes understanding beyond misleading ideas of actual speakers and thinkers and speech and thought events to a recognition of writing as discourse.

Bray's chapter falls into two clear sections, an informed and purposive review of the field as it bears on his own research into the relation of uses of this stylistic device to effects on readers, and then an empirical experiment to test the theoreticians' claims against the reported experience of his undergraduate readers with two versions of two relevant novel extracts. Crucially, Bray tests critics' proposals for greater empathy as a predictable effect of FIT, whether formally or more pragmatically identified.

The relation of linguistic forms to effects on readers is of course central to the endeavour of stylistics, and empathy even arguably central to developing an understanding of literariness and the value of literature. Bray's extension of existing work to reader response, and then still more topically to concerns of cognitive poetics represents a state of the art intervention.

Some will have reservations about the empirical research presented, though Bray does this kind of thing here probably as well as it can be done. Extracts read in a group for purposes of psychology experimentation are not natural readings of fiction chosen by oneself, particularly when followed up by questionnaires. Transformed extracts take us still further from the real world. The study comes most alive as we hear the more discursive comments of the participants underlining the need for the researcher into response to know more of the reading histories and practices of these 'subjects' (actually they are people).

To return to a founding text in the study of FID and still one of the most profound, Vološinov (1986) would have seen the interest in empathy as an example of 'individualistic subjectivism', one of the two weaknesses he identified in stylistic practice of his time (the other being abstract objectivism, such as Bally's search for the precise forms of what he called 'style indirect libre'). 'Characters' or 'narrators' are language effects rather than primary ontological realities as they are usually discussed in the FID literature. The empathy which post-Romantic literature exists to promote, as Bray shows, is as much in the cognition of the reader as in any linguistic features, which at best provide 'affordances' for the empathetic yearnings of our literary education. It is the value of this incisive chapter that it prompts the reader to more closely interrogate their own under-standings of these centrally important areas.

Geoff Hall

'Nothing about FID is uncontroversial', Brian McHale has recently declared (2005: 189). Certainly free indirect discourse is one of the most keenly debated topics in stylistics, with critics signally failing to agree on, amongst other things, its origins, its distinctive formal properties, whether it is exclusive to literature and whether it contains a 'dual-voice' of narrator and character (see Fludernik 1995). Even its name has provoked disagreement. Among the most popular alternatives that have been proposed are 'style indirect libre' (Bally 1912), 'narrated mono-logue' (Cohn 1978) and 'represented speech and thought' (Banfield 1982), each of which suggests a different approach to defining the style. In characterising FID as 'a swamp that I had originally intended to avoid completely', Alan Palmer notes that 'the precise nature of free indirect discourse has been the subject of a lengthy, technical, and fiercely contested narratological debate for a number of years' (2004: 56).

There has been more consensus, however, over the literary effects that free indirect discourse is supposed to create. McHale's earlier observation that 'it is routinely naturalized both as a mode of ironic distancing from characters and as a mode of empathetic identification with characters' (1978: 275) has continued to be the standard line. Stefan Oltean, for example, claims that 'the evaluative function of FID can be of two different types, depending upon whether the narrator conveys his/her distance from or identification with a character in the representation of the latter's verbal, preverbal, or non-verbal states, namely, *irony* and *empathy*' (1993: 706). For Oltean, 'the natural conjunction of irony with FID arises from the fact that FID articulates a double significance produced by the contrast of values associated with the two positions' (p. 706), while 'empathy is closely associated with the rendering of a character's personal perspective through FID, which presupposes the narrator's identification with his/her subjectivity' (p. 708).

Most critics typically associate irony with the free indirect representation of speech (FIS) and empathy with its counterpart in thought representation (FIT). Leech and Short, for example, note that since direct speech is the 'norm or baseline for the portrayal of speech', free indirect speech 'is normally viewed as a form where the authorial voice is interposed between the reader and what the character says, so that the reader is distanced from the character's words' (1981: 334). It is this distancing 'which allows FIS to be used as a vehicle of irony' (p.334). In contrast, according to Leech and Short, the 'norm or baseline' for the presentation of thought is indirect thought, and hence the free indirect form 'signifies a movement towards the exact representation of a character's thought as it occurs' (p.344). For them, 'while FIS distances us somewhat from the characters producing the speech, FIT has the opposite effect, apparently putting us directly inside the character's mind' (p.344). Monika Fludernik endorses this contrast, observing that 'empathetic thought representations in free indirect discourse are quantitatively more prominent than ironic ones, whereas free indirect discourse renderings of speech acts typically tend to be either ironic or neutral (objective): one usually does not talk about empathy in this case' (Fludernik 1993: 5–6).

Care needs to be taken, however, when considering how exactly these 'empathetic' or 'ironic' representations are created. Critics often seem to assume that 'irony' and 'empathy' are the natural outcomes of the blending of narrator's and character's 'voices' in free indirect discourse. In explaining how it is possible for his two 'evaluative functions' to merge, Oltean claims that 'with FID, empathy (character), as one of the constitutive dimensions of bivocality, is coupled with distancing (narrator) since in this case the narrator expresses his/her identification with the character in the *narrative act of telling*, that is, without entirely yielding the floor to that character, as happens with interior monologue' (Oltean 1993: 708). Oltean's emphasis on the style's 'bivocality', then, leads him to the conclusion that 'it may be unsatisfactory to conceptualize FID exclusively in terms of its empathetic or ironic function' (p.708). Yet the assumptions behind 'empathy (character)' and 'distancing (narrator)' need more examination. In particular, the view that empathy and irony are automatically present in the text as a result of the interaction of character and narrator in the so-called 'dual voice' of free indirect discourse neglects the role of the reader, a crucial figure vital to any discussion of the style's effects.

Fludernik has emphasized how 'irony' is an effect of reading, even in the standard cases of 'ironic contradiction':

> Irony is always a pragmatic phenomenon of an implicational nature; textual contradictions and inconsistencies alongside semantic infelicities, or discrepancies between utterance and action (in the case of hypocrisy), merely *signal* the interpretational incompatibility, the break in the argument, the crack in the mirror which then requires a recuperatory move on the reader's part – aligning the discrepancy with an intended higher-level significance: irony.
>
> (Fludernik 1993: 352)

Fludernik thus rejects the view that irony is caused by any kind of a 'dual voice' interaction at the textual level, arguing that 'within the free indirect discourse of course the pronominal and temporal alignment of the narrative provides a clear frame for the embedded dialogue that is being represented, but to speak of a narrator's voice intermingling with the figural idiom – or even juxtaposed to it *within* the free indirect discourse – is clearly incorrect' (p.354). Though she does acknowledge that readers often experience 'a dual voice *effect* on a higher interpretative plane' (p.356), for her the style's formal features do not themselves create irony, but instead 'facilitat[e] the effects of implicit irony' (p.355).

This chapter argues that, in the context of free indirect discourse, empathy also needs to be considered as, at least in part, a construction of the reader, rather than as an intrinsic feature of the text. After some consideration of critical approaches to the term itself, I discuss a small-scale reading task designed to investigate whether FID does evoke empathy in readers. Originally from the German 'einfühlung', 'empathy' is defined by the *OED* as 'the power of projecting one's personality into (and so fully comprehending) the object of contemplation'. The term began to be used with this sense of 'projection' in German aesthetics at the turn of the century (see Lipps 1900), and soon spread into psychology, where it became linked to the concept of 'identification' (see Zillmann 1994: 34–5, 39–40). As Susumu Kuno puts it, 'Empathy is the speaker's identification, which may vary in degree, with a person/thing that participates in the event or state that he describes in a sentence' (Kuno 1987: 206). Yet recent critics have been sceptical about the possibility of 'identification' in the reception of art. In his discussion of empathetic responses to film, Ed S.-H. Tan notes that 'identification in a literal sense is characterized by the viewers' experience of the very same emotion that the character is imagined to have' (Tan 1994: 24). He then describes some problems with this notion:

> The viewers' presumed sharing of concerns is the difficult part of the identification concept. For viewers to share completely the concerns of the character in his or her situation, would mean that they do not understand or imagine those concerns, but *have* them – an obviously impossible situation. Incomplete sharing of concerns makes it doubtful whether viewers can have emotions similar to the imaginary ones of the character.
>
> (Tan 1994: 24–5)

Tan concludes that 'we can, at best, assume that it is possible for viewers to imagine actually having a concern, which in turn results in an experience that parallels the character's "emotion" as closely as possible', and that 'all in all, it seems doubtful whether there is any use at all for the concept of identification in describing film viewing and concomitant emotion' (p.25). He proposes an alternative model of empathy, according to which 'the viewers are led to imagine themselves an *invisible witness* in the fictional world' (pp.16–17), and claims that 'the witnesses' situation is completely analogous to that of the observer in the real world, who is neither called upon to intervene nor physically able to react' (p.17). Thus an 'empathic emotion', for Tan, is simply one in which 'the viewers "relate to" the character's experience of the fictional world' (p.18). This brings 'empathy' closer to its related term 'sympathy'; Tan claims that 'most, though not all, empathic emotions are sympathetic, that is, they depend on a basic sympathy concern' (p.23). In fact the terms have often been used interchangeably, as Keith Oatley observes, 'under the heading of *sympathy*, empathic processes have received much attention and have been scrutinized by numerous scholars' (1994: 39). 'Sympathy' has usually been defined as fellow feeling rather than 'einfüh-lung'; one of the senses in the *OED* is 'the quality or state of being affected by the condition of another with a feeling similar or corresponding to that of the other' (*OED*, 3b). Philosophers of 'sympathy' have often emphasised the ways in which it differs from 'identification'. For Adam Smith in *The Theory of Moral Sentiments*, for example, the crucial point about our sympathy with others is that it can never give us direct access to their feelings. He argues that 'as we have no immediate experience of what other men feel, we can form no idea of the manner in which they are affected, but by conceiving what we ourselves should feel in the like situation. Though our brother is upon the rack, as long as we ourselves are at ease, our senses will never inform us of what he suffers. They never did, and never can, carry us beyond our own person' (Smith 1976: 9). As Charles L. Griswold observes of Smith's theory, 'sympathy does not dissolve the sense of separateness of either party' as 'in no case of sympathy [...] do we simply identify with the other' (1999: 88).

It is clear then that the term 'empathy' can involve a range of meanings; from 'identification' at one end of the continuum to 'sympathy' at the other. The relationship between these three feelings, and the ways in which they are generated by literary texts, have rarely been investigated empirically, as Don Kuiken, David S. Miall and Shelley Sikora observe, 'although narrative feelings are most frequently discussed by object-relations theorists [...], the effects of empathy, identification, and their associated narrative feelings have not been systematically examined in empirical studies' (2004: 175) (see also Keen 2006). Furthermore, though some work has been done on readers' responses to changes in narrative perspective (see for example Ludwig and Faulstich 1985; László 1986; Andringa 1996; and van Peer and Pander Maat 1996), empirical studies focused specifically on the effects of free indirect discourse remain rare, as Marisa Bortolussi and Peter Dixon note, 'how precisely readers process free-indirect speech, especially when faced with ambiguities concerning whose voice or point of view is represented, is something that has still not been studied' (2003: 208). Bortolussi and Dixon do attempt to remedy this, though their interest is solely in how readers assessed the 'rationality' of characters in FID, on the hypothesis that the style generates 'narrator-character associations' (p.229), and that 'when an association is formed between the narrator and a character, that character will be seen as more rational (a characteristic normally associated with the narrator)' (p.231). The broader range of emotive responses that FID generates in readers remains underinvestigated. The small-scale reading task outlined in the rest of this essay represents a first step at remedying this lack.

The task focuses specifically on the representation of thought since, as noted above, FIT is more commonly associated with empathy than FIS. Extracts from two novels were chosen: Frances Burney's *Camilla* (1796) and Tom Wolfe's *I Am*

Charlotte Simmons (2004) (hereafter *Charlotte*). The task therefore also tests whether there is a difference in the response of readers to a relatively early example of the style, when it was just beginning to enter into the English novel in extended form, and to a contemporary example over 200 years later, by which time FIT has become an omnipresent feature of the novel. Despite the historical difference, there are similarities between the two texts. *Camilla* is often cited as an example of the 'novel of manners', a genre in which the leading character (usually female) enters into society and is forced to negotiate its complexities, frequently stumbling into embarrassing situations along the way (see Bowers and Brothers 1990). Charlotte Simmons is similarly plunged into a new and bewildering social world as she starts life at Dupont University, a fictional American college. Like Camilla, she is forced to learn how to deal with being pursued aggressively by a series of unsuitable men.

The passages chosen for the task from the two novels both involve the heroine reflecting on an awkward recent experience with the opposite sex in which she feels she has compromised herself beyond all hope of repair. Below are the passages as they were given to the subjects (with some brief context in square brackets). I have numbered the sentences for ease of reference.

Extract 1A

[Camilla's admirer, Sir Sedley Clarendel, has given her a gift of £200, in order to help her penniless brother Lionel. Her first thought was to return the money at once, but Lionel has seized the cheque and she now fears she is in Sir Sedley's debt]

(1) Camilla was too much confounded either to laugh or explain, and hastily wishing them good-night, retired to her chamber.

(2) Here, in the extremest perturbation, she saw the full extent of her difficulties, without perceiving any means of extrication. (3) She had no hope of recovering the draft from Lionel, whom she had every reason to conclude already journeying from Tunbridge. (4) What could she say the next day to Sir Sedley? (5) How account for so sudden, so gross an acceptance of pecuniary obligation? (6) What inference might he not draw? (7) And how could she undeceive him, while retaining so improper a mark of his dependence upon her favour? (8) The displeasure she felt that he should venture to suppose she would owe to him such a debt, rendered but still more palpable the species of expectation it might authorise.

Extract 2A

[Charlotte Simmons, a fresher at Dupont University, has been to her first fraternity party the night before, at which one of the coolest students on campus, Hoyt Thorpe, spent much of the evening with his arm around her]

(1) Well past ten o'clock the next morning, Charlotte was still in bed, lying flat on her back, eyes shut … eyes open … long enough to gaze idly at the

brilliant lines of light where the shades didn't quite meet the windowsill ... eyes shut ... listening for sounds of Beverly, who occasionally sighed or moaned faintly in her sleep ... eyes open, eyes shut, running the night before through her mind over and over to determine just how much of a fool she had made of herself. (2) She was at her most vulnerable, her most anxious, during this interlude between waking and getting up and facing the world ... which she knew, but that didn't make the feeling any less real ... how could she have let him keep *touching* her that way? (3) Right in front of everybody! (4) Right in front of Bettina and Mimi! (5) She had fled the Saint Ray house without even trying to look for them ... walked back to Little yard through monstrous shadows in the dead of the night. (6) How could she ever look them in the eye?

There are significant differences between the type of FIT in each passage, perhaps reflecting the development of the style in the centuries that separate the two. In the first example the proximal deictic 'Here' in sentence 2 is the first sign that Camilla's point of view is about to enter into the narrative, though this sentence otherwise remains the narrator's report. In sentence 3, 'She had no hope of recovering the draft from Lionel' appears to be the character's opinion, though 'whom she had every reason to conclude already journeying from Tunbridge' reintroduces the narrator's perspective (a free indirect version would be 'who was surely already journeying from Tunbridge'). The next four questions (sentences 4–7) are clearer examples of FIT, coming from Camilla's point of view while retaining the third person and past tense of the modal verbs ('could', 'might'). Yet in sentence 4 the deictic expression 'the next day' suggests the narrator's perspective rather than the character's, indicating that free indirect thought has not fully emerged from narratorial control (a 'freer' version would be 'What could she say tomorrow to Sir Sedley?'). The lingering presence of the narrator is also indicated by the formal lexis ('so gross an acceptance of pecuniary obligation'). Sentence 8 appears to return to indirect thought. Throughout the passage then the character's and narrator's perspectives are hard to untangle, perhaps reflecting the fact that the style is still in its early stages of development in the late-eighteenth-century novel, and not yet being commonly used for the extended representation of a character's thoughts.

In the example from *Charlotte* (Extract 2A), on the other hand, FIT seems freer from narratorial control. Sentence 1 starts from an external perspective, until the ellipses take us inside Charlotte's barely conscious thought processes. Her perception is implied in 'the brilliant lines of light where the shades didn't quite meet the windowsill', and it is clearly her opinion that she has 'made a fool of herself'. Sentence 2 seems to start as narratorial comment, yet the ellipsis again marks a transition to Charlotte's perspective. It is her judgement that the feeling is 'real', and the following question is clearly FIT, with the italics emphasising her mortification at what she sees as the most incriminating aspect of the evening. The lack of verbs in the following exclamations (sentences 3 and 4) suggests direct thought, as the passage slips into interior monologue. In sentence 5 ellipsis is again used to suggest a transition to Charlotte's perspective, with 'monstrous shadows in the dead of the night' indicating her overheated Gothic imagination. Sentence 6 returns to unambiguous FIT. In comparison with the example from *Camilla* then, this extract contains more sophisticated techniques for representing the character's thought processes, and less narratorial intrusion, giving the impression that Charlotte's thoughts and feelings are being represented with more directness.

Half the subjects in the reading task received the passages 1A and 2A given above. The other half read the following versions, in which instances of FIT were rewritten as indirect thought (IT) (subjects were supplied with the same context in square brackets):

Extract 1B

(1) Camilla was too much confounded either to laugh or explain, and hastily wishing them good-night, retired to her chamber.

(2) Here, in the extremest perturbation, she saw the full extent of her difficulties, without perceiving any means of extrication. (3) She realized that she had no hope of recovering the draft from Lionel, whom she had every reason to conclude already journeying from Tunbridge. (4) She wondered what she could say the next day to Sir Sedley. (5) She was unsure how she would account for so sudden, so gross an acceptance of pecuniary obligation, and was concerned about the inference he might draw. (6) In addition she did not know how she could undeceive him, while retaining so improper a mark of his dependence upon her favour. (7) The displeasure she felt that he should venture to suppose she would owe to him such a debt, rendered but still more palpable the species of expectation it might authorize.

Extract 2B

(1) Well past ten o'clock the next morning, Charlotte was still in bed, lying flat on her back, intermittently opening her eyes long enough to gaze idly at the brilliant lines of light where the shades didn't quite meet the windowsill, and listening for sounds of Beverly, who occasionally sighed or moaned faintly in her sleep. (2) As she continued to doze she ran the night before through her mind over and over to determine just how much of a fool she had made of herself. (3) She knew that she was at her most vulnerable, her most anxious, during this interlude between waking and getting up and facing the world, but that didn't make the feeling any less real. (4) She was incredulous and mortified that she had let him keep touching her inappropriately, right in front of everybody, especially Bettina and Mimi. (5) She had fled the Saint Ray house without even trying to look for them, and walked back to Little yard through monstrous shadows in the dead of the night. (6) She wondered how she would ever be able to look them in the eye again.

It should first be noted that in keeping with the relative absence of the narrator in the passage 2A, the transposing of 1A into 1B was easier than 2A into 2B. For example, 'What could she say the next day to Sir Sedley?' can be rendered relatively unproblematically in IT as 'She wondered what she could say the next day to Sir Sedley', whereas 'How could she have let him keep *touching* her that way? Right in front of everybody! Right in front of Bettina and Mimi!' requires more invention to convey the strength of feeling. I eventually decided on two adjectives ('incredulous and mortified'), though other indirect versions are of course possible and equally valid.

Twenty-four subjects completed the task. All were second or third-year undergraduates at the University of Sheffield, and native speakers of English. Fourteen were reading English Literature and ten English Language and Literature. All were female; it was supposed that male readers might experience a different (not necessarily lesser) degree of empathy to the heroines in these examples. A future experiment testing the responses of male readers to the same passages could obviously yield interesting comparisons. All subjects were asked if they had read either novel; none had. Twelve were given passage 1A and 12 1B. In a different combination 12 read 2A and 12 2B. All subjects therefore read one passage from *Camilla* and one from *Charlotte*. Below each passage the subjects were asked the following:

> Rank on a scale of 1–10 how close you felt to the character Camilla/Charlotte while reading this passage (10 = I felt I was in her position, 1 = I couldn't understand why she was making such a fuss).

> Comment below on the features of the language of the passage that led you to your ranking.

I decided to ask the subjects about their 'closeness' to the character rather than use the more specific term 'empathy' for three reasons. I was worried that the latter might confuse subjects who were not sure of its meaning, or, worse, lead them to ask me for an exact definition. Second, I was interested in whether, unprompted, they would use the term (or related terms such as 'sympathy' or 'identification') in their comments. Finally, as some of the subjects would have come across specific discussion of free indirect discourse and its effects on their course, I feared that the term 'empathy' might trigger a recognition of free indirect discourse and lead to a more self-conscious response than would otherwise have been the case. In fact only one subject mentioned FIT in her comments, and this did not seem to affect her perception of her closeness to the character (see below). Though it is of course true that 'closeness' is not synonymous with 'empathy', the use of a scale of 'closeness' from 1 to 10 (with 1 representing a complete lack of 'sympathy' and 10 the traditional definition of 'identification') does reflect the range of the term 'empathy' in the critical literature.

Based on most criticism of FID, my hypothesis was that the passages from the two novels containing FIT (1A and 2A) would evoke more feelings of closeness than those without FIT (2A and 2B). I also predicted that the difference between responses to 2A and 2B would be greater than that between 1A and 1B, since, as discussed above, 1A is a less 'free' form of FIT than 2A and contains more signs of the narrator's presence. Finally, given that the subjects were all university students and may have encountered similar experiences to Charlotte it was supposed that overall the empathy for Charlotte would be greater than that for Camilla, whose predicament seems more particular to that of an eighteenth-century heroine and less obviously relatable to student experience.

The subjects were given up to 10 minutes to make their rankings and comment on the two passages. The average ranking for each passage was as follows:

Camilla	1A:	5.96
	1B:	4.75
Charlotte	2A:	7.08
	2B:	6.5

First it is not surprising that more empathy was experienced as a whole for Charlotte than for Camilla; the indirect version from *Charlotte* evoked more empathy than the FIT version from *Camilla*. Also as expected was that in the case of both novels the passages containing FIT generated more empathy than those without, though in both cases the difference is quite small. If empathy is the predominant effect of FIT, one would have expected the differences between the rankings for passages A and B in both cases to have been greater. It was also surprising that the gap was greater for the *Camilla* examples than the *Charlotte* ones (1.21 vs 0.58), given that, as discussed above, passage 2A seems a 'freer' form of FIT. Some possible explanations for these unexpected results are discussed below.

The subjects' comments in response to the second part of the task turned out to be as, if not more, revealing than their rankings. Four responses included the word 'empathy' or 'empathise', with another five referring to 'sympathy' and its derivatives and two to 'pathos'. The difficulty of experiencing these feelings was a recurring theme, however. In particular, ten subjects cited the high register of the *Camilla* passages as a barrier to empathy. For example, in response to passage 1A one subject wrote, 'Use of fairly high register – Latinate words – perturbation, extrication, pecuniary – distanced me – harder to read and respond/empathise'. Five of those who read passage 1B commented on the use of the third person rather than the first as affecting their response, with one writing for example that 'is written in 3rd person so doesn't feel like a 1st hand experience/personal experience'. However, this reader nevertheless ranked her 'closeness' to Camilla as 6, and another who described the 'measured and logical' style of the narrator as 'slightly distancing' added that 'the feelings do seem believable so I felt quite a lot of empathy', and also gave a ranking of 6. Somewhat paradoxically, a subject who commented on the combination of the third person in passage 1A with the questions which provide 'a sense of her feelings' ranked her 'closeness' as 3, and the subject who noted the use of free indirect thought added that there are 'no real comments about her feelings', and gave a ranking of 5. The recognition of the presence of both narrator's and character's perspectives in passage 1A, in other words, does not seem to result automatically in a higher degree of empathy.

Similarly, of those who read passage 2A, few commented on the relatively direct way in which the character's thoughts were represented. One subject, who ranked her 'closeness' to Charlotte as 8, did observe that the passage was 'more like stream of consciousness, exclamation marks and "..." help to add to tension and bring the situation alive', while another, who gave a ranking of 7, noted that 'writer logs her thoughts, e.g. "Right in front of everybody!" – makes the reader feel closer to the character as are able to enter character's thoughts'. In general though, observations on the language of 2A tended to be accompanied by a comment on its relevance to student experience. Thus one subject wrote that 'the fractured language represents her thoughts and the fact that this piece is relevant to student life makes it more accessible'. Five subjects said they could 'relate' more to Charlotte, either because of her 'age' or 'the situation', with one commenting that the passage represents a 'frequent female experience'. Similarly, several responses to 1A and 1B mentioned the unfamiliarity of Camilla's situation; one subject, who gave a ranking of 5, wrote that 'Gender, social conditions influence the relationship with the character', while another, who gave a ranking of 3, simply noted 'Never been in that situation'.

In other words, despite the instruction to focus on 'features of language', the amount of empathy that subjects felt for the two characters often seemed to depend, from the evidence of their comments, on non-linguistic factors. Even when the language was thought to evoke empathy, rankings could be swayed by other influences. Thus a subject who noted of passage 1B that 'use of omniscient narrator rather than 1st person made it more difficult to empathise', gave a ranking of 7 on the basis that 'her situation definitely arouses pity'. The same subject then ranked her 'closeness' to Charlotte in 2A as 5, revealingly commenting that:

> The language makes it easier to empathise as more dramatic words like 'vulnerable' are used, and the more colloquial style allows the reader to identify with her more (perhaps because it is more modern), but the situation is not as serious.

This reading task represents a preliminary investigation only of the effects of FID, and clearly much more empirical work is required. Its findings do suggest, however, that though 'empathy' may indeed be an effect of FIT, it may not be as pervasive and as defining a feature of the style as critics have tended to assume. The degree to which readers feel 'close' to characters in literary texts may, at least on the evidence of the responses given here, depend less on the language of a particular passage than on a reader's assessment of the 'seriousness' of 'the situation', and its relevance to his/her own life. Most criticism of the effects of FID is based on the textual interaction of narrator and character that results from its supposed 'dual voice'. This task suggests, however, that the way readers respond to FIT is more complex than has been supposed, and that empathy is not generated automatically. In particular, it seems that formal features may be overriden by non-linguistic considerations, including the extent to which the reader can 'relate' to the character represented.

The Stylistics of Cappuccino Fiction: A Socio-cognitive Perspective

Rocio Montoro

Montoro's renaming of Chick Lit as 'Cappuccino Fiction' certainly foregrounds one effect of reading these novels, where neat narrative resolution induces a feel-good factor for some; for others it's the incipient nausea of one frothy coffee too many. Beryl Bainbridge's infamous dismissal of Chick Lit as 'froth' gives this epithet further resonance, and Chick Litter Marian Keyes recently exploited this factor to its extreme, having a character 'write a story where everyone lived happily ever after, in a fictional world where good things happened and people were kind' (Keyes 2004: 24). This embedded novel acts as a counterpoise to Keyes's own, perhaps intended to prompt the response that Keyes is much less anodyne and that Chick Lit is more heterogeneous in its scope, not least in its ability to absorb contradictions and criticisms (see Whelehan 2005: 192–4).

'Chick Lit', however, does allow for a number of more complex and contradictory resonances. The term 'chick' like so many other slang terms for 'woman', has emerged from second wave feminist censure to enjoy a new dynamism as a playful word which women and men can use ironically, knowingly, while still unsettling those who feel infantilized (and even dehumanized) by it. In common with 'Chick Flick' it reminds us that the market for these books is, as Montoro acknowledges, exclusively women, and their scope is almost always limited to that of the white middle-class heterosexual. Such texts as 'brand' are ripe for socio-cognitive analysis because they are packed with character types and relationships which fit into conventional social schemata, because fictional women are so often identified by their relationship to the domestic social institutions of marriage and the family, and ideologies of romantic love. Chick Lit draws on our recognition of such schemas and effectively depends upon our ultimate endorsement of them, as Montoro points out.

This requirement for endorsement in order to participate in reading pleasure is also the cause of the genre's problematic relationship to contemporary feminism. The young women portrayed, despite their promising professional status, are characterized by traits traditionally associated as negative feminine characteristics, their life goals more often coupled with romance or consumption (rather than self-definition or social responsibility, explored within feminist novels of the

1970s and 80s). Montoro notes, too, that these characters are always located as daughters; but sisterhood is not explicitly powerful within the pages of Chick Lit.

A reassessment of these novels' preoccupations from a stylistic point of view reminds us that their feel-good factor is about our postmodern identification with the popular cultural world around us. The types and traits we are supposed to recognise are as much the creation of popular television, film and magazine features. The pleasure of reading and talking about Chick Lit is in drawing on a whole lexicon of contemporary social meanings where there is some cultural capital to be had out of simply knowing them. Their features are at once infinitely repeatable and at the same time developing into new mutations, new anxieties, reflected in shifting lifestyle trends and the will to consume to excess.

An equal pleasure, touched upon in Montoro's concluding discussion, is that of the vicissitudes of romance; and, I would suggest, this is the point at which Chick Lit's scarcely buried 'feminist' anger at men is exposed. Romance, it is claimed, is a means whereby women can exert power over men, and, according to Tania Modleski

> [a] great deal of our satisfaction in reading [romance] novels comes, I am convinced, from the elements of a revenge fantasy, from our conviction that the woman is bringing the man to his knees and that all the while he is being so hateful, he is internally grovelling, grovelling, grovelling.
>
> (Modleski 1982: 45)
>
> *Imelda Whelehan*

Introduction

Cappuccino Fiction emerged as a popular genre in the latter part of the twentieth century and offers works written by women, for women of a specific social, cultural and financial status. Central to a definition of this genre is an engagement with modern relationship issues viewed from a heterosexual female perspective, while combining characteristics typical of romance fiction. Additionally, these novels aim to incorporate a fictional representation of a new generation of urban professionals for whom a hedonistic view of life, based on materialistic possessions, seems central.

This chapter argues for the applicability of a socio-cognitive framework to help describe Cappuccino Fiction's ironic and/or contradictory, certainly problematic, view of femininity. I want to assess whether such a representation is based on a paradoxical perpetuation of patriarchal values using the 'romance' fiction formula (one in which the woman always 'gets' her man), or whether it is otherwise built upon a twenty-first-century take on certain feminist concerns previously dealt with in the 1960s and 1970s.

As stated elsewhere (Montoro 2003), I favour my original coinage Cappuccino

Fiction, to the more commonly used 'Chick Lit'. Although I am aware of the problematic nature of labels, Cappuccino Fiction seems to embody better than Chick Lit an aspect which I consider essential for a definition of this genre, namely the 'feel-good' factor that accompanies the reading of these novels: 'like after drinking a cappuccino, one is left with a sweet taste' (Montoro 2003: 470). Space restrictions, however, will not allow for a full insight into how theories of emotion can also shed light on the way the extreme popularity of these novels is due to the positive emotions experienced by their readers (see Cupchik *et al.* 1998; Niedenthal *et al.* 2003; and Winton 1990).

Social Cognition

Social cognition is generally defined as:

> A branch of social psychology that involves the study of the processes and structures that determine and are determined by knowledge of self and others.
> (McCann and Higgins 1990: 15)

Pennington's elaboration on the likely realms of this discipline establishes that there are:

> Three cognitive processes [...] that we apply to our social world. First, information we receive about other people (and ourselves, for that matter) is *interpreted*; this means that information is given meaning often by both the social context and our previous experience, cultural values, etc. [...] Second, social information is *analysed*, this means that an initial interpretation may be adjusted, changed or even rejected. [...] Third, social information is *stored in memory* from which it may be recalled or retrieved. [...] Theory and research in social cognition may equally be about other people, ourselves, and, which is most likely, about ourselves in interaction with other people.
> (Pennington 2000: 2)

Thus, the way people perceive and interact with the social world can be described in terms of a three-part process: 'interpretation' of information surrounding us, 'analysis' of such input and 'storage' for possible future recall. Central to this definition is Pennington's reference to the 'social world' encompassing both other individuals and ourselves. It is this focusing on 'people's perception of other people' that I deem useful for an analysis of the presentation of female characters in Cappuccino Fiction.

Social cognitivists find it advantageous to use the concept of social schemas (or schemata), defined by Fiske and Taylor as:

> A cognitive structure that represents knowledge about a concept or type of stimulus, including its attributes and the relations among those attributes.
> (Fiske and Taylor 1991: 98)

These social schemas draw together 'clusters of information' about the social world, formed after the interpretation, analysis and storage processes Pennington defines above. My argument in relation to Cappuccino Fiction is that at least part of the success of this genre relies on readers recognizing these clusters and, on occasions, even on their embracing them as pertinent to their own social situation.

Nevertheless, despite the applicability of socio-cognitive models to the analysis of female characters in these works, their fictional nature needs discussion too. Character comprehension and recognition entails not only being aware of the actual social world but also of a typology of fictional characters. Culpeper underscores the need to accept both types of knowledge if we are to provide a realistic account of the way readers handle the characterization process in fiction:

> I would argue that first impressions of characters are guided by the implicit models offered by social schemata. Such schemata, once activated, offer a scaffolding for incoming character information. Moreover, they allow us to make further knowledge-based inferences and thereby flesh out our impressions of character [...] However [...] we also need to take on board knowledge about fictional character types.
>
> (Culpeper 2001: 87)

Whereas the cognitive processes involved in character recognition and comprehension emerge from the marriage of two clearly distinct types of knowledge, in the real world social schemas would suffice for an assessment of social beings. The acclaimed success of the genre apparently justifies the agreeable marriage mentioned above, as these female characters seem to 'remind' readers of real-life people. I am suggesting here that behind these narratives' success lies an attempt at a quasi-faithful representation of certain female values and beliefs drawn from our social world so that their readership can recognize, sympathize and maybe even empathize with those values. Consequently, a positive response to those 'implicit models' offered by social schemas has apparently allowed this genre to grow so rapidly. Such is the case that the original Cappuccino Fiction heroines from the latter part of the twentieth-century are now getting married, having children or generally growing up, giving way to further branchings-out of the genre in what is known as Mommy Lit, Ethnick Lit or Nanny Lit (Ferris and Young 2006).

For a more detailed analysis of the way real-life knowledge determines our processing of these characters, I propose to use Culpeper's classification (2001) of social categories. He suggests three broad groupings for the social categories deployed when perceiving others and forming social schemas:

- Personal categories: including knowledge of people's preferences and interests, habits, traits and goals.
- Social role categories: including knowledge about people's social functions, such as kinship roles, occupational roles and relational roles.

- Group membership categories: including knowledge about social groups, such as sex, race, class, age, nationality, religion and so on.

Van Dijk (1987) provides a fourth category, namely that of 'appearance', separating it from the group membership category. Unlike the latter, the appearance category refers to those features of a person's physical aspect that are reasonably controllable, that is, can be easily changed, enhanced or adorned. In these novels, physical appearance turns out to be not just another factor in the general description of that female, but almost her defining trait as she incessantly obsesses about her weight (mainly), fashionable clothes and beauty routines. Appearance issues feature in these novels to such an extent that I would argue for their inclusion in Culpeper's 'group membership category', because our perception (positive or negative) of these characters is as much determined by their preoccupation with appearance as it is by their sex, race, class or nationality.

Five novels have been looked at in order to assess the possible repetition of social schemas. These are Imogen Edward-Jones's *My Canapé Hell* (2000), Helen Fielding's *Bridget Jones's Diary* (1996), Sophie Kinsella's *Can you Keep a Secret?* (2003), Adele Parks's *Game Over* (2001) and Fiona Walker's *Lucy Talk* (2000). As far as 'Personal categories' are concerned (inclusive of people's preferences, habits, traits and goals), three of the main females coincide in sharing an interest in 'reading self-help books', for instance. The traits by which all of these women are mostly characterized comprise epithets such as 'scatterbrained', 'talkative', 'inefficient' and 'needy'. Their goals in life include concerns with 'recovering from break-up with boyfriend', 'achieving or maintaining a successful career' or 'losing weight'. As an illustration, consider the following:

Dear Mo,
Very productive weekend so far. Have sent out invitations for Halloween party, sorted my tights drawer, thrown everything past its sell-by date out of the fridge and cleaned the bathroom even though it's Jane's turn on the roster. As you know, she never uses enough Jif. [...] She says I'm suffering from displacement activity syndrome because Greg hasn't called me. I told her that was rubbish and set about polishing the telephone for the fifth time. [...] She tried to persuade me to go with her to a line-dancing night at her riding school, but I was far too busy removing built-in grime from cooker hob, and cleaning lime-scale from the kitchen taps with the toothbrush Greg keeps here for overnight stays. [...] Might just tidy my bedroom again.

(Walker 2000: 5–6)

Lucy is an example of the stereotypical representation of women in this genre. Her obsessions, overdependence on her partner and overreactions, features reminiscent of a paranoid behaviour, are caused by her apparent emotional instability. The cleaning spree in the above quotation, for instance, is prompted by the fact that a woman has answered her boyfriend's phone.

The 'Social role categories' (kinship, occupational and relational roles) also exhibit many similarities among the five novels. These women always feature as 'daughters', so their kinship role and family connections are an important factor, especially as their parents also tend to play a part. Their occupational role varies but only within the 'professional' bracketing denominator, that is, these females are never manual workers or simply housewives, for instance. As stated before, they form part of a new generation of urban professionals whose careers determine their lives to a considerable extent. Their relational role is, nevertheless, the trait these characters are mainly known for, especially since and probably because of, *Bridget Jones's Diary*, so far the most famous Cappuccino Fiction work. These females are either single at the beginning of the novel or have a boyfriend who ends up being replaced by the figure of the new and better man. In this respect, the connections with the prototypical romance fiction of the Mills & Boon type have been amply discussed (Montoro 2003; Whelehan 2000, 2005) but limitations of space prevent me from developing this issue any further.

The final grouping is 'Group membership category'. The type of knowledge in this category is based on sex, race, class, age, nationality, religion and, as discussed earlier, appearance. The variations between the characters are now even less marked than among the previous categories. Only the protagonist of *Game Over* belongs to a higher social class. The rest are all middle-class females, in their late 20s or early 30s, white, British and profess an obsessive preoccupation with their appearance, as in the next extracts:

> I've championed the 'what normal people look like in designer clothes' corner. I've been dressed up in hipsters, bumsters, I've donned blonde and dark wigs to see if blondes really do have more fun. I've [...] test driven the micro skirt, the tube skirt, the split up the side skirt and all in the name of fashion.
>
> (Edward-Jones 2000:4)

> Am now convinced that I have the figure of a TellyTubby. Feel so paranoid that I rejected the sexy little mini-dress I'd packed for tonight [...] We ate in a country pub [...] I had a small tuna salad. Feel famished.
>
> (Walker 2000:109)

In relation to person perception, Culpeper states that there are two possible ways of forming our impressions:

> Sometimes a category may indeed suffice, and sometimes we may form an impression more on the basis of information about a particular individual than any category [...] The first alternative involves a greater emphasis on top-down processing and results in a 'category-based' impression [...] The second alternative involves a greater emphasis on bottom-up processing and results in a 'person-based' or 'attribute-based' impression: the impression is made up of the individual attributes of the target person.
>
> (Culpeper 2001: 83)

In Cappuccino Fiction, I would claim, impression formation hardly ever occurs as a result of bottom-up processes, that is to say, as a result of an application of 'person-based' impressions. Instead, perceptions seem to be mainly 'category-based' or top-down processes as shown by the similarities in the 'social groupings' analysis applied above, which greatly limits the scope for individuality in the portrayal of these females. Despite the repetitive nature that this lack of distinctiveness causes, the genre's undeniable popularity needs to be accounted for, with the reader's expectations concerning the presence of this particular character type confirmed as the most likely reason. The social schemas forming the skeleton of the character give way to a more particularized recognition of a specific character typology, as defined by Culpeper. The female characters resemble one another because Cappuccino Fiction writers are following very closely certain generic conventions in the depiction of these women. Consequently, what could initially be understood as a stereotypical presentation, reminiscent of a quasi-reactionary sterile depiction of women, can be equally justified by the authors' interest in adhering to the specific 'ideal woman' somehow expected from these works.

Feminism

Recognizing the role that social schemas play in forming character impression is not the only way in which a socio-cognitive analysis can shed light on Cappuccino Fiction characters. Social schemas are high-level cognitive formations that function as part of a network, not as isolated structures, which carries further repercussions for the structuring of social knowledge. As Culpeper states:

> It is particularly important to note that social schemata include links across the three category groupings [Personal categories, Social categories and Group membership categories] [...] Note that some of these links form evaluative beliefs (that is, may be considered positive or negative features). Such evaluations constitute what van Dijk (1987, 1988) refers to as 'attitude schemata', and provide a link to the notion of ideology. Different groups would have had different attitudes, or different attitude schemata, associated with the schema for a particular group.
>
> (Culpeper 2001: 77–8)

It appears that social schemas on their own cannot fully account for the way people's impression formation is achieved. It is the evaluative beliefs associated with certain social schemas, that is, attitude schemas, that are similarly employed in our perception of individuals. These evaluations of beliefs and knowledge, Culpeper states, are closely linked to the concept of ideology, which again seems relevant for the fictional representation of females in Cappuccino Fiction. I am particularly interested in the role played by ideological feminist concerns, because of the open relationship these novels set up between their female characters and feminist beliefs and values. For example:

'I'm being a feminist, actually,' retorts Jemima. 'We women have to stand up for our rights. You know, before she married my father, Mummy went out with this scientist chap who practically jilted her. He changed his mind three weeks before the wedding, can you believe it? So one night she crept into his lab and pulled out all the plugs of his stupid machines. His whole research was ruined!'

(Kinsella 2003: 280)

The possible traits that a 'feminism' schema could comprise would, most certainly, vary from one individual to another but some of the most likely cognitive connections would include knowledge of 'women's rights', 'inequalities for women', 'denouncement of such inequalities', at times 'activism' and so on. The quotation above, however, seems to portray a rather peculiar definition of feminism, more akin to a display of revengeful rage by the character of Jemima's mother. Similarly in Colgan's *Amanda's Wedding*, the flippant Amanda justifies her decision to keep her maiden name as a feminist stance:

'Darlings!' said Amanda, with an edge in her voice. This is my BIG NEWS!'
[...] 'Anyway, by sheer coincidence I spoke to the castle's people and they gave me his mother's number, and she had his home number and it was just across London, so we got together and we had so much in common; [...] and now I am going to be Lairdess Amanda Phillips-McConnald!' finished Amanda, all in one breath.
There was a silence.
'Hey, his name's Phillips too?' said Fran.
'No, no! You see, I'm keeping my name and taking his name. It's a feminist statement, really.'

(Colgan 1999: 11–12)

These women's take on feminism sounds, at the very least, rather unorthodox. Their apparent adherence to a feminist ideology is not used as a platform to fight for women's rights or to denounce inequalities, but instead generally to serve as a source of comedy which, nonetheless, can have some additional implications for the reader's expectations concerning fictional character schemas, as developed below.

Feminism and its associated study of gendered uses of language are topics long established and discussed. In relation to the generation of gendered texts, Walsh describes the construction of meaning in the following manner:

It is assumed [...] that the choices text producers make are not random, but are motivated, often by a desire to position listeners/readers as compliant subjects. Such choices impose constraints on the process of interpretation by acting as traces and cues which promote certain readings, while seeking to suppress others. In this way, they can serve to reinforce or challenge dominant conceptual frames, including those involved in the reproduction of normative gendered identities and gendered relations. Listeners/readers construct hypotheses about the preferred meaning of texts on the basis of the traces and cues they perceive to be present 'in' the texts, as well as on the basis of their own, often gendered, assumptions about the communicative event. Interpreters are not passive, then, but active, since they often have to do a good deal of inferential work to make connections that are not always made explicit in a text.

(Walsh 2001: 31)

Walsh's analysis consolidates the role of mental structures and textual devices as the mechanisms that permit text comprehension. Cognitive or 'top-down' strategies as well as textual or 'bottom-up' processes play a seemingly equal part when inferring meaning from texts. But Walsh also highlights the responsibility of text producers in making the significant linguistic choices that determine the bottom-up processes mentioned before. These linguistic preferences, she suggests, far from being innocuous are, instead, selected in an attempt to make the readership compliant with the text-producer's beliefs. In Cappuccino Fiction, the mocking nature in which feminist issues seem to be presented could possibly validate an anti-feminist reading of these novels. The 'producers' of Cappuccino Fiction texts, being women themselves, are leaving open the possibility for a kind of 'rebuke' of their novels as quasi-reactionary. In fact, the novelist Beryl Bainbridge has famously dismissed them as inconsequential 'froth' (Bainbridge 2001). An unsympathetic reading by some critics and readers could be justified, I would suggest, because of the compliance of these works with somewhat 'conservative' values typical of heterosexual romance fiction:

'Where were we?'
She smiled at him. 'You were offering me a job.'
'Yes.'
But they were standing absurdly close to one another. It was impossible to concentrate. She cleared her throat. 'It, er, yes. It sounds very tempting. Especially after what happened to, er, Y'know...'
'What?'
'The – Grey ... In the pub ... Horrible.'
'Or shall we get just married?'
'What?' It brought her to her senses. [...]
'Charlie! I mean I love you and everything. But marriage? It's – Marriage is just a bit –'
'Say "old-fashioned",' he said, 'and I'll die of boredom and withdraw the offer.' [...]
'Shall we do it?' She grinned at him. 'Why not? We could give it a try!' [...]
They paused, just for a second, to gaze at one another, to revel in their own wonderful good fortune. He bent to kiss her, she put her arms around his neck, their lips were just a millimetre apart [...]

(Waugh 2002: 292–3)

These novels' explicit but, equally 'oblique' relationship with feminism has, in fact, provided critics with much scope for discussion. Whelehan, for instance, originally expressed certain uneasiness with the rather unconventional treatment of feminist concerns in Cappuccino Fiction novels:

> The second crucial lesson is that 'after all there is nothing so unattractive to a man as strident feminism [Fielding 1996: 20].' *Bridget Jones* might be seen as a 'post-feminist' text in the sense that feminist values are situated as somewhere in the past or as an uneasy conscience to a woman who finds the newspeak of 'biological' accounts of sexual difference more comforting.
>
> (Whelehan 2000: 137)

She furthers her assessment by asserting that *Bridget Jones's* confessional style ultimately condemns feminism as 'too prudish, judgemental and unattractive' (Whelehan 2000: 138). However, I would claim that halting any appreciation of Cappuccino Fiction at this level would simply elude tackling the real issues, as Whelehan also remarks in relation to Bainbridge's derogatory consideration of these works as 'froth':

> In previous publications I have found myself being more dismissive about these works, since it is easy to classify them as retroactive and merely souped-up, sexed-up versions of the classic Mills & Boon romance.
>
> (Whelehan 2005: 16)

Her analysis concludes that these novels are exhibiting certain developments in relation to the prototypical feminist publications of the 1960s or 1970s. Cappuccino Fiction has been able to accommodate feminist concerns by voicing those issues that older forms of feminism apparently failed to address. The schemas that gave rise to the formulation of first and second wave feminism do not appear to suffice to account for the specific situations of twentieth and twenty-first-century women and the obvious popularity of the genre apparently confirms that this is the case. In her comparison with the feminist best-sellers of the 70s, Whelehan observes:

> Both groups of books tell us something about their contemporary cultural context and both suggest that, much as feminism of the second wave was truly life-changing in the impact it has had on social policy, the law and politics over the years, there were mistakes and deficiencies which left certain women out in the cold.
>
> (Whelehan 2005: 5)

Although accusing these authors of a 'sitting-on-the-fence' mentality could be an alluring proposition for some, contextual factors affecting twenty-first-century readers in their application of social schemas clearly need to be borne in mind too. Insofar as these female figures fail to display the type of political commitment of their 1970s counterparts, for instance, Cappuccino Fiction's relationship with feminism is, simply, flawed. But in as much as this genre attempts a faithful representation of current social concerns, inclusive of the career, relationship or appearance pressures women are under, these novels' connection with feminism is atypical but, still, similarly valid. The many branchings-out of the genre recently identified certainly seem to support this new take on the connections between Cappuccino Fiction and feminism:

> In the decade from *Bridget Jones,* it [Chick Lit] has crossed the divides of generation, ethnicity, nationality [...] Leaping the generation gap, it has given rise on one side to 'hen lit' [...] and on the other to [...] 'Chick Lit jr.' [...] Between these two extremes 'mommy lit' finds its place, adding new complexity to the old question, 'Can women have it all?' [...] Crossing the racial divide, we find Ethnick lit, including such subgenres as 'Sistah lit' and 'Chica lit.' [...] Perhaps even more surprising than these transformations has been the development of Christian Chick Lit, or 'church lit'.
>
> (Ferris and Young 2006: 5–6)

In order to evaluate further these new elements in social schemas, a return to the appearance issue can help to conclude this section. Walsh highlights this long-established concern:

> Lakoff (1995: 45) points out that the disproportionate focus on women's appearance is effectively a form of silencing, since it deflects attention away from what they are actually saying. Ward's (1984) observation that this is true whether the woman in question 'defies or exemplifies a popular stereotype' (cited in Lee 1992: 111) is supported by my research. Indeed, despite the wide range of images and sartorial codes adopted by women in public life, they tend to be portrayed either as 'femmes' or 'frumps', signalling to them that they are women in a male-dominated environment.
>
> (Walsh 2001: 45)

This assessment underscores how showing preoccupation for women's looks might actually be used simply to camouflage the true ulterior motive of smothering their voices, by drawing attention away from what they have to say. However, I would claim that the obsessive interest in physical aspects present in Cappuccino Fiction does not do so. Instead, these women writers endow their female characters with voices that relish in the discussion of beauty routines, fashion interests or weight worries. It seems that, nowadays, a characterization of twenty-first-century femininity does not conflict with, but is instead fully endorsed by, an extensive treatment of appearance schemas as an attempt, I would suggest, to acknowledge the type of external contextual pressures that a *Cosmopolitan*-reading generation of women seems to be under.

Concluding Remarks

Attitude schemas, as defined above, have been used to explain the cognitive ideological links which can prevail in readers' mechanisms for text processing. But there seems to be another significant link related to the existence of these cognitive structures:

> Van Dijk also suggests that these evaluative beliefs may be associated with emotive aspects, such as like and dislike (1987: 188–9). How emotive and affective aspects are dealt with in a cognitive model and whether they belong there at all is controversial [...] With regard to characterisation, my model needs to cope with emotive aspects, since sometimes authors construct characters in order to create particular emotional effects.
>
> (Culpeper 2001:78)

The complexity of including emotion in a cognitive model of analysis has been amply discussed by scholars (Semino 1997). Nevertheless, Culpeper's defence of character construction based on the possible emotional effects on the reader seems extremely relevant to my analysis. In Cappuccino Fiction, the social schemas evoked appear to give way to an important affective side, in as much as these authors expect a positive response to the characters in their novels. Frameworks of analysis based on emotion would certainly aid a description of the affective aspects but there is no space here to develop such a stance. Suffice it to repeat my favouring the label Cappuccino Fiction to Chick Lit in order to underscore the 'feel-good' factor that characterizes the reading of these works. The upbeat emotive aspects that these novels evoke in the reader are not a mere accident but an integral part of their definition as a specific genre, and these positive 'affective schemas', as I would like to call them, stand at the core of the commercial success enjoyed by these books.

Another aspect I hope to have made clear in this chapter concerns my discussion of the type of knowledge needed for character impression. The real-life knowledge acting as basis for social schemas can only represent a first half in text comprehension, the second being realized by knowledge of character types or, as Culpeper calls them, dramatic roles:

> Dramatic roles are closely tied to genre. Our knowledge about different genres – comedies, tragedies, romances, Westerns, detective stories, and so on – includes a set of associated dramatic roles. Thus, recognising the genre one encounters can lead to the activation of a set of dramatic roles, which in turn may guide one's perception of the characters.
>
> (Culpeper 2001: 87)

The fact that readers of Cappuccino Fiction expect certain character traits in their novels would support, once more, its consolidation as a distinctive narrative genre. For instance, the atypical treatment of feminist concerns as a basis for comic scenarios has been examined previously. Rather than dismissing these matters as light-hearted or unserious, the readership seems to be more interested in the humorous possibilities that such a disruption of old schemas can convey. It is not the case that these women writers are unable to incorporate traditional feminist debates in their stories and as part of their female characters' discourse, but rather, that they choose not to. Doing so as a group of narratives belonging to a particular genre inevitably results in the repetitive nature of these novels, but it appears that the readership of Cappuccino Fiction knowingly accepts such repetition as they approach these works with a specific set of social and dramatic schemas in mind.

For my final observations, I would like to quote the feminist critic Stevi Jackson whose remarks provide food for thought concerning a possible alternative reading of femininity in Cappuccino Fiction. She states:

> The chronic insecurity so often suffered by lovers is not, I think, merely a result of romantic passion but is fundamental to its continuance: being 'in love' appears to wear off once lovers feel secure with each other. Insecure and compulsive passion centred on a unique other can engender feelings of powerlessness, of being at the mercy of the beloved. It also, however, holds out the promise of power – of being the loved one, of ensnaring another into total psychic dependence. The attraction that love has for women may in part be because it is a means by which they can aspire to power over men. This is a central theme of romantic narrative (Modleski 1984) – in both fairy-tales and romantic fiction love tames and transforms the beast.
>
> (Jackson 1993: 43)

Jackson questions a possible evaluation of romantic love as an act of submission for female characters. Instead, she defends romantic love as women's attempt at exerting power over men. Viewed from this perspective, the romantic resolution of these novels defines not a compliance with patriarchal conservative values whereby women only achieve fulfilment via romantic liaisons, but instead an ironic treatment of such traditional values. My own understanding would underscore the fact that these novels consciously play upon such a double possibility and successfully manage to merge and accommodate both points of view.

Attribution Theory: Action and Emotion in Dickens and Pynchon

Alan Palmer

Alan Palmer's chapter is based on the fundamental claim that 'novel reading is mind-reading': in order to understand novels, and narratives generally, readers have to construct and monitor the workings of the minds of fictional characters. Palmer considers more specifically how mental functioning is attributed to characters by narrators and (other) characters within the texts of novels, and by readers in the process of interpretation. Two short extracts are used for exemplification, respectively from Charles Dickens' *Little Dorrit* and Thomas Pynchon's *The Crying of Lot 49*.

Although the study of the presentation of thought and consciousness has a long tradition in stylistics and narratology, Palmer's contribution is innovative in a number of ways. First, the way in which Palmer privileges the notion of fictional mind over those of text world and plot constitutes a departure from more established approaches to the study of prose fiction, but is in line with the recent work of narratologists such as Monika Fludernik and Uri Margolin.

Second, Palmer shows how the textual means that enable readers to attribute mental functioning to characters go well beyond the categories of thought presentation that are normally considered by stylisticians. In particular, Palmer points out how references to actions and emotions often play a crucial role in triggering inferences about characters' mental functioning. Palmer's notion of a 'thought-action' continuum is therefore highly relevant for the stylistic analysis of the novel, since it acknowledges that the boundary between pure narrative and thought presentation is fuzzy, and that the extent to which particular linguistic expressions reveal the mental functioning of characters is a matter of degree.

Third, Palmer emphasizes the way in which cognitions and emotions are inextricably linked, both in the mental lives of 'real' people and in textual references to the mental lives of fictional characters. While stylisticians and narratologists have developed sophisticated accounts of the presentation of cognitive activities, less detailed attention has been paid to the presentation of emotions, and its interrelationship with thought presentation.

Fourth, Palmer considers an area that has been largely overlooked in the study of point of view and thought presentation, namely the ways in which mental states and activities are attributed to groups, rather than individual characters. As Palmer has persuasively shown in his book *Fictional Minds*, the mental functioning of different kinds of 'intermental' units often plays an important part in fictional worlds and plots, as does the formation, development and dissolution of these group minds.

Fifth, Palmer draws from discursive psychology in order to discuss how linguistic choices in the description of actions and emotions are never neutral, but tend to have evaluative implications. Overall, Palmer's integration of textual analysis with psychological theories makes an important contribution to current cognitive approaches in stylistics, particularly in relation to the study of fictional narratives and characterisation.

Elena Semino

A very useful conceptual tool for analysing the fictional minds of characters in novels is *attribution theory*: the study of how attributions of states of mind are made (see Heider 1958, Kelley 1973 and Wilson 2002). It involves such questions as: How do narrators attribute states of mind to characters? How do characters attribute mental states to themselves and to other characters? How do readers make attributions and thereby build up a sense of a character's whole personality? This chapter discusses attribution theory in relation to two key elements in narrative fiction: action and emotions. It will apply the theory to the actions described in a passage from Charles Dickens' *Little Dorrit* and to the emotions contained in a passage from *The Crying of Lot 49* by Thomas Pynchon. I aim to show how the presentations of actions and emotions contained in novels are extremely informative about the mental functioning of fictional characters, and, in particular, I will consider what discursive purposes are served by these presentations.

Towards the end of *Little Dorrit*, the firm Doyce and Clennam is ruined by the collapse of Merdle's financial empire. Clennam knows that it is his fault and decides to do all he can to spare his partner Doyce. He tells his solicitor, Mr Rugg, that he will publicly accept all the responsibility for the bankruptcy.

(1) Clennam then proceeded to state to Mr Rugg his fixed resolution. (2) He told Mr Rugg that his partner was a man of great simplicity and integrity, and that in all he meant to do, he was guided above all things by a knowledge of his partner's character, and a respect for his feelings. (3) He explained that his partner was then absent on an enterprise of importance, and that it particularly behoved himself publicly to accept the blame of what he had rashly done, and publicly to exonerate his partner from all participation in the responsibility of it...
(4) The disclosure was made, and the storm raged fearfully. (5) Thousands of people were wildly staring about for somebody alive to heap reproaches on; and this notable case, courting publicity, set the living somebody so much

wanted, on a scaffold. (6) When people who had nothing to do with the case were so sensible of its flagrancy, people who lost money by it could scarcely be expected to deal mildly with it. (7) Letters of reproach and invective showered in from the creditors; and Mr Rugg, who sat upon the high stool every day and read them all, informed his client within a week that he feared that there were writs out.

(8) 'I must take the consequences of what I have done,' said Clennam. (9) 'The writs will find me here.'

(Dickens 1967: 781–3, sentence numbering added)

The background to the passage from *The Crying of Lot 49* is that Oedipa Maas knows that her husband, Mucho, regularly sleeps with young girls. (Oedipa will herself be unfaithful later in the novel.)

(1) She knew the pattern because it had happened a few times already, though Oedipa had been most scrupulously fair about it, mentioning the practice only once, in fact, another three in the morning and out of a dark dawn sky asking if he wasn't worried about the penal code. (2) 'Of course', said Mucho after a while, that was all; but in his tone of voice she thought she heard more, something between annoyance and agony. (3) She wondered then if worrying affected his performance. (4) Having once been seventeen and ready to laugh at almost anything, she found herself then overcome by, call it a tenderness she'd never go quite to the back of lest she get bogged. (5) It kept her from asking him any more questions. (6) Like all their inabilities to communicate, this too had a virtuous motive.

(Pynchon 1996: 30, sentence numbering added)

Theory of Mind

Theory of mind is the term used by philosophers and psychologists to describe our awareness of the existence of other minds, our knowledge of how to interpret other people's thought processes, our mind-reading abilities in the real world. Readers of novels have to use their theory of mind in order to try to follow the workings of characters' minds. Otherwise, they will lose the plot. The only way in which the reader can understand the above texts is by trying to follow the workings of characters' minds and thereby attributing states of minds to them. This mind-reading involves trying to follow characters' attempts to read other characters' minds. Anyone who has a condition such as autism or Asperger's syndrome, and who therefore suffers from what is called *mind blindness*, will find it difficult to understand a novel. Novel reading is mind-reading. (For more on theory of mind and the novel, see Palmer 2004 and the excellent account contained in Zunshine 2006).

The characters in the Dickens passage do a good deal of mind-reading. This is a summary:

1. Clennam explains his view of the workings of Doyce's mind (he is simple and has integrity).
2. Clennam also explains his view of the workings of his own mind (he has been rash).
3. Clennam wants to make sure that the public mind will understand his intention to accept responsibility.
4. Clennam knows that Rugg, as a lawyer, is unhappy about his intention.
5. So, to achieve his purpose, Clennam has to make sure that Rugg understands his 'fixed resolution' to make the disclosure.
6. Rugg conveys to Clennam that he does in fact understand his intention (because he arranges for the disclosure).
7. Rugg deduces from the letters of reproach and invective that writs will follow.
8. The public forms a view on Clennam's intentions (that he is wantonly seeking publicity).
9. Rugg and Clennam become aware of the public's view.

In fact, though, this list, detailed as it is, is an oversimplification. For example, item 1 can be broken down into much more detail as follows: (a) Clennam thinks that (b) Doyce will think that (c) the public will think that (d) Doyce will think that (e) the public will acquiesce in (f) Doyce trying to get away with not paying his debts.

The same sort of theory of mind work is also required by a reader of the Pynchon novel. For example: (1) Oedipa does not want (2) Mucho to believe that (3) she thinks that (4) the young girls would (5) make Mucho feel humiliated.

Attributions and Action

The reader of the Dickens passage has to undertake this complex theory of mind processing without being able to rely on any explicit representations of consciousness by the narrator. The extract is simply a presentation of a number of actions, including speech acts. As shown above, the reader, as part of the process of understanding narrative, has to translate action descriptions into mind descriptions. As a result, the various thought processes become clear. Clennam feels the emotions of guilt, remorse, shame and embarrassment. He decides that the bankruptcy is his fault and that he should accept the blame for it. By following Clennam's actions, the reader is able to follow the workings of his mind. The mental events and states that comprise these workings and that provide the causal network behind his actions are just as much a part of the story world of the novel as the physical environment of events and happenings.

What appear to be simple action descriptions in novels often contain a good deal of explicit information about characters' consciousnesses. It can be very difficult to establish whether or not a statement refers to an action or to a state of consciousness. In the *Philosophical Investigations*, Ludwig Wittgenstein quotes the sentence, 'I noticed that he was out of humour', and asks, 'Is this a report about his behaviour or his state of mind?' (Wittgenstein 1958: 179). He is drawing attention to the fact that the mental and physical sides of action and behaviour coexist and interpenetrate to the point where they are difficult to disentangle. The mental network that lies behind all actions contains intentions, reasons, motives, purposes and causes, and elements of this network are often present in the discourse that is used to describe an action. For example, the causal network in this case is Clennam's intention to take responsibility because his conscience is troubling him and he wishes to mitigate the harm done to Doyce, and this is made entirely explicit because Clennam explains to Rugg the reasons for his action. Often, there is more work for the reader to do. However, there are various characteristics of fictional discourse that help readers to do this work.

Take a statement such as 'He hid behind the curtain'. It seems at first glance to be merely a description of an action. However, it tells the reader much more about that character's mental processes than a statement such as 'He stood behind the curtain'. This is because the first statement tells us *why* he is performing this action. It contains the reason or motive for, or the intention behind, the action. I use the term *thought-action continuum* to describe this phenomenon. The word 'stood' is at the action end of the continuum; 'hid' is nearer the thought end. A phrase such as 'wildly staring about for somebody alive to heap reproaches on' in sentence 5 is another example. It is a description of an action, wildly staring, and a hypothetical or potential action, heaping reproaches. However, both phrases are also descriptions of states of mind: feeling wild and feeling reproachful. The two phrases are therefore in the middle of the continuum.

Readers also rely on *cue reason words*. These are words that signal that the causal network behind an action is about to be made explicit. 'Because', 'so that', 'in order to' and 'for' are common examples. In sentence 5, the description of the action of wildly staring is followed, after the cue reason word 'for', by the reason why people were doing so. Or take this statement: 'Clennam watched her face for some explanation of what she did mean' (Dickens 1967: 365). The first four words describe the action; the words following the cue reason word 'for' explain the reason for the action. Novels tend to contain few action descriptions that simply describe only the surface of physical behaviour. As with Clennam's action of watching, the accompanying mental event is often made part of the action description, rather than left implicit.

The stress within the philosophy of action (for example, Mele 1997) on the importance of such concepts as intentions, reasons, motives, purposes and causes dovetails neatly with the sociocultural concept of *teleological action*: a person attaining an end or bringing about the occurrence of a desired state by choosing the means that have the promise of being successful in a given situation and applying them in a suitable manner. The central concept is that of a decision among alternative courses of action, based upon an interpretation of the situation, in order to realize an end (Wertsch 1991: 9–10). This is clearly an accurate description of this text. Clennam wishes to bring about the desired state of minimizing the effect of the catastrophe on Doyce. The means he chooses involve making a public disclosure of his responsibility. He has made a decision that this course of action is the best means of achieving his end.

Attributions and Emotions

Psychologists and philosophers stress repeatedly that cognition and emotion are inextricably linked (for example, Damasio 2000 and Le Doux 1999). Cognitions cause emotions; emotions cause cognitions; cognitions tend to have some sort of emotional component; emotions contain cognitive elements. There are a number of cognitions in the Pynchon passage: Oedipa *knows* that the practice occurs; she *wonders* if Mucho is worried; Mucho *decides* that he is worried; Oedipa *decides* that she hears 'more' in his voice; she *decides* not to ask any more questions. In every case it is impossible to disentangle these cognitions from the emotions that are discussed below and that are attached in various ways to them.

The background to the following discussion is the notion of what we are supposed to feel: the cognitive and emotional *scripts* that we all follow by default unless something exceptional happens and we have to improvise. In other words, readers bring to any fictional text folk psychology notions that guide them on the appropriateness of emotions to particular situations. The default script in this case would consist, I think, of Oedipa's anger and disgust and Mucho's guilt and embarrassment. However, a close examination of the text shows that it does not go according to script and that the two characters may not be feeling precisely what they are supposed to feel. In addition to the strong sense of implicit feelings and emotions such as tension, fear, love and so on, we find the following explicit attributions of emotion or feelings: worry (1) and (3); annoyance (2); agony (2); tenderness (5); and feeling 'bogged' (5). The terms are italicized in the following extract from the passage under discussion so that you can see how the terms work in context:

> (1) She knew the pattern because it had happened a few times already, though Oedipa had been most scrupulously fair about it, mentioning the practice only once, in fact, another three in the morning and out of a dark dawn sky asking if he wasn't *worried* about the penal code. (2) 'Of course', said Mucho after a while, that was all; but in his tone of voice she thought she heard more, something between *annoyance* and *agony*. (3) She wondered then if *worrying* affected his performance. (4) Having once been seventeen and ready to laugh at almost anything, she found herself then overcome by, call it a *tenderness* she'd never go quite to the back of lest she get *bogged*.

These attributions are made in the following ways:

Worry This is a speculative hypothetical attribution by Oedipa to Mucho that he confirms as true. It is the only one that unproblematically fits the script, in the sense that it appears to cohere well with our folk psychology notions of how somebody would typically feel in that situation.

Annoyance and *Agony* These are used as alternatives in an implicit tentative attribution by Oedipa to Mucho. We do not find out what Mucho was 'actually' feeling. They make a very strange pairing. Although either would fit the script separately, it is the juxtaposition of the two that is odd. There is something very unsettling for the reader in being given such a grotesquely wide choice between something as mild as annoyance and something as intense as agony. This unsettling conjunction jolts readers out of their default mode. It amounts to a kind of defamiliarization of, or estrangement from, the whole process of attributing emotions. This kind of challenge is precisely what would be expected from a postmodern novel, of course.

Tenderness The responsibility for this attribution is unclear. Is it the narrator who is attributing this state of mind to Oedipa; or is it Oedipa who is aware of her own state of mind? (An interesting characteristic of attributions is that it can often be difficult to know whether attributions are the responsibility of the narrator or the character whose thought is being reported.) The phrase '*call it* a tenderness' adds to the effect of estrangement mentioned earlier and suggests that it is the narrator who is taking the responsibility for naming the emotion that Oedipa herself is not prepared to accept. On the other hand, the fact that Oedipa would never quite go to the back of it suggests that she is at least half aware of it, and has made a conscious decision not to recognize it further.

Bogged This attribution appears to lie with Oedipa, rather than the narrator. The word 'lest' seems to indicate that Oedipa is self-consciously aware of her motive for not wanting to get to the back of the tenderness that she feels for Mucho.

Intermental Attribution

Intermental thought is joint, group, shared or collective thought. It is also known as *distributed* or *situated cognition*, and also, especially in literary studies, as *intersubjectivity* (see Wertsch 1991, Hutchins 1995; and Clark and Chalmers 1998). Intermental thought is a crucially important component of fictional narrative because much of the mental functioning that occurs in novels is done by large organisations, small groups, work colleagues, friends, families, couples and other intermental units. (For more on intermental thought in the novel, see Palmer 2006.)

Given the close links between thought and action that are described above, it follows that action as well as thought can be joint, group, shared or collective. This type of action is known as *communicative action*. It is the interaction of at least two persons. The actors seek to reach an understanding about the present situation in order to coordinate their actions by way of agreement (Wertsch 1991: 11, following Habermas 1984: 86). For example: 'The three statesmen hid themselves behind the curtain' (Waugh 1996: 86). Teun van Dijk (1976: 296) describes communicative or intermental action as interactions between several agents which include all forms of cooperative social behaviour, such as the use of language. The simplest examples are those cases where two agents together accomplish the same action, while having the same intention. More complex are the cases where the intended actions are the same, but where the purpose is different, and so the action is done for different reasons. Alternatively, the purposes may coincide, but the actions are different. For example, the joint action may be preparing dinner, but each agent fulfils different tasks within the overall action. Some actions can be carried out by either one or more agents, while others, such as marrying or fighting, must have at least two agents (van Dijk 1976: 298).

In my view, it is possible to make use of a looser notion of intermental or communicative action than that used by van Dijk. You may have noticed that I have been using the term *the public* when discussing the reaction to Clennam's declaration. This term designates the intermental unit which undertakes the communicative actions that are described in the second half of sentence 4, all of 5 and 6 and the first half of sentence 7. Although sentence 4 is quite oblique, the phrase 'the storm raged fearfully' can only be understood as a metaphorical presentation of intermental action. This action arises out of the intermental view of the members of the public on Clennam's actions in investing the money in Merdle's empire and then accepting responsibility for the loss of the money. Because a very large number of people are involved, there is not the explicit joint understanding and coordination that Wertsch, Habermas and van Dijk have in mind (although van Dijk concedes the possibility that people may take part in a communicative action for different reasons and purposes). Nevertheless, the group behaviour being described here is very different from individual action. We recognise this difference in phrases such as 'mob rule', 'group hysteria' and so on. As Nietzsche put it, 'madness is rare in individuals, but common in parties, groups and organisations' (*Beyond Good and Evil*, Part 4, aphorism 72). The fact that it is so easy to use a phrase such as 'the public thinks ...' shows that we are well aware in practice of the phenomenon of intermental thought. In a sense these are individual actions – it is individuals who are heaping reproaches and sending letters – but in another sense they are also collective. The individual actions make more sense when they are regarded as part of a joint action because people have become caught up in a group mind that is made up of wildness, reproach and invective. They are behaving differently from the way in which they would behave as individuals because they have become part of this group mind.

I said above that fictional intermental units vary greatly in size. In the Dickens case, it is a large ill-defined mass of people. In the Pynchon text, the intermental unit is a marriage. So, different questions arise: How well do Oedipa and Mucho know what the other is thinking? Do they think as intermentally as you would expect a married couple to? (This question assumes that you have high expectations of the intermental thought processes of married couples!) Well, it seems that their knowledge of each other's mind is patchy. Oedipa knows that Mucho likes to sleep with young girls, but she does not know if he worries about the penal code or if worrying affects his performance, and she is not quite sure what she can hear in his tone of voice. The very approximate attribution by Oedipa of Mucho's state of mind (between annoyance and agony) suggests that the intermental unit of their marriage is not working well. And, of course, the passage actually explicitly refers in the final sentence to their inabilities to communicate. However, there is an apparent paradox here. As they *share* a virtuous motive for their inability to communicate, is there a tacit intermental understanding that they will not communicate intermentally? I will come back to this question later by approaching it from the perspective of discursive psychology.

Discursive Attribution

Discursive psychologists (Edwards and Potter 1992; Harré and Gillett 1994; and Edwards 1997) see the mind 'as dynamic and essentially embedded in historical, political, cultural, social, and interpersonal contexts' (Harré and Gillett 1994: 25). The fundamental premise of discursive psychology is that 'no description of anything is the only one that is reasonable or possible' (Edwards 1997: 8). Furthermore, 'descriptions *constitute* events as understandable sorts of human actions' (Edwards 1997: 6). 'Accounts *of* actions are invariably, and at the same time, accounts *for* actions' (Edwards 1997: 8). Specifically, 'versions of mind, of thought and error, inference and reason, are constructed and implied in order to bolster or undermine versions of events, to accuse or criticize, blame or excuse and so on' (Edwards and Potter 1992: 16). These 'causal inferences and implications are often handled indirectly via ostensibly descriptive or factual accounts' (Edwards and Potter 1992: 78). Put simply, 'attributional work is *accomplished by* descriptions' (Edwards and Potter 1992: 91).

Action is a discursive concept because any consideration of an action is inseparable from its description as an action. These descriptions are performative speech acts that occur within complex language games and are always embedded in specific social contexts. Action descriptions tend to be discursively constructed as apparently factual and objective, but they often contain self-interested attributions of motives. 'Pure' action descriptions are rare. An action will be described in a certain way and not in other ways for a particular purpose, and these alternatives can vary greatly as to how they ascribe agency, impose responsibility, justify behaviour, explain motivations, assign praise, deflect criticism and blame and so on. This approach has obvious relevance to the novel, where actions can only exist as descriptions by narrators within a fictional discourse. Also, the point that a good deal of attributional work is accomplished by descriptions has obvious relevance to this chapter. As I have been arguing, it is difficult to disentangle pure action description from attribution because descriptions will usually contain hidden attribution cues. So, what discursive purposes are served by the attributions that have been described in the previous sections?

The Dickens passage is marked by a deliberate and self-conscious use of discourse in order to achieve discursive purposes. The narrator shows Clennam to be choosing his words very carefully in order to give credit to Doyce's character ('simplicity' and 'integrity'), to emphasise his need to be guided by 'respect' for his feelings, to acknowledge the pressure of social and moral norms (feeling 'behoved'), and 'to accept the blame for what he had *rashly* done'. In the language of discursive psychologists, he is *positioning* himself (Bamberg 2005) as the person responsible for the calamity. Also, Clennam's language in the third paragraph is principled and direct in that he does not portray himself as a passive, hapless or reluctant recipient of the writs. Any description of an action is never the only one: it is the one that is chosen, successfully or not, for a particular discursive purpose. It is easy to imagine the various, very different ways in which Clennam could have talked to Rugg if, say, his purpose had been to avoid responsibility. Much of the theory on discursive psychology assumes that people generally try to avoid responsibility for bad things, acquire responsibility for good things, avoid blame and acquire praise. However, while this may true in general terms, characters in novels tend to be more complex than that. In this case, the whole purpose of Clennam's discursive construction of his actions is to accept responsibility for a bad thing and to acquire blame.

Also of relevance to Clennam's behaviour is the sociocultural notion of *dramaturgical action*. A person evokes in their public audience a certain image or impression of themselves by purposefully disclosing their subjectivity. Each agent can monitor public access to the system of their own intentions, thoughts, attitudes, desires, feelings and so on. Thus, the presentation of the self does not signify spontaneous behaviour: it stylizes the expression of experience with a view to the audience (Wertsch 1991: 10). This perspective on action as impression management fits the first and third paragraphs extremely well. Clennam's presentation of his proposed action, sentence 3 in particular, has a very stylized feel to the language. His directly quoted language in sentence 8 also has the air of a public declaration.

The point made above that the same action can be described in different ways is vividly demonstrated in the second paragraph, where Clennam's action of disclosure is pejoratively referred to as 'courting publicity'. This presentation by the narrator of the viewpoint of the public is very different from Clennam's positioning. It is also worth noting how cleverly the narrator frames the discourse in the second paragraph to encourage the reader to come to a negative judgement on the behaviour of the public. There is a deliberately exaggerated style to the descriptions of the public's actions: 'storm raged fearfully', 'wildly staring', 'scaffold', and 'reproach and invective'. This exaggeration makes it clear that the apparent justification for the public's behaviour in sentence 6 (the 'flagrancy' of Clennam's actions, the appeal to disinterested parties, people who had lost money 'could scarcely be expected to deal mildly with it') is ironic. The reader is well aware that the narrator is indicating that this apparent justification for the public's actions is insufficient to excuse it. It is this irony that distinguishes the narrator's appeal to the consensus view and a supposed objective moral standard from the typical everyday positioning that is analysed by discursive psychologists. And again, the narrator could have used any number of other rhetorical devices in order to achieve very different discursive purposes.

Emotion is as much a discursive concept as action. Just as in the case of action, any consideration of an emotion is inseparable from its description as an emotion. Because the labelling that we apply to the feelings that we have is culturally constructed, no clear distinction can be drawn between emotions themselves and emotion discourse. To discuss the Pynchon text from a discursive perspective, let us go back to the annoyance/agony dichotomy. There is a difference in what might be called *emotional direction* here. 'Annoyance' is usually *outward* (being annoyed with others), although it can also be inward (being annoyed with one-self). 'Agony', by contrast, is always an extremely *inward* emotion. This amounts to a difference in the acceptance of responsibility. 'Annoyance' suggests an avoid-ance of moral responsibility by locating it in others (if outward) or suggesting that it is irrelevant (if inward). 'Agony', though, very definitely involves an acceptance of moral responsibility and the resulting guilt. By hearing something between the two, Oedipa is locating a profound ambivalence in Mucho regarding the moral responsibility for the consequences of his actions that he is prepared to accept.

Although, as I have said, a good deal of discursive psychology is about how people use discourse to assign blame to others, this passage seems to be precisely about Oedipa *not* blaming Mucho. This avoidance of blame and therefore of the responsibility for confronting a major factor in their marriage is achieved by various means. For example, according to the script, Mucho's infidelities should be constructed by the discourse as grounds for Oedipa's condemnation, but they are in fact constructed as difficult and emotionally dangerous events for *Mucho*. Blame is also avoided by means of the intensely controlled nature of the emotion discourse. This is particularly noticeable in the reference to 'scrupulous fairness' in sentence 1. Finally, there is an avoidance of introspection in Oedipa not wanting to get to the back of the tenderness that she feels, not wanting to get bogged, and, as a result, not asking any more questions.

The cognitive work on the emotions that I referred to earlier suggests that they are psychological states or processes that function in the management of goals. Oedipa's goal is the maintenance of their marriage, while Mucho's goal is less clear. Oedipa's objective is to let Mucho know that she cares for him and Mucho's, it *is* clear, is to let Oedipa know that he understands and appreciates that. Oedipa feels pity and tenderness towards Mucho and a kind of embarrass-ment or humiliation by proxy. She is worried about Mucho being laughed at by the young girls and does not want him to experience the resulting feelings of embarrassment and humiliation. The fact that these are sexual matters intensifies the problem. But she is unable to communicate this feeling to Mucho because it would only add to the embarrassment. The virtuous motive for the inabilities to communicate is their love for each other, or at least their affection for each other, or at least their desire not to hurt each other. This intermental interpretation explains the apparent paradox of the final sentence. Their feelings for each other have led them to a tacit shared understanding that they should maintain their inability to communicate with each other in order to be with each other.

Conclusion

I hope to have shown that readers have to undertake a continual stream of attribution of mental functioning to characters in order to understand novels. In addition, I have described a few, but only a few, of the various means by which readers undertake this attribution work. It was also part of my purpose to demonstrate that the descriptions of actions and emotions that readers rely on for these attributive purposes are not neutral. Many different choices can be made by narrators regarding the wording of such descriptions and by readers regarding their interpretations of such wording. These choices have a profound effect, not only on the cognitive attribution of a wide range of mental states, but also on the discursive attribution of responsibility, criticism, praise and blame.

Bridget Jones's Diary and Feminist Narratology

Ruth Page

Ruth Page's chapter analyses the relation between feminist narratology and feminist stylistics, particularly focusing on the way that feminist narratology has tended to focus on the macro-level of analysis, including analysis of plot, voice and focalization, whilst feminist stylistics has tended to focus on the micro-level, including analysis of nouns, pronouns and phrases. These two fields of study have become more distinct since they have tended to focus on different types of texts and draw on different models of analysis. Nevertheless, Page argues that these two fields, despite their differences, can usefully be drawn on when analysing texts.

Page analyses the notion of linearity in texts in order to illustrate the way that feminist stylistics and feminist narratology have approached similar issues and topics differently; in the process she demonstrates the way in which the concept of ideology is handled in a more nuanced way in current feminist narratological work. Focusing on *Bridget Jones's Diary*, Page analyses the way that temporal sequencing and plot are handled, particularly exploring the way that these can be discussed in relation to feminism. She challenges the notion that open-ended narrative sequences are necessarily feminist, and instead turns from content-analysis to an analysis which draws on Hoey's work (2001) in order to identify the patterns of goal-achievement. Through focusing on the way that romance is used as a 'solution' to Bridget Jones's problems and the way that Bridget's goals are endlessly undercut and satirized, Page manages to highlight the way that this novel challenges a great deal of self-help ideology which underpins feminist discourses. Thus through drawing on both a more linguistically oriented type of analysis together with one which focuses on sequencing and plot, Page is able to evaluate the complex relationship between this text and discourses of feminism.

Furthermore she has been able to foreground the way that gender inequality is mediated through texts such as this. Whilst I would challenge the notion that feminist stylistics has been subsumed within critical stylistics, this type of close linguistic analysis combined with broader analysis of the workings of ideology is an excellent example of a combined feminist stylistics/narratological analysis.

Sara Mills

Introduction

Feminist narratology gained currency in the mid–1980s and has since burgeoned into one of the most prolific streams of postclassical narrative analysis. In this chapter I critically re-examine the relationship between gendered values and narrative form with reference to the macro-level concepts of linearity and narrative closure. Through an analysis of *Bridget Jones's Diary* (Fielding 1996), I show that feminist interpretations of narrative form might be enhanced through the use of Hoey's (2001) predictable patterns of textual organization, especially as these intersect with the patterning of the self-help genre and the contemporary romance. Before beginning the analysis, I provide an overview of feminist narratology and its place within contemporary stylistics.

Definitions and History

Feminist narratology has many areas of intersection with the concerns of contemporary stylistics, particularly the contingent subfield of feminist stylistics. Recent definitions of feminist narratology and feminist stylistics suggest strong similarities between the two. Mills outlines feminist stylistics as 'concerned with the analysis of the way that questions of gender impact on the production and interpretation of texts' (2006: 221). As such, the gender-conscious close reading offered by feminist narratology seems to fall within the broad remit of feminist stylistics. However, to regard the two terms as synonymous obscures important further differences between them. Given that feminism, narratology and stylistics all stretch across a range of disciplines, and as terms of reference are not transparent or used in unified ways, the parallels and divergences between feminist narratology and stylistics are not neatly discrete, but better understood as embedded within the historical developments of each area.

Both feminist narratology and feminist stylistics began in the 1980s as part of the contextualist move away from the abstract and universalizing tendencies of structuralism. They reach beyond an analysis of the text alone to draw attention to the influence of contextual matters, although what is meant by 'context' can vary considerably. Both fields have also been shaped by developments in feminist theories over the last three decades. Broadly speaking, their inception can be seen as the result of feminism's shift away from the material concerns of 1970s radical feminism into 'the discursive concerns of literary and cultural theory prominent in the 1980s and into the 1990s' (Kavka 2001: xii). However, despite the similarities in the point of impetus, there are crucial contrasts which relate primarily to the differing ways in which stylistics and narratology interface with linguistics and literature.

While both analyse written texts, stylistics has never been bound by the limits of literature, nor by narrative as a specific genre. Indeed, Mills' most extensive treatment of feminist stylistics argues forcefully for the inclusion of a broader selection of text types in which literature might be situated (1995: 17). On the other hand, narratology proper has concerned itself with describing systems of literary meaning (Warhol 2003: 24), and feminist narratology has followed suit to focus for the most part on literary texts, although this has widened in recent years to include films and folklore.

Shen (2005a) points to the contrasting toolkits which stylistics and narratology have developed from linguistic origins. While stylistics has used the findings and methodology of linguistics to analyse verbal texts, narratology uses textual analysis to focus on supra-linguistic elements such as plot structure, narrative voice, focalization or temporal ordering. Although this should not be taken as a binary or exclusive distinction, this has led to a tendency where feminist stylistics has focused on sexism as manifest through micro-level features (such as lexis or syntax) whereas feminist narratology has been more concerned with tracing associations between gender and macro-level structures, particularly plot and voice.

The differences in text type and application of linguistics correspond to the variation in the feminist theory that is drawn upon. In line with its closer allegiance to linguistics, feminist stylistics explicitly takes account of work in feminist linguistics, specifically sociolinguistics and critical linguistics. Following Burton's (1996) lead, feminist stylistics understands language as a form of social action, thus it is the stylistic analysis itself that becomes politicized as feminist resistance. Although feminist narratology proceeds from the same theoretical premises: that is, that no analysis can be objective and ideologically neutral, feminist narratology has taken relatively little notice of work on gender and narrative carried out in sociolinguistics. Instead, the 'feminism' of feminist narratology is derived more closely from the feminist literary criticism of the late 1970s and early 1980s, particularly Anglo-American gynocriticism and the work of French theorists Cixous and Kristeva. Subsequently, the challenges posed by feminist narratology are more closely associated with literary criticism, and use the recovery of neglected women's texts in order to both extend narrative criticism and re-evaluate narrative theory itself.

The result of this is that some 20 years on from their beginnings, the positions of feminist narratology and feminist stylistics have come to be rather different. At the beginning of the new millennium, feminist narratology finds itself clearly situated in narratological criticism with interests in cultural studies (Bal 1999; Warhol 2002), associated most prominently with the work of North American scholars. The feminist dimension of this research has become increasingly theoretical and is often integrated with queer studies (Lanser 1995; Warhol 2003). In contrast, the term 'feminist stylistics' is seen less frequently these days, and has become difficult to distinguish from post-feminist text analysis (Mills 1998; Bucholz 2003) or is subsumed within the superordinate term 'critical stylistics' (Hall and Gavins 2004). The 'feminism' of feminist stylistics has also altered under the influence of postmodernism, recognising the need to take account of changes in both sexism and feminist linguistic analysis (Mills 1998). It is no longer the case that either field are asking simplistic questions about gender difference, but rather have come to respond to texts of different kinds with localized contexts. Indeed, despite superficial similarities in practice there is surprisingly little cross-reference between researchers working within these communities. This leads me to question the ways that future synergies might be forged in order to bring about mutual benefit.

Although I have stressed points of difference, the relationship between feminist narratology and feminist stylistics should not be taken as mutually exclusive, but rather the means of offering complementary perspectives. At this point in time, a further degree of integration might be particularly salient. Mills argues for a new phase of post-feminist text analysis which 'must analyse words at the level of discourse as well as at the local level of occurrence' (1998: 241). Moving away from a micro-level focus, the tools of narratology might lend further precision to this kind of stylistic analysis. In turn, the narratological analysis of literature might be usefully informed by the findings of sociolinguistic research, and reconceptualize its politics through the lens of critical linguistics. I will demonstrate the potential benefit of this interchange with reference to an issue of relevance to both feminist narratology and feminist stylistics: linearity.

Linearity and Ideology

At the outset, it is important to recognise that the concept of 'linearity' might entail a number of separate but overlapping dimensions including textuality (the physical representation of the verbal text as signs in a sequence), content (the perception of logical relations such as causality or time sequence) and form (such as normative patterns of syntax). Narratology and stylistics have been concerned with the last two of these, but address them in different respects. Feminist stylistics has focused on linearity at the level of syntax while feminist narratology transposes the matter onto the macro-level issues of temporal sequence (Wallace 2000) or plot teleology (Winnett 1990; Anderson 1995). Feminist stylistics and feminist narratology are united in imbuing textual features with ideological value, where boundaries, be that of the sentence, time sequence or plot closure, apparently represent a form of patriarchal oppression. The gendered equation results in a binary opposition between conventional narrative forms, which are derived from a male-authored corpus and thus deemed to be masculine or patriarchal, and experimental feminine writing. In terms of narrativity, these associations polarize conventional narrative structures against the 'female' alternatives, which are characterized instead as open-ended, episodic, with multiple climaxes or none at all.

The attempt to invest different forms of linearity with gendered meaning and political potential are best understood as the product of particular theoretical trends which have since come under fierce critique. It reflects the priorities of second wave feminist literary criticism which both sought to insert women's voices into the literary canon and subjected a range of academic theory to feminist scrutiny. This went hand in hand with the increasing prominence of French theorists, who in turn derived much of their thinking from revisions of psychoanalytic theory. Both the metaphorical abstraction and binary thinking inherent in this phase of textual feminism have been problematised. Later work has critiqued the gendered discussion of linearity for its lack of linguistic precision and shown that in the face of empirical data, a simplistic correlation between linearity and gender at any level cannot hold (Mills 1995; Richardson 2000; Livia 2003; Page 2006). More broadly, binary classifications have been found reductive, obscuring the diverse range of gendered experiences and the rich variation in narrative technique that might be involved in matters of linearity. As a result, Richardson (2000: 693) concludes that 'the quest to find an easy symmetry between form and ideology should be abandoned, along with other comparably simplistic and undialectical claims made in the name of ideological purity or commitment'. While I agree that a quest for 'easy symmetry' is untenable, I maintain that ideology should not be discounted from our discussions of narrative form, theory and analysis. Instead, any such discussion needs to be open-ended and context-sensitive.

From the outset, Lanser implied a position for feminist narratology that was 'cautious in its construction of systems and favour[ed] flexible categories over fixed sets' (1986: 345). That said, it should be noted that much of the early work in feminist narratology was strongly influenced by binary paradigms, for example, questioning 'whether men and women do write differently' (Lanser 1986: 346). The kinds of questions now asked by feminist narratology are rather different, and treat the matter of ideology in a more mediated manner. Therefore in the following analysis I am not so much interested in claiming that the text is an example of feminine or feminist narrative style. Instead I set out to demonstrate how the tools of narratology can be helpful (or not) in exploring how the analysis of linearity and its related concerns can help us understand how gendered meanings are constructed in my chosen text.

Bridget Jones's Diary – a Postfeminist Narrative?

I turn now to analyse *Bridget Jones's Diary* (henceforth *BJD*), which was originally serialized in the British newspaper, the *Independent*, then later published as a novel (1996) and adapted for film (in 2001). All quoted references are from Fielding (1996). Like many other women-centred texts, *BJD* is a rich site for exploring the contradictions of women's lives and their identifications (Hanson 2004: 25). However, *BJD* has attracted most academic interest for the complex way in which it engages with postfeminist concerns. On one level, *BJD* ventriloquizes feminist theory (for example through Bridget's mother and the character 'Sharon') and Bridget herself exemplifies the outcome of second wave feminism in her self-determination, career success and sexual freedom. On another level, *BJD* also seems to reinforce sexist stereotypes as shown through Bridget's compliance in constructing herself as a sexualized object of the male gaze, and the fact that she seeks pleasure in desiring romance-plot closure for the narrative, ultimately reaffirming heterosexual and patriarchal social structures. The content of the narrative suggests multiple gendered interpretations. The task of feminist narratology is to explicate the part that narrative patterning plays in helping to construct the ambivalent feminist reaction to this text.

BJD does not manipulate narrative structures in an experimental fashion. In many respects, the narrative format is conventionally straightforward. Following a pseudo-diary format, the entries are sequenced in a ruthlessly chronological order, and even within the entries themselves reiterate a linear time sequence as Bridget recounts the events of her day. Some entries do contain flashbacks and projections, such as the opening entry which returns back to the previous August (Fielding 1996: 8) and moves forward with predictions of what the future might hold. However, while Bridget repeatedly returns to her ongoing singleness, 'once again I am humiliatingly spending Christmas Eve alone in my parents' house in a single bed' (p.299), there is little in the temporal structure of *BJD* that suggests the repetitive cyclical nature or timelessness associated with the feminist reading of Kristeva's (1997) 'women's time'.

Similarly, the teleological focus of the plot structure does not suggest feminist emancipation. Given that the end point of the narrative carries particular ideological weight, *BJD* seems remarkably conservative, finishing with the implied consummation of Bridget and Mark Darcy's relationship. In the film adaptation, the traditional romance plot is all the more strongly enforced with the closing scene of Bridget and Mark embracing. However, the novel's ultimate summary undercuts the finality of this union, listing the outcome of the year as including 'Boyfriends 2 (but one only for six days *so far*)' (p. 310, emphasis added). Thus Bridget evaluates the summary as 'An *excellent* year's progress' (p.310), but the permanence of the romance closure is thrown into doubt and a sense of open-endedness introduced.

The extent to which the ambiguous closure of *BJD* might be interpreted as a feminist feature is open to question. While superficially it undermines the finality of the romance plot and suggests that Bridget's narrative is not yet over, it is difficult to argue that this feature alone functions as a form of feminist resistance that challenges patriarchal boundaries. It might equally be explained from a contextual point of view as a reflection of social changes where the romance closure of marriage has been replaced by serial monogamy. From a generic perspective, the open-endedness is also in keeping with the original serialization of the diary entries. In either case, the correlation of feminist intent and narrative lack of closure is problematized by two further factors. First, the interpretation of closure is based on narrative content, rather than linguistic or structural analysis. Therefore it is limited in terms of comparability. Second, even a brief survey of other literature suggests that open-ended narratives are by no means exclusively woman-centred, feminine or feminist. One only has to refer to Victorian serial writers such as Dickens and Trollope to bear this out. This being the case, it would seem that conventional feminist approaches to linearity in *BJD* have little to tell us about the feminist controversy surrounding this text.

Instead, I argue that an analysis that combines feminist and narratological perspectives is possible, but would benefit from moving away from metaphorical concepts such as 'linearity' and 'closure' and instead interrogate the plot structure using linguistically informed models from text analysis. Here I draw on the work of Michael Hoey (2001) who presents a schematic outline of what he terms 'culturally popular, predictable patterns of text organisation'. These patterns include problem-solution, goal-achievement, desire-arousal and gap in knowledge progressions, many of which have strong parallels with existing narrative outlines (for example, Labov's (1972) model).

Crucially, Hoey's account of the predictable patterns is heavily contextualized and emphasises the role of the reader in textual interaction. He argues that predictable patterns of text organisation can function as forms of narrative schemata, thus contributing to a sense of how a story 'should go' within particular cultures. Where expectations of that sequencing are thwarted, this may result in a sense that a narrative is unfinished, even if the text on the page has stopped. This more cognitively oriented approach to textual organisation thus provides an alternative perspective on narrative progression, and in particular the question of closure.

BJD contains a multitude of predictable patterns. I focus on the two which feature most prominently in the textual organization. *BJD* opens as a novel with a double spread of resolutions, listing Bridget's projected achievements under the headings 'I will not' and 'I will'. At the outset, the narrative is framed by the initiation of a series of goal-achievement patterns, which follow the schematic progression:

What was the situation?
What goal did x want to achieve?
What method did x or y use to achieve it?
How successful was this in the opinion of x, y, or z?

(Hoey 2001: 146)

The precise nature of each of the goals varies, including Bridget's attempts to improve her body 'I will stop smoking, drink no more than fourteen alcohol units a week, reduce circumference of thighs by 3 inches', her environment 'purge flat of all extraneous matter', her character 'be kinder and help others more' but above all else, her relationships with men (pp.2–3), with the following entries recording the means by which Bridget attempts to achieve these goals and the headings of each entry evaluating her relative success, albeit in contradictory and shifting terms.

Sunday 19 February
8 st 13 (v.g. but purely through worry), alcohol units 2 (but the Lord's day), cigarettes 7, calories 2100

(Fielding 1996: 55)

Thursday 23 February
8 st 13 (if only could stay under 9 st and not keep bobbing up and down like a drowning corpse – drowning in fat), alcohol units 2, cigarettes 17 (pre-shag

nerves – understandable), calories 775 (last-ditch attempt to get down to 8st 7 before tomorrow)

(Fielding 1996: 58)

What is perhaps most interesting is the way that the goal-achievement patterns here allude to the self-help genre. The structural features of the self-help genre are not inherently gendered or political any more than any linguistic form can be. Nonetheless, the social uses of the self-help discourse have gained gendered currency, where Cameron (1995) claims it is associated particularly with a female audience and concerned with feminine behaviour.

Bridget Jones's Diary and the Self-help Genre

BJD is littered with references to self-help texts, such that Marsh (2004) goes as far as to call it a 'self help satire'. However, the feminist implications of this form of the goal-achievement pattern are open to debate. Self-help literature seems to suggest the individual's empowerment, self-determination and agency: all quali-ties one might associate with the demands of second wave feminism. Indeed, in narrative terms, these are realized by placing Bridget in the agentive position of the one seeking to achieve her goals, and the controlling position of evaluating and justifying her own success, 'An *excellent* year's progress'. To this extent, *BJD* seems to have followed the historical development of plot in feminist literature where the heroine moves from being a passive figure to a questing hero (Gutenberg 2000).

Alternatively, the self-help discourse poses problematic issues for feminists, particularly as it is narrativized through the goal-achievement patterns in *BJD*. Generally, feminists have argued that self-help literature in fact might lead to the 'devaluation of women' (Cameron 1995: 204), and, in its insistence on the per-sonal, fails to address the wider political issues at stake. Thus, allowing Bridget to initiate goal-achievement patterns is of limited value given the nature of the goals she projects and the means by which she chooses to fulfil them. Nowhere is this more clear than in the specific subgenre of self-help that Fielding centres on. Cameron (1995) divides self-help discourse into two types: one focused on career advice, as distinct from the other which deals with relationships. *BJD* draws almost exclusively on the latter of these.

It is not only the content of the predictable patterns but the way they are structured that is of interest in *BJD*. Bridget's resolutions ostensibly negate the need for romantic relationships, but they simultaneously contradict this by cast-ing her independence as the means by which the secondary goal of obtaining a 'boyfriend' can be achieved. The pattern runs as follows:

What goal (1) did Bridget want to achieve?
'I will not sulk about having no boyfriend,'

What method (1) did Bridget use to achieve it?
'but develop inner poise and authority and sense of self as woman of substance, complete without boyfriend...'
What goal (2) did Bridget want to achieve?
'...as best way to obtain boyfriend' (p.2)
What method did x or y use to achieve it?
Implied by method (1) above, that is, 'develop inner poise'.

The reassertion of a romance plot emerges more prominently when throughout the narrative, the text repeatedly constructs Bridget's singleness as a problem which should be solved, for example through the attitudes of Bridget's family and friends,

'How's your love life anyway? ... So you *still* haven't got a feller!' (p.11)
'Yes, why aren't you married yet, Bridget?' sneered Woney. (p.40)

So although Bridget superficially rejects the romance plot of 'love' in favour of self-help achievements, 'It is proved by surveys that happiness does not come from love, wealth or power but the pursuit of attainable goals: and what is a diet if not that?' (p.18), ultimately the narrative structure of the diary in turn rejects the possibility of feminist self-help transformation.

The false promise of the self-help genre is indicated through two narrative strategies. First, the nature of the self-help patterns which underpin *BJD* is such that they either endlessly recycle and thereby generate a sense of incompleteness, or that they fail to bring about transformation at all. The sense of incompletion is generated through the use of negative evaluation. For example, Bridget positively evaluates the goal of reducing her body weight, 'Today is an historic and joyous day. After eighteen years of trying to get down to 8st 7 I have finally achieved it. It is no trick of the scales, but confirmed by jeans. I am thin' (p.105). However, the success of completing this pattern is short-lived and immediately negated,

'Did you see how thin I am?' Silence.
'Tom?'
'I think you looked better before, hon.'
[...] I feel like a scientist who discovers that his life's work has been a total mistake.

(Fielding 1996: 107)

In terms of predictable patterning, this negative evaluation results in the expectation that the text will recycle until a positive conclusion is reached (Hoey 2001: 130–1), a conclusion which is impossible for Bridget to attain, 'I am a child of *Cosmopolitan* culture, have been traumatized by supermodels and too many quizzes and know that neither my personality nor my body is up to it if left to its own devices' (p. 59). The nature of the goal-achievement patterns in *BJD* thus suggests feminist self-empowerment to be a myth. The ambiguous closure and serial continuation in *BJD* thus remains of interest from a feminist perspective, not in an abstract sense but contextualized as a realisation of the problematic self-help discourse which offers only illusory empowerment and instead perpetrates restrictive stereotypes and anxieties.

The apparent empowerment of the self-help goal-achievement patterns is undermined by a second strategy in *BJD*. Bridget's adoption of a self-help attitude is juxtaposed and ultimately displaced by another predictable pattern: the desire-arousal pattern more often (although not exclusively) associated with love stories or erotic narratives. The schematic outline of the desire-arousal pattern is as follows:

> What was the situation?
> Who or what within this situation was particularly attractive?
> What effect did this have on x?
> What did x do about it?
> What was the result?
>
> (Hoey 2001: 157)

This is evident in the entry for Tuesday 3 January where the readers are first introduced to the character, Daniel Cleaver. Bridget begins by endorsing the power of self-help discourse. However, by the end of the entry, this pattern has been replaced by the desire-arousal schema:

> *What was the situation?*
> Bridget concludes that 'happiness does not come from love'
> *Who within this situation was particularly attractive?*
> 'Mmmm. Daniel Cleaver, though. Love his wicked dissolute air, while being v. successful and clever.' (p.2)
> *What effect did this have on Bridget?*
> 'Think might wear short black skirt tomorrow' (p.2)
> *What did Bridget do about it?*
> Carries out intention to dress in 'short black skirt'
> *What was the result?*
> Flirtation between Cleaver and Bridget begins (Thursday 5 January) ending with Bridget's positive evaluation, 'Yessss! Yesssss! Daniel Cleaver wants my phone no. Am marvellous. Am irresistible Sex Goddess. Hurrah!' (p.26)

In narrative terms, the appropriation of this pattern by a female character seems a clear move away from associating masculinity with desire and action in the manner of Brooks (1984). Indeed, positioning the male character as an object of attraction initially seems to align *BJD* with feminist writing of recent decades, which Whelehan (2004: 34) describes as developing 'a female language of hetero-sexual desire'. Contrary to the arguments critically summarised by Wallace (2000), narrative, it seems, can after all express feminine desire.

The feminist potential of the desire-arousal pattern in *BJD* is nonetheless short-lived. The response that Bridget makes is to construct herself as an object of the male gaze, interpreting her power primarily in terms of sexual attraction. A feminist interpretation might find this problematic for two reasons. First, Bridget's flirtation with Daniel reveals not only her compliance with but approbation of a discourse that might in other real-world contexts be deemed sexist, 'Think will cross last bit out as contains mild accusation of sexual harassment whereas v. much enjoying being sexually harassed by Daniel Cleaver' (p. 25). Second, Bridget's repositioning of herself as the object of attraction forces the male characters back into the conventional romance roles which reinstate the old equation of masculinity with desire and agency. In terms of narrative content it is Mark who finally rescues Bridget and resolves the textually created problems (in the novel, the ill-fated liaison between Bridget's mother and the criminal Julio). Although it is important not to equate syntactic patterns simplistically with social patterns of power (Mills 1998: 239), it is notable that by the end of the novel, the heterosexual union is narrated so that Bridget is the acted-upon object (italicized below):

> Then he took the champagne glass out of my hand, kissed *me* and said, 'Right, Bridget Jones, I'm going to give *you* pardon for,' picked *me* up in his arms, carried *me* off into the bedroom.
>
> (Fielding 1996: 307)

While it may be that the nature of sexism has changed and that we are not supposed to take Fielding's depiction of Bridget seriously, a gender-conscious interpretation of the narrative structures in *BJD* reveals the points of contradiction between feminist and conservative positions in this text. Both the self-help goal-achievement and romance desire-arousal patterns show the same slippage. At first the heroine appears to be agentive, initiating a quest-like sequence, but the goals she wishes to achieve and the means she chooses to attain them invoke sexist attitudes and stereotypes for both masculine and feminine behaviour.

Whether or not we take Fielding's satire ironically, played for comic effect alone, there are serious social inequalities which lie behind these narrative patterns. The emphasis on romance and relational self-help in these predictable patterns separates the public and private domains. Indeed, *BJD* neglects career advice literature almost entirely and overwrites professional development with personal desire. In so doing, the content of the narrative both reflects and reinforces the split between progressive and traditional gender identities highlighted by the narrative analysis. In turn, this is rooted in a wider ideological context where separating private and public domains has problematic consequences for at least some groups of women (and men). In the private domain, the predictable patterns in *BJD* position Bridget (and not the male characters) as the maker of relationships, the one for whom being without a partner and children is a problem she must address. This value system not only lags behind the apparent success of women in the public domain but also creates further asymmetries within the workplace, where for example, men's familial identities are less well recognised and women continue to carry the primary burden of domestic responsibility (Leonard 2001). The heroine's agency in these predictable patterns is not the feminist empowerment it might seem, but rather reinforces a conservative value system in place of personal or political change.

Summary and Closing Remarks

The discussion has demonstrated the ways in which the analysis of the predictable patterns in *BJD* can contribute to a gender-conscious interpretation of the text. The application of the narrative frameworks highlights the ambivalence between the apparent feminist agency of the heroine, Bridget, and the retention of conservative gender identities. The open-endedness of the diary is not seen in this context as an abstract form of feminist resistance to a metaphorical form of patriarchal silence. Instead, I have argued that the open-endedness is generated at least in part by Fielding's satirical evocation of the self-help genre. Thus I am not trying to claim that the perception of open-endedness is an unequivocally feminist feature, nor that the self-help discourse is a defining feature of feminist narratology (say as a distinctive plot type). Rather, the interplay between the predictable patterns, self-help discourse and feminist perspectives highlights that it is social narratives and their contexts, not the formal properties of a narrative alone that bring gendered meanings to a text.

I close, then, by reflecting on what the modifier 'feminist' might mean for feminist narratology within the context of contemporary stylistics. The textual interpretation I have carried out in this chapter is in many respects typical of much feminist narratology, and demonstrates its key strength as a form of close reading. However, the influence of 'feminism' as a political movement in relation to this kind of criticism is open to question. Although feminist narratology has refined narrative theory in important ways, the theoretical distinctions drawn by Warhol and Lanser remain of necessity abstract and decontextualized (Shen 2005b) and do not constitute an explicitly gendered alternative to existing narrative frameworks. Instead of deeming this problematic, the failure to 'gender' narratology might be seen as a benefit, avoiding a binary and potentially hierarchical pairing between a supposedly neutral 'narratology' and a 'feminist' opposite (Page 2006).

More provocatively, it is clear that producing a gender-conscious analysis of a narrative need not entail a feminist dimension, just as a woman-centred text need not be inflected by feminist values. To the extent that my interpretation of *BJD* has exposed points of gender inequality as refracted through this text, then feminism as a means of challenging gender politics remains an appropriate term of reference. Indeed, many have argued that exposing points of inequality is a prerequisite step towards changing those asymmetries. But therein lies the crux of the matter for feminist narratology and for its use in stylistics more generally. As critical linguistics challenges us, we have yet to move beyond interpretation alone to ask 'What can be done about this text?' (Fairclough 1995). Outside the academic domain, the analyses produced by feminist narratology or feminist stylistics cannot be said to have produced much impact. The reasons behind this must remain speculative and are inevitably manifold, but reflect the at least superficial split between feminist theory and practice, the effects of postmodern fragmentation and the conservative anti-feminist 'backlash' cited in current years (McRobbie 2004).

Does this mean that feminist narratology is a misnomer and will eventually be replaced by a non-gender specific modifier as in the case of feminist stylistics' subordination to critical stylistics? The answer remains to be seen, but the ongoing necessity of feminism (Bryson 1999: 5) points to the case for feminist narratology remaining open. While there are clearly limitations within which this field operates, the potential to generate new categories for formal narratology, and to sensitize critics to gendered inequalities through the interpretation of texts continues to produce new work. As contemporary stylistics broadens its theoretical and textual horizons, the close reading and contextualisation of feminist narratology are offered fresh territory to explore.

9

Schema Poetics and Crossover Fiction

Clare Walsh

Mark Haddon's novel *The Curious Incident of the Dog in the Night-time* has become one of the most successful of recent 'crossover' novels – fiction that appeals to both adult and younger readers. It is one of the most widely read modern British novels in the context of overseas secondary education, being widely adopted as a class reader, a main title and a reading group mainstay in several countries. I have myself worked on preparing a stylistic/pedagogic apparatus for it in a project on 'reading diversity' in Slovenia, and work done on it in Hungary is likewise beginning to reach a wide audience.

Clare Walsh usefully applies schema poetics to study various ways in which this novel works. As she suggests, the widespread multifaceted readership the novel has reached has come about in part because of and in part despite the novel's unique take on the events it narrates. She says

> the presence of metafictive devices in *The Curious Incident* could be said to *reduce* the experiential gap that generally exists between adult and younger readers in that the radical newness of such texts means *all* readers are without a ready-made text schema to guide them through the work.

That the novel manages to combine that 'radical newness' with wide readerly appeal is something that Walsh's analysis endeavours to account for, and in the attempt she makes some very significant points, which deserve to be taken up by those working on the pedagogical aspects of stylistic approaches to such a text. Questions of intertextuality, of identification and sympathy, of shared and unshared perceptions all come into play. Where this approach leads us ultimately is to questions of cultural interface, of how readers perceive embedded cultural references and the strategies writers use while they engage in the necessary processes of creating a familiar fictional world while defamiliarizing, as Haddon does, many aspects of quotidian experience.

Walsh approvingly quotes Cook (1994: 130) on this very subject: 'the essence of schema theory is that discourse proceeds and achieves coherence by successfully locating the unexpected within a framework of expectations'. Non-fictional case studies of Asperger's syndrome, frequently referred to in the pedagogic context of work on Haddon's novel, make an exactly similar point. This interface between scientific case studies, a schema theory approach to this particular fictional text and the pedagogic implications for a worldwide readership, both in English and in translation, would open up a wide range of ways of building upon Clare Walsh's basic findings.

Taking this approach further might lead to useful contrastive analyses, which would bring out similarities and differences between novels, and their degree of 'crossover' potential. One recent example that springs to mind is *Runt* by Niall Griffiths: a similarly 'challenged' protagonist, but a rather different and highly distinctive approach and function to the novel. Stylistics, and its use of schema theory among many other tools, will thus be seen to be more and more illuminating about a range of texts rather than only in the study of single texts. The benefits to literary linguistic studies and to the teaching of texts will be considerable.

John McRae

Introduction

Schema poetics involves the application of insights from work in the fields of Artificial Intelligence (AI) and cognitive psychology to an understanding of the process of literary reading. One of the major advantages of schema poetics is that it can account for different interpretations of the same literary text. In practice, however, critics have understandably tended to privilege their own expert readings, although they generally include the caveat that other interpretations are, of course, possible (de Beaugrande 1987; Cook 1994; Semino 1995; Stockwell 2002). Yet schema poetics also has the potential to account for readings by 'interpretative communities' (Fish 1980) of readers, including, I will argue, those based on age and readerly experience. This chapter will provide a brief account of the origins of schema theory and will outline one particular application of this theory to literary texts (Cook 1994). It will then provide a definition of the relatively recent hybrid genre of 'crossover fiction'. The remainder of the chapter will explore how schema poetics can help to illuminate the potential benefits for young readers of challenging works of crossover fiction that offer them 'mental disruption, refreshment and play' (Cook 1994: 255).

Schema Poetics

Schema poetics has its origins in the work of AI theorists, most notably Roger Schank (Schank and Abelson 1977; Schank 1982, 1984, 1986), who developed schema theory to enable computer programs to process language in a context sensitive way. To this end, AI theorists posit the existence of interpretative scripts or *schemas* which individuals store in background memory in order to make sense of events in the world. Stockwell notes that: 'The classic example given is the "restaurant" schema, which gives an understanding of what restaurants are, what they look like, what sorts of things one would expect to find in them, how to go about ordering food, paying, and so on' (2003: 255). In his later work, Schank (1982) emphasises the dynamic nature of schematic knowledge and the way in which it is continually adjusted to match new incoming information. Thus visits to different kinds of restaurants, such as a self-service café or a sushi bar, will require modifications to one's existing restaurant schema.

It is this dynamic aspect of schema theory that is taken up by Cook in his account of literariness as discourse deviation: 'the essence of schema theory is that discourse proceeds and achieves coherence by successfully locating the unexpected within a framework of expectations' (1994: 130). However, Cook is critical of AI theorists for failing to pay sufficient attention to the role played by language and text structure in the process of schematic change. His own approach, by contrast, focuses on the 'author-reader-text' dynamic (Cook 1994: 129). He proposes a hierarchy of different types of schema, comprising world, text and language schemas (Cook 1994: 181). He argues that texts can be schema reinforcing, schema preserving or schema disrupting at any or all of these levels, depending on their degree of divergence from readers' existing schematic knowledge (Cook 1994: 191). Schema disruption is triggered by deviation at one or both of the linguistic and text-structure levels and has the potential to effect a change in the reader's world schema (p.198). According to Cook, it is perhaps *the* defining criterion of literary discourse that it is schema disrupting, thus offering the potential for schema refreshment and 'cognitive change' (p.44). This somewhat narrow focus on *cognitive* change downplays the importance of the affective dimension of literary reading, something which is arguably even more significant for young readers. By contrast, in his discussion of 'mind style' in fiction, Palmer extends this concept beyond cognitive functioning to a character's 'dispositions, feelings, beliefs and emotions' (2004: 19).

Crossover Fiction

Cook's definition of literature as discourse deviation would seem to preclude traditional works of fiction for young readers, since these tend to be schema reinforcing at all three schematic levels. Thus Nodelman and Reimer (2003: 186–217) argue that, through a gradual process of accretion, a relatively closed set of generic conventions has emerged as characteristic of children's literature based on the socially conditioned assumptions adult writers have made about the limitations of children as readers. Yet, as Beckett notes: 'Contemporary children's literature has become a field of innovation and experimentation, challenging the conventions, codes and norms that traditionally governed the genre' (1999: xvi). This may account for the relatively recent phenomenon whereby fiction for children and adolescents has been appropriated by adult readers and has been published with alternative book jackets featuring a more appropriate (read 'less childish') layout and design. Notable amongst such works of crossover fiction have been the hugely successful Harry Potter books by J. K. Rowling (1997–2007) and the critically acclaimed *His Dark Materials* trilogy by Philip Pullman (1995–2000). Somewhat predictably, this phenomenon has been dismissed by some as the 'juvenilization' of adult literature and has been used as evidence of a regressive nostalgia amongst 'kidults' for more traditional linear narratives involving empathetic characters (Kenward 2005). Such a view ignores the complex pleasures offered by the densely intertextual nature of books by Pullman, David Almond, Cornelia Funk and Daniel Handler, amongst numerous others.

Nor does such a view account for the popularity amongst young readers of Mark Haddon's challenging novel *The Curious Incident of the Dog in the Night-time* (2003, hereafter *The Curious Incident*). The novel's crossover status is, I would suggest, not simply an opportunistic marketing ploy to maximize book sales in an increasingly competitive market. What an experienced children's publisher, David Fickling, recognized in the book is its genuine hybridity in terms of audience appeal. I will argue that the reason for the novel's appeal to young readers is that there is a sufficient 'fit' with their existing language, text and world schemas to make it accessible to them, while at the same time including unexpected elements which offer the potential for schema refreshment, which may in turn lead to cognitive and affective change.

Schema Poetics and Alternative Readings of Mark Haddon's *The Curious Incident*

Although marketed as a crossover novel, Haddon insists that he wrote *The Curious Incident* (2003) with an implied *adult* reader in mind. He explains his disappointment when the decision was taken to publish it simultaneously under a children's imprint: 'I'd spent a lot of effort trying to move away from writing for children. Here I thought, "Maybe I'm about to slip back inside the ghetto again"' (cited in Welch 2003). This seems to lend some weight to John Rowe Townsend's contention that 'The only practical definition of a children's book today – absurd as it sounds – is "a book which appears on the children's list of a publisher"' (cited in Hollindale 1997: 27). Haddon's ambivalence about writing for children is hardly surprising, given that he was described by many reviewers as a first-time novelist, despite the fact that he had previously written no fewer than 15 books for children. Other reviewers sought to distance *The Curious Incident* from his previous work by describing it as a 'literary novel', making it clear that, despite the critical acclaim achieved by children's writers such as Philip Pullman and Michael Morpurgo, books for children are still routinely excluded from the category of 'literary fiction'. The appropriation by child readers of this ostensibly adult and literary book renders this exclusion, at the very least, open to contestation. This is not surprising given that there are children, such as the younger self that Frances Spufford (2002) describes in *The Child that Books Built*, who are voracious readers from a very early age, just as there are adults, many of them young men, who gave up on reading fiction in their early teens. This would suggest that readerly experience is a more important determinant of literary competence than age *per se.*

Haddon has nonetheless evinced surprise that *actual* child readers have taken pleasure in a novel that he thought would be beyond their interpretative competence, but intriguingly he goes on to imply that adults and children may well *not* be reading the same book at all. Thus he suggests that the child or young adult reader is more likely to read it as a straightforward 'issues' novel about disability, a genre with which they are all too familiar, since a good deal of contemporary realist fiction written for them falls rather predictably into what might be broadly termed 'bibliotherapy' (Crago 1999). By definition, this is a genre which calls for a very personal identificatory reading. Haddon's *ideal* reader, on the other hand, is an adult who is more likely to realize the novel's full meaning potential as a multilayered text and who will thus read it 'aright' from a more detached reading position as a barely disguised work of metafiction. This illustrates Stockwell's contention that, from the perspective of schema poetics, 'genre and judgements about genre are matters of readerly experience' (2003: 253). Haddon acknowledges that on one level the book is indeed 'about' disability, but that 'on another level, *and this is the level that I think only perhaps adults will get,* it's a book about books, about what you can do with words and what it means to communicate with someone in a book' (cited in Welch 2003, my italics).

The cautious modality Haddon employs here suggests that he does not rule out the possibility that children and young adults *might* be able to recognize metafictive devices in the novel, but it is clear that he believes such precocious readings to be the exception, rather than the rule. The assumption that young readers are unable to grasp fictions that draw attention to their own fictionality remains widespread, in spite of the highly metafictive nature of books now produced for even the youngest child readers, not to mention the self-consciously intertextual nature of 'new young adult' fiction (Wilkie 1999: 135) and popular films, such as *Shrek* (2001) and *Finding Nemo* (2003), whose primary audience comprises children and young adults. Younger readers/viewers seem to respond in particular to the *playful* aspect of such metafictive texts. In any case, as Peter Hunt observes, 'it may be correct to assume that child-readers will not bring to the text a complete or sophisticated system of codes, but is this any reason to deny them access to texts with a potential of rich codes?' (1991: 101). On the contrary, I will argue that Haddon's deceptively simple, yet richly textured, novel is ideally placed to fulfil what Margaret Meek has identified as one of the most important functions of literature for young readers, namely the ability to educate their sense of story (Meek 1988). In other words, Haddon's novel has the potential to offer children and young adults the kind of 'scaffolding' that Nodelman and Reimer (2003: 99) suggest can lead them towards a new understanding of themselves and of the pleasures offered by more critical reading.

As a work of metafiction, *The Curious Incident* lays bare the literary codes and conventions involved in the schizophrenic process of writing for *children,* a process about which Haddon is, as has already been noted, ambivalent. In imagining himself inside the head of a first person narrator with Asperger's syndrome, Haddon has had to perform, only in a more exaggerated and more contradictory way, precisely the kind of world schema shift which all successful writers for children aim to accomplish. This process, described by numerous children's authors, entails taking on the perspective of a younger self, with a more limited language schema and a cognitively more restricted world view. Writers who are capable of achieving this successfully seem to possess what Hollindale (1997) refers to as a quality of 'childness'. Haddon's apprenticeship as a writer of children's fiction was obviously an ideal training ground for the kind of radical schema shift required of the author in *The Curious Incident*. On one level, then, the book can be read as a kind of metafictive comment on the cognitive and linguistic limitations writers for children have to impose upon themselves. This does not, of course, explain why young readers have read the book with enthusiasm; it must have inherent qualities that afford them pleasures. In what follows, and with reference to schema theory, I intend to consider what these qualities might be.

I would suggest that the reason why young readers have responded to a novel that was not intended for them is that there are numerous ways in which it realizes their readerly expectations. As in many fictions written for children and young adults, the story is narrated from the point of view of a sensitive young person, in this case 15-year-old Christopher Boone. The restricted language and childlike logic used in the opening paragraph of the novel are likely to lead the reader, adult or child, to the erroneous conclusion that the protagonist-narrator is a much younger child:

> But *the dog* was not running or asleep. *The dog* was dead. There was a garden fork sticking out of *the dog*. The points of the fork must have gone all the way through *the dog* and into the ground because the fork had not fallen over. I decided that *the dog* was probably killed with the fork because I could not see any other wounds in *the dog* and I do not think you would stick a garden fork into a dog after it had died for some other reason, like cancer for example, or a road accident. But I could not be certain about this.
>
> (Haddon 2003: 1, my italics)

The truncated syntax and the frequent repetition of the noun phrase 'the dog' where one would expect it to be pronominalized are features which characterize young children's writing. It is not until the beginning of the second chapter that a disjunction occurs which makes it clear that this assumption has constituted a miscue and that Christopher is, in fact, autistic, although this has to be inferred, since it is never made explicit in the novel. (The cover blurb on the adult edition is explicit about Christopher's autism; in schema theory terms this knowledge would act as a precondition header). One textual clue that assists the reader is the fact that the chapters are numbered according to prime numbers. The lack of cohesion between chapters, which recurs throughout the book, replicates Christopher's fragmented and often disjointed mind style (Semino 2007). One textual effect created by this condition is the fact that his language schema is generally accessible to young readers, although, because of Christopher's precocious gift for understanding mathematical and scientific concepts, there are sudden shifts into language and ideas that are probably beyond the grasp of many readers of all ages.

The book is full of riddles and puzzles which have been shown to function as textual 'hooks' for young readers, even when it is beyond their ability to solve them (Styles and Arizpe 2001). There is also an almost complete absence of metaphor. Christopher offers the reader the benefit of his metapoetic reflections on the limitations of this kind of figurative language by explaining why metaphorical mapping is, in his literal-minded opinion, a wholly illogical activity: 'imagining an apple in someone's eye has nothing to do with liking them' (p.20). Similes, on the other hand, earn his approval because, 'a simile is not a lie, unless it is a bad simile' (p.22). The similes he uses to describe the workings of his own mind, drawing upon a variety of sources, notably a DVD player (p.113) and a computer (pp.117–18), give a whole new meaning to the concept of cognitive metaphors and he even invents a few of his own for good measure: RED IS GOOD, YELLOW IS BAD (pp. 105–7).

The novel we read is the one Christopher's teacher, Siobhan, encourages him to write and which he insists is a true story since he cannot tell a lie. The narrative is interspersed throughout with diagrams, tables, graphs, pictures and various graphological effects, making it much more medium dependent (Carter and Nash 1990: 38) than most literary novels for adults. Paradoxically, this mixing of verbal and visual texts is likely to cause greater schema disruption for adult readers, given that visual material rarely features in adult literary fictions and is, indeed, often regarded as antithetical to it. Likewise, the kind of switching between aesthetic and efferent readings (Rosenblatt 1995) required by the frequent register shifts between fiction and non-fiction may be less alien to children than adults, since studies have shown that dominant pedagogic practices often invite children to adopt an efferent stance towards the literature they read (Zarrillo and Cox 1992). In one sense, then, the presence of metafictive devices in *The Curious Incident* could be said to *reduce* the experiential gap that generally exists between adult and younger readers in that the radical newness of such texts means *all* readers are without a ready-made text schema to guide them through the work. McCallum (1999: 139) points out that Hutcheon's description of the cognitive processes involved in the reading of metafictions is analogous to those engaged in by an inexperienced child reader, 'one of learning and constructing a new sign-system, a new set of verbal relations' (Hutcheon 1980: 19).

Wilkie notes that younger readers may not, however, be able to engage *fully* with intertextual allusions in metafictive texts for the very pragmatic reason that their 'intertextual knowledge cannot be assumed' (1999: 133). This is not really a problem in *The Curious Incident*, since Christopher obligingly fills in the intertextual gap for any reader unfamiliar with the main intertext, Conan Doyle's *The Hound of the Baskervilles*, by devoting an entire chapter to a detailed summary of the plot (pp. 88–93). This led one exasperated young reader to comment that she now knows 'everything there is to know about *Hound of the Baskervilles*' (Robyn Hislop, cited in *Cool-reads* 2007). In any case, Sherlock Holmes is a figure familiar to many children from numerous media versions of the books and, as Carpenter and Prichard (1984: 146–7) point out, the genre of detective fiction has proven popular with children since its inception, perhaps because of the problem-solving element involved, as well as the superiority over adults most children's versions of the genre accord to their child detectives. As Gilbert observes, in Christopher's case it has the added advantage of 'satisf[ying] his desire for order' (2005: 244).

Younger readers are likely to recognize, if not identify with, Christopher's decision to project himself into the role of a fictional character, in this case Sherlock Holmes, in order to solve the 'murder' mystery of Mrs Shears' poodle. (Holmes' methodical thought processes and meticulous attention to detail are, of course, very much like Christopher's own, hence the speculation that Holmes may, in fact, have been a savant.) This practice of 'role playing' characters from fiction, a habit Haddon is no doubt gently mocking here, is one in which young children often engage, leading many critics to make the patronizing assumption that children cannot distinguish between literature and real life. Most young readers are likely to be in a position to map their existing schematic knowledge of the conventions of the whodunit on to the first half of Haddon's text, although the fact that the murder victim is a dog, rather than a human being, will obviously require some modification to this text schema. The effect of this adjustment for readers of all ages is likely to be a humorous one, although this is not Christopher's intention, since, as he makes very clear to the reader, he cannot tell jokes and is unable to appreciate them (p.10). The joke for the knowing reader, however, is that the only real parallel between the plot of *The Hound of the Baskervilles* and *The Curious Incident* is that both books feature dead dogs.

In many ways, then, Haddon's book could be said to be more schema reinforcing for young readers than for adults. However, it also offers them many opportunities for schema refreshment and even for a radical restructuring of their existing schemas, depending on the extent to which they engage with the many metafictive devices in the novel. Stephens refers to the potential for writers to manipulate the child's point of view by employing a child protagonist-narrator: 'a child-narrator who lacks the verbal sophistication of an adult tends to produce a discourse very restricted in vocabulary, register and syntax, and to create extremely solipsistic subject positions for character-narrators *which are then replicated by readers*' (1992: 252, italics in the original). This is, however, highly unlikely in the case of *The Curious Incident*, unless, of course, the child reader also happens to be autistic in a similar way to Christopher. The estranging effect created by Christopher's autistic mind style prevents the young reader from taking up a simple identificatory reading position, a position that is generally regarded as the natural point of entry into the text world of a novel for young readers. Instead, he/she is forced to occupy a mental space alongside Christopher's, a role that Benton (2000) refers to as the 'spectator role', but which, for the first half of Haddon's novel at least, is more like the role of a knowing detective, invited to read aright the signs that Christopher so often *misreads*. This is likely to prove particularly empowering for young readers, since it offers a rare opportunity to match their world schema against one which, in many respects, is much less sophisticated than their own.

For instance, one of the symptoms of Christopher's condition is his inability to draw a clear distinction between figure and ground: 'For the autistic person, most stimuli register with equal impact, and because these little pieces of information cannot usually be processed effectively, life becomes a very confusing mess of constantly competing signals' (Whipple 2003). As a consequence, Christopher's attention is selective in ways that are at best eccentric. Thus he has a disconcerting tendency to thematize objects before people. By contrast, as Stockwell points out: 'In most narrative fiction ... characters are figures against the ground of their settings' (2002: 15). When he does describe people, Christopher focuses on arbitrary aspects of their appearance, such as the detail that his teacher, Mr Jeavons, 'wears brown shoes that have approximately 60 tiny circular holes in each of them' (p.5), while a policeman has 'a big orange leaf stuck to the bottom of his shoe which was poking out from one side' (p.7). The fact that neither of these details is 'telling', in the sense of giving us an insight into their character or behaviour, is for the experienced reader a humorous subversion of the metonymic mode for conveying aspects of character in realist fiction.

Readers of all ages are challenged to empathize with a character whose condition means that he has a chronic inability to empathize with others (something often said, of course, about children and young adults). Christopher is the ultimate detached narrator and, as such, Haddon regards him as ideal: 'he never tries to make the reader react in one way or another. He simply explains what happens' (Random House interview, 2003). He is, therefore, very different from the strongly evaluative extradiegetic narrators who traditionally guide young readers' responses to characters and events in fictions written primarily for them. This forces the reader, child or adult, to do a good deal of emotional 'filling in'. A vivid example of Christopher's inability to read the emotional cues of others occurs when he sees his father crying and asks him whether he is sad about the dead poodle, Wellington: 'He looked at me for a long time and sucked air through his nose. Then he said, "Yes, Christopher, you could say that. You could very well say that"' (p.27). An inexperienced reader may accept this at face value, but the more experienced reader will be able to deduce from the clues in the surrounding co-text that this is an evasive response designed to protect Christopher from the hurtful truth that it was in fact his father who had killed the dog.

As Lim observes, 'it's remarkable how fully the other characters emerge, how palpably their pain registers despite Christopher's obliviousness' (2003). Paradoxically, then, *The Curious Incident* is a novel which involves the reader very directly and powerfully in the production of affect. This offsets to a large extent the 'inhibition of return' (Stockwell 2002: 19–20) that might otherwise arise from the fact that Christopher is a relatively static character. In a review of the book, Carol Ann Duffy (2003) refers to it as 'a moving education in difference' suitable for readers from 11 upwards. While this is undoubtedly true, young readers are also likely to derive illicit pleasure from the fact that, however powerless they may feel themselves to be and however dependent upon adults, who from their point of view constrict their freedoms, they have a great deal of agency compared to a young person like Christopher. At the same time, there are opportunities for young readers to view Christopher's extreme fear of strangers and the outside world as a metaphor for the highly circumscribed condition of childhood in the West in the twenty-first century.

While in other ways Christopher is not an easy character with whom children and young adults can identify, not least because his condition precludes him from experiencing the usual adolescent anxieties about sex, in his own way he manages to expose the hypocrisies and contradictions of the adult world as devastatingly as Holden Caulfield, but as a catalyst for provoking their erratic behaviour, rather than as a critical commentator on it. For instance, one of the things that young people who have read the novel seem to find particularly shocking is the way in which adults, including parents, scream and swear at Christopher. Swearing is perhaps *the* last taboo in children's literature and the fact that Haddon did not need to censor himself in this respect once again has the effect of extending the possibilities of fiction for young readers, this time in terms of the language appropriate to it. Indeed, in the case of one 10-year-old reader, the taboo language was the most transgressive aspect of the novel for him (Sam Loake, personal correspondence with the author). Christopher's father in particular is likely to alienate young readers because he keeps him in ignorance of his mother's existence, rationalizing his actions on the spurious grounds that he knows what's best for his son.

The resolution of the murder mystery half way through the novel (p.150) involves a further disruption of the text schema for reading the whodunnit, since such a resolution normally marks the point of closure. Instead, in *The Curious Incident* it effects a shift to an identity quest schema. Duffy (2003) describes the novel as a 'double mystery': 'the boy's detective work on the small crime leads him to the dark heart of a lie'. This lie is the trigger for his departure from home and his journey from Swindon to London in search of his mother, before returning to Swindon again. Nodelman and Reimer argue that, 'This home/away/home pattern is *the* most common storyline in children's literature' (2003: 197–8). It is, of course, a variation on the underlying cognitive metaphor: LIFE IS A JOURNEY. Even an inexperienced reader is likely to recognize, however, that the journey on which Christopher embarks is hardly of the symbolic order of those undertaken by Max in *Where the Wild Things Are* (Sendac 1971) or Jim in *Treasure Island* (Stevenson 1883), yet so effective is Haddon's technique of suggesting the way Christopher's mind is assaulted by a bewildering array of new signs that the sensitive reader, adult or child, will realize that to Christopher it is just as harrowing as anything undergone by the most daring of fictional protagonists. Haddon conveys this by having Christopher reproduce the effect graphically as a literal jumble of signs (p.209). Lim (2003) records his own feelings when Christopher finally arrives at his mother's house in London: 'the magnitude of his challenge and the joy in his achievement are over-whelming', a feeling that is likely to be shared by the majority of readers of all ages.

A perhaps unsettling instance of schema refreshment is likely to occur for the young reader at the end of *The Curious Incident*, since, although Christopher returns to his home town, he does not return to the same *home*. Instead, he moves into a bedsit with his mother. As Murray points out: '[the novel] resists the obvious narrative conclusion that would reunite Christopher's family' (2006: 35). Clausen sees the device of the 'return home' in children's literature as *the* most significant criterion for distinguishing it from fiction for older adolescents and adults:

> When home is a privileged place exempt from the most serious problems of life and civilization – when home is where we ought, on the whole, to stay – we are probably dealing with a story for children. When home is the chief place from which we must escape, either to grow up or ... to remain innocent, then we are involved in a story for adolescents or adults.
>
> (Clausen 1982: 142)

Christopher's ambivalent view of home at the end of his identity quest arises quite naturally from the generically hybrid nature of the novel. Less easy to accommodate is the idea that Christopher has changed very little as a result of his experiences. As Stockwell says of static characters: 'A character that does not develop at all is, in effect, a static object and our natural inhibition of return is likely to mean that we lose interest in this boring character' (2002: 19). However, the reader, whether adult or child, is likely to recognize this stasis as a symptom of Christopher's Asperger's syndrome. The implication at the end of the novel is that in time he will learn to trust his father again and will re-enter the home he escaped, albeit as a visitor (p.267). The fact that his father buys him a dog is at least a partial act of restitution for the loss of Wellington. Christopher informs us proudly that he has passed his Maths A Level and plans to go to university. While the optimistic note on which the book ends is likely to be schema reinforcing for young readers, it offers schema *refreshment* for the adult reader, since even qualified happy endings tend to be anathema in contemporary literary fiction for adults.

Conclusion

To conclude, I hope to have shown that schema poetics offers a fruitful way of accounting for an adultist and childist reading of a complex novel like *The Curious Incident*. Equally, the enthusiastic reception of the novel by readers both young and old makes clear that the boundary between these two kinds of reading is permeable and open to change. The children's author Jill Patton Walsh (1971, cited in Hollindale 1997: 40) refers to a fundamental tension between meaning and form in writing for children. She says that the responsibility of the writer for children is to make a 'fully serious adult statement', but in a form that is accessible. This is precisely what Haddon manages to achieve in *The Curious Incident*. I would argue, then, that exposure to challenging crossover texts, including works of metafiction, is a potentially pleasurable way for young readers to develop their literary competence. An unremitting diet of such texts is by no means what is called for, but I agree with Nodelman and Reimer (2003) that adult gatekeepers of children's literature should not prejudge the limitations of children's literary competence, since this has the effect of becoming a self-fulfilling prophecy. Chambers' belief that, 'Wide, voracious, *indiscriminate* reading is the best soil from which discrimination and taste eventually grow' (1973: 94, italics in the original) is a much more promising approach, although interestingly not one adopted by Haddon, who revealed in an interview that he read almost exclusively non-fiction as a child (cited in Kellaway 2003).

10

Deixis, Cognition and the Construction of Viewpoint

Dan McIntyre

In this chapter, Dan McIntyre brings a cognitive perspective to an important area of stylistic inquiry: *point of view*. Traditionally, the stylistic analysis of point of view has been concerned with developing toolkits that can deal systematically with different types of focalization or 'angles of telling' in stories and with the distinction, common in much narrative, between 'who tells' and 'who sees'. The rationale for these toolkits, and for grounding them in explicit linguistic criteria, was that they provided a welcome antidote to the unprincipled impressionism that had characterized many literary-critical accounts of viewpoint in narrative. Against this theoretical backdrop, there emerged through the 1980s and 1990s various stylistic templates for identifying categories of point of view in fiction, templates which have since become part of the broader analytic armoury of modern narrative stylistics.

McIntyre begins his chapter with a useful survey of a number of these traditional models of point of view, including Roger Fowler's four-part taxonomy, Mick Short's checklist of indicators of viewpoint as well as my own 'modal grammar' of point of view. Quite correctly, McIntyre characterizes this body of work as a stylistics of narrative technique, where the principal indices of point of view are identified through key reflexes in the text. Using the concept of *deixis* as a theoretical bridge, McIntyre gradually shifts the emphasis away from narrative technique towards the conceptual framework that informs the process of reading. Beginning with an assessment of the traditional definitions of the concept of deixis – as the grammatical encoding of orientation in space, time and person – McIntyre reworks the definition in progressively more cognitive terms, leading to a model of point of view that helps us understand better how *readers* take up different positions in a story world. He argues that Deictic Shift Theory (DST) is well suited to explaining how readers enter and move around in the worlds of the text. McIntyre eventually arrives at a synthesis of models, where the traditional text-based approach is overlain with a conception of point of view that enables us to track the cognitive mechanisms of both reading and interpretation.

This chapter is an important contribution to point of view studies for a number of reasons. In no small measure, it is an excellent and lucid exposition of how point of view functions across different genres of writing. While illustrative examples from prose fiction canonically form the material of analysis, McIntyre's argument is strengthened considerably here through illuminating examples from poetry, film and pictorial narrative. His analysis of Seamus Heaney's poem 'Mossbawn' is the centrepiece of the chapter, striking a delicate balance between the application of DST and the close analysis of the stylistic fabric of the text. But one of the most significant contributions of the chapter, on which McIntyre himself is clear, is that it builds upon the foundations laid in earlier traditional studies of point of view. Rather than rejecting wholesale the more textually orientated studies of the twentieth century, McIntyre seeks to enrich those models by incorporating the newer analytic paradigms of the twenty-first. This 'complementarity of approach' is very much the essence of contemporary stylistics.

Paul Simpson

Narrative Point of View

Part way through Jonathan Coe's *The Rotters' Club*, a comic novel set in the mid-1970s, the teenage hero of the story, Benjamin Trotter, awakens the morning after a particularly wild party held at his friend Doug's house, and is not at all sure where he is:

> There was a sound of a hand groping along the surface of the wood and then the creaking of a door being pushed open, and then a rectangle of faint orange light appeared. Benjamin could now see out into a bedroom, lit dimly by the glow of a streetlamp, containing a double bed on which three half-naked bodies lay entangled beneath a pile of coats.
>
> (Coe 2002: 276–7)

As the narrative progresses it transpires that Benjamin is actually inside a wardrobe, where he passed out following an amorous encounter the previous night. Much of the humour in the passage comes from the fact that, although the story is told by a third-person narrator, it is from Benjamin's point of view that events are described. Benjamin's viewpoint is reflected in part through the syntactic structure of some of the sentences. So, for example, he hears 'the creaking of a door being pushed open', but the narrator conceals from us the agent of this action, since presumably, Benjamin himself has not yet realized who is in the wardrobe with him. Similarly, 'the rectangle of orange light' is only visible to Benjamin once the door of the wardrobe has been opened. In effect, what the reader is presented with is the sequence of events in the order that Benjamin experiences them.

This manipulation of viewpoint is something that has received considerable attention within stylistics, with numerous taxonomies proposed to account for the complexities of point of view in narrative texts. Many of these have categorised narrators as a means of doing this. Among the most influential of these taxonomies is that proposed by Simpson (1993), which is itself a development of

Fowler's (1986) work on viewpoint. Simpson distinguishes between what he terms category A narratives (those narrated by a first-person narrator who is a participant in the story he/she is telling) and category B narratives (narrated by a third-person narrator either from inside or outside a particular character's consciousness). The narrator of *The Rotters' Club* is a category B narrator. Simpson's taxonomy pays particular attention to the concept of modality, with each of his categories of narration displaying different types and degrees of modality, accounting for specific viewpoint effects. Within other taxonomies of viewpoint we find different categories. Chatman (1990), for example, distinguishes between *perceptual* and *conceptual* point of view. Broadly speaking, this is the same as Fowler's (1986) spatio-temporal viewpoint and ideological viewpoint, which essentially covers the difference between literal viewpoint (what someone is able to physically see) and metaphorical viewpoint (i.e. someone's opinion). Short's (1996) approach to the analysis of viewpoint is also category-based, but rather than categorising narrators, Short instead concentrates on those small-scale linguistic indicators of viewpoint that are to be found in texts.

There are, then, many different stylistic approaches to the analysis of viewpoint in texts. There are pros and cons to each of them. Nevertheless, one thing that most have in common is that they tend not to take account of the cognitive processes by which readers come to infer particular points of view as they read a text. It is this element of the stylistic analysis of viewpoint that I will concentrate on in this chapter. In particular, I will outline how recent advances in cognitive science can be applied in conjunction with traditional stylistic approaches to point of view to further our understanding of the construction of viewpoint in language. First, though, we will revisit some of the fundamental linguistic aspects of point of view.

Encoding Point of View in Language

The extract above from *The Rotters' Club*, where the reader is presented with events in the order that Benjamin himself experiences them, demonstrates what Leech and Short (1981) call 'psychological sequencing', and which Short (1996) refers to as 'event-coding'. This is just one way in which point of view can be encoded in language. There are many others and Short (1996: 263–87) outlines some of these in a checklist of linguistic indicators of viewpoint. Short's point is that certain linguistic items create the effect of the narrative in question being told from a particular point of view, and that identifying these linguistic indicators can enable us to understand how these viewpoint effects are brought about. We can see some examples of linguistic indicators of viewpoint in the following short extract from Sebastian Faulks' novel, *Charlotte Gray*, set during the Second World War. Charlotte is a British agent, about to make her first parachute drop into occupied France to work behind enemy lines. 'Yves' is also a British agent, working with Charlotte. In this passage, Charlotte and 'Yves' are getting into the aeroplane that is going to drop them into France. It is Charlotte's first experience of working as an agent:

The Whitley smelled of raw machinery: oil, tin, rivet. Charlotte felt a pair of hands pushing on her backside, then a shoulder being added to the shove. She sprawled inside, almost unable to move for the bulk of the parachute, and lay down as instructed by an RAF sergeant across the bomb bay with her head and shoulders propped against the side of the fuselage. Somehow, despite the training, she had been expecting seats. 'Yves' followed her into the plane and took up his position opposite. He gave her an encouraging wink. Charlotte was filled with a sudden certainty that she was going to feel sick. The lack of any view, the mechanical smell and her sense of anxiety reminded her of sitting in the back of her father's shooting brake on long drives across the Highlands, with the windows half fogged by rain, the air heavy with pipe smoke, her view bounded by the back of her parents' heads and Roderick's bare knees beside her.

(Faulks 1999: 161)

The *Charlotte Gray* extract is an example of third-person narration; i.e. the narrator of the passage is not a character in the story he/she is telling. Third-person narration can be either omniscient (where the narrator knows everything about the fictional world and the characters that he/she is describing, including those characters' thoughts and feelings) or restricted. The *Charlotte Gray* extract is an example of a restricted third-person narration in that it seems that the narration is biased towards Charlotte's point of view of the events described. It is, then, what Simpson (1993) would call a category B narrative in reflector mode; that is, it is a third-person narration where the narrator has moved into the consciousness of a particular character (in this case Charlotte) who then becomes the 'reflector' of the fiction. This viewpoint effect is suggested by a number of linguistic indicators. For example, if we look at the verbs of cognition in the text ('felt', 'had been expecting', 'reminded') we can see that they all have 'Charlotte' as their grammatical subject. Conversely, we are not given any information about the cognitive behaviour of the other characters (i.e. the RAF sergeant, 'Yves', Charlotte's parents, her brother).

There is also schema-oriented language that is consistent with Charlotte's point of view. So, for instance, there is the reference to 'The Whitley' (the Second World War Armstrong-Whitworth Whitley bomber), rather than, say, 'the aeroplane', and mention of 'the bomb bay' and 'the fuselage'. We can expect that Charlotte would know these technical terms, having been trained for a parachute drop. If the author were not presenting Charlotte's viewpoint but instead that of a detached outsider, we might expect him to have had the narrator use different, less precise, terms; in effect, we might have expected what Fowler (1986) terms *underlexicalization*.

There is event-coding of the kind we noted in the example from *The Rotters' Club*. Charlotte feels 'a pair of hands' and 'a shoulder' pushing her. The indefinite reference to body parts rather than a definite reference to a particular person is indicative of the fact that the RAF officer (presumably the one doing the pushing) is behind Charlotte. Consequently, he would be outside her range of vision. The event-coding, then, is consistent with Charlotte's perceptual viewpoint. We might even see a viewpoint effect in the listing of 'oil, tin, rivet' in the first sentence of the passage. In effect this sequence may be seen to reflect Charlotte's perceptions as she gets closer to the plane. First she smells the oil, then she is close enough to be aware that its body is made up of sheets of metal, and as she moves closer she is able to see the rivets holding the sheets together.

In addition to all of these linguistic indicators, we can also note that the only character whose thoughts we are privy to is Charlotte: 'somehow, despite the training, she had been expecting seats'. Furthermore, the inverted commas around the name *Yves* suggests that this is a pseudonym but note that the narrator does not tell us what the character's real name is. This again is consistent with Charlotte's viewpoint – the narrator only tells us what Charlotte herself knows.

The list of linguistic indicators of point of view provided by Short is useful, then, for uncovering the ways in which viewpoint effects are created in texts. Of course, there are other indicators of viewpoint in addition to those in Short's checklist. Graphological deviation, for instance, can be used to reflect point of view, especially in multimodal texts. In the example below taken from the graphic novel *From Hell* (Moore and Campbell 2004), a retelling of the Jack the Ripper story, the dialogue in the speech bubble in the second frame is too small to read. This suggests that the reader's position within the fictional world is one where the men pictured are too far away for the reader to hear clearly what they are saying. In this sense, what we have is a graphological equivalent of what Semino and Short (2004), in their work on discourse presentation, refer to as the 'narrator's report of voice'. This refers to instances when we know that verbal activity occurred, but where we know nothing about the form and content of the utterance, nor what speech acts were performed.

This example also makes clear one of the basic tenets of point of view, and this is the notion that, as we read, we take up a position within the story world. The means by which this process occurs is something that, traditionally, has not been well explained by point of view frameworks. However, the advent of cognitive

models of text-processing provides us with a means of understanding more fully how this happens. The cognitive model that best explains this is known as *deictic shift theory* (DST). As we will see, DST provides a useful account of how we, as readers, enter and move around the worlds of the text. To understand DST we first need to know about the concept of deixis.

Deixis

Perhaps the most important of all Short's (1996) linguistic indicators of viewpoint is *deixis*. This is because a speaker's use of deictic terms indicates where they are in relation to the objects, places and people they describe. For example, I would refer to the computer I am currently using as I type this chapter as '*this* computer', the deictic term *this* indicating that the computer is in close proximity to me. On the other hand, I would refer to the computer that is in the next room from me as '*that* computer', since the deictic term *that* indicates distance from me. What should be apparent from this example is that deictic terms are always interpreted in relation to where the speaker is situated. The location of a speaker in time and space is referred to as their *deictic centre*. Needless to say, everyone's deictic centre is different. The term *deixis* comes originally from Greek and means 'pointing' or 'indicating'. Deictic terms indicate the position of something or someone in relation to the speaker's deictic centre.

The words *this* and *that* are examples of place deictics. These are deictic terms that indicate the proximity of a particular referent relative to the speaker. *This* indicates something that is close to the speaker whereas *that* refers to something that is not so close. They are also examples of what Levinson (1983: 79) calls 'pure' deictic words; that is, words that, in and of themselves, encode perceived distance in relation to the speaker. Deictic terms often come in pairs and other examples of pure place deictics include the demonstratives *these* and *those*, the adverbs *here* and *there* and the dynamic verbs *come* and *go* (which respectively indicate movement towards and away from the speaker's deictic centre). Apart from via pure deictic terms, position in space can be suggested by locational deictic expressions. These are expressions which, to be interpreted fully, require knowledge of the position of other referents within the situational context in question. So, if I were to tell you that my computer is *next to my bookcase*, you would need to know where my bookcase is in order to understand the location of my computer.

In addition to place deictics, Levinson (1983) identifies four other types of deixis: temporal deixis, person deixis, social deixis and empathetic deixis. Temporal deictics indicate metaphorical proximity and distance from the speaker in relation to the point in time at which the speaker makes their utterance (e.g. *now* and *then*, *yesterday*, *today* and *tomorrow*). Person deixis is most obviously represented by the pronoun system, and encodes the speakers and addressees within a speech event (e.g. *me* and *you*). Social deixis is, in effect, another analogous development of place deixis and encodes how close to someone we feel in terms of our social relationship with them. For instance, the naming system in English allows us to express either metaphorical distance or proximity in relation to our interlocutor depending on what we call them. As an example, I am fortunate to work in a department where people tend to get on well together and the use of first names is normal unmarked behaviour. It would therefore be unusual if I were to suddenly start calling the head of department 'Dr Burrow', since the use of title-plus-surname typically indicates social distance, which would not be con- sistent with the working relationship that we have. Finally, empathetic deixis is similar to social deixis and indicates psychological closeness or distance from whatever person, place or object is being described. For example, 'Tell me about *that* new colleague of yours' seems to indicate a more negative view of the col- league in question than 'Tell me about *this* new colleague of yours', because *this* and *that* indicate proximity and distance respectively (as we have seen in the example of place deixis), and are here being used analogically.

   This, then, is deixis. Deictic shift theory suggests that this concept is central to understanding how we as readers become involved in the world of a text. Con- sequently it follows that DST is relevant to the explanation of how viewpoint effects are created in language.

Deictic Shift Theory

Deictic shift theory (outlined in full in Duchan *et al.* 1995) is described by Segal as a way of accounting for how the reader of a text 'often takes a cognitive stance within the world of a narrative and interprets the text from that perspective' (1995: 15). The suggestion is that when we read a text we suspend our normal egocentric assumptions about deictic references (i.e. that they are to be inter- preted from our own position in time and space) and instead interpret events in the text world from a different deictic centre. This happens because of deictic shifts that we make as we read, cued by certain textual and sometimes non- linguistic triggers, that change the deictic centre from which the events in the narrative are to be interpreted. Galbraith (1995), in her own summary of DST, explains that all fictional narration is made up of a number of deictic fields, defined by Stockwell (2002: 47) as a set of deictic expressions all relating to the same deictic centre. Galbraith suggests that as we read and respond to deictic cues in the text, we take up a cognitive stance in the fictional world within a particular deictic field. This might belong to the narrator or to a specific character. Nevertheless, this is not necessarily fixed for the whole text, and, as a result of further linguistic or non-linguistic cues, we might shift our deictic position and start to interpret events from a different deictic centre again. The key point here is that, as we read, we assume that spatial, temporal, social, person-related and empathetic deictic coordinates are not to be interpreted with reference to our own deictic centre, but instead in relation to a deictic centre somewhere within the fictional world. Consequently, we 'project' a deictic centre that is different to our own.

   The process of reading often necessitates a large number of deictic shifts and consequently a complex series of cognitive actions. For instance, the action of picking up a novel and starting to read causes us to shift into a deictic field within the fictional world. Once within the fictional world we might immediately shift into another deictic field constituted within a flashback in the narrative. We might then shift from *that* deictic field into another one belonging to another character and constituted within a separate time frame in the narrative. Some of these shifts can be described as movements between what text world theorists call the 'discourse world' and the 'text world'. Others are of a different type and can involve shifting along the temporal continuum of the story (for example, when we experience a flashback) or shifting between the deictic fields of the different characters in the novel. Whatever the shifts we make as we read, Galbraith (1995) makes the point that our background knowledge about how stories work causes us to expect to return from any deictic fields that we have shifted into during the course of reading. So, if we shift into a fictional world that is *embedded* within the larger fictional world (as happens in *A Midsummer Night's Dream* during the mechanicals' play within a play), we expect to return from that embedded fictional world to the world that frames it. Finally, a deictic field will decay if we are not regularly reminded of its boundaries. This often happens in films that begin with voice-over narration which does not then continue throughout the whole film (for example, Roberto Benigni's *La Vita è Bella* (1997) and Steven Spielberg's *War of the Worlds* (2005)). The initial narration sets up a fictional world in which the narrator is telling a story, but if that narration is not continued, the deictic field of the narrator decays and we forget that the story we are watching is embedded within a higher order fictional world. If the narration is reinstantiated at the end of the film (as it is in the two examples referred to above) we shift back into the initial fictional world. If not, we remain in the embedded fictional world until we shift directly back to our real world deictic field.

Now that we have the basics of DST in place, let us consider how it might be applied in the stylistic analysis of viewpoint.

Applying Deictic Shift Theory to Prose Fiction

DST can help us to understand how we as readers process textual indicators of viewpoint in even the shortest of texts. The following brief extract is from the beginning of Ellis Peters' *Monk's Hood*, a murder/mystery novel set in twelfth-century Shrewsbury, featuring the sleuthing monk, Brother Cadfael:

> On this particular morning at the beginning of December, in the year 1138, Brother Cadfael came to chapter in tranquillity of mind, prepared to be tolerant even towards the dull, pedestrian readings of Brother Francis, and long-winded, legal haverings of Brother Benedict the sacristan. Men were variable, fallible, and to be humoured.
>
> (Peters 1980: 7)

On reading this passage, interpretatively it seems that we are fairly close to Brother Cadfael in spatial, temporal and psychological terms. There is a sense of being in the same physical space as him, as events are unfolding in his immediate time and space. The narrator does not seem to be reporting events from a perspective in the modern world, but instead seems relatively close in temporal terms to the events described. In Simpson's (1993) terms this appears to be a category B narrative in reflector mode, with Brother Cadfael as reflector. DST can help us to be more specific about the cognitive processes we go through in order to arrive at this interpretation.

When we start to read the novel, the first deictic shift we make is to recentre ourselves within the text world as opposed to the actual world (notice that, obviously, deictic fields occur within text worlds; see McIntyre (2006) for more on this aspect of DST, and Gavins in this volume for a full explanation of text worlds). The act of opening the book and starting to read constitutes a shift into the text world. Once within the text world we then need to locate ourselves deictically. The three prepositional phrases preceding the main clause (each of which serve to indicate the temporal position from which events in the text world are to be interpreted) act as a trigger to the reader to shift into a new temporal deictic centre. Our physical location within the text world is specified by the spatially deictic verb 'came', indicating movement *towards* a deictic centre and suggesting that the reader's position within the text world at this moment is within the chapter house. As Cadfael arrives at the chapter house, the narrator indicates Cadfael's cognitive state ('Cadfael came to chapter *in tranquillity of mind*') as well as his thoughts. He regards Brother Francis's readings as 'dull' and 'pedestrian' (note the negatively charged lexis) and Brother Benedict's 'legal haverings' as 'long-winded'. Of course, this evaluative lexis reflects the narrator's point of view, but it also reflects Brother Cadfael's viewpoint. The narrator tells us that Brother Cadfael was 'prepared to be tolerant' which would suggest that he must at least share the narrator's characterisation of Brother Francis and Brother Benedict, even if this is not his viewpoint alone. At this point, then, the reader's position in the text world is very similar, spatially and temporally, to that of Brother Cadfael. Add to this the fact that we have knowledge of Brother Cadfael's thoughts and cognitive state and there is a strong indication that we will interpret events, at least for the time being, from Brother Cadfael's point of view. It may be that later in the novel there is a viewpoint shift to that of another character, in which case, according to deictic shift theory, we will shift out of the deictic field that we share with Brother Cadfael and into a new one.

Applying Deictic Shift Theory to Poetry

Although, prototypically, viewpoint effects are found most often in prose fiction, it is also the case that they occur in other text types. Jeffries (2000), for example, has looked at point of view in poetry (see also Semino's (1997) work on deixis in poetry), and I have examined point of view in dramatic texts (McIntyre 2004, 2006). Limitations of space mean that I can't consider both these text types here, but to highlight the usefulness of the DST approach beyond prose fiction, let's have a look at how it can help explain viewpoint effects in the first part of Seamus

Heaney's poem, 'Mossbawn'. In doing this, we can also combine DST with elements of text world theory to further elucidate our analysis. The poem is reproduced below:

'Mossbawn: Two Poems in Dedication'
For Mary Heaney

1. Sunlight

There was a sunlit absence.   [1]
The helmeted pump in the yard
heated its iron,
water honeyed   [4]

in the slung bucket
and the sun stood
like a griddle cooling
against the wall   [8]

of each long afternoon.
So, her hands scuffled
over the bakeboard,
the reddening stove   [12]

sent its plaque of heat
against her where she stood
in a floury apron
by the window.   [16]

Now she dusts the board
with a goose's wing,
now sits, broad-lapped,
with whitened nails   [20]

and measling shins:
here is a space
again, the scone rising
to the tick of two clocks.   [24]

And here is love
like a tinsmith's scoop
sunk past its gleam
in the meal bin.   [28]

(Heaney 1990)

'Mossbawn' was the name of the farm on which Seamus Heaney grew up (the family left the farm when Heaney was 14), and the poem is dedicated to his aunt, Mary Heaney. The first part of the poem, 'Sunlight', appears to be a reflection on the depth of feeling Heaney has for his aunt through a description of his memory of her baking bread on a warm afternoon (notice that the dedication that precedes the poem, and our background knowledge of who Mary Heaney was, preempts us to suppose that the woman described in 'Sunlight' may very well be Heaney's aunt). The recollection seems to increase in intensity as the poem progresses, and what is initially a fairly vague portrayal of the woman moves to become an increasingly detailed portrait of her, culminating in a concentrated evaluation in the final verse of what she represented to Heaney. It seems to me that the deictic references in the poem are particularly significant in explaining this interpretation, and applying DST can help us to be clear about some of the cognitive processes it seems likely we engage in as we read the text.

In text world theory terms (see Gavins 2007), the first two verses of the poem provide us with a number of world-building elements that together 'constitute the background against which the foreground events of the text will take place' (Stockwell 2002: 137). These include objects specified by the noun phrases 'the helmeted pump', 'water' and 'the slung bucket', as well as information about the location, specified in the prepositional phrase 'in the yard'. This information, and any contextual information that we bring from the discourse world (e.g. our knowledge that 'Mossbawn' was the name of the farm where Heaney lived), allows us to build up a picture of the farmyard. In terms of the other world-building elements we might prototypically expect as we construct a text world, what are missing at this point are a specification of time and mention of characters, this latter element usually defined through a noun phrase. This is particularly interesting when we consider that the first line of the poem is semantically deviant in that it states the presence of 'a sunlit absence'. Given that one of the world-building elements that is missing is a specification of character(s), we might assume that the 'sunlit absence' referred to is the absence of a person, possibly Heaney's aunt. What is significant here is that she is not present in the text world at this point; she is marked by her absence. The reference to 'a sunlit absence' might therefore lead us to suppose that at the outset of the poem, Heaney is remembering the farm, Mossbawn, but from a perspective in the discourse world where Mary Heaney is now dead. The connotations surrounding her are resolutely positive, as a result of the positively charged adjective 'sunlit' which premodifies 'absence'.

The use of definite reference in line 2 of the poem ('*The* helmeted pump', '*the* yard') gives us the impression that the speaker is assuming that we know which pump and which yard he is referring to, since definite reference tends to be used in relation to information that is already known by the reader. We are therefore led to project a viewpoint that is Heaney's rather than our own.

In DST terms, the locative adverbial 'in the yard' in line 2 begins to specify the deictic field from which we interpret events in the text world. However, the past tense verbs indicating past time suggest a degree of temporal distance from the events being described.

In the third verse, a female character is introduced into the text world, though it is still not specified who this woman is and she is referred to only through the possessive pronoun 'her'. Notice, though, that 'her hands' are described as scuffling 'over the bakeboard' and this in itself implies a shift in our spatial viewpoint (which, as we have seen, is a projection of the narrator's viewpoint) from outside in the farmyard to inside in the kitchen (this must be the case if the narrator is able to describe what the woman is doing). The figure of the woman is then specified further through a reference to her 'floury apron' and an indication of her spatial location 'by the window'.

The most dramatic deictic shift comes in the fifth verse. Here the verb phrases are present simple as opposed to the earlier past simple, and the proximal deictic 'now' suggests a temporal shift towards a time that is closer to the narrator's temporal deictic centre than we have previously been. This is potentially an amalgam of the narrator's temporal deictic field in the discourse world (the proximal deictic 'now' perhaps indicating that the memory is becoming more vivid) and a dramatising shift within the past-time zone that has the effect of bringing us closer to the past events that are being described. In cognitive terms, we shift rapidly back and forth between these two deictic fields.

In the sixth verse there is another proximal deictic reference, this time the spatial deictic 'here' ('here is a space again'). As DST suggests, when we read a text we suspend our egocentric conception of deixis and instead interpret deictic references from a deictic centre within the text world. The proximal spatial deictic appears to refer to the space in which the narrator is watching the woman, and Heaney's use of 'here' suggests that we as readers are at this point located in a similar position to the narrator within the text world. The proximal deictic coordinates are restated in the final verse, where the love that Heaney associates with his aunt is compared with 'a tinsmith's scoop/sunk past its gleam/in the meal bin'. This would appear to suggest that the woman described was the kind of person who concealed her love behind ordinary everyday actions, such as, for example, baking scones. Heaney's point appears to be that love is not shown best by overt declarations but by the little things we do for our families and friends. What is significant here is that the poem ends with us having shifted in deictic terms to become closer spatially and temporally to the narrator's position within the text world in relation to the woman in the poem. In DST terms there is no shift back to the spatial and temporal location we were in at the outset of the poem. DST, then, can usefully explain one aspect of how the poet/speaker's recollection of the woman appears to become more intense as the poem progresses.

Conclusion

I hope to have shown in this chapter how recent advances in cognitive stylistics can complement more traditional frameworks for the analysis of viewpoint in language, and help us to account for the point of view effects we encounter as we read literary and non-literary texts. An important point to make here is that cognitive stylistic frameworks are not intended to supersede more traditional approaches; rather they are aimed at facilitating a greater degree of analytical precision in stylistic analysis. In this case, DST complements a traditional stylistic approach by providing a means of hypothesizing about the cognitive processing involved in inferring particular viewpoints. In actual fact, any good stylistician has always considered the cognitive aspects of text comprehension anyway, even if this has not been couched in the terms currently used. Stylistic analysis should not, of course, be a simple matter of using the latest fashionable terminology to describe a text; but considering the terminological nuances of recently developed cognitive frameworks such as DST can be useful in that it forces us to think through the analytical and interpretative consequences of using such terms. This, in turn, can lead us to greater analytical and interpretative accuracy, which is, of course, the goal of all stylistic analysis.

Stylistics of Poetry

CHAPTER

11

'And everyone and I stopped breathing': Familiarity and Ambiguity in the Text World of 'The day lady died'

Joanna Gavins

One of the key challenges for cognitive poetics researchers in contemporary stylistics is to explain how readers interpret literary texts by bridging the gap between their own worlds and the author's world. Joanna Gavins develops Paul Werth's Text World Theory in order to address this issue, illustrating her model with a detailed stylistic analysis of Frank O'Hara's 'The day lady died', an enigmatic poem which describes the day of the death of the jazz singer, Billie Holiday. Gavins builds on Werth's notion of the discourse world, the outer communication level of the author and reader, and argues for the idea of a 'split discourse-world' in which enactors of the author and reader appear in the text-world. This provides an important new way of conceptualising the writing and reading process.

The split discourse-world model is particularly appropriate for Gavins' interpretation of the O'Hara poem because author and reader are temporally, spatially and culturally separate in her own reading of the text, and separation from the author will be the case to a greater or lesser extent for many other readers. Literary critics have traditionally approached the poem differently, focusing on the historical-cultural and biographical background to explain the author's representation of himself and his environment in the poem. Gavins complements this type of approach by drawing on the resources of modern stylistics to examine reference, tense and deixis in the poem and to explain how these linguistic forms create such a vivid representation of the text world that readers can become immersed in it. In particular, Gavins draws attention to the unusual mix of both highly specific details and heavily ambiguous expressions that together allow readers to create a rich and realistic text world which is nonetheless interpretable at multiple levels.

Gavins' article is successful because it not only provides a new analysis that casts fresh light on O'Hara's poem, but also because it presents a model of literary interpretation which is highly suggestive in a number of ways for future work by other researchers. First, the split discourse-world model is of relevance to any text where the worlds of the author and reader are distinct, so is of value in studying the vast majority of literary readings. Second, this model may also have major practical uses, such as in explaining different cultural interpretations in the study of literature in the foreign language classroom. Third, the chapter raises important questions about how linguistic items facilitate the readers' immersion in a text world, an issue which links with the current significant interest in embodiment in cognitive linguistics and psychology. Fourth, a particularly exciting application of Gavins' work would be empirical testing of real readers to see how they construct mental representations of this poem which reflect their individual responses, but nevertheless allow intersubjective appreciation of the work in literary critical discussions.

Overall, Gavins provides here a fine example of cognitive poetics research at its best, presenting not only a new interpretation of a particular text, but also important insights into the reading process in general.

Catherine Emmott

Introduction

In this chapter, I present a twenty-first-century analysis of a twentieth-century text: Frank O'Hara's (1964) poem 'The day lady died'. First published in his *Lunch Poems* collection in 1964, 'The day lady died' has since become O'Hara's most anthologized work. In fact, for many twenty-first-century readers, it is prototypical not only of O'Hara's writing but of the work of the whole group of New York Poets of which O'Hara was a part (see Perloff 1977: 125). The poem itself describes in minute detail the poet's experience of the day in 1959 on which the jazz singer, Billie Holiday, died. It is simultaneously representative, then, of an historical event, a personal experience, a poet and a literary movement. In the discussion which follows, I examine the relationships between the world in which the poem was written, the world depicted in the poem itself and the world in which my own analysis of the poem takes place. My aim is to uncover the connections and disconnections between these different worlds and to explore some of the conceptual effects which result from their existence.

Context-sensitive versus Context-restricted

Here is O'Hara's poem in full:

It is 12:20 in New York a Friday
three days after Bastille day, yes
it is 1959 and I go get a shoeshine
because I will get off the 4:19 in Easthampton
at 7:15 and then go straight to dinner
and I don't know the people who will feed me

I walk up the muggy street beginning to sun
and have a hamburger and a malted and buy
an ugly NEW WORLD WRITING to see what the poets
in Ghana are doing these days
                  I go on to the bank
and Miss Stillwagon (first name Linda I once heard)
doesn't even look up my balance for once in her life
and in the GOLDEN GRIFFIN I get a little Verlaine
for Patsy with drawings by Bonnard although I do
think of Hesiod, trans. Richmond Lattimore or
Brendan Behan's new play or *Le Balcon* or *Les Nègres*
of Genet, but I don't, I stick with Verlaine
after practically going to sleep with quandariness

and for Mike I just stroll into the PARK LANE
Liquor Store and ask for a bottle of Strega and
then I go back where I came from to 6th Avenue
and the tobacconist in the Ziegfeld Theatre and
casually ask for a carton of Gauloises and a carton
of Picayunes, and a NEW YORK POST with her face on it

and I am sweating a lot by now and thinking of
leaning on the john door in the 5 SPOT
while she whispered a song along the keyboard
to Mal Waldron and everyone and I stopped breathing

Critical opinions on this text vary, but the vast majority of literary critics choose to examine the climate – historical, artistic, political – in which the poem was produced. For example, some (e.g. Ashbery 1971; Stein 1996) discuss O'Hara's poetic experimentalism in comparison with the more conservative style of many of his contemporaries in the United States, arguing that 'The day lady died' is representative of an 'anti-literary' quality which pervades O'Hara's work in general (Stein 1996: 43–56). Others expand upon this view by arguing that the text's experimental form gives primacy to personal experience and trivia over public history (e.g. Libby 1976; Vendler 1980; Blasing 1995; Stein 1996). Such critics often point to O'Hara's poetic celebration of the everyday in 'The day lady died', explaining this as an example of 'personism' (O'Hara 1971: 498), O'Hara's own tongue-in-cheek description of his work. Most frequently, however, 'The day lady died' is described, like many of O'Hara's other poems, in terms of its strong visuality. Fruitful speculations are made about the possible connections between O'Hara's writing style and the abstract paintings of contemporary artists such as Jackson Pollock, Willem de Kooning and Jasper Johns, some of whom O'Hara collaborated with during his career (see Libby 1976; Perloff 1977 and 2001; Ferguson 1999; and Smith 2000).

All these differing approaches to O'Hara's work share a common focus on the context in which 'The day lady died' was written, rather than that in which it might be read. Perhaps more surprisingly, this focus is normally also maintained at the expense of any substantial attention to the poem itself. Despite O'Hara's painstaking recreation of New York at 12:20 on 17 July 1959, relatively little exploration of the precise nature of this description has been undertaken in any detail (see Perloff 1977: 179–82 for an exception to this rule). The remainder of this chapter uses Text World Theory (Werth 1999; Gavins 2007) to examine the complex conceptual structures created by the text and relates them to both the context of production and the context of reception. My aim is to unearth some of the possible reasons for the enduring popular appeal which 'The day lady died' has sustained from its first publication in 1964 to the present day. The use of Text World Theory as an analytical framework for this exploration enables an approach to O'Hara's text which is context-sensitive, rather than context-restricted. The focus of most text-world theorists is primarily textual, but based on an essential recognition of the importance of contextual input into both the creation and reception of a given text.

The Split Discourse-world

The careful consideration which has so far been given in literary criticism to O'Hara's personal life, his relationships with contemporary visual artists, his position within an identifiable literary group, his opinions on art and poetry and his political beliefs, all contribute to a detailed picture of one half of the discourse-world of 'The day lady died'. In Text World Theory terms, the discourse-world is the immediate physical and conceptual environment in which a particular act of communication takes place. It is populated with thinking communicating human beings, whose personal knowledge, beliefs and experiences have the potential greatly to influence the discourse they produce. Existing discussions of O'Hara's work provide some useful clues about the sorts of contextual factors which may have affected the writer's contribution to the discourse of 'The day lady died'. Exhaustive biographies of O'Hara are available in abundance, as are more general historical accounts of the 1950s and 1960s art scene in New York, of which O'Hara was an active member, and these often form the basis for literary-critical interpretations of O'Hara's poetry.

However, in written communication the discourse world is often split between two or more participants, the writer and the reader(s), who may be occupying separate spatio-temporal locations. Unlike in face-to-face discourse situations, the participants do not have a shared perception of one another's immediate surroundings, from which information helpful to their processing of the discourse might be drawn. Readers must rely far more heavily on the text and on their own existing background knowledge in order to make sense of the discourse at hand. For example, in the discourse world of my reading of 'The day lady died' I am separated in time from my co-participant by more than 40 years, and in space by over 3,000 miles. I am not in New York in 1959, but in Sheffield in 2007. I have in fact never been to New York, so must base my mental representation of the city described in O'Hara's poem on the knowledge of New York I have accrued throughout my life from its frequent representation in other literary texts, in films, on television and so on. This kind of spatio-temporal, and indeed cultural, split is by no means an uncommon phenomenon in literary discourse; the vast majority of readers of literature are separated from the writers communicating with them. Bridging this gap by utilising our existing knowledge frames to facilitate the creation of a text world, a mental representation of the discourse, is second nature to most literate human beings.

Nevertheless, the varying distances between the point of production and the point of reception of a discourse – spatial, temporal, cultural – have the potential to impact significantly upon the precise structure of the text-worlds created in readers' minds. For example, the text-world I construct of 'The day lady died' is likely to differ considerably from that created by a New Yorker, because of the greater distance which exists between my physical and cultural context and that of O'Hara, compared with someone who shares O'Hara's geographical location, if not his temporal coordinates. However, this is not to say that a New Yorker's text-world of 'The day lady died' is somehow more authentic, more rich or more valid than my own. As the enduring popularity of the poem testifies, the rich deictic detail contained in O'Hara's poem has just as striking an effect on a reader lacking personal experience and direct knowledge of the scenes and events depicted in the text. The remainder of this chapter presents a reading of 'The day lady died' from this remote readerly perspective and investigates the means by which such a reader's relative alienation from, or inclusion in, the text-world is managed within the poem.

Experiencing the Text-World of 'The day lady died'

As already noted earlier in this chapter, the temporal location of 'The day lady died' is made particularly prominent from the very opening of the poem. O'Hara uses four temporal locatives ('12:20', 'Friday', 'three days after Bastille day', '1959') within the first three lines in order to establish the precise temporal parameters of the text-world he is constructing. In Text-World Theory, these locatives are known as *world-building elements* (see Werth 1999: 180–90; Gavins 2007: 35–52), deictic features which locate a text in time and space. Time is further foregrounded by the use of the present tense throughout the majority of the text, another world-building element which adds a sense of immediacy to the scene being described. O'Hara also makes a number of temporally restricted references. For example, he talks about buying a copy of 'NEW WORLD WRITING', a poetry journal showcasing the work of new international poets which ran from 1952 to 1959, and one of five proper nouns highlighted in upper case in the text ('GOLDEN GRIFFIN', 'PARK LANE', 'NEW YORK POST', and '5 SPOT' being the other four). He later also considers buying 'Brendan Behan's *new* play' (my emphasis), which in 1959 may have been either *The Hostage* or *Borstal Boy*. Both of these cultural references help to tie the text-world yet more closely to a specific moment in time, more than 40 years away from my own position in the split discourse world.

In his study of deixis in lyric poetry, Green outlines the difference between the 'content time' of a poem, the time to which the poem itself refers, and the 'coding time', the time at which the poem is 'transmitted' (Green 1992: 126–7). He notes that many lyric poems dramatize coding time and content time as synchronous, and this can be seen to happen too in 'The day lady died'. O'Hara's use of the present tense creates an illusion whereby the reader experiences the text-world from the perspective of the author's poetic persona as if the scene were unfolding in real time for both participants. Although O'Hara's half of the discourse world, his writing of 'The day lady died', is likely to have occurred some time after the death of Billie Holiday, in the poem it appears that the author's discourse world and the text-world are co-located on 17 July 1959. In my own reading of the text, I too am 'transported' (Gerrig 1993) from my location in Sheffield in 2007 into the spatio-temporal parameters of the text-world. The text-world is inhabited, then, by an enactor of the author and an enactor of the reader, who share a moving perspective on the scene (see Emmott 1997; Gavins 2007: 40–2). This movement is indicated through the frequent present-tense verbs of motion, often combined with spatial adverbs (for example, 'I go', 'I walk up', 'I go on', 'I just stroll into', 'I go back where I came from'). These help to establish the spatial relationships which exist between objects and entities in the text-world, and therefore also come under the category of world-building elements. However, they act at the same time as *function-advancing propositions*, which give information about actions, states and events in the text-world and thus propel the discourse forwards (see Gavins 2007: 53–72, and Lahey 2006 for further discussion).

Other spatial world-builders are also present in abundance throughout the poem. Most obvious are the nouns and pronouns which refer to and give other descriptive detail about the objects and entities in the text-world. O'Hara introduces these elements with an almost 50/50 split of definite articles (for example, 'the 4:19', 'the bank', 'the tobacconist', 'the Ziegfeld Theatre', 'the john door' and so on) versus indefinite articles ('a Friday', 'a shoeshine', 'a hamburger', 'a bottle of Strega', and so on). All but two of the nouns taking definite articles in the poem are specific in nature. Only 'the people who will feed me' (people O'Hara says he does not know), and 'the poets in Ghana' (whose work he is yet to discover in his copy of *New World Writing*) are non-specific exceptions to this rule. The rest of the definite specific nouns in the text add to the emerging rich deictic detail of the text-world, with which, it is made clear, the poet is highly familiar. Crucially, although I have never seen the 'PARK LANE liquor store' or 'the Ziegfeld Theatre' in my real life, O'Hara presents these world-building elements as everyday features of the world of the poem into which the reader must transport him/herself if a coherent mental representation is to be constructed. It matters not, then, that I do not possess sufficient background knowledge in my discourse world in Sheffield in 2007 to visualize accurately the objects and textual entities to which O'Hara refers. What matters is that I understand the familiarity of these items *to him*. O'Hara's use of deixis creates for readers, regardless of their previous real-world experiences and existing knowledge, a strong sense of the commonplace nature of the scene.

This sense is further enhanced by the inclusion of an equal number of nouns taking indefinite articles in the poem. Despite the temporal specificity of the text-world, the New York landscape is given a timeless quality by O'Hara's addition of a wide range of indefinites. Hamburgers, shoeshines, malteds, Gauloises cigarettes, copies of the *New York Post* and other objects are presented as habitual items, present not just in this particular moment in time, but regularly and recurrently in the poet's everyday life. Indeed, on one occasion in the text O'Hara appears to make a deliberate choice to exclude the definite article in favour of something more imprecise. In the middle of the second stanza, he first makes a first reference to considering buying 'a little Verlaine for Patsy'. In his second mention of this object later in the same stanza, his final choice of it as a gift, one might expect the indefinite article to switch to the definite, but O'Hara instead omits the article altogether: 'I stick with Verlaine'.

Focalization and Familiarity

The presence of an enactor of the author in the text-world is, of course, the result of the first-person narration of the poem. This also means that 'The day lady died' is a text with a fixed focalisation and that all the world-building and function-advancing information available to the reader is filtered through the perspective of a textual entity. This is a common phenomenon in literary discourse, which normally takes places in a split discourse-world where the reader has access to the author only through the text he/she creates. The 'I' of 'The day lady died' is not the author, a co-participant in the discourse-world, but an enactor of him inhabiting the text-world, his poetic persona. Where participants communicating face to face have the ability to question one another, to clarify and to assess the reliability of the material being exchanged, participants in a split discourse-world do not. The textual information upon which their text-worlds are based is often presented by text-world enactors who exist at a different ontological level from the participants and whose reliability is consequently unverifiable. As a result, text-worlds which relate to an enactor's perspective, such as those created by focalized narration, exist at a greater epistemic distance from the reader than unfocalized text-worlds (see also Gavins 2005; Gavins 2007: 126–35). Having said this, in a fixed focalization no other narratorial voice is present and the reader has no choice but to accept the world-building and function-advancing elements presented to him/her by the focalizer as reliable if a text-world is to be constructed at all. Many prose fiction texts, of course, take advantage of the trust the reader must necessarily place in the focalizer in order to facilitate narrative tricks, deceptions and twists in the tale. The effectiveness of these tricks is entirely dependent on readers conceptualising what is in fact an example of a remote *modal world* (see Gavins 2005; Gavins 2007: 91–145) as if it were a text-world.

In 'The day lady died', however, no such deception is carried out and the first-person fixed focalization of the poem instead enhances the informal conversation-like tone O'Hara adopts and which other critics have identified as a primary component of the poet's anti-literariness (see Stein 1996). Once again, the predominant present tense in the poem plays an important role here, as does the recurrent conjunction 'and', and the conversational 'yes' in line 2 of the text, suggestive of a direct address to the reader. Where other writers and artists are referred to formally, either by both first name and surname or by surname only (for example, 'Verlaine', 'Bonnard', 'Brendan Behan'), O'Hara's friends are referred to informally by their first names, 'Patsy' and 'Mike', as if the reader too already has an acquaintance with them. The chatty informality of the poem is further accentuated by O'Hara's inclusion of a number of drifts into other epistemic meanderings yet more remote from the reader than the epistemic modal-world functioning as the main text-world. The remoteness of these embedded modal worlds acts to secure the reliability of the world from which they have sprung. The epistemic modal world of the main focalized text appears all the more text-world-like because of the existence of embedded mental activity.

The fact that the reader must rely upon the author-enactor's perspective throughout the poem is underscored by the use of epistemic modality at the end of the first stanza: 'I don't *know* the people who will feed me'. Like all modality, this negative construction creates a new epistemic modal-world, embedded within the existing epistemic modal-world formed by the main body of the poem. Its negated nature actually means, as Hidalgo Downing (2000) has suggested, that its content becomes foregrounded in the mind of the reader. A little later in the text, our attention is drawn once again to the workings of the author-enactor's mind, as he admits, 'I do *think* of Hesiod, trans. Richard Lattimore'. The representation of thought here creates a new epistemic modal-world embedded within the main world of the poem through which the thoughts of the poetic persona can be conceptualized. Notice here how O'Hara distinguishes his inner thought processes clearly from the conversationality of the rest of the poem through his use of a markedly un-speech-like form 'trans.'. His omission of the preposition 'by' suggests an unmediated representation of the written words on the cover of the book as he looks at it.

Modalized World Switches and Ambiguity

A number of other new worlds are constructed within 'The day lady died' as the result of some variation in the spatio-temporal parameters of the main focalized text-world. In Text World Theory, such variations are known as *world-switches* (see Gavins 2007: 45–52). For example, in line 4 the predominant simple present tense of the poem shifts temporarily to create a new world set in a future time-zone: 'I will get off the 4:19 in Easthampton/at 7:15 and then go straight to dinner'. Here, O'Hara describes an unrealized situation which has both a different spatial location (Easthampton) and a different temporal location (7:15) from its originating world. Once again, it is the temporal coordinates of the new world that are particularly emphasised, with O'Hara providing to-the-minute detail about when his train arrives in Easthampton. Literary critics have noted the frequency with which such time shifts occur in O'Hara's poetry, with Perloff (1977: 122) going so far as to describe them as 'one of O'Hara's trademarks'. It is important to note, however, that the description of a new time zone which takes place over lines 4 to 6 in 'The day lady died' is not the straightforward time shift it might at first appear to be. We have already seen earlier in this analysis that line 6, 'and I don't know the people who will feed me', contains a negated epistemic modal world. This world is oddly sandwiched in the middle of the future world-switch: O'Hara 'doesn't know' in the time zone of the main text-world, but 'the people who will feed him' are doing so in the unrealized future. Furthermore, all future constructions of this kind are essentially speculative in nature. Whether or not the events being predicted in the world switch will actually happen at some point in time is a matter of subjective opinion. Thus, future world switches are often also modalized to some degree, since they are based on an expression of speaker judgement. Since the speaker in this case is a text-world enactor, the reliability of the world switch he creates is unverifiable by the discourse-world participants.

Indeed, 'The day lady died' contains a number of shifts in time and space and each of them, regardless of whether they relate to future or past events, is a mixture of world switch and modal world. For example, line 12 reads 'and Miss Stillwagon (first name Linda I once heard)'. The information provided in brackets describes a report given to the focaliser by some other unnamed textual entity about Miss Stillwagon. This report also took place at a time preceding the content time of the main text. It is, therefore, a world-switch to a past time zone but one which relates to unverifiable enactor information which must be conceptualized at a considerable epistemic distance from the main text-world. A further example of a modalized world-switch can be found in the flashback contained in line 19: 'after practically going to sleep with quandariness'. In lines 15–17, the representation of the poet's thoughts in the Golden Griffin bookshop, examined in the preceding section of this chapter, first occurs: 'I do think of Hesiod ...'. In line 18, the epistemic modal-world relating to this representation ends and we return to the main text-world for the focaliser to report his final actions, 'I don't, I stick with Verlaine'. In line 19, however, an anaphoric reference is made back to the decision process again, causing a world-switch to a past-time zone and a modalized world.

The final and most significant world-switch in the poem, however, occurs in the final stanza. Once again, it presents a curious mix of spatio-temporal shift within a modal-world. Here is the entire stanza again, for ease of reference:

and I am sweating a lot by now and thinking of
leaning on the john door in the 5 SPOT
while she whispered a song along the keyboard
to Mal Waldron and everyone and I stopped breathing

The first line of this stanza sees a shift from the simple present tense which predominates in the poem to the present continuous, but the text world remains within the same temporal parameters as the majority of the rest of the text. It also contains the beginnings of another representation of the focaliser's inner thoughts. However, the combination of 'thinking' with the preposition 'of' creates an ambiguity in the first line and in the line which follows. On my own first reading of the poem, I had to reread the first two lines of this stanza in order to ascertain whether 'thinking of leaning on the john door' was a report of a memory of a past event, or whether it expressed an intention to lean on a john door in the main text-world. Although there is no shift in tense to signal a world switch and the previously abundant temporal clues used to mark time changes elsewhere in the text are strangely absent, the reference to a different spatial location, 'in the 5 SPOT', which closes the second line allows a swift world-repair (see Emmott 1997; Gavins 2007: 141–3) and confirms that this is indeed another flashback.

The semantic ambiguities contained within this final stanza do not end here. Once able to mentally represent a new past-time world in which the poet is leaning on the door of a toilet in a jazz club, the reader must then decode a series of concluding textual puzzles. First of all, the world of the 5 Spot is difficult to populate with textual entities. We know that an enactor of the poet is present in this world, along with the jazz pianist Mal Waldron. Billie Holiday herself is never referred to by name, however, so the reader is left to infer her presence through the female personal pronoun 'she' in this stanza and 'her' at the end of the preceding stanza. We are told 'she whispered a song along the keyboard', but once again ambiguity is created with the use of a single preposition: in this case 'to'. Reading the final line 'to Mal Waldron and everyone and I stopped breathing', it is unclear whether Holiday whispers her song to Mal Waldron alone, or 'to Mal Waldron and everyone'. Inferring the latter is difficult without any textual information on who 'everyone' might be. The reader can assume a nightclub full of people, but this is likely to remain an indistinct mental image. A further possibility is to extend the clause to include 'to Mal Waldron and everyone and I', but this leaves an odd verbal group, 'stopped breathing', hanging at the end of the line without an apparent subject. Again, an inference is possible, but perhaps not entirely satisfactory: does this verbal group in fact refer to Holiday herself and to the moment of her death?

More logical, perhaps, is to link 'stopped breathing' to the nearest possible human agent in the text. However, if the ambiguity of the line is resolved through a mental representation of Holiday singing 'to Mal Waldron and everyone' in the nightclub and of the focaliser as the agent who 'stopped breathing', a further question immediately arises: in which text-world does this happen? The match of simple past tense between 'she whispered' and 'I stopped' might at first suggest that the focaliser is still situated against the toilet door in the 5 Spot and that his extreme physiological reaction is a reaction to the beauty of the song. If this interpretative route is selected, the line can be reread once more and the agency extended to 'and everyone and I stopped breathing', portraying an entire audience transfixed by Holiday's talent. And yet, this is a poem entitled 'The day lady died', in which painstaking detail has been provided about a specific moment in time in a specific location. Despite occasional world-switching and diversions into the modal-worlds of inner thoughts and opinions, the text-world in which O'Hara's enactor moves around the New York landscape on 17 July 1959 remains the world most richly detailed and most prominent. It would seem, also, that stopping breathing is a more appropriate response to the news of a death than it is to just a singer singing a song. According to this reading, Holiday sings 'to Mal Waldron and everyone' in the flashback world before the poem switches back to the focaliser in the main text-world as his breath (and everyone's?) is taken away by the front cover of the *New York Times*.

In the end, however, it is practically impossible to disentangle the ambiguity of O'Hara's final lines into a single coherent text-world and the enduring appeal of the poem lies perhaps in its creation of many worlds to be conceptualized somehow simultaneously in its closing stanza. Throughout 'The day lady died', O'Hara manages to balance a remarkable level of social, historical and cultural specificity in the text-worlds he creates with an informality and familiarity which makes this readerly experience hospitable even to the most remote co-participant in the split discourse-world. In so doing, O'Hara encapsulates Holiday's phenomenally broad-ranging appeal: to an entire audience in the 5 Spot nightclub whose breath is taken away the night she sings to Mal Waldron; to everyone in New York on the day she died; to Frank O'Hara in both of these contexts; and to everyone experiencing these moments through O'Hara's focalisation. More importantly, however, it is the irresolvable multiplicity of readings O'Hara includes in his text, the permeability he allows between worlds, which enables the distance between the poet and his reader, between 'everyone and I', to be bridged.

'Progress is a Comfortable Disease': Cognition in a Stylistic Analysis of e.e. cummings

Michael Burke

Stylistics traces its origins back through the study of rhetoric across the twentieth century and the modern era, and into the study of *elocutio* in the ancient past. In this chapter, Michael Burke shows how stylistics continues to cement its connections with the ancient art of literary analysis and appreciation. One of the latest and most powerful innovations in stylistics has been the addition of a systematic means of understanding context through cognition. In an analysis of a poem by e.e. cummings – the stylisticians' favourite – Burke demonstrates how a cognitive poetic analysis follows naturally on from a traditional stylistic account, working to enrich our understanding of how literary reading works.

The chapter stands as an example of stylistic practice in that it engages with literary critical viewpoints in order to make apparent and explicit what is often impressionistic and implicit. Of course, stylistics *is* literary criticism, but of a progressive, open and falsifiable kind. Burke acknowledges and celebrates the subjectivity and humanity in his reading, but the invitation to intersubjectivity represented by this chapter comes with the proviso that the reader engages with the technical idiom as a means of ensuring a common currency of critical discourse. In short, the stylistician invites the student to do some work.

In connecting the latest developments in stylistics with the earliest named patterns in rhetoric, Burke is not merely cycling back through scholarly history but is showing how stylistics represents the long view of the conscious analysis of verbal art. Stylistics is progressive: less workable frameworks and perspectives are abandoned, adapted or augmented in favour of a better understanding, as linguistics and language study more broadly develop new tools and more reliable or generalizable methods. In the beginning, Aristotle delineated *logos, pathos* and *ethos* as the key dimensions of human discourse. Stylistics in the first phase of its modern history has developed a science of *logos*. Cognitive poetic developments in stylistics have begun to reconnect us with a systematic and rigorous understanding of *pathos*. And stylistics has always had the sociolinguistic and rich social theoretical means of addressing questions of discursive ethics, power and authority: onwards to *ethos*. If we can bend our minds to a synthesis of these, then we will really be doing literary criticism properly.

Peter Stockwell

Introduction

Stylistics in its default linguistic-analytic form is sometimes viewed as traditional, while stylistics in its cognitive guise is often considered somewhat reductive and perhaps even 'threatening' (see Downes 1993 and Freeman 1993 for the first salvoes in an ongoing debate). I believe that not only are the premises drawn from such classifications fallacious but the categorizations themselves are, since the domains of written language and of mental processes are not isolated and independent, rather they operate in the same text-processing human-cognitive system. Stylistic analysis in the twenty-first century should, where possible, attempt to mirror this reality. This means blending the 'sign-fed' system of apprehending words on a page or screen, with the 'mind-fed' aspects of what is brought to bear on such semiotic signs during the maelstrom of meaning-making that must take place when a reader sits down to engage with a work of literature. In this chapter I will start at the linguistic end of what I see as a continuum of stylistic tools and end at the cognitive end. Also, in order to show that one can use tools from the past as well as those from the present I will include a classical rhetorical dimension to my analysis. In doing so I am seeking to draw on 'all the available means of (stylistic) analysis' to paraphrase Aristotle from his *Art of Rhetoric*. In essence, what I hope to show, as I have already started to argue elsewhere (Burke 2005), is that cognitive linguistics does not threaten or replace stylistic analysis; rather it augments it, and further that rhetoric, linguistics and cognition co-exist in the same methodological stylistic toolkit.

Stylistics and Cognitive Linguistics

Stylistics or 'literary linguistics' as it is often termed is broadly acknowledged as 'an approach to the analysis of (literary) texts using *linguistic* description' (Short 1996: 1). It is centrally concerned 'with the study of style in language' (Verdonk 2002: 3). Together, these quotations emphasize the written, 'bottom-up' essence of stylistic analysis. When a stylistician sits down to conduct a stylistic analysis he/she can choose any number of tools from the extensive linguistic stylistic toolkit that is at his/her disposal. These are then brought to bear on a text through a close analysis of the language and style in order to draw out meanings that otherwise might have remained hidden. There is no definitive list of stylistic tools that the student can employ. Short (1996), however, draws up a useful selection, which he sets out at the end of each chapter in the form of ten student-friendly check-sheets. These are:

(i) deviation, parallelism and foregrounding
(ii) style variation

     (iii)   phonetic structure
     (iv)   metrical structure
      (v)   discourse structure and speech realism
     (vi)   turn-taking, speech acts and politeness
    (vii)   inferring meaning
   (viii)   linguistic indicators of point of view
     (ix)   speech and thought presentation
      (x)   style features of narrative description

The first of these involves a list of linguistic categories that can be systematically deployed when analysing a text for foregrounded features. This list includes levels of phonetics, morphology, graphology, metre, lexis, semantics, syntax, discourse and pragmatics. A stylistic observation may also fall simultaneously into two or more categories. The beauty of such checklists is that once learned they can be used as a heuristic by students and deployed almost automatically in a similar way to how the ancient orators used their own rhetorical checklists to generate arguments at the levels of discovery, arrangement and stylization. Indeed, it is the level of stylization, traditionally seen as the third of the five canons of rhetoric, from which current stylisticians take their cue.

    Unlike stylistics, cognitive linguistics has less of a direct link to the ancient rhetorical past. It developed in the late 1970s as a result of inputs from cognitive psychology, artificial intelligence and philosophy. One of the most influential books in this early period of cognitive linguistics is Lakoff and Johnson's *Metaphors We Live By* (1980) which focuses primarily on the notion of cognitive or 'conceptual' metaphor. Cognitive metaphor works by firstly identifying a source domain and a target domain in an utterance. Specific characteristics or qualities from that source domain get mapped onto the target. This is the basic mechanism by which almost all metaphors work. There are three main types of cognitive metaphor: structural, ontological and orientational. An example of a structural cognitive metaphor is LIFE IS A JOURNEY. Here, elements from the source (journey), such as distance, endurance, having to go around obstacles, etc., get mapped back onto the target (life). This is realized in many everyday linguistic expressions such as 'I have got to get around this problem', 'he still has a long way to go', etc. An example of an ontological cognitive metaphor is THE MIND IS AN OCEAN, which maps qualities onto the mind such as depth, dynamism, inscrutability, etc. Orientational cognitive metaphors represent spatial relationships which are not arbitrary but rather have a basis in our physical and cultural experience. These are expressed in abstract conceptualisations like UP IS GOOD and DOWN IS BAD. Linguistic examples include 'he is down in the dumps today' versus 'she is over the moon', and 'she is downcast' versus 'he jumped for joy', etc.

    Another important concept in cognitive linguistics is image-schemata, which can be loosely described as being the recurring patterns of our everyday perceptual interactions and bodily experiences. For instance, whenever we stand up from a chair or sit down in one, or whenever we go into, or out of, a building or room we experience the image-schematic distinction between 'up and down' and 'in and out' respectively. Image schemata are like dynamic skeletal narratives that are grounded in embodied patterns of meaningfully organized experience. There are a number of identifiable structures that can be highlighted as emerging from our bodily interaction with the world. These include CONTAINERS, BALANCE, COMPULSION, BLOCKAGE, ATTRACTION, PATHS, LINKS, SCALES, CYCLES, CENTRE-PERIPHERY, etc. (see Johnson 1987: 206). Other main cognitive linguistic tools that will not be expanded on here include space grammar, schema theory, figure and ground, prototypes and categories, etc. Unlike mainstream stylistics, no checklist currently exists for cognitive stylistic tools. This last observation concludes this section on some relevant methodological tools for this chapter. In the next section I will introduce the poem that is to be analysed.

The Poet and the Poem

Born in 1894, Edward Estlin Cummings was one of the most influential American poets of the twentieth century. His first major breakthrough was in 1923 with the publication of a collection of poems entitled *Tulips & Chimneys*. He went on to publish many volumes of verse before his death in 1962. Like Eliot and Joyce, he is looked upon now as one of the great innovators of twentieth century English literature. When people speak of cummings, they invariably comment on his idiosyncratic use of language (he even insisted his name be written as 'e.e. cummings'). As Kennedy (1996: xv) notes, cummings' unique poetic style made him famous for being, among other things, an individualist and an iconoclast. Influenced by the likes of Pound, he wrote in an extreme free verse style. In his introduction to *Tulips & Chimneys*, Kennedy refers to cummings' 'free play with punctuation and the scattering of words on the page' and his 'unconventional visual arrangements' (1996: xvii). Kennedy further observes though that despite this deviation, many of cummings' poems have at their centre a simple and coherent view (Kennedy 1996: xviii). This is echoed later in his observation that in cummings' poetry there is an emphasis on what is 'simple, natural, individual and unique', adding 'it values whatever is instinctively human' (Kennedy 1996: xix).

It may not have gone unnoticed that the above literary critical comments appear to contradict each other in places. On the one hand, there is cummings' poetry that is 'iconoclastic', 'unreal' and 'highly individualistic', yet, on the other, there is his poetry that is 'simple', 'coherent' and 'instinctively human'. But how can this be the case? I agree intuitively that there seems to be the uneasy paradox that Kennedy suggests. Unfortunately, this is where the literary critic stops and we as readers must take his/her word for it. It is here, as Short (1996: 3) has cogently argued, where stylistics as a textual analytic methodology can be brought to bear to show both sides of the literary critical argument: the 'individualist' subjective side and the 'instinctively human' social side. In what follows I will go a step further and show that by combining a literary linguistic analysis with a cognitive linguistic one, both sides of Kennedy's literary critical claim can be brought to the surface in a more illuminating fashion than had been the case were I solely to have employed a traditional stylistic analysis.

Below is the poem. Like almost all of cummings' poetry the first line is the poem's title. The theme of the poem loosely appears to be a description of a day in the life of a city. I have numbered each line to the left in order to make my analysis easier to follow.

```
 1    the hours rise up putting off stars and it is
 2    dawn
 3    into the street of the sky light walks scattering poems

 4    on earth a candle is
 5    extinguished   the city
 6    wakes
 7    with a song upon her
 8    mouth having death in her eyes

 9    and it is dawn
10    the world
11    goes forth to murder dreams....

12    i see in the street where strong
13    men are digging bread
14    and i see the brutal faces of
15    people contented hideous hopeless cruel happy

16    and it is day,

17    in the mirror
18    i see a frail
19    man
20    dreaming
21    dreams
22    dreams in the mirror

23    and it
24    is dusk   on earth
25    a candle is lighted
26    and it is dark.
27    the people are in their houses
28    the frail man is in his bed
29    the city

30    sleeps with death upon her mouth having a song in her eyes
31    the hours descend,
```

32   putting on stars. . . .

33   in the street of the sky night walks scattering poems
                                     e.e. cummings (1923) from *Tulips & Chimneys*

A Cognitive Linguistic–Stylistic Analysis of an e.e. cummings Poem

I will start with a traditional literary linguistic analysis and move to a cognitive linguistic one, interspersing both with classical rhetorical observations, thus showing how it is both feasible and beneficial to work on one single continuum, blending stylistic analytic methods from the past, present and future. For ease of understanding I will go through the linguistic categories set out in Short's first checksheet on foregrounding; where possible I will proceed from the smallest units to the largest. I will not discuss every category; rather I will focus on just a small selection of 'all the available stylistic tools'. Remember, this is my own reading: yours may differ. Since I know of the general reputation surrounding cummings' poetic style, I expect that his poetry will be somewhat deviant. My knowledge of his imagist roots suggests to me that this deviation will primarily, if not exclusively, occur at the graphological level. So even though I do not know what to expect, I do know that I can expect something. Let us then begin with this graphological category. My initial focus in this part of the analysis will be on deviation.

I anticipated that if there were one thing that I could be almost sure of, it would be that cummings will not use capitalization in this poem as he is famous for not doing so in his work. Fittingly, there is no sentence-initial capitalization, as well as no line-initial or even stanza-initial capitalization and no capitalization of the first-person pronoun 'I'. The punctuation in this poem is for the most part non-existent. There are just two commas, at the ends of lines 16 and 31 and just one full stop, at the end of line 26. There are two instances of four ellipsis dots, in lines 11 and 32. This lack of full stops is not down to long sentences in the poem, e.g. complex sentences with extensive multiple sub-clauses, rather the endings of sentences are sort of 'alluded to' either by the end of a line as in line 2, the end of a stanza as in line 11, or irregular spacing in the middle of lines as in line 5. Such deviation is as much a question of layout as it is punctuation. The missing punctuation and odd layout make comprehension and meaning-making difficult for the reader. From an analytic perspective this stylistic observation is not just a question of graphological deviation but rather of semantic-syntactic-graphological deviation as it arguably transcends all three categories. At a kind of macro level, the layout of the poem is also graphologically deviant as there appears to be neither order nor pattern to the stanzas.

The poem is extremely deviant at the semantic level, and although I could go on later to highlight deviance at other levels such as phonetics or syntax, I will instead explore this semantic category in some depth. Let us begin unconventionally, in true cummings style, with the final line of the poem, which in itself is highly foregrounded internally because of its positioning. The line in question, which mirrors an earlier line (3) is 'in the street of the sky night walks scattering poems' (33). This line is not easy to read. In fact, I find my own physical reading of the poem gets held up here. So why does cummings do this in the final line and what kind of effect might this momentary jarring have on a person's reading experience? I will return to this question in a moment after we have looked at the line in more grammatical detail. After some puzzling, let us presume that 'night' is the subject of the sentence, 'walks' the main verb and 'scattering poems' an adverbial. This leaves 'in the street of the sky', which can now be seen as a semantically deviant prepositional phrase. The deviation here is at the level of the poetic metaphor, since (a) there appears to be a 'street in the sky' and (b) 'night', which is an inanimate noun, is personified here. As stated, the effect of this on me, and perhaps on you too, is that it slows down my reading process, when what I really want to do is speed up to finish the poem. I find that one of the results of this resistance is that I am forced to focus more on the actual words in this final line. One effect of this is that the final word 'poems' is left ringing in my ears. This appears to become exacerbated by the fact that the poem does not end with a full stop but instead seems to carry on in some way. This sense of continuation is something I will return to later.

There are many further examples of semantic deviation. This commences in the very first line of the poem. One might think that dawn would figuratively 'put *out*' stars since our world knowledge tells us that lights can be extinguished; here though it 'puts them *off*' (1). The manipulation of this verb phrase goes against a reader's expectations and thus estranges him/her from the discourse. Verbs and nouns are juxtaposed in deviant semantic ways. How does one 'dig bread?' (13) or 'murder dreams?' (11) or 'dream dreams in the mirror?' (20–2) or 'have a song in one's eyes?' (30). Odd personifications add to this sense of semantic deviance. For example, as we have seen 'light' and 'night' 'walk' and 'scatter poems' (3), the city has a 'mouth' and 'eyes' (8), the world is a potential 'murderer' (11), the city 'wakes' (6) and 'sleeps' (30). Thus far we have seen how this poem is not just deviant at the graphological level as expected, but also at the semantic level, and had there been time this could have been extended to other levels too. Let us now move on and look at the other aspects of foregrounding: parallelism and repetition.

Before proceeding, a question we need to ask ourselves is 'what can parallelism do to a reader?' and further, 'what effect might it have on meaning-making for that reader?' There is no definitive answer to these questions even though we know that humans take great pleasure from noticing and discovering patterns at many levels of sensual appraisal: visual, auditory, tactile, etc. Short offers us an explanation with his 'parallelism rule' when he says 'what is interesting about parallel structures, in addition to their perceptual prominence, is that they invite the reader to search for meaning connections between the parallel structures' (Short 1996: 14), adding 'thus parallelism has the power not just to foreground parts of a text for us, but also to make us look for parallel or contrastive meaning links between those parallel parts' (Short 1996: 15). There is then a fundamental invitational emotive essence to parallelism that readers/listeners can pick up on and are enchanted by. This was something not lost on the style experts of the past. As classical rhetoricians Corbett and Connors state in their discussion on style figures 'repetition is one of the characteristics of highly emotional language' (1999: 392). With all this in mind, let us return to the text.

At the phonetic level of analysis it can be observed that there is some parallel alliteration and assonance. For example, in line 3 we can see the alliteration between 'sky' and 'scattering' and later in the poem the juxtaposed words 'city' and 'sleeps' (29–30). In the first example we have a blend of voiceless alveolar fricative /s/ in combination with voiceless velar plosive /k/. The combination of these consonants produces a hard voiceless fricative-plosive sound /sk/, but in the second example just the /s/ sound is repeated. This similarity between 'sky' and 'scattering', on the one hand, and 'city' and 'sleeps', on the other, may invite readers to consider the connection between the words in question at a deeper level of sound symbolism, as Short suggests in his 'parallelism rule'. In line 15 the voiceless velar plosive /k/ sounds of 'contented' and 'cruel' and the soft glottal fricative /h/ sounds of 'hideous', 'hopeless' and 'happy' are not just juxtaposed at the semantic level but also at this phonetic level. From an assonance perspective, i.e. the repetition of vowel sounds in close proximity, we have the examples 'see' /si:/ and 'street' /stri:t/ in line 12, which are close front vowels.

Moving up the linguistic scale there is a prominent example of lexical repetition in the stanza that makes up lines 17–22, namely, 'in the mirror/i see a frail/man/dreaming/dreams/dreams in the mirror'. First, there is the adverbial 'dreaming' followed twice by the noun 'dreams'. This repetition of a word derived from the same root is a common style figure, known more commonly in classical rhetoric as *polyptoton*. There are many more literal repetitions at the syntactic level such as the steady repetitive flow, known as *polysyndeton* in classical rhetoric, of '*and* it is dawn' (1–2); '*and* it is dawn' (9); '*and* it is day' (16), '*and* it is dusk' (23–4), '*and* it is dark' (26). The effect of *polysyndeton* is that something is made to seem even more extensive than it actually is, as opposed to *asyndeton*, which gives the opposite effect. Also note the phonological repetition of the /d/ sound in /d/awn, /d/awn, /d/ay, /d/usk, /d/ark. This is a well-spaced voiced alveolar plosive 'thudding' effect that moves throughout the poem from beginning to end. For me personally in my reading this is in some sense sound-symbolic of the tolling of a division bell: a chronological device traditionally used to partition the day into units, as heard in the '/d/ing-/d/ong' sound that bells are said to make in the English folk understandings of the terms.

At this lexical level there are also parallelisms in the form of opposites. This notion of 'parallel-deviation', known as *antithesis* in classical rhetoric, is still one of the most prevalent and persuasive of all style figures: as Aristotle noted already in his *Rhetoric* more than 2000 years ago (233–7 BC). Consider the following: 'the hours rise up' (1) versus 'the hours descend' (31); 'putting off stars' (1) versus 'putting on stars' (32); 'and it is dawn' (1–2) versus 'and it is dusk' (23–4), 'and it is day (16) versus 'and it is dark' (26). These, to me, are compelling – almost hypnotic. There are also much longer parallel constructions such as: 'into the street of the sky light walks scattering poems' (3) versus 'in the street of the sky night walks scattering poems' (33); and 'on earth a candle is extinguished' (4–5) versus 'on earth a candle is lighted' (24–5) and 'the city wakes with a song upon her mouth having death in her eyes' (5–8) versus 'the city sleeps with death upon her mouth having a song in her eyes' (29–30). In this last example some of the verbs and nouns have swapped places in the second line, blending the concepts even more and thus producing a potentially powerful effect on the reader.

There are also other aspects of repetition and parallelism worth noting. In the lexical section of this analysis we saw how there was repetition in lines 17–22. In that same section, there is an even more significant example of repetition, which occurs not just at the syntactic level but also at a semantic-syntactic level. This involves the prepositional phrase 'in the mirror' which both commences the stanza in line 17 and closes it in line 22. From a classical rhetorical perspective, this is similar to the scheme *epanalepsis*: a device said to 'spring spontaneously from intense emotion' (Corbett and Connors 1999: 392). At the stanza level therefore one can say that the semantic sense of mirroring is quite literally 'reflected' by the 'book-ending' or mirroring of this prepositional phrase. This increases the effect of the mirroring in deeper and more embodied ways for engaged readers. Such 'semantic-symbolism' is often highly effective in eliciting emotive responses.

In the analysis so far we have seen how a literary linguistic approach addresses both sides of Kennedy's literary critical comments set out earlier: the ones pertaining to the 'individual', 'iconoclastic' side of cummings' poetry, highlighted by deviant aspects in foregrounding, and the ones pertaining to the 'simple', 'human' side of cummings' poetry, highlighted by parallel and repetitive aspects of foregrounding. Upon reflection the deviant/iconoclastic side of the analysis appears to me to have been slightly more prevalent than the parallel/simple part, perhaps because there was extensive deviation in some of the parallelisms in the form of antithesis. A traditional literary linguistic analysis would end here and that would be that – but not this one. Let us consider just one of Kennedy's earlier claims in more detail, namely that 'many of cummings' poems have at their centre 'a simple and coherent view' (Kennedy 1996: xviii). My discussion of the mirror stanza in the middle of the poem provides some evidence for this, but surely this literal example is far too obvious and is not what Kennedy meant? It is at this point that we turn to our cognitive linguistic tools to search for more fundamental evidence of that simple coherent view at the core of cummings' poetry.

There are a number of conceptual metaphors in this poem. One of these is the dual notion that CITIES ARE FEMALE/CITIES ARE SPACES. Another aspect to this ongoing metaphor is arguably CITIES ARE FIELDS, which I will return to below. However, there is a parallel set of metaphors to these which begins with the dual metaphor LIGHT IS MALE/LIGHT IS A TRAVELLER, which at a more abstract level might be represented as LIGHT IS A SOWER, an individual who moves from one edge of a space to the opposite edge. Later in the poem the same can also be said for 'night'. Embedded in all of these is the metaphor POEMS ARE SEEDS. The parallelism at work here, even at this essentially non-linguistic level, is a very affective form of foregrounding for me as a reader, which appears to have a kind of delayed affect on me, perhaps because it is not entirely at the surface level of discourse processing. I will now look more closely at the female and male aspects of these metaphors and in doing so draw in other types of cognitive metaphor.

CITIES ARE FEMALE/CITIES ARE SPACES and are inhabited with men who are both 'strong' (12–13) and 'frail' (18–19 and 28). The qualities which are attributed to the city are mixed: in the morning one would expect 'her' to be associated with positive things, but here although she has 'a song *upon* her mouth' (7–8), she has 'death *in* her eyes' (8). This is also supported at an orientational level of cognitive metaphor since from an abstract spatial perspective 'upon' or 'on' is almost always more elevated than 'in': e.g. I would be physically higher were I to be 'on' a house than 'in' one. What we arguably have here is deviation, and thus foregrounding, at the cognitive stylistic level of cognitive metaphor in that the positive feeling set up by GOOD IS UP, from the opening words 'the hours rise up' (1), and continued by 'song *upon* her mouth' is then challenged by the negativity of 'death *in* her eyes'. Had this line read death 'on' her eyes, this would have continued the orientational pattern rather than breaking with it. The mirror image of this occurs at the end of the poem: thus showing that the deviant cognitive structures are also parallel. This supports my earlier observation that the poem itself is a mirror. Here, where one might expect BAD IS DOWN type orientational metaphors, we find 'the hours *descend*' (31) and 'a song *in* her eyes' (30) juxtaposed with 'death *upon* her mouth' (30) and 'putting *on* stars' (32). In this case the explicit downward motion of 'descend' and the implicit sense of 'in' fit the pattern, but a song 'upon' her eyes and putting 'on' stars does not. In sum, we see here how the GOOD IS UP/BAD IS DOWN orientational cognitive metaphor is initially upheld but then deviates. This similar pattern occurs both at the beginning and the end of the poem. What we therefore see at this cognitive metaphorical level is foregrounding in both the form of deviation and repetition.

LIGHT IS MALE/LIGHT IS A TRAVELLER since he 'walks' and 'scatters' (3). He is like a sower in a ploughed field, moving steadily from one end of a furrow to the other, only here he is not a sower of seeds but of poems. Implicit are, therefore, the metaphors POEMS ARE SEEDS and CITIES ARE FIELDS. Since seeds are the essence of life's beginnings, represented linguistically in expressions such as 'a budding career', 'the green shoots of youth', etc., I am tempted to take the inductive leap in my own cognitive meaning-making mind and say that POEMS ARE SEEDS can allude to the notion that poetry is the essence of life itself. Perhaps coincidentally, and perhaps not, this idea was prevalent in the ideology of the 'art for art's sake' movement which was active at the time cummings was writing. Also, if CITIES ARE FIELDS, as stated above, and cumming's city here is quite clearly female, confirmed by the pronouns in lines 7 and 30, then there is the overriding cognitive cultural metaphor at work here that WOMAN IS FIELD. This taps into all of our cultural cognitive knowledge. From a Western cultural perspective, 'woman as earth' or 'mother earth' is a concept that has been embodied in our Western cultural knowledge since our Greek ancestors worshipped Ge, goddess of the earth, and later, Demeter, goddess of the harvest. Juxtapose this with masculine creations associated with light such as Uranus (heaven) and later Apollo (sun) as well as the lesser known god of light, Aether. In addition to the 'seeder' connotation, this also supports my male 'light the sower' claim.

In addition to the above, however, there is a much more explicit cognitive metaphor at work in this poem: one might even see it as the overriding cognitive metaphor. As mentioned earlier, the poem is essentially about 'a day in the life of a city', more abstractly portrayed as a progression through space from the beginning to the end. Almost all of these observations are supported and triggered linguistically in the text. For example, the verbs 'walks' (3), 'wakes' (6), 'goes forth' (11) and 'walks' once again in the final line (33) all support the notion of progression through space. That space is structurally demarcated with 'dawn' (2 and 9), 'day' (16), 'dusk' (24) and 'dark' (26), which act like milestones on the pathway of time. Metaphors that are triggered by these words are first and foremost DAYS ARE JOURNEYS, which at a more abstract level alludes to A DAY IS A LIFE and perhaps, by extension, A YEAR IS A LIFE. All of these are embodied in Lakoff and Johnson's structural cognitive metaphor *par excellence*: LIFE IS A JOURNEY. This metaphor has embodied in its structure the abstract notion of PATH which as we have seen is one of the many abstract cognitive constructs that belong to the domain of image schemata. This finds form particularly in the SOURCE-PATH-GOAL image-schematic construction. This structure is linear, but cummings seems to offer us much more than that. We can say that in the opening lines 'the hours rise up' (1) is the SOURCE in the image-schematic projection. As we have seen UP IS GOOD: it represents daylight and at a more abstract level the notions of renewal and birth. The main bulk of the poem is the PATH part of the image schema. This is also supported by the aforementioned verbs of movement as well as the reflective stanza involving the man looking into the mirror. This is a stationary moment at the centre of the poem that is perhaps meant to reflect mid-life: a philosophical period where hopes for the future, turn into memories of the past. The GOAL part of the structure takes place in the final stanza with the clause 'the hours descend' (31). Here, DOWN IS BAD as the city 'is dark' (26) and 'sleeps with death upon her mouth' (30). Does the poem end with death then? Is there no hope? Is life a linear path with a definitive starting point and an equally definitive end, like the structure of a day? Just as we draw on our world knowledge that it is not only darkness that follows light (dawn leading inevitably to dusk) but also, that light follows darkness (dusk inevitably leading to dawn), so, we sense some alternative, some escape hatch to break the inevitability of this linearity. The final word in the final line of any poem arguably occupies the most prominent, most foregrounded place. So what does cummings offer us? Gods? Heavens? Immortality? None of these. Instead, he gives us 'poems', and as we have seen POEMS ARE SEEDS and we know from our world knowledge 'seeds are new life'. At this cognitive level cummings, or at least the speaking voice in the poem, seems to be saying that poetry and art itself offer some kind of life beyond life. The message then in this poem might be that life is not simply linear, as expressed in the LIFE IS A JOURNEY metaphor, rather life – like the world around us: our days, seasons and years – is about renewal: new art, new hope, new life. In short, LIFE IS A CIRCLE.

Now that this cognitive part of the analysis is complete we need to ask ourselves whether it has added anything to the literary linguistic analysis and whether we have found more fundamental evidence in support of Kennedy's (1996) claim that cummings' poetry has a 'simple, coherent, view at its centre'? The final answer will be up to you, but I would argue that the discovery and the subsequent bringing to light of the basic, yet essential, abstract PATH metaphor running though the very heart of this poem, both in its default guise of LIFE IS A JOURNEY and its variant of LIFE IS A CIRCLE, has gone some way to doing just that.

Conclusion

The integration of cognitive linguistic implements into the traditional literary linguistic toolkit of the stylistician, interspersed throughout with rhetorical observations, may have succeeded in offering a richer account than a traditional stylistic analysis might. The general methodological expansion from language and style to cognition is, I believe, not a threat to more traditional methods of stylistic analysis – no more so than the arrival of literary stylistics was a threat to the style figures of classical rhetoric. Rather it is an opportunity to develop and thus enhance our stylistic analytic framework. All we are doing is following Aristotle's sound advice in his *Art of Rhetoric* to attempt to employ 'all the available means of (stylistic) method' (1959). Can there be anything reproachable in that? Progress, in any domain, can be an uncertain and unsettling business, but it need not be viewed in solely negative terms. As cummings (1944) himself once famously noted in somewhat oxymoronic fashion in his poem 'pity this monster, manunkind' – 'progress is a comfortable disease'.

Note
I am indebted to Helle K. Hochscheid for bringing this wonderful cummings poem (her favourite) to my attention. For this reason, I dedicate this chapter to her.

Megametaphorical Mappings and the Landscapes of Canadian Poetry

Ernestine Lahey

Through the centuries philosophers, painters, writers and poets have made use of landscape as a metaphor to put across a particular message or idea. For instance, in his dream allegory *The Pilgrim's Progress*, John Bunyan uses landscape as a metaphor for life. Thus the hero Christian passes through metaphorical landscapes significantly named the Slough of Despond, the Valley of Humiliation and the Delectable Mountains.

In continuance of this literary tradition, Canadian cultural historians and critics have frequently noted that in present-day fiction and poetry the lonely and rugged landscape of the country often symbolizes the history and the character of its people in that it is strongly associated with the early pioneer spirit and the process of nation-building.

Obviously because she had developed a fascination for this cultural and literary phenomenon, Ernestine Lahey carried out her doctoral research by making a systematic linguistic and stylistic analysis of 150 poems by three twentieth-century English-speaking Canadian poets: Al Purdy, Milton Acorn and Alden Nowlan. In order to assess the precise nature of the landscape-consciousness of these poets as well as that of their readers, she attempted, with the help of Text World Theory, to reconstruct the enabling cognitive space created by both poets and readers of how in modern Canadian poetry the rural landscape is used as a metaphor of building a cultural and national identity.

The outcomes of this earlier research project laid a firm foundation for the present chapter in which the author focuses on four basic metaphorical sequences which manifest themselves in the works of all three poets and which prove to lend solid support to earlier claims made by a variety of scholars and critics that there exists a reciprocal symbolic relationship between the Canadian landscape, the literature it engendered and the intersubjective cultural identity of the Canadian people.

The author's analysis shows that the core meanings of these longer metaphorical sequences cannot be related direct to clearly recognisable structures on phrase or sentence level. Typically, they accumulate as sustained undercurrents. Therefore, one of the many benefits of this research is that the author's sensitive stylistic analysis of the basic metaphorical patterns in this poetry supports the hypothesis of the originator of the text-worlds approach, the late Paul Werth, that 'sustained metaphors' or 'megametaphors', as he called them, 'represent the most proto- typical and primitive frames in our culture and are the basic building-blocks of our world view' (1999: 328). At this point Lahey rightly observes that the assumption that these recurrent underlying metaphorical structures reflect the fundamental culturally specific knowledge frames as well as the shared values of a society may well provide a powerful incentive to research which seeks to relate the production and reception of literary texts to their relevant cultural contexts. Since the goal of such research verges on that of cognitive anthropology, I feel tempted to introduce the term *anthropological stylistics* (by analogy with anthro- pological linguistics) which seeks to reveal culturally specific meaning sequences.

Peter Verdonk

Towards a Poetics of Landscape

Scholars of Canadian literature have long recognised that the establishment of a national literature for Canada has traditionally both influenced and been informed by the concurrent process of nation building that began in earnest in post-Confederation Canada, a process that itself relied on the explication and promotion of a landscape ethos that would serve as the hallmark of the Canadian identity (Russell 1966: 239; Keith 1985: 13; Garrett-Petts 1988: 920; Schafer 1995: 9; Angus 1997; Corse 1997). The result of this mutual reliance was the develop- ment of a national literature for Canada in which the Canadian landscape found itself extensively represented. Accordingly, much has been written about the presence of landscapes in Canadian literature (see, for example, Jones 1970; Frye 1971; Marshall 1979; Norcliffe and Simpson-Housley 1992; Atwood 1996; Glick- man 1998; New 1997). However, no attempt has yet been made to explicate the precise manner in which these literary landscapes are linguistically determined, or to provide a systematic account of how these landscapes function stylistically. This chapter represents a contribution to a poetics of landscape that will seek to fill this need.

Following research which outlined some of the ways in which poetic landscapes are cued linguistically (see Lahey 2006), the present discussion turns to a con- sideration of how these landscapes function metaphorically within their respec- tive discourses. Drawing on my earlier (Lahey 2005) Text World Theory analysis of 150 poems by three twentieth-century English-Canadian poets – Al Purdy (1918–2000), Milton Acorn (1923–86) and Alden Nowlan (1933–83) – the findings below reveal four key metaphorical patterns explicit in the works of all three poets. The identification of these metaphorical patterns provides transparent and systematic analytical support to the claims of interdependence between land- scape, literature and cultural/national identity made by some of the scholars cited above. It furthermore reveals the aesthetic import of literary landscapes, too often regarded merely as backdrops against which the stories of literary texts are enacted.

In the traditional literary critical distinction between setting and plot, the stylistic distinction between foreground and background, and the cognitive linguistic distinction between figure and ground, it is the plot, the foreground, the figure that have typically enjoyed theoretical pride of place, since these represent the most dynamic elements of a text-world, and therefore attract the attention of the reader (Ungerer and Schmid 1996: 156–204). Text World Theory centralizes the world-building process through which the spatio-temporal contexts of literary texts are negotiated and updated, thereby providing an ideal analytical framework for careful examination of the background spaces against which a text's foregrounded elements are in fact made meaningful.

The Metaphorical Functions of Poetic Landscapes

Analysis of the 150 poems on which this study's findings are based was carried out using the cognitive and experientialist theory of discourse known as Text World Theory (Werth 1999; Gavins 2001, 2007). The basic premise of Text World Theory is that all discourses are characterized by the construction of a set of richly defined conceptualized spaces known as 'worlds', of which three levels are recognised. The discourse-world is the conceptualisation of the immediate spatio-temporal context in which the discourse takes place, and contains at least two discourse participants (one speaker or writer and one or more listeners or readers) and a naturally occurring language event (i.e. discourse). The text-world is the representation of the subject matter of the discourse and relies for its construction on a text-driven process whereby linguistic cues activate relevant general or specific knowledge upon which further inferences about the parameters of the text-world space may be drawn. 'World-building' propositions in the text provide deictic and referential information which partially establish the text-world's situational variables (time, location, entities and the interrelationships between them), while information pertaining to the actions, mental processes, states and attributes of entities in the text-world is provided by 'function-advancing propositions', which may be path-expressions, denoting actions or processes, or modifications, advancing description of entities in the text-world.

Finally, sub-worlds arise as the result of perceived deictic or modal shifts away from the parameters of the matrix world out of which they arise. Flashbacks, for instance, are treated as prompting the construction of new deictic spaces which contrast with their matrix text-world spaces for the variable of time. Modal world switches are cued by propositions which are modalized according to the conventional separation between deontic, boulomaic and epistemic contexts, and account for such things as expressions of beliefs, desires and obligations. At all levels of discourse, the activation of participant knowledge frames contributes crucially to the world-building process.

Metaphor is classified as a sub-world in the Text World Theory framework, although Werth (1999) is never specific about precisely what type of sub-world metaphor represents. However, insofar as metaphor sets up a context which is psychologically 'remote' in relation to some (presumed) equivalent literal expression, one might classify metaphor as a type of epistemic modal sub-world (Werth 1997; Gavins 2001: 113). Werth's treatment of metaphor, which is in line with contemporary cognitivist accounts such as Lakoff and Johnson (1980) and Lakoff and Turner (1989), focuses not on the individual 'surface' metaphors of a discourse, but on sustained or extended 'megametaphors' which result from a succession of related instances of individual surface metaphors (Werth 1999: 319). Megametaphors, according to Werth, represent 'the most prototypical and primitive [knowledge] frames in our culture' and provide an overarching metaphorical sub-text which draws on the available cultural knowledge of the discourse participants in communicating something of the general 'gist' of the discourse (Werth 1999: 323). This understanding of metaphor as a device by which the cultural norms and values of a society are communicated is of considerable value for studies that seek to situate the production and reception of literary texts within their relevant cultural contexts.

Analysis of the sample of 150 poems revealed a number of distinct megametaphors mapping a relationship between the represented poetic landscape and some other aspect of, or entity within, the poetic text-world. Although some patterns were specific to the works of individual poets, my concern was with those landscape-based metaphors which were common to works by all three. My analysis revealed the following four metaphors to be especially prominent:

1. The external landscape is a metaphorical representation of the internal landscape (self) of the poetic persona (EXTERNAL AS INTERNAL).
2. The landscape is a metaphorical representation of a character in the text-world (the landscape is personified) (LANDSCAPE AS CHARACTER).
3. A character other than the poetic persona is described metaphorically as if he/she were a landscape (CHARACTER AS LANDSCAPE).
4. The poem itself is a metaphorical representation of a landscape (POEM AS LANDSCAPE).

In metaphors belonging to the first category, description of the poetic persona's state of mind relies on landscape as a source or target domain in the metaphorical mapping. My analysis has shown that in most cases, though the description of the poetic persona as landscape may ultimately be interpreted as a description of his state of mind, this comparison is usually achieved through a mapping with some aspect of his physical body. In Milton Acorn's 'Music point', for instance, landscape, history and the poetic persona are implicated in a metaphor which maps the beating of a traditional First Nations drum onto the beating of the poetic persona's own heart. The final stanza of the poem makes this relationship explicit:

> Thus I hear a single drum
> Above the sound of ripples meeting

The land; am frozen for a moment
Till I know it for my own heart beating.
(Acorn 1988: 28)

In this example, the sound of the drum seems at first to come from the land itself ('I hear a single drum/*Above the sound of ripples meeting*') until the persona recognises the sound for '[his] own heart beating'. Through the association of the drum first with the landscape and then with the poetic persona's body, the poetic persona's understanding of the relationship between himself, his heritage and his environment is made manifest. Likewise, in 'Live with me on earth under the invisible daylight moon', also by Acorn, the love that the poetic persona feels for his addressee is expressed via a metaphor that equates their emotional union with mingling shadows, as seen in the line 'walk with me and sometimes cover your shadow with mine' (Acorn 1983: 98). Again in this example, the mindset of the poetic persona with regard to his lover is revealed through a metaphor utilizing a land-based source domain.

Metaphors which map landscape to poetic persona are also explicit in the work of Al Purdy, who likewise achieves this mapping through reference to some aspect of the poetic persona's body. Purdy often describes the poetic persona's organs – typically his brain – in landscape terms, and in one instance (see 3 below) suggests a poetic persona who ingests landscape. In each case below, the specific surface metaphor that contributes to the realisation of the broader EXTERNAL AS INTERNAL megametaphor has been specified in BOLD:

1. 'Listen to your blood negotiate/interior roads in the *brain's* back country' ('Ten thousand pianos' (Purdy 1976: 96, emphasis added)) A BRAIN IS A COUNTRY
2. 'Canada/inside the *brain's* bone country.../carve up my *brain* into small ivory fossils' ('Joint account' (Purdy 1970: 66, emphasis added)). A BRAIN IS A COUNTRY
3. 'After a while the eyes *digest* a country .../a mapmaker's vision/... spurts *through blood stream*/campaigns in *the lower intestine*' ('Transient' (Purdy 2000: 95, emphasis added)) A LANDSCAPE IS A HUMAN BODY

At other times Purdy envisions the poetic persona and his/her ancestors as mythically or symbolically connected to the landscape in a manner reminiscent of Acorn's 'Music point', above:

4. 'Standing knee-deep in the joined earth/the hunters silent and women/ bending over dark fires./I hear their broken consonants' ('Remains of an Indian village' (Purdy 2000: 51)) A PERSON'S CULTURAL HERITAGE IS LANDSCAPE

Of the three poets, it is Nowlan who tends least towards this focus on the physical body in metaphors which map landscape and poetic persona, instead preferring metaphors linking landscape and mind directly. Nowlan is particularly interested in the figure of a poetic persona who compares his childhood self to his adult self using a HOMETOWN IS CHILDHOOD metaphor. In some cases, as with example 6, below, the HOMETOWN IS CHILDHOOD metaphor is realized in part through the title; in Nowlan's 'You can't get there from here', the deictics 'there' and 'here' must be understood as at once spatial, temporal and psychological, as the poetic persona reflects both on his childhood home and his former childhood self. The same is true for example 7, in which the 'here' refers both to Nowlan's eventual home in New Brunswick (having been born and raised in the neighbouring province of Nova Scotia) and to his adulthood as conceptualized in contrast to the implied 'there' of his childhood:

5. 'It is nowhere so dark as/in the country where I was born/... and it wasn't until tonight/... I began to realize/how much I was afraid' ('The Mosherville Road' (Nowlan 1996: 60)) A HOMETOWN IS A CHILDHOOD
6. 'the road maps indicate/that I live less than/five miles/from my birthplace./ There are truer charts' ('What colour is Manitoba' (Nowlan 1977: 41–3)) A HOMETOWN IS A CHILDHOOD
7. 'You can't get there from here' (title); 'lilac was the smell/of my childhood, a ... smell that sets colts galloping/along cool rivers in my mind' ('You can't get there from here' (Nowlan 1996: 155)) A HOMETOWN IS A CHILDHOOD
8. 'here/where there is no/defense against/the night/I am no longer/afraid of/the dark' ('Sleeping out' (Nowlan 1967: 31)) A HOMETOWN IS A CHILDHOOD

Landscapes may not always map the states of minds of the poetic personas in the poems, but may sometimes be involved in metaphors which relate landscape to other characters. It was found that these metaphors are available in two forms in the poems analysed: either (1) landscape is treated as though it were a character in the text-world (it is personified), hence LANDSCAPE AS CHARACTER, or (2) a character in the text-world is described as though he/she were landscape, hence CHARACTER AS LANDSCAPE. LANDSCAPE AS CHARACTER, or personification, was the more common metaphor of the two in the poetry of all three poets, which is unremarkable given the commonality of personification metaphors generally (Lakoff and Johnson 1980: 33). The prevalence of the LANDSCAPE AS CHARACTER metaphor throughout the sample means that a complete list of examples of its occurrence cannot be provided here; however, one example of the metaphor as it is realized in each poet's work is provided below:

9. **Al Purdy**: 'Waves ... rant now/on the still listening beach/pounding motherless bergs/to death on rocks' ('Still life in a tent' (Purdy 1967: 68–9)) AN ICEBERG IS A PERSON
10. **Milton Acorn**: 'the clouds/growing and raising heads to look at themselves,/ opening mouths to say what should be said' ('If you're stronghearted' (Acorn 1983: 150)) A CLOUD IS A PERSON

11. **Alden Nowlan**: 'the cornflowers are not yet/aware they will die soon' ('Cornflowers' (Nowlan 1971: 109)) A CORNFLOWER IS A PERSON

In the above examples, the LANDSCAPE AS CHARACTER megametaphor is manifested in surface metaphors in which only particular elements of the text-world landscape are personified. In most cases in the poems analysed, metaphors which implicate one element of the landscape in the mapping between landscape and character do not occur singly, but throughout the poem, with different landscape elements serving as target domains. Hence, the broader LANDSCAPE IS CHARACTER megametaphor is realized through the accumulation of these numerous X ARE PEOPLE metaphors, in which 'x' represents one entity in the landscape.

In the third category of metaphor outlined above, CHARACTER AS LANDSCAPE, a character in the text-world of the poem is described using land-based metaphors. Again, this mapping is usually achieved through an association between the landscape and the character's physical body or some aspect of it. As with the LANDSCAPE AS CHARACTER category discussed above, the prevalence of this metaphor throughout the sample of poems analysed means that an exhaustive account cannot be provided here. However, one example is again provided from each poet's work with the underlying surface metaphor specified:

12. **Al Purdy**: 'as if she were a stone or a fallen tree,/her temperature the same as the landscape's' ('At Evergreen Cemetery' (Purdy 1973: 56)) A HUMAN BODY IS A LANDSCAPE
13. **Milton Acorn**: 'His beard may be a sprucetree upside down' ('The figure in the landscape made the landscape' (Acorn 1983: 152)) A HUMAN BODY IS A LANDSCAPE
14. **Alden Nowlan**: 'your body consists of so many provinces' ('A song to be whispered' (Nowlan: 1996: 154)) A HUMAN BODY IS A LANDSCAPE

In example 12, the poetic persona visits the grave site of his deceased mother, likening her body to 'a stone or a fallen tree'. In 13, the physical appearance of the poetic persona is partly achieved through the description of his beard as an upside-down spruce tree. Finally, in 14, the body of the poetic persona's lover is a nation of many provinces; this last example is interesting not only for the CHARACTER AS LANDSCAPE metaphor at work within it, but also for its allusion to Canada in its choice of the word 'provinces'. Although Canada is not the only nation whose secondary levels of government are designated provinces, the reader who is aware that he/she is reading a poem by a Canadian poet and who is privy to the relevant knowledge about Canada will likely infer that the landscape to which the character of this poem is being compared is a Canadian one.

In some instances, the textual cues for both LANDSCAPE AS CHARACTER and CHARACTER AS LANDSCAPE metaphors appear to be the same. In Milton Acorn's 'On speaking Ojibway', for instance, an association between landscape and heritage is made which results in the presence of both LANDSCAPE AS CHARACTER and CHARACTER AS LANDSCAPE metaphors, each cued by the same unit of text. Consider the first two stanzas of the poem:

In speaking Ojibway you've got to watch the clouds
turning, twisting, raising their heads
to look at each other and you.
You've got to have their thoughts for them
and thoughts there'll be which would never
exist had there been no clouds.

Best speak in the woods beside a lake
getting in time with the watersounds.
Let vibrations of waves sing right through you
and always be alert for the next word
which will be yours and also the water's.
                                                (Acorn 1975: 110)

In this example, the addressee-character invoked through the use of the generalized second-person pronoun 'you', the land ('the clouds', 'the woods', 'a lake') and the Ojibway language are described as in union with each other. As the clouds rely on the addressee for expression of their thoughts in Ojibway ('You've got to have their thoughts for them'), so the addressee must rely on the clouds to have the thoughts that can be spoken ('and thoughts there'll be which would never/exist had there been no clouds'). Thus the land and the Ojibway-speaking addressee become a unified embodiment, the clouds the thinking component and the addressee the component for expressing those thoughts. In the second stanza this unification of addressee and land through language continues; now the land speaks but its words are indistinguishable from the addressee's ('the next word/which will be yours but also the water's').

In this example the overriding mapping is not, strictly speaking, between character and landscape, but between *language* and landscape. The landscape-character relationship is resolved in this instance through the construction of a metaphor which nonetheless implicates the character by virtue of the fact that the character is speaking the language. The LANGUAGE AS LANDSCAPE metaphor serves to associate landscape and character in such a way that it is impossible to say whether the landscape is being described as if it were a character (i.e. whether it is being personified), or a character is being described in terms of landscape, since the overriding metaphor means that both mappings are equally possible. This type of relationship between character and landscape unified under some broader megametaphorical construction is one seen in several other examples, and especially, though not exclusively, in those poems which draw on ancestry and history; it is particularly prevalent in the poetry of Al Purdy, whose tendency towards attending to such themes in his work has been noted (Duffy 1971: 25; Winkler 1988; Atwood 1996: 112).

A fourth pattern of metaphor identified in the poems analysed was the POEM AS

LANDSCAPE metaphor, in which the metaphorical mapping is between the text-world landscape and *the poem itself.* Since this type of mapping implicates the text under consideration, this type of metaphor, though it necessarily occurs at the text-world level, appears to occur at the discourse-world level because it makes reference to the discourse itself. In many cases, deixis drives the construction of the metaphor, and may do so independently or in conjunction with cues provided by the poem's formal features (i.e. the spatial patterning of the poem's lines and stanzas).

Although deixis, for most linguists, encompasses a great deal more than spatial deixis (see, for example, Stockwell 2002: 45–6), it is spatial deixis which is of primary importance for the current discussion. Spatial deixis is essential for indicating the placement of entities in relation to each other, the poetic persona and other characters in the poetic text-world. Spatial deictics may be locative adverbs such as 'here' or 'there', locative adverbials (usually prepositional phrases) such as 'in the mountains' and 'at the entrance', demonstratives such as 'this' and 'that' and certain egocentric verbs such as 'come' and 'go' and 'give' and 'take' (Bühler 1982; Levinson 1983; Green 1992, 1995; Stockwell 2002: 46). Most examples of spatial deictic expressions in the sample are conventional and do not demand special attention. However, some examples stand out for their exploitation of readers' expectations about grammatical conventions and/or spatial relationships, and are foregrounded as a result. One such example is Acorn's description of wind 'like a train *from no direction*' in his 'Lee side in a gale', which captures the all-encompassing nature of the wind by capitalising both on the reader's expectations for which elements typically follow the preposition 'from', and his/her understanding of paths and goals for moving objects (Acorn 1983: 32, emphasis added).

A second example of foregrounded spatial deixis from Purdy's 'Archaeology of snow' exploits the orienting effects of the proximal locative adverb 'here' and the world-building abilities of poetic form:

```
Bawdy tale at first
              what happened
   in the snow
   what happens
              in bed or anywhere I said
                            oh Anna
              here –
                    here –
   here –
        here –
            here –
              (Purdy 1970: 30–4)
```

In this example the placement of the words 'here –/here –/here –/here –/here –' on the page is suggestive of the marks left in the snow by the lovemaking of the poetic persona and his lover, 'Anna'. But the choice of word here is also significant, for 'here' is a deictic; it *points* and it does so from some embodied and egocentric zero-point or *origo*, in this case the poetic persona's (Bühler 1982). The effect of this combination of form and deixis is to force the reader to embrace the poetic persona's stance and to see the world from his perspective; in this stance the reader may see what is referred to by 'here' (Green 1992, 1995; Semino 1992). In the actual situation of the discourse-world, of course, the reader's gaze is directed only at the text; the text then itself serves as a representation of that which is perceived in the text-world – in this case the impressions left in the snow. One of the effects of the POEM AS LANDSCAPE metaphor is thus to allow the reader to experience something in his/her discourse-world – the text – in a manner similar to the way in which the poetic persona experiences something in the text-world.

Another example of the POEM AS LANDSCAPE metaphor, also from Purdy, can be found in 'The country of the young'. The opening stanza to that poem reads:

> A. Y. Jackson for instance
> 83 years old
> halfway up a mountain
> standing in a patch of snow
> to paint a picture that says
> "Look here
> You've never seen this country
> It's not the way you thought it was
> Look again"

The poem then ends as follows:

> ...an old man's voice
> in the country of the young
> that says
> "Look here –"
> (Purdy 2000: 126)

In this example, as in 'Archaeology of snow' above, the deixis serves to orient the reader according to the origo of a character in the text-world, in this case the persona, who is the addressee of the directive 'Look here –' from Group of Seven painter A. Y. Jackson. 'Look here' in this example works on several levels: look at 'this country' (Canada), look at an A. Y. Jackson canvas which, as a representation of Canadian landscape, also invites one to 'Look here' (at Canada), and 'look here' as an idiomatic scolding directive (as in 'Now look here young man'). Finally, 'Look here –' employs the imperative to invite the reader to look 'here', *at the text* from a discourse-world perspective at a poem that, like an A. Y. Jackson painting, provides a vision of 'this country/it's not the way you thought it was'. The reference to the artistic legacy of the Group of Seven is significant here, the archetypal subject matter for this early-twentieth-century Canadian school being uninhabited Canadian landscapes (Silcox 2003).

In some cases deixis works to cue a discourse-world-level association between poem and landscape which speaks to something about the poet himself. In Nowlan's 'Sleeping out', the lines 'here/where there is no/defense against/the night/I am no longer/afraid of/the dark' may be interpreted as simply describing the poetic persona's lack of fear about sleeping outdoors (Nowlan 1967: 31). However, I argued above that these lines may also cue a HOMETOWN IS A CHILDHOOD metaphor which serves the broader EXTERNAL AS INTERNAL mega-metaphor in which a relationship between a poetic persona and a landscape is mapped. Such an interpretation relies on three factors: the presence and activation of knowledge about Nowlan's childhood move from Nova Scotia to New Brunswick; an assumption that the poetic persona is a counterpart of the poet (one which is not unreasonable for most lyric poetry); and an interpretation of the deictic 'here' as spatial ('here' in New Brunswick versus 'there' in Nova Scotia), temporal ('here' in adulthood versus 'there' in childhood) and psychological ('here' in the current mindset versus 'there' in the childhood mindset). However, a third interpretation of these lines as contributing to the POEM AS LANDSCAPE metaphor is also possible, and again relies on knowledge about Nowlan's life and, in particular, his development as a young writer in rural Nova Scotia.

Michael Oliver addresses the incompatibility between Nowlan's working-class maritime upbringing and his early literary ambitions (Nowlan wrote his first poem at the age of 11) when he says: 'Being a writer in Hants County, Nova Scotia, in the 1940s was, by definition, a secret occupation. [...] It was a tough, puritanically masculine world ... a world where literacy – let alone literature – was useless' (Oliver 1991: 3). The sentiment is echoed by Nowlan, who refers to himself as the product of a society of 'psychosomatic mutes', and a culture 'that fears self-discovery and self-revelation as it fears physical nakedness' (Nowlan 1978: 87). Consequently, for the young Nowlan, literature was associated with the forbidden; even in adulthood, his shame and embarrassment was such that he 'developed a habit of quickly covering his work whenever someone would come into the room where he was writing' (Toner 2000: 51).

Although Nowlan may have been embarrassed about his writing, he was not embarrassed in it, and was unafraid of exposing himself in his poems (Guns 2004). Thus when Nowlan writes 'here/where there is no/defense against/the night/I am no longer/afraid of/the dark', 'here' is not just the dark landscape of the text-world, nor is it simply the temporal and psychological past of Nowlan's childhood. 'Here' also refers to the poem, and the 'I' to a counterpart poet. Although the Nowlan in the discourse world is vulnerable and insecure, 'defenseless' against the attitudes and values of those who would see his poetic self-expression as a weakness, in his poems, where his true self is most honestly expressed, Nowlan finds himself 'unafraid of the dark'.

The POEM AS LANDSCAPE relationship appears at first to be problematic for current Text World Theory which views the three levels of discourse as hierarchically configured such that there is no 'upward access' from the sub-world or text-world levels to the level of the discourse world (Werth 1999: 213–16). What this means is that any reference to the text cannot be a reference to the same text currently under consideration by the discourse participants, since the poetic persona who makes the reference has no access to that text. However, as the above examples demonstrate, the effect of the POEM AS LANDSCAPE metaphor is to implicate the current text in the metaphorical mapping. The problem of access can be resolved in Text World Theory through a consideration of 'transworld identity'.

Transworld identity refers to a mapping between entities in two different worlds, and posits that the existence of 'the same' entities in two or more worlds can be explained by understanding the entities as counterparts of one another (Doležel 1998b: 788–9; Ryan 1991: 52; Werth 1999: 294). Although prototypical transworld identity involves places or characters, in theory transworld identity may exist for all types of entities. In texts which are self-referential, like those cited above, because it is understood that the poetic persona cannot be referring to the text in which he/she is a character, it must be conceded that there exists in the text-world a counterpart of the text currently under consideration. In other words, in each case above, the poem in question may be said to have transworld identity with a counterpart poem in the text-world in which the poetic persona exists. At the discourse-world level, the POEM AS LANDSCAPE megametaphor is perhaps the most powerful of the four sustained metaphors examined here in terms of what the metaphorical sub-text suggests about the relationship between literature and landscape in Canadian literature generally. In its direct association between text and landscape, the POEM AS LANDSCAPE metaphor represents the most explicit metaphorical realisation of the interdependence of landscape, literature and cultural identity in Canadian literature to which its scholars have so often pointed.

Conclusion

My aim in the foregoing analysis has been to reveal some of the most pervasive patterns of landscape metaphors identified in the works of three twentieth-century Canadian poets, and in so doing to move closer to a comprehensive poetics of landscape that considers the ways in which those landscapes are cued linguistically and how they function within a broader aesthetic and cultural framework. The identification of four 'megametaphors' mapping a relationship between the poetic landscape and some other aspect of the poetic text-world provides stylistic support for claims by scholars of Canadian literature about the significance of landscape as a trope in the Canadian literary canon. Furthermore, if, as Werth (1999) suggests, megametaphors represent the most prototypical and primitive of a culture's knowledge frames, the findings presented here suggest that space, place and landscape have been crucial to the process through which Canada has made sense of its own cultural distinctiveness.

Perception and the Lyric: The Emerging Mind of the Poem

Sharon Lattig

Many of the earliest modern stylistic treatments of lyrical poetry focused on formal properties (such as metre and sound patterning). In doing so, they reflected several interlocking influences: concern with the supposed distinctiveness of 'poetic language'; methods in descriptive linguistics; and a sense that stylistics should complement, rather than transform or replace impressionistic literary criticism of the time. Other topics, such as figurative language, parallelism and ambiguity, raised questions more central to interpretation. But until more recent engagements between stylistics and different currents of literary theory, stylistics often left general questions about discourse interpretation to established fields with which stylistics had in any case always been interwoven: literary criticism, cultural history and aesthetics. More recent work in stylistics, however, that combines the ambitions of literary theory with developments in cognitive linguistics, has not only shifted the field to some extent away from formal description, but opened up new interdisciplinary fields for further exploration. Sharon Lattig's chapter extends such avenues of interdisciplinarity. She addresses questions always recognised to be important but constructed differently in the established fields: questions about how a sense of subjectivity is created in lyrical poetry.

Lattig begins by arguing that the notion of a presiding subjectivity has been central to definitions of lyrical poetry, but remained resistant to analysis from different perspectives and across major changes of poetic practice. She points in particular to the historical shift, with literary modernism, from subjectivity viewed as something carried over into writing from oral traditions of a bardic speaker (that had the effect of authorizing or sponsoring perception and reflection) through to something more fragmented and displaced, often reflexive about its own composition.

Lattig's main arguments discuss how far our understanding of the representation of perception, consciousness and subjectivity in lyric poetry can be extended by insights in contemporary neuroscience. To investigate possibilities in this area, Lattig draws particular attention to the idea of 'obscurity', which links perception and interpretive difficulty, and challenges any settled presumption of the poetic mind speaking. Drawing on the formalist concept of foregrounding, the psychological concept of gestalt, and linguistic concepts including deixis, Lattig outlines a view of subjectivity in lyrical poetry that is always what she calls an 'intermediate stage' between the human body alive in a surrounding environment and the apparent self-presence of a speaking poetic persona. Lyrical poetry, for Lattig, achieves its effects by 'enacting a perceiving mind in the stages of cognition that precede self-awareness'.

These are large questions, and there is no scope in the chapter for Lattig to show in detail how that enactment of cognition can be traced in a particular text. Such work remains for others. In the meantime, Lattig's essay identifies two areas for discussion: the value of interdisciplinary work drawing on neuroscience, as further development of the transformation of stylistics already brought about by cognitive linguistics; and analysis of lyrical poetry in terms of how different linguistic devices construct, rather than convey, processes of cognition that appear collectively as poetic consciousness.

Alan Durant

Introduction

The modern lyric is distinguished as a poem of subjectivity, a personal, indeed a private utterance expressive of a sacred vision of individuality. Two centuries past, Hegel (1993) [original 1886] codified the genre in fixing an identifiable subjective presence within it. Like most such absolutist assertions, his claim was called into question by those who believed the lyric to be burdened by the overbearing presence of an empirical author or his sanctioned substitute, the speaker. Postwar poetry and poetics etherealized the subject, recasting it as a voice to loosen the strictures imposed by 'the lyrical interference of the individual as ego' (Olson 1951: 24). Poststructuralism came to regard the poetic voice as disembodied, an airy evanescent vehicle detached from an explicit subjectivity. As a trope, 'voice' serves to emphasise the linguistic materiality of the poetic artefact and thus the semantic fluidity of the poem. Yet the idea of 'voice' also presumes embodiment – a physical instrumentation consisting of a diaphragm, vocal chords, a throat, and a mouth – and therefore an orality that recuperates the premodern lyric singer, a figure who vocalizes sometimes as a mere conveyance, an anonymous *jongleur*, and at others as an implicated and expressive subjectivity.

The determination of expressive source, of who or what speaks in the presentation of a poem and on behalf of whom, remains to a great extent a matter of aesthetic preference. My present aim is to defend in some minimal way the assertion that the term 'lyric' necessarily refers to both of these extreme forms of poetry as well as all positions that might be considered intermediate. The lyric genre, I shall argue, is a continuum embracing degrees of conscious emergence that may or may not evolve self-awareness. It is the enunciation of a mental act recapitulating the same structural dynamic that is deployed within the neurology, and eventually the experience, of perception. At one end of the continuum lie romantic acts of self-expression; at the other are situated the impersonal poems of the contemporary avant-garde.

Perception re-cognized

A generation into the revision to cognitivism, the dominant trend in neuroscience and its sister disciplines has at last admitted the implications of conceiving of the mind as an embedded, embodied and evolved entity. The revolution (which is, as far as I know, unnamed) overturned the cognitivist model of the mind as a machine, a disembodied processor that, like a computer or Turing machine, manipulates symbols representing independent events in the world. The corrections put forth by the new way of thinking are major. As they are apt to seem counter-intuitive to minds schooled on representative epistemologies, they bear reviewing here.

1. The mind is embodied. The mind is a body, and the impulse to separate a non-physical executive mind from a subordinate physicality is ultimately a false one occasioned or at least furthered by the dualistic legacy of Descartes. The division of the *res cogitans* from the *res extensa* maintains a persistent grasp on our imaginations. What I believe to be the weak definition of embodiment follows from a strict materialist stance; it holds that the brain itself is a physical entity – often referred to as a substrate – whose functioning not only corresponds to or causes mental experience, but also constitutes it. (In theorizing the emergence of consciousness, the philosopher John Searle (1992: 111–12) defines and classifies it as a 'causally emergent system feature' of the brain, that is, one that exists as both an effect and a feature of systemic functioning). The mind is also embodied in the sense that the neurological activity of the periphery is part of a single system that includes the central nervous system and influences it. In the strong sense of embodiment, the experience of inhabiting a particular body plays a formative role in cognition (Iverson and Thelen 1999: 19). The actions and the experiences of a specific constrained physicality qualitatively shape the contents of the mind. Each sense of embodiment is significant herein.

2. The mind has evolved and, in the process of evolving, the environment supporting the mind has evolved co-extensively. This fact assumes that mind and environment are mutually co-constructed, meaning that each continuously shapes the other. The evolved organism is constructed (including genetically constructed) within an environment it concurrently constructs. Adaptation consists of the assimilation of environmental flux by an organism within an overarching system that includes the adapting organism. As it is a constituent of an environment, changes within an organism necessarily impact an environment. The dynamic at stake in evolutionary processes presupposes the third assumption – that of embeddedness.

3. Minds are embedded. Differentiating an organism from its environment is a *decision* in the root sense of a severing or a cutting off (after Alfred North

Whitehead 1978), a fiction that serves to enable actions and cognitive activities such as grasping – both the literal and metaphorical varieties. It is not possible to fully distinguish an organism from the encompassing whole in which it develops for the two are never fully distinct from one another (see Oyama 1985). For example, an animal's exchange of oxygen for carbon dioxide is a seamless mutual process of conversion. Its cessation results in organismic death and a qualitatively different integration of the organism into an ecosystem. Often, the points of continuity between an organism and its environment are unavailable perceptually. It is therefore only *apparently* possible to fully distinguish a unit as such from its context and consider it discrete. It is at all times within it and of it. The directionalities of constituting influence between organisms and environments are multiple, and they are constantly engaged. To speak of immediate environing conditions or a singular environment that pertains to an organism is to make an artificial limitation and thus a determination.

4. Perception is inseparable from action. I also take for granted the enactionist stance of the late neuroscientist and Buddhist scholar Francisco Varela. His theory of enactionism incorporates two major premises. The first is that perception and action cannot be disentangled: as he writes, 'Perception consists in perceptually-guided action'. His second tenet holds that active perception is the basis of all 'higher' cognitive functions such as conception and category formation: '... cognitive structures emerge from the recurrent sensorimotor patterns that enable action to be perceptually guided' (Varela *et al.* 1991: 173).

Once the foregoing tenets of perception are acknowledged, and the poem is regarded as a live artefact embodying and inspiring a dynamic akin to a perceptual dynamic, the lyric poem may be understood to construct an embodied mind that emerges from its embeddedness to some extent. This statement suggests a semiotic revision, an altered understanding of language that will be only loosely outlined here. The approach to poetry foregrounded by such a revision is not, strictly speaking, new; it is what attuned readers, as the owners of embedded and embodied minds, do intuitively. Understanding the poem as a perceptual and therefore a cognitive emergence from embeddedness does, however, suggest a shift of analytical emphasis as well as a basis for considering the validity and the interrelations of extreme forms of lyric poetry. It also assumes that the cognitive processes transpiring for the reader are homologous to those transpiring for the writer.

Obscurity or the Poem as an Environment

In theorising poetic obscurity, a collection of subtly nuanced terms has evolved that implicate perceptual functioning. In addition to 'obscurity' itself (implying a darkening), 'opacity' (meaning not transmitting light) suggests the perceptual occlusion Orpheus, as the figure of the poet, is asked to tolerate. Complementing these terms is another set designating the logical effect of occlusion–disorientation. Empson's 'ambiguity', Bernadette Mayer's 'bewilderment', de Man's 'undecidability', the lingering modernist 'indeterminacy' and the general 'equivocation' further embroil perception because they imply a hesitation to act and to consummate, or fully accomplish, the perceptual process. As previously mentioned, in Varela's radical understanding of organismic functioning, action is both an integral component of perception and its *raison d'être* (Varela *et al.* 1991: 173).

Given the amount of critical attention a set of concepts like obscurity has received within the twentieth century, the phenomenon would seem to exist predominantly, or even exclusively, as an effect of modernist or postmodernist poetry. When obscurity is considered to be a recent phenomenon, it is often linked to an ethos of detachment, or alienation. While indeterminacy indeed thrives within poetic expression of the modernist and postmodernist eras, obscurity in lyric pre-exists self-conscious movement-making in art. (One might adduce courtly alienation, the metaphysical conceit or the non-referentiality of music itself as pre-existing vehicles of obscurity.) It is not in any event controversial that lyric skews towards the non-discursive, the non-expository and does not, as a rule, stoop to explain itself. John Stuart Mill's (1965: 46) caricature of the lyric poem as an 'utterance that is overheard' implies that the genre may encompass even inarticulate mumblings, to invoke the ideological extreme that is the expressionist reduction. To claim that obscurity boasts a centrality within the lyric genre is to reiterate the rather conservative assertion made by structuralist critic Jonathan Culler (1981: 178–9) in appropriating Wallace Stevens' version of obscurity, 'resistance', to make it one of four defining criteria for the lyric poem. Stevens conceived of resistance as a condition to be transcended: 'Poetry must resist the intelligence almost successfully', he writes aphoristically (1957: 197), suggesting that there must be a final capitulation of the poem's obscurity to the lucidity afforded by the comprehending intellect. Culler accordingly opposes 'recuperation' to resistance in setting up a dyadic schema that suggests an emergence forestalling the dead end of obscurantism. He is not alone in assuming that obscurity is a necessary precondition within the poem. The lyric critic Daniel Tiffany asks '... what precisely does obscurity yield in the act of reading – in the absence of clear, cognitive meaning – if not a sense, strange indeed, of poetic *materials*' (2001: 83). The 'out-of-the-ordinary' quality of poetic language may be conferred by any of a number of technical and linguistic conventions: enjambment, line breaks, collage, mélange, elision and liaison, allusion, mixed discourses, disarranged syntax, vague antecedents, conceit, repetition, parallelism, subject/object confusion, strange diction and, above all, sound comprise but a partial compendium of techniques serving to preserve the preconditions or raw materials of decisiveness.

Obscure or opaque writings, those in which meaning is least likely to yield to arrest, tend to evince and to invite theories of language that emphasize its materiality, and the material coextensiveness of the signifier and the signified is precisely what is at stake here. In the early twentieth century, structural linguistics was instrumental in emphasizing the relational nature of meaning made within a system of signification (de Saussure 1916: 165–6). While the insight that meaning arises relationally, as between signifiers, was pivotal, it bears supplementation if semiotics and poetics are to be accountable to basic biological functioning. Given the mutual cross-constitution of organism and environment, any apparently discrete entity must consist within itself of other constituting, and therefore extant, entities; by simply existing, it subsumes a limitless web of embodied relation. If one is to regard language in a material sense, then the word must subsume a range of potential denotative and connotative significance that in turn subsumes a continuum of potential lexical meaning. Obscurity is a symptom of the *embeddedness* of the signifier; it is lexical to the extent that words refer beyond themselves in a chain of constituting effect that is without end. Words therefore embody their denotations and connotations and thus a lingering sense of potentiality. Especially in poetry, the linguistic unit exists in the fullness of its evocative power, bringing into the present the totality of its past experience, its accruals and purgings, expansions, revisions, scars, what corresponds to its genetic and, in turn, its evolutionary memory.

In presenting what has not yet been determined, the lyric renders the fullness of its supporting context rather than masking it. A constituting environment is admitted into the poem as a consequence of obscurity and as a reflection of the poem's rendering of an embodied voice. In restoring language's full functional, that is semantic, potential into the milieu of the poem, poetic obscurity puts language into epistemological and ontological alignment with a theory of embedded cognition and thereby makes possible the inference of the immediate or more extensive conditions embedding each utterance. It is my premise that the obscurity of the poetic artefact mirrors the elusive preconditions of perceptual awareness (and therefore of certainty), that what are invisible are the ways that we embody the ramifying system that supports us. Lyric embodies its performance, a mandate I am taking literally to make an homologous connection between a neurological physical embodiment and the poem. In the myth of Orpheus, the mandate that Eurydice must follow her husband as they climb from out of the depths of Hades and that he must trust implicitly in her proximity, serves to obscure her – the object of his poeticizing – from his view. The condition that Eurydice must follow her husband functions as a trope for the couple's implicit yet tenuous continuity, which must be acknowledged symbolically as long as they remain in the realm in which a greater order holds sway over human agency. The test of Orpheus's faith in a logic that is not immediately apparent to him is a hard lesson in the mysterious interconnectedness of all things. It assumes the truth that his bride is with him despite the fact that her presence cannot be empirically verified. Obscurity is a symptom of the poet's embeddedness, of the fact that within the poem the full constituting environment is both present and imperceptibly continuous.

The lyric feature of obscurity is then both an index of the poem's perceptual investment and a functional presence or 'font' from which consciousness, and perhaps self-consciousness, might arise. As it reflects (and as we shall see, effects) connectedness, lyric obscurity may become practically inexhaustible – the *raison* for the poem's durability. The assertions of the organism, verbal or otherwise, alter the constituting environment, constantly changing the texture of obscurity. The presence of Eurydice that pre-exists Orpheus's determining gaze also finally survives it, though differently. The fluid semiotic dynamic at play in lyric is therefore not the oscillating motion of reference suggested by the amplifications of Derridean post-structuralism. Although post-structuralism shifts the nature of the referent to a linguistic object, it does not finally transcend or complicate representation itself. Embodiment assumes that what is referenced is always *present*, that it is always evolving and never simply alternating. The idea of reference involves, then, the designation of some thing exterior to the signifier and stable only when the referential object is abstracted, that is, only once perception has transpired.

Form and Prosody, or the Poem as Mind

Now that the preconditions of perception have been acknowledged, it is possible to introduce four characteristics of perceptual processing that enable the mind to distinguish itself from its embeddedness so that the corresponding processes in force within the lyric poem may be specified.

Perception is selective. Perceptual systems have evolved to register particular sorts of potential information or stimuli. Each sensory apparatus is, first of all, compatible with only one specific form of energy or potential energy and is therefore capable of perceiving a rather limited portion of the environment. To be precise, the visual system is receptive to a limited spectrum of electromagnetic radiation. Taste and smell register chemical energy while touch and hearing are sensitive to disturbances in the form of mechanical energy. Underscoring the primacy of action in relation to perception, neuroscientist Walter Freeman (2000: 28–36) stresses the fact that organisms continually position themselves to perceive, selecting prospective objects of perception by physically orienting themselves to potential sets of stimuli. An orienting motion may be as simple as a tilt of the head or an extension of the hand, and, more often than not, the selection of a perceptual field by positioning the body is carried out subconsciously. Further, receptor neurons within sensory systems specialize, that is they respond maximally to the limited ranges of energy that constitute their receptive fields. Receptive fields are themselves defined in probabalistic terms, that is, a receptor's range is delimited according to the probability that it will capture a stimulus falling within a said range. The act of perceiving involves the deployment of several mechanisms for selecting stimuli from among a host of potentially perceivable events.

The act of composition, of committing (no matter how briefly) to words is, naturally, an act of selection from among a plenitude. As the word or linguistic unit selected is composed of potential meanings, it exists as a conglomeration of other words that it coincidentally constructs. In culling meaning, the reader tracks the inscribed processes of the mind of the poet and selects which meaning or meanings from a set of potential meanings he/she will choose to interpret, or translate, in the loose sense of the word, for the sake of making his/her experience with the poem cohesive. The selective process of interpretation is mandated by the phenomenon of resistance: interpretative acts select from the potential veiled by obscurity in order to determine and to bring into relief.

Perception translates. The act of selection begins a process of determination through which information from the environment is synthesized within the brain. In order for this reintegration to occur, input must be transmuted so that it is materially consistent with the brain. For example, in the visual system, electromagnetic radiation is converted to electrochemical energy that will take on significance when integrated into patterns within a neuronal system. The process of translation, which takes the form of an energy conversion within perception, enables embodiment. The reconception of translation as an embodiment is necessary to explain the processes of sense-making within a self-contained system.

The compositional process likewise involves a translation of experience (including verbal experience) into words. The experience of reading includes the translation of language into meaning. Of course, this claim may be made about non-lyrical literature as well. But in lyric, the reader's homologous re-enactment of the emergent experience of the writer is occasioned by the poem's preservation of structures, via its technique and form, that permit the dynamic of emergence.

Perception renders distinction. Perception is to a large extent the perception of difference. The sensory systems are, first of all, more likely to take note of anomaly than the customary. Perceptual systems tend to habituate, that is, to grow inured to the meaningless constancies of circumstance in order to tend disproportionately to interruptions into the perceptual field. The work of perception is the work of distinguishing. Vision and touch in particular concentrate inordinately on the borders delineating the features of objects and the borders between objects and their surrounds, and function by bringing detail into relief (Gibson 1979: 189–202). Neurologically speaking, perception is a force that renders objects discrete from their supporting environments by discerning borders. In the early phases of visual perception, neuronal activity is parallel; neurons do not interact with one another but serve to isolate or 'articulate' (Skarda 1999) their triggering stimuli into what will become the features of the percept. The brain engages in a bottom-up series of compare-and-contrast mechanisms in order to tease out information from the energy it has segregated: articulation is a scalar process during which progressively larger units of information are contrasted by neuronal activity ranging the firing of a single neuron to the oscillation of larger and larger gestalts emerging finally as hemisphere-wide neuronal networks (Bateson 1979: 102–6; Freeman 2000: 56). Perception is significantly an articulating mechanism whose function is to select input from the environment and to differentiate it into features by means of neuronal contrast mechanisms.

And here the formal tendencies of lyric poetry are credited with the full extent of their functionality, for the formal presentation of lyric poetry (in both its written and oral incarnations) is laden with interruptions which force one to refocus from the flow of words within a cohesive unit to the new line, the new stanza, the strange figure and, in so doing, to draw newly significant contours. Like the brain, the form of the poem is scalar, demarcating units of different size ranging from the word or even the phoneme – which is more likely to be isolated and thrown into relief in poetry – to the stanza and the section. Contrast is also an operative principle in the enactment of rhythm (whether it is organized on the basis of stress, quantity or another principle) as well as other sound patternings, including alliteration, assonance and rhyme. Like the brain, the units created by the poem nest within one another. The hinges between these units are vital in characterizing the poem, in giving it features that can be translated and integrated within the mind of the reader.

A further form of differentiation enacted within the lyric is deixis, another of Culler's (1981) defining genre characteristics. For instance, the shifter 'this' is brought into relief as against its sometimes implicit, sometimes explicit complement 'that' in what is usually an early stage of the emergence of meaning. Deixis is language's orienting function, the making of spatial and temporal relation through the deployment of shifters, words whose referents can only be understood from context. Deictics operate in accordance with a contrastive principle, and contrast has its limit in indication. They are often the first resort of one for whom the sheer chaos of the untranslated impinges on the senses and threatens perception, a quasi-gestural linguistic strategy in which tentative or preliminary designations establish proximity: a 'there' takes on significance in relation to the 'here' with which one is newly acquainted. The effect of deixis is to render meaning nascent, to mark as potentially significant pending the emergence of the referent through the transcendence of context. Perception is a divisive faculty, rendering borders and contours and thereby bringing its objects into relief. The turn that brings Eurydice into Orpheus's perceptual field is, paradoxically, the gesture that divides them irremediably as the inevitable resort to vision causes her to recede back into the depths of the underworld. The symbolic serpent bite that renders their 'fall' into separateness, or separation, is reiterated as the glance that inflicts an everlasting schism between earthly lovers. The poem embodying, functioning as a perceptual act, must account for a level of relation that precedes the abstraction of subject and object that vision in particular effects. The poetic act – the act of poeticizing – must recur to a state of embeddedness and successfully perpetuate that embeddedness, folding it into the effective poem as a precondition to the emergence of poignant meaning, of persuasive voice.

Perception is creative. Finally for present purposes, the mind, via its perceptual systems, selects, translates and determines in order to maintain the consistent categorizations that enable its 'hold' on reality. It synthesizes information into gestalts it has created to function efficiently and is likely to interpret subsequent input to fit it into pre-existing categories, conferring a regularity and a consistency that are not necessarily paralleled in the outside world. This revelation follows, for example, the discovery that the correspondence between electromagnetic wavelength and perceived colour is at best tenuous and not at all consistent (Land 1977). Gestalt creation provides the continuity and the relevance that might eventually lead to identity formation, self-awareness and ideas about subjectivity. The mind's ability to actively create categories within its own self-consistent system suggests that it does not represent or mirror the world as it is, but rather specifies it. The songs informed by Eurydice are not replicas of Eurydice.

Veronica Forrest-Thomson (1978) was one of the first critics to systematically address the ways in which poetic meaning is made predominately within the structures and the strictures of the poem and only secondarily as between words and referents that pre-exist the poem and are external to it. This emphasis within her work places it within the vein of structuralism. Thomson's focus is on the creative function of metaphor within the poem; however, internal complexes of meaning cohere through other relation-making techniques, such as shared positioning within a line and repetition, echoes that when sounded may be integrated so that nascent categories may congeal. Despite the lyric poem's systemic tendency to focus inwards and to make meaning internally, the semantic emergence it fosters must also respond to exterior constraints that are to some degree specified as relevant to the mind in question – if they did not, it would not be possible to negotiate the poem's obscurity. It is through poetic techniques enabling selection, translation, distinguishing and reintegration that the poet reshuffles existing sets of connotations in order to restore an efficacy to the words Shelley sought in order to enable lawmakers to enact wisely (Forrest-Thomson 1978: 312).

Towards an explication

In approaching a poem, one would need, then, to restore the abundance it embodies. As continuity tends not to be perceptually available, it must be inferred and, in some instances, surmised. The human's ability to deduce the constituting environment of an organism is curtailed severely in relation to his ability to infer the environment that informs a linguistic expression: the reconstitution of a supporting environment is far less daunting when construed as linguistic task. A complete encounter with a lyric poem must allow the potential of poetic language to resonate by giving air to the trains of associations, connotations and denotations that are potentially specified by linguistic units. It would also need to focus on points of contrast or rupture at which features and details are brought into relief in order to integrate those details into evolving clusters of meaning. The directionality of scaling may be either bottom up or top down. To an extent, the coherence of larger units presumes that a degree of internal differentiation has occurred; however one may also limn the contours of the face and its major features before noticing a freckle on a cheek.

By way of demonstration, a snippet from Susan Howe's (1980) poem 'White foolscap' has been chosen for its overall brevity and for the fact that it presents a speaking 'I' who is not clearly rooted in biographical circumstance. The following reading is by necessity sketchy and selective, but suggestive of an approach nevertheless.

I can re
trac

my steps

iwho

crawl

between thwarts

Do not come down the ladder

ifor I

haveaten

it a

way

Much of the obscurity of this passage derives from its short fragmentary lines. Line 1 ends precipitously with the severed syllable 're': the enjambment created by breaking the line in mid-word (exaggerated, as postmodern technique often is) evokes, for an instant, a plethora of ensuing syllables, the entire stock of roots that might complete the abandoned prefix. It is, for the nonce, a line denoting the possibility of recursion, of turning back or performing again. If enjambment intensifies the indetermination triggered by the line break and is a site where the floodgates of meaning are opened and obscurity vented, the ensuing line limits the potential so-aired in affixing the selected root 'trac' to the prefix 're.' In differentiating the two halves of the word, the line break throws them into perceptual relief, rendering a distinction that makes each salient and graspable. The unconventional spelling of 'trac' then permits the word reconstituted by the reader to be read as either 'retrace' or 'retrack,' conferring a further ambiguity that remains active with the addition of the object 'my steps'. The complicated embeddedness inscribed within the poem continues to tug against its propensity to determine, to clarify. The prosaic statement 'I can retrace my steps' is a simple assertion that a method of recursion is possible, whereas the poetically formatted passage 'I can re/trac/my steps' articulates a consciousness defined by the potential power of reversal and repetition at its disposal, one composed of its own environmentally constrained ability to go backwards, to repeat, to remember, perhaps to regress into a predetermined state within an implicit environment.

The ultimate deictic negotiation within the lyric poem transpires between the verbalizing *I* and the potentially audient *you* that is sometimes explicitly and always implicitly present with it. The trope apostrophe (addressing and therefore bringing into being an absent you) and its visual counterpart prosopopoeia (giving face to the faceless) are large-scale elaborations of the articulating objectifying processes of perception embodied in the oscillating motion of neuronal networks. The ode and the elegy, as central subgenres of the lyric, ensconce the lyric near the culmination of its emergence. In poems in which an 'I' does not expressly identify itself (and is therefore not fully articulated from its environment), one can nevertheless identify its contents as they are selected; one can mark the struggle to distinguish within a poem indicative of and enacting a perceiving mind in the stages of cognition that precede self-awareness. In fact, lyric subjectivity always exists as an intermediate stage. Poetic articulation suggests neither a bounded, stable and self-assured subjectivity, nor the utter absence of one. It cannot be subject to an absenting oscillation that ultimately forestalls subjective action, for the gestures of the poem are building blocks in an emergence implicating history, memory and presence, including the present force of an ambiguous constituting environment.

Significantly, Howe's lines appear earlier in 'White foolscap' without the stanza break between lines 6 and 7. The division inflicted as part of the reiteration of this passage serves to articulate the 'I' (in both senses of the word) by means of the command that distinguishes it in the attempt to effect control over an addressee. Absent the stanza break, one might grant syntactical continuity to the two-stanza unit and read the line 'Do not come down the ladder' as the predicate of the subject 'I': 'Iwho crawl between thwarts do not come down the ladder'. With the isolation of this unit as a line, the mood shifts from the indicative to the imperative, and the 'I' and the 'you' emerge in tandem as the former commands each into existence.

The desire to strand the 'you' atop the ladder at a distance from the 'I' expressed in the second stanza might then be interpreted as the will to remain intact as against the tendency to meld into the indistinction of embeddedness (iwho, ifor). The eating away of the ladder can suggest either the forestalling of remerger or an attempt to consume what mediates between the coterminous destinations of emergence and thus restore their contiguity and continuity. The 'I' here cannot be equated with a personality: it is tenuous and enacts a perceiving mind in the stages of cognition that precede self-awareness. Selection through distinction-making informs (in the literal sense) and thus creates it. Even in the most I-centred of lyric poems, the speaking entity is more tenuous than its persistent self-reference might lead one to believe. Obscure poems stress the context that is physically entrained in the acts of selection, transmutation and reintegration and motivate a centrifugal directionality tugging against subject cohesion, while personal confessional poems give the centripetal directionalities at play in subject emergence greater impetus. It is ancillary to my thesis that to flirt with the precipice of biography, in which the self is no longer emergent in the complex sense suggested here, but is rather determined, or, conversely, to verge upon its counterpart, an utter obscurity that does not yield to a degree of coherence, is to risk tipping off the lyric plateau.

15

Stylistics and Language Teaching: Deviant Collocation in Literature as a Tool for Vocabulary Expansion

Dany Badran

Dany Badran's chapter raises some key questions in the study and teaching of literature in the context of learning English as a second or foreign language, while maintaining throughout an awareness of previous investigations in the field of pedagogic stylistics and making in a non-restrictive way important points concerning definitions of style and literariness. The same spirit of openness is carried through into suggestions for pedagogic activity involving an exploration of the kinds of lexical patterning commonly found in literary texts and of the kinds of language learning, most particularly vocabulary acquisition, made possible by classroom interaction and 'involvement' with such patterns. Emphasis is placed on the value for learners of the relationship between semantic elaboration, inferencing and vocabulary retention. However, what is particularly impressive about the chapter is that the focus on vocabulary is also seen as a springboard for wider questions about the nature of literature, about the practice of critical reading and about the nature of textual evidence when forming interpretations.

What I like about the chapter, that is a refusal to see vocabulary simply as words but rather as signifying patterns, is also what I would propose can form the basis for two further areas of exploration:

- *Data-driven learning*: the possibilities created by recent work in corpus analysis and corpus stylistics allow a more top-down discourse-driven view of language which contrasts effectively with the bottom-up lexical processing investigated in this chapter. Corpus analysis generates both links with contexts for word meaning and access to the most frequent patterns in a text (the latter certainly useful in collocational analysis of novels) and affords opportunities for both statistical (quantitative) and interpretive (qualitative) investigation. The existence (often with web-based access) of multi-million-word databases for English at different periods of history also allows comparison with the norms from which literary collocations provide surprising and, as Badran puts it, 'memorable' departures. For valuable further reading see Adolphs (2006) Stubbs

(2005) and Louw (1993) and (2006), the last offering a suggestive span of work grounded theoretically in a view of meaning in language as collocational and pedagogically attuned to the advantages of discourse-based data-driven learning.

- *Working with collocations*: the dangers for non-native users of a language in attempting to predict and interpret gaps in collocational patterns have been alerted by Mackay (1992) and followed up by Weston (1996) who argues against Mackay to show that a widely used language teaching strategy (cloze-procedure) can be, as Dany Badran argues here, sensitively applied to a wide range of texts in ways which foster enhanced sensitivity to literary language use. Weston also points out that this kind of vocabulary development can also be stimulated by activities that are productive as well as receptive, involving students in generating their own texts and word choices, a pedagogic move that follows on from Dany Badran's explorations.

The significance of this chapter lies above all in its open and retrievable search for ways of allowing language learners to move beyond single words and referential meanings and to embrace a view of language as patterned representation. Future development of the ideas and examples in this chapter will owe much to these fundamental insights.

Ron Carter

Style and Literature

Stylistics: a linguistic approach to analysing style in literature. This is one accepted definition of stylistics. Yet within this definition are embedded two problematic concepts: style and literature. The trouble with these concepts is the degree of controversy with regard to the way they have evolved and, consequently, the way they are currently approached. The non-distinctiveness and relative narrowness associated with style, on the one hand, and the difficulties faced in answering the question '*What* is literature?' on the other, have discouraged some practitioners, increased the determination of others but confused many.

Starting with literature, the majority of interest generated by the term has been in attempts to address its *specialness* through trying to find objective, sometimes measurable, justification for what at most is an intersubjective reader reaction. Traditionally, literature was considered as a special *type* of discourse mainly because it displayed a distinctive type of language, thus placing it in a position of contrast, sometimes opposition, with other types of texts.

Yet in reviewing mainstream views of literature and literary language, there is no consensus with regard to what this specialness really entails. Some argue for specialness, even superiority of literature in terms of structural distinction (Chapman 1973). Others see partial distinctions between the literary and non-literary discourse based on exclusive functional grounds (Jakobson 1960), dominant functional grounds (Leech 1987) or even reader-response grounds (Fish 1980). And yet others see no justification whatsoever for distinguishing literary discourse from non-literary discourse either at the structural level (Pratt 1981) or at the functional levels (Kress 1988; Weber 1992; and Simpson 1997).

Brumfit and Carter (1986) make a more general proposition in terms of a continuum of literariness. And a more specific view may even argue for several continua of literariness:

a.   *A structural continuum:* while structural constraints are necessary and sufficient conditions in more structurally rigid cases in literature (a sonnet for instance) they are less so in others (such as free verse).

b.   *A functional continuum:* the more dominant Jakobson's (1960) 'poetic func-tion' is, the more 'literature-like' a work is. Informative texts lie on the other extreme.

c.   *A chronological/traditional continuum:* what is more likely to qualify as literature from a traditional institutional/institutionalized view would be closer to older, more traditional works (usually described as the 'great' literatures of the past) and less so with more modern works. The question is thus properly phrased as 'when' as opposed to 'what is literature' (Heath 1998).

d.   *A reader-response continuum:* the more a text is read as literature, the more literary it becomes (see Fish 1980).

Literature is, in fact, all of the above and more. The concept is dependent on each of these continua as well as an interaction among them. Yet the most important and currently relevant part of any definition of literature is not *what* it is in terms of the presence and/or absence of some broad structural and/or functional criteria, but the question of how it is regarded by readers. Whatever literature may be (structurally and functionally speaking), it is still the result of a long-standing sociohistorical institutional educational tradition, which promotes its image to readers and is consequently viewed as a special type of discourse. As Birch properly phrases it, literature is approached by readers as a 'complex and opaque' form of discourse 'because the experiences [it] describe[s] and elicit[s] in the reader are considered necessarily to be complex and deep' (1989: 86). And this view is constantly reinforced whenever students are asked what literature is. In fact, this question was asked in an introductory lecture to a sophomore Rhetoric course, a course which focuses on argumentation in literature, taught in an EFL context at the Lebanese American University, Beirut. The written answers of the overwhelming majority used words and phrases like: 'expressing sentiments in a special way, deep and beautiful writing, all writing that is of value, all writings that have a unique style, deep meanings, analytical, creative, artistic and original.'

Certainly, there are arguments concerning why this is the case or how that, historically, came to be; instead, the more productive argument should start from the factual premise that literature is approached in the above manner, and that it may, subsequently, be used productively in ESL/EFL contexts. While there is, and has been, a dominant tendency for ESL/EFL instructors to favour non-literary 'informative' texts (frequently by consciously avoiding literary texts) for language learning reasons, I argue that literature may still play a central and unique role in an ESL/EFL context.

The same is the case with style. Whether defined in terms of a 'DEPARTURE' from a set of linguistic patterns labelled as a 'norm' or the 'syntactically neutral or unmarked', an 'ADDITION' of stylistic traits to expressions deemed as 'neutral or styleless, or pre-stylistic', and/or 'CONNOTATION', whereby linguistic features acquire their value from the 'textual and situational environment' (Enkvist 1973: 15), style is still useful from the perspective of the reader and his/her expectations. All pseudo-scientific/objective definitions of style will find themselves making style a non-distinctive redundant term. In escaping the earlier structural traps (of deciding what neutral language is), Birch and O'Toole propose a more inclusive, less distinctive, view of style where stylistic choices are partly determined by the *functional* and *ideological* needs of the producer of the text and partly by 'the norms of the socially appropriate *genre* for these functions' (1988: 1, emphasis mine). A similar inclusive view is that of Carter and Nash who see style as 'a textual phenomenon [which] should be studied both in terms of particular linguistic *forms* in a text and as *effects* generated by those same forms on the consumer (the *reader*) by the producer of the text (the *writer*)' (1990: 21, emphasis mine). Unfortunately, according to these latter views, there would be little justification for singling out the notion of style since stylistic choices would be identical with linguistic choices at the syntagmatic and paradigmatic levels, and one's style indistinguishable from one's discourse. In other words, in the absence of styleless discourse, style would, at best, be a redundant notion. Style is, in fact, precisely what Tinker argues it is: 'difficult to define, you know it when you see it' (2003: 86).

In short, the difficulties in approaching the notions of style and literature can be avoided through a shift of focus from questions like *what* is literature? and *what* is style? to those trying to make use of the reader's perception of literature and style for productive purposes. In this chapter, these are precisely the type of questions that will be asked and, hopefully, answered:

1. In the light of the problems associated with these two notions – style and literature – why would we want to use literature for language teaching?
2. What is special about literary texts as perceived by readers?
3. How can literature be used in an ESL/EFL context?
4. In what ways can literary discourse prove superior in an ESL/EFL context?

We are all familiar with those traditional views arguing for the value of literary discourse for human experience, helping humans cope with the complexities of life. With any discussion of literature, predictable collocations seem to accompany such discussion: words like 'emotional', 'moral', 'ethical' and 'aesthetic' (see Rothery and Stenglin 2000: 25; and Zyngier and Shepherd 2003: 13) as well as 'value', 'elevated, unique, or impressively difficult to achieve' (MacDonald 2002: 618). Literature allows involved readers to 'grapple with the emotions of a parallel life', providing them with the unique opportunity 'to enter and inhabit the landscape of a text that touches emotions and invites personal involvement' (Hess 2003: 19). Ultimately, in answering the question, 'What is Literature, Really?' Zyngier and Shepherd (2003: 14) see conventional literary ability from the educators' perspectives as students 'becom[ing] involved in their reading experience' and consequently making 'emotional, ethical and moral responses to [literary] texts'. Here, the key term is *involvement* since, as Hess argues, approaching literature 'under the guidance of appropriate teaching, brings about the kind of participation almost no other text can produce' (2003: 20).

Literature, Deviance and Memorability in an EFL Classroom

Stylistic deviation, though not exclusive to literary discourse, is more common and anticipated and therefore accepted in literature, especially poetry. This is of particular practical value. In the context of what are labelled 'informative texts', bumping into collocational deviations at the level found in literary discourse is usually deemed illogical, possibly incomprehensible and ultimately even un-acceptable. In this chapter, my argument is that through close conscious analyses of such deviations (collocational deviations) in literature (particularly poetry), linguistic awareness (and vocabulary acquisition) can be raised to a level un-achievable through other means.

Recent studies in vocabulary acquisition all point in the same direction:

1. that word knowledge is essentially 'multifaceted' (Nation 1990) though attempting a full implementation in an ESL/EFL context is simply not feas-ible (Schmitt 1998: 285);
2. that *size* as well as *depth* of a learner's vocabulary are equally important in predicting academic performance (Qian 2002: 513);
3. that 'word comprehension does not automatically predict correct use of the word' (Laufer and Paribakht 1998: 368–9). The first is labelled passive vo-cabulary knowledge, the second active;
4. that 'the activation of passive vocabulary seems to depend on multiple exposures to words and broad opportunities to use them' (Laufer and Par-ibakht 1998: 387);
5. and finally, that passive interaction with the language for the purpose of vocabulary acquisition through, for instance, 'inferencing' as an activity does not necessarily lead to retention (Paribakht 2005: 705).

In other words, the most promising and potentially reliable means for eventual vocabulary expansion and retention are: *multiple exposures* to, as well as *conscious, dynamic* and *varied interaction* with, the language. And I argue that literature, more specifically poetry, provides one of the most economically feasible channels for all that to be developed and achieved.

First, there is general consensus regarding the amount of time and attention that students give to literature. According to Hall, literature is considerably more demanding 'than more predictable genres like the business letter or a medical report' (2005: 37), and this is reflected in the fact that 'readers of literature ... particularly second language readers, do indeed pause longer over works and remember surface forms better than ... other kinds of writing' (Hall 2005: 15). To that effect, there is ample empirical evidence to show how readers are more likely 'to repay equally deliberate and careful processing' with 'deliberately carefully constructed text[s], such as a poem' (Hall 2005: 101).

Second, this level of attention, time and effort put into literature in particular, is partly in response to the type of linguistic ambiguity resulting from linguistic deviation (foregrounding) characterising literary text since 'things are often deliberately left unclear in literary text' (Brumfit and Carter 1986: 14). The significance of foregrounding (through deviation) to the learning process is crucial. As McIntyre points out, 'memorable lectures are more effective in terms of student learning' and 'anything that is foregrounded is ... arguably more memorable' (2003: 1,4). Although his attempt to make lectures more memorable through foregrounding takes non-linguistic physical form, the argument still stands at the level of linguistic foregrounding through deviance.

Third, linguistic ambiguity as mentioned above necessarily gives rise to multiple interpretative possibilities which endow the text not only with a unique type of conscious processing, but also with a type of dynamic involvement with overwhelmingly positive language learning outcomes. This is the type of activity referred to by Jeffries (2003: 70–1) when discussing the importance and 'richness of open-endedness' and 'exploration' (as opposed to explanation) in language learning. In other words, I argue, the need to force cohesion and coherence onto literary texts in order to be able to 'infer meaning' (Brumfit and Carter 1989: 14) partly explains the level of conscious effort (through interaction with the text) that readers will put into the process of reading literature.

Yet at the heart of this argument is the following claim: a crucial factor for the high level of involvement that readers experience when approaching literature in particular is, I argue, the *interplay* within their expectations between the *macro* and *micro* levels of the literary textual make-up. Here is an example of exactly how that works in an EFL setting.

In October 2006, I ran the following activity in an introductory lecture to the above-mentioned course on argumentation. The purpose of that activity was to show how different perspectives come into play and how each can be equally valid. The poem (lyrics of a song displaying traditional and easily identifiable elements of poetry – such as rhyme and rhythm) that I used is entitled 'A boy named Sue' by Johnny Cash. The story is of a narrator whose father left him (ran away and hid) at the age of three, leaving him and his mother very little to live on. Moreover, he was named Sue. That caused the boy a lot of grief, and he struggled considerably in order to get over people making fun of him. He also swore to kill his father if he ever found him. Of course he does find his father, and when the boy has his gun out to shoot, the father smiles and explains to him that the reason he named him Sue was precisely because he could not be there for him and he needed to make sure his son survived. That name would guarantee that he would either 'get tough or die'. In fact, his son ought to thank him for being given that name.

In class, as I read out the last stanza, I deliberately stop before the 'last word' (which actually turns out to be another line), and all students, without exception, hurriedly and cheerfully filled in the word: 'Sue'.

> I got all choked up and I threw down my gun
> And I called him my pa, and he called me his son,
> And I came away with a different point of view.
> And I think about him, now and then,
> Every time I try and every time I win,
> And if I ever have a son, I think I'm gonna name him ... (pause)

The point that subsequently follows this deviation (of the poem rhyming all along except in the last line) is that following the literary norms of rhyme (at the macro level) makes the whole argument (at the micro level) partly absurd. In fact, after a few seconds of everyone shouting out 'Sue', some students began to look dissatisfied, arguing that the conclusion was rather illogical. They argued that although the boy might understand why his father named him Sue (in the circumstances), it would be foolish if he did the same to his own son considering the amount of misery, unhappiness and difficulty the name had caused him. Different interpretations by readers arise mainly as a result of a clash between reader expectations (as encouraged by traditional norms in literature – namely rhyme in poetry), and commonsensical clues in the language and content of the poem. In other words, while, on the one hand, the relative rigidity and demands of *genre* within literature systematizes literature at the inter-textual level, and greatly limits reader expectations, linguistic deviations within literary discourse at the intra-textual level, on the other, open up countless possibilities. The paradox is that as far as readers are concerned, literature offers a relatively limitless range of variance, yet within a limited set frame. And it is this interplay which, I argue, keeps readers 'on their toes' and endows the classroom with a high level of reader involvement and dynamism. Indeed, the amount of generated discussion and meticulous textual re-examination that followed were extremely rewarding for students being introduced to argumentation.

Finally, as mentioned above from studies in vocabulary acquisition, there is evidence that the likelihood that new information will be retained is greatly increased when greater attention is paid to various aspects of words. In other words, 'rich (qualitative) and numerous (quantitative) associations with existing knowledge increase the chances that the new information will be retained ... [and] ... this is known as elaboration in both its qualitative and quantitative sense' (Hulstijn and Laufer 2001: 541). This is also what Barcroft refers to as 'semantic elaboration' which arises from the same basic premise that 'semantic elaboration can lead to greater recall and recognition of items' (2002: 323–4), both acquired and new. And this semantic elaboration is essential in the meaning-inferencing process characteristic of reading literature.

In the following section, I will demonstrate how focusing on deviant collocations in a literary text can provide a context for elaboration at the linguistic, literary and topical levels, ultimately raising linguistic awareness, leading to sensitivity and refinement in the use of qualification in writing, all within an EFL context.

Deviant Collocation, Literature and Vocabulary Expansion

The practical application which follows focuses on deviant collocation in a literary text (a poem entitled 'Awake' written by Jim Morrison of the band The Doors) as a tool for vocabulary expansion. The reasons I have emphasized collocation (more precisely, deviant collocation) for the mentioned purpose in this exercise are the following.

First, collocation is an essential part of meaning, usually associated with advanced meaning knowledge as Schmitt (1998) argues. The better one can explain the semantic relations/features that bind two or more words within a collocative tie, the deeper is one's word/meaning knowledge. Second, as Barcroft explains, 'semantic elaboration can lead to greater recall and recognition of items' (2002: 324). In other words, collocational elaboration as one dimension of semantic elaboration is fundamental for the purpose of vocabulary retention. Finally, when it comes to deviance, the high level of attention in trying to explain collocational deviances makes the process of exploring meaning quite 'rich', serving to raise consciousness, ultimately increasing retention possibilities (Hulstijn and Laufer 2001: 540).

The exercise undertaken below has been used in more than one context with the same objective in mind. I have used it on several occasions in a sophomore Rhetoric class, a Practical Semantics course as well as a Principles of Translation lecture. What binds these classes, whether the focus is on linguistics, translation or evaluations/responses to arguments and argumentation, is the centrality of, as well as the need for, accuracy and sensitivity to vocabulary usage. The chosen text and approach to its analysis have not, in short, been used in literary studies although they can be seen to constitute an essential part of literary analysis. Consequently, those specific findings reported below are the outcome of running this activity in two sections of sophomore Rhetoric, a class which focuses on argumentation and rhetoric with particular emphasis on, and utilization of, literary texts.

Despite the relatively advanced level of English that students generally possess when they are majoring in Translation, Applied Linguistics or taking a Rhetoric class, there is prevalent weakness (in an ESL context) when it comes to uses of words which extend beyond what Carter (1998) labels 'core vocabulary'. Despite the fact that in reading comprehension, 'difficult' words are often recognized and understood, when it comes to production (whether spoken or in writing), students predominantly resort to the more basic and elementary 'core vocabulary'. Nouns like 'thing' and adjectives like 'nice', 'good' and 'bad' are customary in students' expressions of description and evaluation. Moreover, preset phrases which come straight out of dominant television advertisements and news reports are often rehearsed without much contemplation. When students are challenged with regard to the meaning of individual words within the whole utterance structure, they often find them difficult to explain.

Consequently, the purpose of this exercise is to raise the students' critical awareness and consciousness regarding 'familiarized' phrases as well as increase their sensitivity towards providing more accurate, specific and therefore expressive descriptions and evaluations. This exercise is aimed more at fine-tuning existing word knowledge for it to become more actively used rather than simply increasing the size of students' passive vocabulary. Yet both objectives are in no way mutually exclusive.

The poem used in this exercise, entitled 'Awake', by The Doors, is not sung but rather read with music in the background on the album *An American Prayer.*

> Shake dreams from your hair
> My pretty child, my *sweet* one.
> Choose the day and choose the sign of your day
> The day's divinity, first thing you see.
>
> A vast *radiant* beach in a *cool jewelled* moon
> Couples naked race down by its quiet side
> And we laugh like *soft*, mad children
> Smug in the *woolly cotton* brains of infancy.
>
> The music and voices are all around us.
>
> Choose, they croon, the Ancient Ones
> The time has come again.
> Choose now, they croon,
> Beneath the moon, beside an *ancient* lake.
> Enter again the *sweet* forest,
> Enter the *hot* dream,
>
> Come with us,
> Everything is broken up and dances.

(Morrison 1978)

Quite notable in this text are the uncommon collocations in some instances and those semantically deviant ones in other instances (these are italicized in the text). And this is one extremely common characteristic of poetry, at least at the level of reader expectations. While it would be hard to predict such collocations, readers would find it easier to explain and justify the poet's use of them by looking for links, semantic or metaphorical, to make the poem more meaningful. And this active, involving, conscious and dynamic search for semantic ties is inextricably linked with the above-mentioned goal.

In order to achieve this objective, the activity as a whole was divided into a set of smaller manageable teacher-led tasks. Initially, students were provided with the following list of decontextualized nouns used in the poem in order to provide qualifiers for these nouns.

1. ____ child
2. ____ beach
3. ____ moon
4. ____ children
5. ____ brains
6. ____ lake
7. ____ forest
8. ____ dream

As expected, the findings reflected a higher frequency of more core vocabulary. With the word 'child', for instance, core vocabulary qualifiers were used in the following manner.

Qualifier for 'child'	Occurrences (%)
beautiful	30
nice	20
ugly	12
dirty	8
good	6
bad	6
young	6
small	4
sweet	2
innocent	2
playful	2
smelly	2

Overall, however, despite the uses of qualifiers like 'playful', 'innocent' and 'smelly, the more dominant qualifiers were 'beautiful', 'nice', 'ugly' and 'dirty'. Other words in the list attracted qualifiers like 'blue', 'green' and 'white' or common collocations such as 'full moon' or 'deep forest'. Some students left the word 'brains' without qualification.

The second step was to contextualize these words. The original poem, 'Awake', was thus presented to students but with its qualifiers missing, as in a cloze test. Students were then asked to fill in the blanks using their self-generated qualifiers. These were discussed with regard to how appropriate or inappropriate the students' choices were in these contexts. In doing so, emphasis was placed on explaining and discussing semantic features and semantic relations within these collocations. It was concluded that adjectives like 'good' or 'beautiful' were too general, common, collocationally inclusive and indistinctive in terms of semantic relations. The more core a word is, the wider its semantic range is, the more used it is, the less precise (and by extension, poetically effective) it is. More specialized, feature-sensitive qualifiers are needed if the poem was to have any effect as poetry. Suggestions were elicited, listed on the board and discussed. Consequently, in applying semantic relations, students were asked to make changes to the qualifiers in such a way for the poem to make more meaningful sense. Through raising awareness with respect to semantic features within the qualifier-qualified collocation, the changes which followed revealed an overall move from the more basic, core vocabulary to the more specialized, keeping in mind the overall unity of the poem. Words like 'charming, disturbed, enormous, ambitious, arrogant and dynamic' started to appear more consistently in the interest of making the poem more meaningful. These changes were further explored with special emphasis on those explicit semantic features which now create this semantic collocational tie.

The poem was then presented in its entirety, and students were encouraged to inspect the existing collocations through interpreting the poem. The first reaction with respect to such collocations as 'soft children', 'cool moon', 'woolly brains', 'sweet forest' and 'hot dream' was that they were, semantically speaking, either incompatible or strange at best. But then again, that was poetry. Yet before encouraging a metaphorical interpretation of these collocations, the meanings of the words 'soft, cool, woolly, sweet and hot' were explored. It was seen that, in fact, the students' knowledge of these meanings corresponded almost exclusively with the most dominant (core) sense of each word. Then, with reference to the *Encarta World English Dictionary*, alternative senses were presented and interpretations of the poem were subsequently elicited in light of the more peripheral senses of these words. In this process, students were consciously involved in validating each sense until they arrived at potentially valid interpretations within the context of the poem. Here is a listing for the word *sweet*:

Sweet:
1. tasting or **smelling** of sugar or a similar substance;
2. containing a relatively large amount of sugar, or retaining some natural sugars;
3. associated with the basic taste sensation that is not bitter, salt or sour;
4. not stale, rancid or soured;
5. not salty or saline;
6. **pleasing to any of the senses**;
7. **desirable, gratifying or satisfying**;
8. **kind, thoughtful or generous**;
9. **having an appearance that is charming or endearing**;
10. used to describe land that contains no acid or corrosive substances;
11. used to describe gasoline or oil that contains little or no sulphur;
12. **dear**, respected or **beloved**.

Following that, students moved from the original reaction to what appeared to them as nonsensical collocative deviances (at the semantic level) towards the imposition of a metaphorical dimension to meaning. In other words, students were actively trying to impose reading conventions consistent with their knowledge of, as well as their expectations from, literature on the poem, ultimately forcing cohesion and coherence on it. This meant that those peripheral senses of the qualifiers under examination (in bold print in the list above) were seen as serious potentials whereby the overall meaning of the poem did not move towards complete nonsensical absurdity. For instance, the collocation of 'soft, mad children' which most students were discontent with if 'soft' related solely to the sense of touch made complete sense and was consistent with the following 'woolly cotton brains of infancy' if soft had the sense: 'lacking intelligence or sound judgement' and woolly had the sense: 'confused, vague and lacking focus.'

In that light, those seemingly nonsensical collocative deviances started to make sense. The poem was then read as one unified text, and collocations were easily explained and justified to serve the unity of the poem. The poet's appeal to the five senses in his descriptions was most dominantly highlighted as the principal unifying theme. Consequently, the author's invitation for readers to join this experience was one taken to its fullest through an immersion of all the five senses in the experience.

Quite interestingly, a large number of readers saw the poem as a narrative. As Hall points out, 'humans are story-telling beings ... [and] ... literature clearly participates in this wider human meaning-making activity ... narrative competence' (2005: 32). This had the noticeable effect of enriching the activity with a lot of dynamism as different students told their different versions of the 'story' of the poem. These stories had such themes as 'freedom', 'nature', 'love and eroticism', 'birth and rebirth', 'death', 'superstition, religion and spirituality', 'absurdity', etc. Yet under each of the above-mentioned themes that were discussed, the related vocabulary which was elicited in the process (and listed on the board under the general theme heading) had a very wide range. One of the more dominant interpretations was that the poet is advising/inviting the typical twenty-first-century corporate worker to wake up from the surrealness of his life and move back to a life which he/she can fully experience and indulge in, to remember life with one's senses as opposed to living a virtual life through one's mind. Although that might seem a foolish childish move, it would be a blissful rich one.

Conclusions and Implications

The main argument in this chapter is that literature, approached from a stylistic perspective, offers students unique opportunities for enhancing their vocabulary by raising their levels of awareness and sensitivity to lexical choices through an analysis of deviant collocation. Exposure to such collocations provides diverse contexts for dynamic, conscious and therefore more memorable interaction with the language, thus moving this sensitivity to lexical choices from the receptive to the productive level.

Based on the poem discussed above, the following conclusions and implications for further applications can be made. Literature, approached from a stylistic perspective, can provide a particularly rich context for interaction:

1. *At the thematic level.* Because of its partial ambiguity, the poem discussed in the above manner was easy to relate to a variety of fields and topics: reading as a movie or a narrative, relating to religion and spirituality, life and death, freedom, love and nature. On top of that, and in all these cases, the learners were extremely motivated due to their personal involvement in the themes and topics of discussion.

2. *At the linguistic level.* A stylistic discussion of the poem offered students the opportunity to explore language, raising awareness with regard to the subtleties of style (or language choice), and ultimately leading to fine-tuning and refining their knowledge of language.

3. *At the literary level.* One interpretation of the poem highlighted the fine line between what is deemed to be sensible and absurd. A stylistic analysis of those collocations considered deviant in the poem, for instance, led to questions of literariness and aesthetics, for example, *when is literature deemed 'good'* and *when is it complete nonsense?* This issue could perhaps be elaborated further in a literature class.

4. *At the critical level,* enhancing critical ability. No interpretation, no matter how far-fetched it was, was allowed to go beyond the linguistic determinants of the text. Despite the potential for variant interpretations as encouraged by linguistic ambiguity in the text, students learned to be dismissive of all interpretations without proper backing. Similarly, collocationally preset phrases (characteristic mainly of a blending of poetry and political rhetoric – especially in an oriental country like Lebanon) were subject to scrutiny through defamiliarization. Critical awareness regarding the process of meaning making and its potential effects was therefore raised.

When it comes to teaching the English language, both to native and non-native speakers, the potential for literature and stylistic analyses is far from being exhausted.

Stylistics of Dialogue and Drama

CHAPTER
16

Oral Accounts of Personal Experiences: When is a Narrative a Recount?

Marina Lambrou

This chapter provides an excellent overview of some of the possibilities and limitations of the approach to narrative analysis established four decades ago in a path-breaking study published by Labov and Waletzky (1967). Extended and refined in subsequent work by Labov himself as well as others working in what has come to be called the 'Labovian' tradition of narrative inquiry, this approach has also been challenged on several fronts. Theorists working in the tradition of Conversation Analysis (e.g. Schegloff 1997) have argued that as originally formulated the approach failed to take into account how the narrative structures it identified were occasioned by the particular discourse environment in which Labov's data were elicited: namely, sociolinguistic interviews designed to gather extended, largely monologic speech productions by informants. Meanwhile, drawing on ideas from systemic-functional grammar, Plum (1988) suggested that to account for the diverse forms and functions of storytelling, the category 'narrative' itself needs to be decomposed into multiple subgenres, including *stories* proper, *anecdotes, exempla* and *recounts* (see Table 16.1 below).

Lambrou's chapter builds on these critiques without completely jettisoning the Labovian framework; her aim is to develop an enriched, empirically grounded method of analysing natural-language narratives. Using Plum's taxonomy of storytelling genres, Lambrou cross-compares accounts of personal experiences produced in a one-on-one interview setting with accounts produced during peer-group interviews (see Table 16.2). (Here, however, the Conversation Analyst might still object: how do these etic categories of analysis, imposed on the data by the researcher *ex post facto*, relate to the emic categories to which participants orient themselves while engaged in talk? To what extent do participants themselves discriminate between anecdotes and recounts, for example, in their own practice, and how would we go about finding that out?) Lambrou also considers whether topic interacts with the production or non-production of fully fledged narratives (that is, the production of narratives versus recounts) concerning past personal experiences (see Table 16.4). Indeed, although multivariate statistical analysis does not feature in Lambrou's chapter, her data would allow her to assign relative weights to the multiple factors she coded for, including age, sex, topic and type of interview setting (see Table 16.3), and to evaluate interactions among all the factors involved. For example, does topic trump interview setting, sex and age when it comes to the production or non-production of fully fledged narratives versus recounts in all environments where stories might be used?

In any case, Lambrou's research outlines productive new directions for post-Labovian narrative analysis. For one thing, the chapter reveals the fruitfulness of studying contrasts between the storytelling practices of different generations within the same speech community; it also suggests that comparing multi-generational data from several speech communities may allow ethnocultural differences to be separated out from universal age-graded processes of narrative acquisition. More generally, Lambrou's discussion points up the advantages of integrating quantitative methods into narrative analysis (Herman 2005) – for instance, to study how the variable of sex interacts with the production or non-production of particular narrative subgenres across different communicative settings. By the same token, the chapter highlights the importance of creating synergy between such quantitative research on narrative and qualitative accounts of how situated storytelling practices help constitute gender, among other aspects of identity (see Bucholtz and Hall 2005).

Especially productive, finally, is the way Lambrou explores correlations between the topic of a given account (e.g. emotional states versus actions that cause or resolve Trouble) and the selection or non-selection of particular discourse genres to encapsulate that topical content. The key question here is, as Lambrou notes, 'Which topics are less likely to produce narrative forms and instead produce, for example, recounts?' In this respect, the chapter has significant metatheoretical implications, suggesting that narrative analysis should set itself predictive as well as descriptive goals. That is to say, research on stories should seek to identify not only what features and functions narratives characteristically embody, but also what kinds of semantic content are most likely to be narrativized, all other things being equal. In this strong predictive form, narrative analysis would be able to contribute importantly to such fields as learning theory, automated story generation and natural language processing.

David Herman

Introduction

It is generally accepted that narrative storytelling is a universal activity and that there is a human propensity to organize experiences into tellable stories to make them interesting and memorable (Bruner 1990; Hymes 1996). Studies in linguistics and anthropology show that through narrative storytelling individuals are able to make sense of their lives; specifically, the exchange of personal experiences is seen as a social transaction whereby individuals represent and shape their lives through events that have happened in the past. According to Bruner, we 'cling to narrative models of reality and use them to shape our everyday experiences' (2003: 7). Anderson critically asserts that humans 'find it easy to lie and deny, to transport both sender and receiver to other actual and imagined situations, and to construct elaborate shared narratives and simultaneously modify and contradict these stories' (1998: 31). It is what Cobley sees as a consequence of language, which 'not only "permits" narratives but practically makes them obligatory in the organization of human experience' (2001: 23).

The notion that storytelling is part of our socialisation is also the view of Culler who states that 'Stories ... are the main way we make sense of things, whether in thinking of our lives as a progression leading somewhere or in telling ourselves what is "happening in the world"' (1997: 83). Schiffrin offers a functional description of narratives as a storytelling discourse by explaining that:

> A story is a reconstruction of an experience, told at a specific time, in a specific place to a specific audience for whom the storyteller seeks to demonstrate the validity of a general claim (e.g. about oneself, one's experience, or the world). Put another way, a story seeks to establish an intersubjectively agreed upon point (a point which may involve the audience as co-author).
>
> (Schiffrin 1994: 7)

Sharing personal narratives, therefore, is part of a wider strategy for asserting and constructing identity: how we tell stories and who we tell them to reflects who we are, while also expressing how we would like to be regarded. By reconstructing real past events, narrators come to share their personal experiences with others, in an act that has greater implications than simply exchanging experiences for entertainment purposes. Moreover, narrators as protagonists of first-hand experiences decide just how far to elaborate or fabricate actual facts and events so that what transpires may be closer to fiction than the truth. In this way, narrators are not only able to construct, and even reconstruct, their identity, but also the identity of other agents in their narrative, to represent them in a positive or negative light. Goffman argues that personal narratives are not only about retelling, constructing or reconstructing experiences, but are also about what is 're-experienced' (1981: 174). Toolan (2001) also foregrounds the functional importance of narratives as 'cognitively enabling' and a 'definingly human activity', drawing attention to the core features of a narrative and seeing both aspects as inseparable. One question this raises is whether all personal experiences are narratives, however, as there is an assumption that past experiences are encoded in this way, or whether there are other types of discourse that provide a similar function. If the latter is the case, what are the distinctions between the different modes of storytelling, where can they be found and can these differences be correlated to specific variables such as the speaker or even the topic of the experience itself?

What is a Narrative?

Attempts to provide a general and functional description of a narrative in terms of storytelling as practice is not so straightforward because of its interdisciplinary concerns (Toolan 2001). Even within the same discipline and under the broad heading of linguistics, cognitive linguists and sociolinguists, for example, work with different theoretical models that reflect specific interests. One overlapping feature, it could be argued, however, is that in order for an audience to comprehend what is being said and to satisfy particular expectations associated with the genre, narrative discourse requires all narrators to adhere to some form of story template. The notion of the existence of a kind of mental model for stories is fundamental to our understanding of narrative processing. Herman puts this simply by stating that 'story recipients, whether readers, viewers or listeners, work to interpret narratives by reconstructing the mental representations that have in turn guided their production' (2002: 1). For the purposes of the discussion in this chapter, the template presented as the central model for analysis and definition of a narrative is the influential, functional model of personal narratives developed by the sociolinguists William Labov and Joshua Waletzky (1967) and later modified by Labov (1972).

Labov and Waletzky primarily set out to investigate linguistic differences in the speech of minority groups in New York (from the African-American and Hispanic communities) as a way of challenging the notion that social deprivation resulted in the use of a 'restricted code', a sort of linguistic deficiency. Labov and Waletzky asked informants to narrate personal experiences on the themes of *danger of death* and *fights,* a strategy that produced elaborated answers beyond word and sentence level. Moreover, asking emotive questions about life-threatening situations caused informants to engage emotionally, resulting in a perceived style shift to a more relaxed and natural speech style called the *vernacular* (Labov 1972). Analysis of these oral narratives showed recurring clausal and structural patterns which led Labov and Waletzky to propose an 'analytical framework for the analysis of oral versions of personal experience in English' (1967: 12). Consequently, they were able to define narratives as 'one method of recapitulating past experience by matching a verbal sequence of clauses to the sequence of events which (it is inferred) actually occurred' (1967: 20).

Specifically, Labov and Waletzky proposed a macrostructure of narrative. This was in the form of six stages or schemas, each composed of 'a group of clauses of a common functional type' (Labov 1997: 403), with its own functional and structural role in the narrative. The six schemas of the narrative model and their functions are presented below, in the sequence given by Labov and Waletzky:

1. Abstract   signals what the story is about;
2. Orientation   provides the *who?, what?, when?* and *where?* of the story, usually descriptive;

3.	Complicating action	provides the *what happened?* part of the story and is the core narrative category;
4.	Evaluation	provides the *so what?* element and highlights what is interesting to narrator or addressee; reveals how participants in story felt;
5.	Resolution	provides the *what finally happened?* element of story;
6.	Coda	signals the end of story and may be in the form of a moral or lesson.

The *complicating action* is essentially the core narrative category of the story so that if the narrative was stripped back to ask the question *what happened?*, only the clauses in this section would remain, thus fulfilling Labov's definition of a minimal narrative as 'a sequence of two clauses which are temporally ordered' (1972: 360). It is this definition of a narrative that is vital and makes the distinction between what is a narrative and what, as we shall see, is not. Later work on personal narratives by Labov (1972) proposed some refinements to the *evaluation* category, which was found as being woven into the narrative rather than present as a distinct stage in the narrative sequence. Labov (1997) returned to the narrative model to re-evaluate the schema categories but commented only on issues of 'reportability', 'credibility', 'objectivity', 'causality', 'assignment of praise and blame' and 'viewpoint', as further criteria for a narrative, making no changes to the six-schema structure of the original model (see Bamberg 1997).

Alternative Story Modes

Recent studies in personal narratives have shown that not all personal stories are narratives. Some retold experiences may, on the surface, appear to fulfil the basic conditions of a narrative in that they describe past experiences. Closer examination, however, shows that the clauses lack the all-important narrative action or *complicating action*, which is the sequence of events that forms the basic narrative unit and is the 'tellable' high point of the story. Without clauses that constitute a *complicating action*, there can be no transformation and so its absence must disqualify any story from being called a narrative. Fludernik identifies various types of 'natural narratives' and other oral modes that are usually found in conversational storytelling, such as a 'narrative report', an 'observational narrative' and 'narratives of vicarious experience'. The narrative report, like any report – whether an eyewitness account of an incident by a police officer or a personal account of a relative's wedding – functions only to 'provide information, not to tell a story' (Fludernik 1996: 71). Consequently, a personal report lacks the necessary 'tellability' factor crucial to personal narratives as well as an evaluative commentary to draw attention to the point of its telling. Linguistically, Fludernik points out that reports are more likely to use *then* clauses instead of the causal *so*, which are commonly found in narratives of personal experience. (Fludernik also identifies the 'joke and/or the anecdote' as one other mode of conversational storytelling, however, this will not be elaborated on here (1996: 81–91).) In narratives of vicarious experience, the events described are ones that have occurred to someone else and so are third-person accounts – often hearsay – rather than autobiographical first-person stories. For this reason, Labov and Waletzky categorise such personal experiences as non-narratives. Observational narratives, on the other hand, may be considered a basic story category which uses the first person, *I*, 'as witness', and conveys 'the narrator's surprise, dismay, shock, fear or frustrated expectation that constitutes the tellability of the story' (Fludernik 1996: 73). However, observational narratives cast the narrator in the role of 'a passive experiencer of the events that usually do not concern him/herself directly' (p.74).

Plum (1988) also provides further insights on genre-based approaches to storytelling. In his data, he found that while some responses from informants conformed to Labov and Waletzky's six-schema structure, other personal experiences did not and this led him to identify four distinct categories or generic structures of storytelling to account for these formal variants, determined by their internal structure. In addition to the *narrative* genre, Plum concluded that personal experiences can be expressed as an *anecdote, exemplum* or *recount*, each a separate speech genre with identical beginnings and endings but with variations in the middle sections of their structure. (For a discussion of Plum's work on storytelling genres, see Eggins and Slade 1997 and Toolan 2001.) Functionally, each storytelling genre is said to be associated with different 'entertainment values'. For a summary of Plum's four storytelling genres, see Table 16.1 below.

Table 16.1 Plum's storytelling genres (adapted from Eggins and Slade (1997))

Genre	Beginning	Middle	End
Narrative	(Abstract) Orientation	Complication – Evaluation – Resolution	(Coda)
Anecdote	(Abstract) Orientation	Remarkable event – Reaction	(Coda)
Exemplum	(Abstract) Orientation	Incident – Interpretation	(Coda)
Recount	(Abstract) Orientation	Record of events – Reorientation	(Coda)

According to Plum, each storytelling genre has a specific social and rhetorical function:

Both anecdote and narrative may be said to be primarily concerned with 'entertaining' a hearer with a textual artefact which, in order to be successful needs to have a status independent of the experience it represents. On the other hand ... exemplum (is) much more concerned with 'making a point' rather than with entertainment, something which is achieved by creating a link between the text as representation of experience and something outside it.

(Plum 1988: 223)

Clearly, the *anecdote, exemplum* and *recount* cannot be described as narrative because they lack a *complicating action*, the all-important core narrative category. What Plum's work emphasises is how genre and form are inextricably linked to social function, and that not all personal experiences are narratives. The question I then ask is, 'Do certain story topics lend themselves better to producing personal narratives than others?' In other words, 'Do personal narratives about danger-of-death experiences, which have a clear social function in terms of their "entertainment value", conform easily to Labov and Waletzky's narrative model, as opposed to other types of experiences?' If that is the case, which topics are less likely to produce narrative forms and instead produce, for example, recounts? By analysing personal experiences of a group of informants, I found it possible to establish how far story topic determines story genre, and the type of storytelling discourse.

Methodology and Informants

As part of a larger study (Lambrou 2003, 2005) to investigate the claim for the existence of a universal narrative model, I interviewed members of the London-based Greek Cypriot community (LGC) for their personal narratives. I focused specifically on culture, age, gender, size of interview group and story topic as variables that might cause differences in the narrative structure. The LGC community was chosen as it represents an alternative speech community to the one investigated by Labov and Waletzky and, moreover, provides one way of testing the presumed universalism of their narrative model.

Three age groups were identified for the study: 9–11, 18–21 and 35–49, which covered two different generations of the LGC community. Typically, informants in the older adult group are second-generation Greek Cypriots, while the younger adult group and children are third-generation Greek Cypriots. Interviews took place in one-to-one settings (that is, the interviewer and one informant) and peer-group settings of up to four informants. All peer-group interviews were single-sex.

Informants in both one-to-one and peer-group interviews were asked to recall personal experiences about the same themes: happy, sad, funny and embarrassing events as well as those involving fights, arguments and the classic danger-of-death scenario, for example:

- Can you tell me about a sad experience?
- Can you tell me about a time you were involved in a fight or an argument that really upset you?

The range of topics was deliberately chosen to be wider than the 'danger-of-death' and 'fight' themes used by Labov and Waletzky (1967) and Labov (1972).

In this way, it is possible to test whether story topic affects or determines story structure to produce variations at both the macrostructure and microstructure level, and therefore creates subgenres of personal experiences that may not conform to Labov and Waletzky's model. In other words, which story topic correlates with which storytelling mode to *guarantee* a narrative or a recount.

Findings: Narrative and Recounts

A total of 45 informants participated in 26 interviews made up of 14 one-to-one interviews and 12 peer-group interviews. The interviews produced a corpus of 279 personal stories which were analysed against Labov and Waletzky's narrative model to identify which were narratives and fulfilled the minimum narrative criteria of having at a minimum, 'a sequence of two clauses' that are temporally ordered. The *complicating action* also had to report actual first-person events.

Of the 279 stories, 171 (61 per cent) were identified as personal narratives while the remaining 108 (39 per cent) were categorised as non-narratives and classified as recounts. This information is summarised in Table 16.2, below:

Table 16.2 Narratives and recounts: summary of LGC informants, interview setting and total number of personal stories

Sex	Age group	Interview setting	Number of interviews	Total number of informants	Number of personal experiences elicited	Experiences which are narratives	Experiences which are recounts
Male	9–11	One-to-one	2	2	9	5	4
		Peer group	3	9	61	43	18
	18–21	One-to-one	2	2	11	8	3
		Peer group	3	8	49	32	17
	35–49	One-to-one	2	2	13	6	7
		Peer-group	1	4	20	15	5
Female	9–11	One-to-one	3	3	14	5	9
		Peer group	2	4	28	12	16
	18–21	One-to-one	2	2	12	5	7
		Peer group	1	2	14	11	3
	35–49	One-to-one	3	3	21	11	10
		Peer group	2	4	27	18	9
			26	45	279	171 (61%)	108 (39%)

An example of a personal narrative that fulfils Labov and Waletzky's criteria is provided in Text 1 below, in order to be able to compare with examples of the non-narrative texts. (The narrative is taken from my data and is presented to show the distinct schemas. Names of informants are not given for reasons of confidentiality.)

1	Int	(And I just wondered if um any other stories in the sort of argument danger happy sad or embarrassing kind of genre have come up at all)	
	L	Em … fights-s …	Abstract
		I've only had one other experience of a fight and that was when	Orientation
5		someone was chasing me in a car because apparently I'd cut him up I'd	Orientation
		the kids in the car … um I parked the car outside my dad's factory he	Orientation
		parked in front of me walked up to the window and started staring and	Orientation
		started shouting at me through the window um the kids had got scared	Orientation
		so I got fed up of this got out kicked him a couple of times … and he	CA
10		drove off so I phoned up the police to tell him what I've done just in	CA
		case he'd gone as well	CA
		and never thought anything of it.	Resolution
		I'm not a very violent person but I can be if I have to be em …	Evaluation

Text 1 Personal narrative about a fight (male; 35–49; one-to-one interview).
CA = complicating action

Speaker L's personal narrative describes an experience of a fight where a crisis ensues and is resolved, whereby the *complicating action* (ll.9–11) lists the sequence of events in the temporal order in which they happened. Despite lacking a coda, L's experience is clearly recognisable as a narrative.

Recounts, however, are another matter. According to Plum (1988), recounts crucially lack a high point or crisis that forms the *complicating action*. Because there is an absence of narrative events, recounts also lack an *evaluation* and *resolution* because nothing reportable happens. Recounts are best described as a 'record of events' rather than a series of events linked through a process of causality. Three examples of recounts are presented below, in Texts 2–4, taken from across the range of informant groups:

1	Int	Tch okay em what about em a sad er experience in your life?
	A	==Hmm tch oh it has to be em … my gran's death and deaths in the family … they're probably the worst experiences in my life … people that I'm close to an
5	Int	Hmm can you think of a particular event the kind of events leading up to er … to one of those experiences that you can tell me about – a story about it
	A	Ehmm … well … actually my my em aunt's death was pretty em unexpected and em we weren't really expecting it at all so its not
10		much leading up to that but my gran em she was in hospital for about a month or two before she actually died so … there was obviously a lot of upset in the family then
	Int	Hmm

Text 2 A recounts a sad personal experience (female, 18–21, one-to-one interview)

1	Int	Great okay emm change the tone a little bit erm can you tell me about a time when you were very happy ... is there a lasting memory a very happy memory
5	L	A very happy memory? um 1986 one of the best holidays I've ever had in Cyprus ah 3 weeks of doing absolutely whatever I wanted ah I'd just started working in a bank pre – 2 years before that and I was on a very very good salary so I was – I had the money to blow and could drive and do whatever I want so it was 3 weeks of sheer bliss in Limmassol, Larnaca, Paphos met my first girlfriend there so
10		yeah that's probably the best memory I've got at the moment ... Could always say kids giving birth but THAT is something I always go back to

Text 3 L recounts a happy experience (male, 35–49, one-to-one)

1	Int	Okay ... what about a happy story can you think of a happy moment in your life?
	H	Em oh yeah when I went on em a jet ski in Greece with my cousin and we saw – we were heading towards this old ship and all the jelly
5		fish were round it and then like all these like and then all these pieces of woods off the ship were just falling down and we were laughing
	Int	You had a really nice time
	H	Yeah

Text 4 H recounts a happy experience (male, 10–11, one-to-one)

As the above three texts illustrate, recounts are descriptive records of the past. Moreover, they also describe recurring facts, in the same way the grammatical 'used to' describes past habits and states. There is no clear high point or record of events pointing to something specifically happening that is resolved. This is best illustrated by Text 5, below, in A's personal experience about fights and arguments.

1	Int	Okay were you ever involved in a fight or an argument that really upset you?
	A	I've been in fights yeah like I've been in a fight the only ones that actually annoy me and anger me is the ones between me and my
5		brother you know because they're the ones that 'cause he means something to me it's like it annoys you when he says something to you but when it's someone else so you don't care it's like no no-one else means anything to you so no matter what they say to you they can't anger me but when it's someone close to you ...
10	Int	Yeah can can you think of a specific argument?

A   yeah oh with my brother em [laugh] just little things like you know
         it's over the most stupid things 'cause he's – he comes home tired
         from work an' its like he takes it out on everyone and ... but so do
         we and we just all take it out on each other an like we argue over
15   stupid things like this shirt like wearing someone's clothes or you
         know who's gonna get in the bath first an' you know things like
         that an' it just like it builds up to like the biggest argument an'
         then you stop and you think yeah an you stop and you think "Wait
20   a minute why am I arguing with you over something like this?
         There's no reason to". It's normally over what he says to my sister
         my little sister as well 'cause like he shouts at her ...

Text 5 A recounts fights and arguments

Speaker A begins with an extended *abstract* on fights (ll.3–9) but his description
is general and not specific to any one incident. The interviewer's attempt to elicit
a narrative about a specific event (l.10), however, fails. What follows is a series of
free clauses, which describe arguments in his family that are general and recurring, as indicated by the word *normally* (l.20). The recurring nature of these
arguments is also signalled by the use of present simple tenses throughout to
suggest habitual behaviour, states or facts. A's recount is in fact an elaboration of
the 'most stupid things' (l.12), otherwise a description of a general state of affairs,
which he then goes on to describe.

The experiences identified as recounts were then analysed more closely by story
topic, sex, age and interview setting to provide a comparative analysis and identify
whether any correlations can be made. See Table 16.3, below.

What emerges from a close analysis of Table 16.3 appears to be a correlation
between recounts and story topic that has not been commented on by other
works, including Plum's. Despite the 108 recounts ranging across six story topics
or themes, over half the recounts (60 per cent) are based around two topics:
happy (31 per cent) and sad (29 per cent) experiences, see Table 16.4 below.
Conversely, both happy and sad experiences provide the lowest proportion of
narratives – only 18 per cent:

Happy and sad personal stories provide the highest proportion of recounts and
the lowest proportion of narratives, while experiences based on danger of death,
fights/arguments and embarrassing events produce the greatest proportion of
narratives. If narratives are descriptions of 'actions' then it can be argued that
recounts are descriptions of 'states', the states being happiness and sadness, as
illustrated in Texts 2–4. These findings provide evidence suggesting that story
topic does go some way towards determining story form. The question this now
raises is, 'Why is it that experiences about happy and sad topics produce recounts,
while stories about danger, fights, arguments and even embarrassing stories are
more likely to produce narratives?'

Table 16.3 Recounts showing story topic, sex, age and interview setting for each informant group

Sex	Age	Interview setting	Stories which are recounts	Danger of death	Fight/ argument	Embar- rassing	**Happy**	**Sad**	*Funny*
Male	9–11	One-to-one	4	0	1	0	2	1	0
		Peer group	18	1	1	3	7	5	1
	18–21	One-to-one	3	0	0	1	1	0	1
		Peer-group	17	2	4	0	6	3	2
	35–49	One-to-one	7	1	0	1	2	2	1
		Peer-group	5	1	2	1	0	0	1
Female	9–11	One-to-one	9	0	1	1	4	3	0
		Peer-group	16	0	3	1	5	6	1
	18–21	One-to-one	7	0	1	1	2	3	0
		Peer-group	3	0	1	0	1	1	0
	35–49	One-to-one	10	1	1	1	2	4	1
		Peer-group	9	1	3	0	2	3	0
			108	7	18	10	34	31	8

Narratives and 'Trouble' with a Capital 'T'

The most likely reason for the correlation with story topic and the schematic differences found in narratives and recounts can be explained by the single concept of 'Trouble' with a capital 'T'. The notion of 'Trouble' was proposed by Bruner (1997) in a critique of Labov and Waletzky's *complicating action*. Bruner builds on the earlier work of Burke (1945) who identified six 'requisite elements' of a story for his 'dramatist Pentad', namely 'Agent, Action, Goal, Instrument and Scene'. Burke argues, however, that 'the "engine" of dramatic narrative is not simply their interaction, but an imbalance between two or more of these elements

Table 16.4 Table showing the high proportion of recounts about happy and sad topics when compared to topics which prompt a narrative

Genre of storytelling	Total elicited	Danger of death	Fight/ argument	Embarrassing	Happy	Sad	Funny
Narrative	171	23%	20%	24%	**8%**	**10%**	15%
Recount	108	6%	17%	9%	**31%**	**29%**	8%

– a mismatch' (1945: 63). According to Bruner, this imbalance generates the sixth element, 'Trouble', which he claims defines complication, going so far as to suggest that 'Trouble' is essential for narrative structure. (See also Bruner 1990.)

> Indeed, Labov and Waletsky take Trouble so much for granted as the heart of complication that they even gathered their corpus of narratives so as to guarantee its presence. Recall that they asked their subjects to tell about a time when their lives were endangered – the ultimate trouble! And, of course, it's virtually in the structure of narrative that if a story contains a troubled complication, it requires some explication about how things were before it got that way – that is, an orientation, telling how things were before the trouble erupted.
>
> (Bruner 1997: 63)

Indeed, nothing guarantees drama, a crisis or a high point more than narratives based on fight, arguments, danger of death and embarrassing experiences. In other words, the reportability of the narrative is at stake as is the reputation of the narrator who must ensure that the personal experience is not only worth telling in the first place but that the reason for its telling is explicitly stated. The presence of 'Trouble' would guarantee a crisis, which is likely to be expressed as a series of narrative actions, linked by causality and having the assignment of praise and blame as central characteristics. Narratives by adults about 'Trouble' also guarantee *evaluation* of some sort, which also ensures their reportability worth, a further core characteristic of a personal narrative. This is exemplified in Text 1 where speaker L resorts to a fight to resolve the crisis that has developed and evaluates his actions in the final part of his narrative. Conversely, a description of less dangerous or dramatic experiences, such as those found in happy and sad stories, do not provoke the same schematic form and stylistic demands, and may typically result in less need for expressions of *evaluation*, self-aggrandizement or appraisal and blame. This can be seen in Texts 2–4 (and even Text 5 despite the prompt for the experience being about fights). Fundamentally, happy and sad experiences describe 'states', where nothing of note happens, as opposed to 'actions' where something leading to a high point or crisis that needs a resolution, is in fact resolved, and this is crucial to understanding the difference between a recount and a narrative.

A further interesting finding in my data is the correlation of recounts with informant age. Children (aged 9–11) of both sexes produced the largest proportion of recounts of the three age groups. Possible explanations are that children have fewer experiences to narrate, or have not yet acquired competency in storytelling to understand the importance of a *complicating action* in their personal experience to justify its telling. Both hypotheses, however, would need further investigation.

Coda

Variations in personal experiences, where they exist and how they can be accounted for, are fundamental for our understanding of different modes of storytelling such as narratives and recounts. The presence of a *complicating action*, as defined by Labov and Waletzky (1967) in their narrative model, is essential if a personal experience is to be recognised as a narrative. Variations at a macro-structure level can produce a range of storytelling subgenres, including recounts, where the internal structure varies significantly from a narrative. Story topic is one variable that determines story structure and, consequently, storytelling genre, by generating different story modes. This has been shown in the correlation with recounts and happy and sad experiences, which tend to describe 'states'; and narratives, which tend to describe 'actions' based on 'Trouble', where a personal disruption or crisis arises. For the narrator to be successful, a personal experience that is encoded as a narrative must be worth reporting in the first place; this is guaranteed by the presence of a personal crisis typically found in danger-of-death, fight, argument and embarrassing experiences, which fulfils not only the expectations of a reportable event but also those of the audience as recipients.

Transcription key

?	question or uncertainty
!	surprise
WORDS IN CAPITALS	emphatic stress and/ or increase in volume
" "	indicates direct speech
"*italics*"	captures the marked change in voice quality in direct speech of narrator or when narrator mimics another
(names and places)	names and locations not given but indicated in brackets
[ ]	non-transcribable speech
[laughs]	paralinguistic and non verbal information
=	interruption
= =	overlap
…	pauses of under 3 seconds
–	false start/restart
a-and	elongation of word

'Never a Truer Word Said in Jest': A Pragmastylistic Analysis of Impoliteness as Banter in *Henry IV, Part I*

Derek Bousfield

The application of ideas from pragmatics to stylistic analysis is an important part of stylistics and an important part of pragmatics. Taking pragmatics to be concerned with the ways in which we understand acts of verbal (and, for some, non-verbal) communication, it is natural to expect that insights from pragmatics will help us to understand how all spoken and written texts are understood, and so make a significant contribution to stylistic analysis. At the same time, the texts considered by stylisticians can be seen as data with which to test particular approaches to pragmatics. Bousfield's chapter simultaneously sheds light on the development of the character of Hal in *Henry IV, Parts I* and *II* and illustrates some key aspects of pragmatic approaches to stylistics: it applies the same methods to this literary text as would be applied to any other kind of verbal communication; it considers particular questions about audiences and communicators raised by fictional texts; it applies particular concepts from the study of pragmatics (in this case the notion of impoliteness) to the analysis of a fictional text; it integrates the pragmatic approach with other stylistic methods; and, finally, it raises interesting questions for further research.

The analysis of Hal's particular kind of face-threatening behaviour in the scene discussed here clearly demonstrates the nature of the difficult situation Falstaff finds himself in, where he simultaneously needs to defend himself and cannot directly do so. It also makes clear some of the ways in which this scene relates to the play as a whole, explaining how the scene helps us to understand the nature of the relationship between Falstaff and Hal and how it contributes to the overall development of Hal's character. The discussion of the complex layering involved makes clear some of the complexities involved in our understanding of the scene, which constitute a large part of its dramatic interest.

For me, the chapter raises three particularly interesting areas for further research. First, it would be interesting to develop a fuller account of the nature of the inferential processes audiences engage in when understanding the play: how exactly do audiences recognise impoliteness, banter and the complex 'discourse architecture' involved in this scene? Second, it would be interesting to explore further to what extent this approach is developing new ways of understanding the play and to what extent it is describing how existing understandings are arrived at. Finally, there is the question of the precise nature of the relationship between a pragmatic approach and existing stylistic models which will no doubt be developed by future work in this area.

Billy Clark

Introduction

The texts, *Henry IV, Parts I* and *II* represent some of Shakespeare's finest work within the history plays. *Henry IV, Part I*, especially, has been popular with the public and with critics from the beginning (Weil and Weil 1997). Set against the backdrop of medieval England during the turbulent period of the Wars of the Roses, the *Henry IV* plays represent the coming of age of a prodigal Prince Hal, tracking his development from the philandering idle coarse-mannered playboy Prince, oft carousing with Falstaff and friends, to his blossoming as, perhaps, one of Shakespeare's most heroic historical figures: *King Henry V*. Hal's apparently lackadaisical attitude to 'appropriate' princely behaviour throughout *Henry IV, Part I* is seen both within the play, and without, as threatening to his father, the titular Henry IV (Humphrey 1960). Indeed, received wisdom (which could be 'confirmed' by a hasty reading) would have it that it's not until *Henry IV, Part II* that Hal, being out from under Falstaff's shadow (as the two are hardly in the same scene in the later play) begins to develop a gravity about his present and future role: that he becomes aware of his need to become more serious and focussed. However, there is evidence from rather early on in *Henry IV, Part I* that Hal is well aware of this aspect of his own growing character, position and role. Nowhere is this more evident than in Falstaff's and Hal's metatheatrical parody (a comedic mocking irreverent 'scene-within-a-scene') in Act II, scene iv, where Hal (who is acting as if he was his father, King Henry IV) *seems* to engage in banter (see Leech 1983) with Falstaff, (who is acting as if he was Hal).

The comedic and highly amusing scene in question, one of *apparent* insincere impoliteness, is actually a cunning characterisation device in which Shakespeare apparently effortlessly signals that Hal is not, in fact, the one-dimensional wastrel and 'drinking buddy' of Falstaff that we have, up to this point, been led to believe. Indeed, Hal, as is apparent from this one early scene (especially when we consider this scene within the context of the play and the immediate series of plays) is beginning to show that he is a capable steely autonomous character: that he is in fact made of 'Kingly stuff'. This can be evidenced through a pragmatic and stylistic, or *pragmastylistic* analysis of Hal's use of *linguistic impoliteness* which is cleverly masked as banter, within, and shielded by, an interestingly deep, multilayered and well-crafted discourse architecture. What this chapter shows is an analysis of the rich and complex interdependence of *impoliteness* and *discourse-structure* within (given the constraints of space here) a single extract. This interplay shows clearly, for the first time in the text, that Hal is truly on a trajectory to becoming a strong, independent and charismatic Henry V; further, it shows that he is as separate and distinct from Sir John Falstaff as he is from his own father, Henry IV. The discussion which follows is, necessarily, brief but it does show that pragmatic models used for the analysis of spoken interaction in *real-life* situations can profitably be deployed with stylistic models of textual understanding to give a greater appreciation of both text and character than each approach, alone, could achieve.

Impoliteness in Shakespeare

The analysis of *impoliteness* as an aid to understanding character in Shakespeare's plays is not new. Culpeper (1996) has shown how impoliteness can contribute to the development and understanding of character in Shakespeare's *Macbeth*, and *The Taming of the Shrew* (Culpeper 1998). Rudanko (2006), building on this, has shown how impoliteness adds to characterization in *Timon of Athens*. What is new here, however, is the dependence (in this scene) of impoliteness on both the nature of *banter* and 'metatheatre' via a manipulation and exploitation of the prototypical discourse architecture relating to theatre. Throughout the remainder of this chapter I shall define and explain what is meant by the term *impoliteness* and the discrete but associated phenomenon of *banter*. I shall then present the scene with which this chapter is most interested in relation to its supposed comedic or banter-like nature. Then I shall discuss the scene in relation to its discourse architecture and, in this way, show how the scene relates not to true banter but to impoliteness-masked-as-banter. The use, therein, of impoliteness, deployed in a complex but enlightening way aids us in understanding the development of Hal's character.

Defining *Impoliteness* and *Banter*

Impoliteness

As with all scholarly definitions, the precise meaning of the term impoliteness is one which is the subject of intense scrutiny. As Watts has noted, '... (im)politeness is a term that is struggled over at present, has been struggled over in the past and will, in all probability, continue to be struggled over in the future' (2003: 9). Attempting to relate and discuss the full definitional struggle that is taking place at present over the term impoliteness is far beyond the scope and scale of the present chapter (though see Bousfield and Locher (2007) for a fuller exploration). For the purposes of this chapter here I take *impoliteness* as constituting the issuing of intentionally gratuitous and conflictive *face-threatening acts* (FTAs) (see Brown and Levinson (1987)) that are purposefully performed:

1) Unmitigated (that is, not *softened*) in contexts where mitigation of what one says is required; and/or,
2) With deliberate aggression, that is, with the *face-threat* exacerbated, boosted, or otherwise maximised in some way to heighten the face damage inflicted.

Furthermore, for impoliteness to be considered successful impoliteness, the intention of the speaker (or *author*) of the impoliteness to *offend* (that is, to threaten or damage face) must be understood by someone (not necessarily the intended recipient) in a receiver role.

(adapted from Bousfield 2007a, 2007b)

Here, for simplicity's sake, I'm following Goffman's definition of *face* as being:

[T]he positive social value a person effectively claims for himself [sic] by the line others assume he has taken during a particular contact. Face is an image of self delineated in terms of approved social attributes – albeit an image that others may share, as when a person makes a good showing for his profession or religion by making a good showing for himself.

(Goffman 1967: 5)

In short, the concept of a person's *face* – their feeling of self-worth or value – can be seen to be co-constructed between a speaker and a hearer (typically). Face, as Brown and Levinson (1987: 61) note is something that is emotionally invested, and it can be lost, maintained or enhanced in interaction. In this way impoliteness can be seen to be broadly, but not entirely, the opposite of the concept of politeness (see Mills 2005; Watts 2003) which is broadly the enhancement or at least the maintenance of face in interaction. Impoliteness (the causing of offence which results in the target(s) losing face (see Culpeper 2005)) can be conveyed in two main ways.

1   On-record impoliteness
    The use of linguistic strategies designed to *explicitly* (a) attack the face of an interactant, (b) construct the face of an interactant in a non-harmonious or outright conflictive way, (c) deny the expected face wants, needs and rights of the interactant, or some combination thereof. The attack is made in an unambiguous way given the context in which it occurs.
2   Off-record impoliteness
    The use of strategies where the threat or damage to an interactant's face is conveyed indirectly by way of an *implicature* that can (potentially) be cancelled (e.g. denied or an account/post-modification/elaboration offered, etc.) but where '... one attributable intention clearly outweighs any others' (Culpeper 2005: 44) given the context in which it occurs.

Sarcasm, and the *withholding of politeness where it is expected* would also come under the heading of off-record impoliteness, as follows:

(a) Sarcasm.

The use of strategies which, *on the surface* appear to be appropriate to the situation, but which are meant to be taken as meaning the opposite in terms of *face-management*. That is, the utterance which appears, on the surface, to maintain or enhance the face of the intended recipient actually attacks and damages the face of the recipient (see Culpeper 2005) given the context in which it occurs. For Leech this effect is caused by the phenomenon of irony, as it is irony which '... enables a speaker to be impolite while seeming to be polite' (Leech 1983: 142).

(b) Withhold Politeness.

Withholding politeness is within the Off-Record category as '... politeness has to be communicated [...] the absence of communicated politeness may, *ceteris paribus*, be taken as the absence of a polite attitude' (Brown and Levinson 1987: 5).

(Adapted from Bousfield 2007c)

Banter

Banter (see Leech 1983: 142–4) can be seen to be the identical-but-opposite phenomenon to what is termed here as *sarcasm*. To put it another way, banter is to politeness what sarcasm is to impoliteness, that is, where sarcasm is an insincere form of politeness which is used to offend one's interlocutor, banter is an insincere form of impoliteness used for the purposes of solidarity or social bonding (see Leech 1983: 144–5; Culpeper 1996). As we might imagine, banter could easily be used between friends (see Daly *et al.* 2004, for example). This is, perhaps, especially true when we consider that for a speaker (S) to engage in banter they must, according to Leech, '... say something which is (i) obviously untrue, and (ii) obviously impolite ...' to the hearer (H) (Leech 1983: 144).

The 'Falstaff–Hal Burlesque'

With the above definitions outlined, we should now move on to look at the extract in question here. By way of contextualisation and exploration the extract is taken from Act II, scene iv and is one described by Humphrey (1960: xlvii) as the 'Falstaff-Hal burlesque'. With *burlesque* meaning 'an artistic composition, esp. literary or dramatic, that, for the sake of laughter, vulgarises lofty material or treats ordinary material with mock dignity; any ludicrous parody or grotesque caricature' (Dictionary.com unabridged, v 1.0.1), then it seems obvious that traditionally this scene is viewed as one of mere high comedy – not one in which serious undercurrents of impoliteness are used to show a developing depth of character.

The scene is set in *Eastcheap, The Boar's Head Tavern*. Falstaff and his company of 'ne'er do wells', Gadshill, Peto and Bardolph have recently arrived at the tavern following their robbery of two hapless gentlemen from whom they have stolen 300 marks in gold. Robbery is the one principal means by which Falstaff's company of rogues have been financing their lifestyle of drink and debauchery, though, of course, Falstaff is attempting to 'groom' Hal so as to be able to profit from a life of luxury at the crown's expense when Prince Hal becomes king. Crucially, despite the risk to the Prince and his position (given that Falstaff's company are known associates of his) Hal manages to keep clear of this debacle and later returns all of the stolen money. This is further evidence of a cool head and independence of action leading to the development of Hal as right, and ripe, for kingship. He has not participated directly in the robbery. Indeed, he is in the tavern when Falstaff, Peto and Bardolph return. By way of contextualising the extract discussed below, the scene from lines 111–433 (Humphrey 1960) sees Falstaff and those in his company give their own version of the encounter they had with the two men they robbed. In this version, comically told with Falstaff who is drinking heavily and exaggerating the number of men he personally faced at every turn, it is claimed by Falstaff that it was he and his company who were subject to an attempted robbery '... by misbegotten knaves in Kendal green ...', which, with great heroism on the part of Falstaff, was defeated after some hours of fighting. Prince Hal is sceptical to say the least, especially given that Falstaff's company admit they instinctively ran from the fight. He has engaged in genuine light-hearted banter and teasing up to this point. He and Falstaff are, after all, both friends (of sorts) and drinking companions. Nothing up to this point has been particularly damaging in terms of the face of either. As the scene changes to the extract below, a messenger – Sir John Bracy – has come from the palace to summon Prince Hal to a meeting with his father, as a rebellion against Henry IV's rule is brewing. Falstaff asks Hal if he is afraid of what the rebellion might bring. Hal answers that he has not Falstaff's instinct to run from a fight. Falstaff points out that Hal will be horribly chided by his father (given his antics up to this point) and advises him to practise answering. Falstaff offers himself up in Hal's father's role. Hal, noting Falstaff's unlikely dialogue and his inability to convincingly play Henry IV, makes them switch roles so that Hal is acting as if he were King Henry IV, and Falstaff is acting as if he were Hal. In this way Hal creates a scene of pure metatheatre – a scene within a scene – which, given the earlier banter-filled exchanges, seems to herald a comic parody or 'burlesque' (Humphrey 1960) of what is to come when Hal actually meets his father. However, what *actually* happens is somewhat different:

1   *Prince~as~King Henry IV.* Now, Harry, whence come you?
       Falstaff~as~Prince Hal. My noble lord, from Eastcheap.
       Prince~as~King Henry IV. The complaints I hear of thee are grievous.
       Falstaff~as~Prince Hal. Sblood, my lord, they are false: nay, I'll tickle
5   thee for a young prince, i'faith.
       Prince~as~King Henry IV. Swearest thou, ungracious boy? Henceforth
           ne'er look on me. Thou art violently carried away from grace,
           there is a devil haunts thee in the likeness of an old fat man, a tun
           of man is thy companion. Why dost thou converse with that trunk of
10   humours, that bolting-hutch of beastliness, that swollen parcel of
           dropsies, that huge bombard of sack, that stuffed cloakbag of guts,

that roasted Manningtree ox with the pudding in his belly, that reverend vice, that grey iniquity, that father ruffian, that vanity in years? Wherein is he good, but to taste sack and drink it?
15 Wherein neat and cleanly, but to carve a capon and eat it, but in villainy? Wherein villainous, but in all things? Wherein worthy, but in nothing?

Falstaff~as~Prince Hal. I would your Grace would take me with you: whom means your Grace?

20 *Prince~as~King Henry IV.* That villainous abominable misleader of youth, Falstaff, that old white-bearded Satan.

Falstaff~as~Prince Hal. My lord, the man I know.

Prince~as~King Henry IV. I know thou dost.

Falstaff~as~Prince Hal. But to say I know more harm in him than in
25 myself were to say more than I know. That he is old, the more the pity, his white hairs do witness it, but that he is, saving your reverence, a whoremaster, that I utterly deny. If sack and sugar be a fault, God help the wicked! If to be old and merry is a sin, then many an old host that I know is damned: if to be fat be to be
30 hated, then Pharoah's lean kine are to be loved. No my good lord; banish Peto, banish Bardolph, banish Poins – but for sweet Jack Falstaff, kind Jack Falstaff, true Jack Falstaff, valiant Jack Falstaff, and therefore more valiant being as he is old Jack Falstaff, banish not him thy Harry's company, banish not him thy Harry's company,
35 banish plump Jack, and banish the world.

Prince~as~King Henry IV. I do, I will.

[*A knocking heard, Exeunt hostess, Francis and Bardolph.*]

[*Re-*]*enter BARDOLPH, running.*

Bardolph. O my lord, my lord, the sheriff with a most monstrous watch is
40 at the door.

Falstaff. Out, ye rogue! Play out the play! I have much to say in the behalf of that Falstaff.

[*Re-*]*enter the Hostess.*

Hostess. O Jesu, my lord, my lord!

45 *Prince.* Heigh, heigh, the devil rides upon a fiddle-stick, what's the matter?

Hostess. The sheriff and all the watch are at the door; they are come to search the house...

(Humphrey 1965: King Henry IV, Part I, II. iv).

A close examination of this extract shows us that *Hal~as~King* begins and intersperses his comments to *Falstaff~as~Hal* with obviously untrue comments. For example, in lines 6–9 we can see *Hal~as~King* chiding *Falstaff~as~Hal* for being '... violently carried away from grace' and that 'there is a devil that haunts thee in the likeness of an old fat man, a tun of man is thy companion'. These comments are obviously literally untrue. Hal is not carried away from grace, rather, as this very scene shows, he has (a) chosen to socialize with these individuals, and (b) continues to develop a grace all of his own. Additionally, the comic banter by which he describes Falstaff as a devil weighing a ton is obviously untrue. Falstaff, for all his faults and size is neither a devil, nor that physically heavy. These all fit Leech's definition of banter in that 'What *s* says is impolite to *h* and is clearly untrue. Therefore what *s* really means is polite to *h* and true' (Leech 1983: 144).

However, from lines 9 until 17 (see below) we see a long string of offensive utterances that *appear* to be banter. However, they cannot be banter in Leech's terms (1983) in that they are impolite but they are *not* clearly untrue. Note the following:

> *Prince~as~King Henry IV.* Swearest thou, ungracious boy? Henceforth ne'er look on me. Thou art violently carried away from grace, there is a devil haunts thee in the likeness of an old fat man, a tun of man is thy companion. Why dost thou converse with **that trunk of humours, that bolting-hutch of beastliness, that swollen parcel of dropsies**, that huge bombard of sack, that stuffed cloakbag of guts, that roasted Manningtree ox with the pudding in his belly, **that reverend vice, that grey iniquity, that father ruffian, that vanity in years? Wherein is he good, but to taste sack and drink it? Wherein neat and cleanly, but to carve a capon and eat it, but in villainy? Wherein villainous, but in all things? Wherein worthy, but in nothing?**

There is evidence elsewhere to suggest that Falstaff *is* in fact diseased (as the insults in 'trunk of humours' and 'swollen parcel of dropsies' would suggest) – the clearest example of such evidence would be his relationship with the prostitute, Doll Tearsheet, in *Henry IV, Part II*. Note also that Falstaff is indeed an old fat heavy-drinking greedy villainous wastrel – all evidenced throughout the text in ways other than by the insults in the dialogue above – insults which are clearly offensive but *not* clearly untrue. It must, therefore, be simply offensive, or, to put it another way such utterances must be *impolite rather than banter*. Indeed, Mills has cast doubts as to the received definition of banter noting that it can be manipulated in the right context so that, although superficially non-serious, it is actually 'closer to [the speaker's] true feelings' than perceived to be by the hearer and, in consequence, is surreptitiously face damaging (Mills 2003: 14; see also Archer 2007). Furthermore, we should perhaps note that *Hal~as~King* is here using *existential presuppositional structures*, e.g. '... why dost thou converse with that trunk of humours, that bolting-hutch of beastliness, that swollen parcel of dropsies ... that reverend vice, that grey iniquity, that father ruffian ...?' Here the existence of Falstaff as a diseased, beastly, foul, roguish, aging leader of vile scoundrels is *presupposed* rather than merely *asserted*. As defeasing or denying presuppositions is much more difficult than defeasing or denying simple assertions, the fact that they are structured thus makes such impolite comments that much stronger and, therefore, that much more damaging. These utterances are used to express and communicate some rather extreme impolite beliefs (see Leech 1983) about Falstaff to Falstaff himself. However, the relationship between Hal and Falstaff is not, for example, descending into a physical altercation and neither is attempting to leave. So just *how* is Hal getting away with offending and damaging the face of Falstaff in this way?

The Discourse Levels

The discourse level under which the scene and the characters are operating is a matter of some significance as to how we view Hal's linguistic behaviour and, thus, his character. As Short (1996: 169) notes, the classic discourse architecture of dramatic texts is a two-level affair, thus:

Producer roles   **Receiver roles**

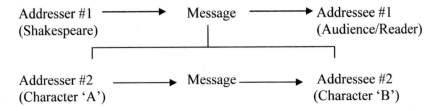

In stage productions, the playwright – in this case Shakespeare – gets his message (including plot lines and character development) across to the audience/reader primarily through what one character within the play says to another. What we have within the metatheatre exchange of the supposedly burlesque scene discussed here, is the following:

Producer roles   **Receiver roles**

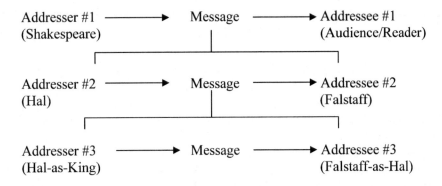

As we can see the dynamics of this scene – where Hal pretends to be his father, and Falstaff pretends to be Hal – mean that a third level is introduced – this, here, produces the type of context which Mills (2003: 14) was suggesting can be surreptitiously face-damaging. In this way Hal and, indeed, Falstaff (where he uses his status as *Falstaff~as~Hal* to suggest that Peto, Bardolph and Poins, but not Falstaff, should be banished from Hal's company) use the safety that is inherent in this extra level as a way of expressing themselves. What is meant by this is that *Hal~as~King Henry IV* can *more safely* utter such impolite comments than he can as Hal. This is because, viewed only on the bottom level of the three-tiered discourse structure (above), such utterances appear to be *on-record impoliteness*. However, because of the metadiscoursal nature of the scene, Hal (on the middle level of the three-tiered discoursal structure) is actually delivering such offensive utterances to Falstaff as *off-record impoliteness* (broadly equating to Mills' (2003) notion of surreptitiously causing face-damage). To put it in simpler terms – Hal would be able to plausibly deny personally meaning any of the things he has said in impolitely calling Falstaff a fat idle diseased wastrel. This is because he said such things *whilst playing the role of his father*, Henry IV. He has, in Holt's (2006) terms, constructed hypothetical enactments of reported speech. This device allows Hal the direct incisive non-ambiguity of uttering on-record comments, whilst simultaneously offering the protection of deniability that off-record comments provide. This is a complex stylistic device *par excellence* for the delivery of impoliteness. In a similar vein it might appear that *Falstaff~as~Hal* has the same opportunity for stylistic manipulation. However, it seems clear that Falstaff is trapped in the role of *Falstaff~as~Hal*. After all, if he rose out of the third (bottom) level to answer or challenge *Hal~as~King* on the second (middle) level then he would have to *admit* that he was offended by what Hal has been saying. To do so would be extremely face-threatening to Hal (whom Falstaff wants to keep sweet) and extremely face-damaging to Falstaff himself (as he would have to admit to being offended by a friend who he thinks is his protégé-of-sorts). Indeed, on this score, we should note the following lines 39–42, again:

> *Bardolph.* O my lord, my lord, the sheriff with a most monstrous
> watch is at the door.
> *Falstaff.* Out, ye rogue! Play out the play! I have much to say in the
> behalf of that Falstaff.

An extremely skilled Hal, by the end of this extract, has linguistically run rings around Falstaff, and Falstaff is aware of this. Indeed, Falstaff is so determined to defend his own face – to win back some points, in effect, all whilst still playing the role of Hal – that he attempts to dismiss Bardolph even though Bardolph has come to warn Falstaff that they are at risk of being imminently arrested for the robbery and theft of 300 marks in gold from two gentlemen. It's not until the Hostess re-enters the room/stage (in line 43) to warn (in line 44) Falstaff that he finally 'snaps' out of the role of Hal. At which point he beseeches Hal for his help which is reluctantly given. The relationship between the two has subtly but irrevocably changed. Hal has shown that he does, indeed, have the *wherewithal* to act in a suitably decisive and incisive manner whilst leaving his opponent(s) reeling – traits upon which he draws throughout the *Henry IV* and *Henry V* plays.

Conclusion

Despite early efforts to account for the phenomenon of impoliteness in real-life and dramatic interactions (Lachenicht 1980; Culpeper 1996), it is only recently that research into impoliteness has really begun to take off (see Culpeper *et al.* 2003; Bousfield and Locher 2007, for example). Indeed, it is only because of this recent research drive that a fuller understanding and appreciation of what Humphrey (1960) describes as the 'Falstaff-Hal burlesque' can be made. That the extract is viewed as a comedic burlesque is testament to the fact that it is a scene which is under-appreciated for its importance in the play with regards to Hal's growing and developing character and his relationship with Falstaff. Hal's linguistic behaviour, in particular, and the scene in general in fact foreshadow and, indeed, foretell the King's genuine reproof (Act III, scene iv) of Hal and his actions. The scene here, which takes place at Hal's instigation, shows that Hal is all too aware of the apparent negative perception that his carousing and popularity-seeking has had with his father. But his ability to play the usually loquacious and oft-insulting Falstaff at his own game, and win, is good preparation for Hal. His overall ability to communicate on this level with the so-called 'common people' or 'lower orders' serves him well during his 'eve of battle' wanderings around the English camp in *Henry V*. Indeed, his ability to connect to his subjects serves him well during the *Harfleur* speech in which Henry V manages to inspire his almost-beaten and thoroughly bedraggled troops into one final victorious charge through the city's breached walls. Further, his understanding of the intricacies of just how impoliteness can be issued serves him well during his meeting with the King of France and the crown prince, the Dauphin. The Dauphin attempts to surreptitiously insult Hal through comments regarding tennis balls. Hal, as Henry V, effortlessly sees through the Dauphin's covert linguistic insults towards him and concisely rebuffs the impoliteness, turning it back on the Dauphin. Hal's linguistic abilities, including his understanding and use of impoliteness, were honed in the *Boar's Head Tavern* in *Eastcheap* during *Henry IV, Part I*.

It seems that at the very least such pragmatic models, deployed within contemporary stylistic models of explanation can help to identify plot themes and characterisation threads much earlier than might otherwise have been thought identifiable. Here, the analysis of the rather complex interplay of impoliteness and banter between Hal and Falstaff in *Henry IV, Part I* (Act II, scene iv) can be seen as being just as powerful as the bare-faced direct on-record impoliteness of Hal (now King Henry V) to Falstaff in *Henry IV, Part II* (Act V, scene v). Impoliteness as a tool for the exhibiting of 'power' (Bousfield 2007c) and causing social disharmony (Culpeper *et al.* 2003) essentially involves the generation of social distance. As such, impoliteness as used in the extract analysed can only be seen as the start of Hal distancing himself from Falstaff, his company and his actions. This finally comes to fruition following Hal's coronation as Henry V in Act V, scene v of *Henry IV, Part II*. Here, hearing that his supposed protégé has been crowned, Falstaff rushes to London to be with Hal. Shouting from the crowd, Falstaff (with Pistol) attempts to gain Hal's attention:

> *Falstaff.* God save thy Grace, King Hal, my royal Hal!
> *Pistol.* The heavens thee guard and keep, most royal imp of fame!
> *Falstaff.* God save thee, my sweet boy!
> *King.* My Lord Chief Justice, speak to that vain man.
> *Chief Justice (to Falstaff).* Have you your wits? Know you what 'tis you speak?
> *Falstaff.* My King! My Jove! I speak to thee, my heart!
> *King.* I know thee not old man. Fall to thy prayers.
>
> (Humphrey 1965: 181)

We should note that Hal, now King Henry V, claiming that he does not know Falstaff is incredibly face-threatening. Hal knows Falstaff all too well. This *on-record impoliteness* here can only serve to distance Hal from Falstaff and, thus, complete the distancing of Henry V from his former life – a process which was begun by Hal in an *Eastcheap* tavern when with impoliteness masked as banter he breathed new life into the old adage, *never a truer word said in jest.*

The Cognitive Rhetoric of Arthur Miller's *The Crucible*

Craig Hamilton

The popular image of stylistics is still often that of a detailed mechanical description of the surface linguistic patterns of literary works. Nothing could be further from the truth. For decades stylistics, drawing upon linguistic pragmatics and discourse analysis, has gone far beyond mere surface linguistic description. Still more recently, its concern with underlying pragmatic inferences and discourse structures has led it to take the 'cognitive turn', to draw upon cognitive psychology, and cognitive science generally, to understand how human minds 'make meaning' out of the often quite fragmentary linguistic structures of literary and dramatic works. Stylistics will never, of course, lose interest in those fragmentary structures. They are the necessary prompts to the process of literary meaning construction. Stylistics consists now, however, of the study of the whole of that process, a process of which the production and reception of linguistic tokens is only a part, though a crucial one. Some of the most important work in contemporary stylistics may therefore pay no direct attention to surface linguistic detail at all, concentrating upon the underlying processes of meaning construction. This is what Craig Hamilton does in his study of *The Crucible*.

Hamilton draws from two theoretical frameworks in contemporary cognitive science to help explain how theatregoers and play readers, and indeed actors and directors, make meaning out of the prompts provided by the language of Miller's play. Malle (2004) cites experimental evidence showing that people tend to adopt simple explanations for desirable events and complicated ones for undesirable ones. In contrast, the characters in *The Crucible* regularly reverse this pattern. This helps to explain why things seem so frighteningly 'wrong' in the imaginative world of this play. The second theoretical framework that Hamilton draws upon is that of blending and parable theory. In an exemplary study of the reception of *The Crucible* he shows that its audiences and readers have from the very beginning consistently drawn a parallel between Salem in 1692 and the McCarthy era America in which it was written, and that Miller had this parallel in mind when he wrote the play. Yet there is no mention in the play of anything other than 1690s New England, so how have audiences and readers been able to draw this parallel? This is done, Hamilton shows, via the identification of generic roles that are filled both by people in Salem and by those of the McCarthyite, or other similar, eras.

When these sets of different values for the same generic roles are blended together, the meaning of a parable is made out of the prompts provided by the play's language.

One final point. Hamilton construes the terms parable and blending in the wide general fashion of Turner (1996). There is of course no single 'correct' way to construe these terms, and Hamilton uses his construal of them to very great effect indeed. Yet narrower construals of them may enable still more insights to be gained.

Peter Crisp

Introduction

Rhetoric is the father of stylistics, but the fruit often falls far from the tree. That is, the concerns of classical rhetoric and contemporary stylistics are not always similar as the variety of topics covered in this collection demonstrates. But stylistics is evolving and exploring new paths of research, especially as the relationship between stylistics and cognitive linguistics becomes clarified (Culpeper and Semino 2002; Hamilton 2006). One of those paths, cognitive rhetoric, locates stylistic research within the rhetorical tradition once again by re-examining the production of textual meaning with reference to findings by cognitive scientists. If putting the adjective 'cognitive' with the noun 'rhetoric' seems odd, we should recall that Aristotle spoke at great length on how the minds of speakers and audiences functioned. This is evident in Book II of Aristotle's *Rhetoric* (1954), for example, where he discusses the creation of persuasive discourse through the manipulation of an audience's emotions and the production of various states of mind. Therefore, since rhetoric in practice and in theory has always been cognitive, 'cognitive rhetoric' is hardly an oxymoron.

That said, 'cognitive rhetoric' has been defined in at least three different ways. In 1975, Dan Sperber used the term for a research programme that would become better known as Relevance Theory in pragmatics in the 1980s (Sperber 1975; Sperber and Wilson 1986). In 1979, Linda Flower began using the term for a research programme in Composition Studies aimed at analysing the thought processes behind writing, especially the writing of American undergraduates (Flower 1979, 1989, 1993). In 1991, Mark Turner began to use the term to define a research programme that tied findings by cognitive scientists to the art of literary criticism. For Turner, cognitive rhetoric referred to 'case studies explaining individual works and elucidating three levels on which cognitive studies form the ground of criticism' (1991: 239); namely, the level of 'local phrasing', the level of the 'whole literary work' and 'the level at which we conceive of literature generally' (1991: 239–45). Referring to cognitive rhetoric more recently, Turner has boldly stated, 'If Aristotle were alive today he would be studying this research and revising his work accordingly' (2002: 10). Hyperbole notwithstanding, Turner's point is that while cognitive rhetoric, like stylistics, has roots in classical rhetoric, its intellectual indebtedness to current cognitive science is rather original.

Although much of my previous research in cognitive rhetoric has analysed the function of figurative language in various texts (Hamilton 2003, 2004, 2005), this chapter is different. Here, I examine character behaviour in Arthur Miller's *The Crucible* (1995) to suggest how the findings of Bertram Malle (2004), a cognitive scientist at the University of Oregon, offer new insights into the peculiar behaviour of some of the play's characters. I also discuss the play's reception history and popularity to suggest that Mark Turner's theory of parable (1996) may explain how audiences interpret *The Crucible* as a political parable. By moving beyond a linguistic analysis of the text, cognitive rhetoric ultimately reveals that cognitive science has plenty to offer to the field of stylistics.

The Play and its Characters

In spring 1952, Arthur Miller went to Salem, Massachusetts for a week of research (Miller 1996: 160). The result of that research was *The Crucible*, which opened on Broadway on 22 January 1953. Although there were at least two other plays about the Salem witch trials being staged in America during the 1952–3 season (Welland 1979: 54), it is Arthur Miller's *The Crucible* that has left its mark on literary history. *The Crucible* unveils a town that is hardly a utopia during America's experiment with theocracy. Indeed, Miller's portrait of 1692 Salem is a portrait of a society falling apart. According to Neil Carson (1982: 65), witch hunts in late seventeenth-century New England were not widespread – they were confined to Salem and a few other nearby villages. The unfortunate uniqueness of Salem is perhaps why, in a moment of despair in Act 1, Salem's pastor, Reverend Parris, openly tells the parishioners before him: 'I cannot understand you people ...' (Miller 1995: 156). Parris, who is Salem's 'third preacher in seven years' (Miller 1995: 156), has learned that Salem is a town full of people who argue over property lines, who file endless lawsuits for libel, and who ironically struggle over firewood (hardly a scarce resource in 1690s Massachusetts). As Klaus-Dieter Gross states, however, 'The end of the seventeenth-century in New England was an era of instability' (2001: 44). King James II was overthrown in England in 1689, which meant that by 1692 – the year in which the play is set – it had been three years since Massachusetts had had a legitimate government (Morgan 1997: 4). In May 1692, when the new governor William Phips arrived, he found gaols full of 'witches' (Morgan 1997: 4). This was the general political context within which the specific events in Salem occurred.

To a certain extent *The Crucible* is tragic because many characters make categorical errors about cause-and-effect relations. According to Miller (2000: 291), 'leaping to conclusions is a wonderful pleasure' for certain people, and the behaviour of many of his play's characters manifests that idea. But what should the cognitive rhetorician make of this? Ever since Turner wrote *Death is the Mother of Beauty* (1987), causality has been a topic of interest in cognitive rhetoric. But as Malle might say, Miller's characters tend to settle for simple explanations when the behaviour they want to explain is grave and complex. In *How the Mind Explains Behaviour* (2004), Malle argues that it is unusual for people to settle for simple causal explanations to explain terrible effects. In fact, we often explain good things that happen in rather simple ways, but we normally offer elaborate causal explanations for bad things that happen (Malle 2004). Malle's conclusions are drawn from research experiments involving thousands of subjects asked to explain various social situations. He found that the more socially unacceptable an event is deemed, the more elaborate our explanations for that event will be. For example, to explain why someone commits suicide, we might offer explanations that refer to mitigating circumstances such as unemployment, divorce or substance abuse. In contrast, we often provide simple explanations for socially acceptable events. For instance, we might say that studying hard was why somebody passed a tough exam. Offering a simple cause (e.g. studying hard) for a socially desirable effect (e.g. passing the test) is something Malle found normal people do on a regular basis. But when the outcome is judged to be less acceptable, then the behaviour explanations become predictably more elaborate.

In Miller's play, however, the opposite is the case. There are at least four instances in the play where characters offer the wrong explanations for the events they hope to explain. First, in Act 1, we learn that Doctor Griggs believes that Betty Parris' illness has a supernatural rather than a natural cause. While Betty is not really ill, her father, Reverend Parris, believes that she is. Moreover, he suspects that the illness has a natural cause. Parris summons Reverend Hale from Beverly in the hope that Hale will contradict the diagnosis of Doctor Griggs by ruling out supernatural causes. The boundaries of medicine and religion are thus confused: while a medical doctor proposes a supernatural cause for the girl's illness, a pastor is called on to offer an expert second opinion about the illness' natural etiology. Unfortunately, Parris invites Hale to Salem without holding a meeting first, which we learn he should have done. His premature invitation is what sparks rumours of witchcraft. The townspeople assume that Reverend Hale from Beverly would only be sent for if Betty's illness were caused by witchcraft. As they see it, why else would Hale be summoned?

Second, despite what others tell him, Parris thinks some young women, including his daughter, Betty, and his niece, Abigail Williams, were engaged in witchcraft the previous night when he found them dancing around a fire outside. Abigail, however, tells him it was merely 'sport' (Miller 1995: 140). Likewise, Rebecca Nurse, a woman over 70 with 11 children and 26 grandchildren, advises Parris not to take this situation seriously since all children go through their 'silly seasons' and cause 'mischief' (Miller 1995: 153). Even in Act 3, when Abigail's friend, Mary Warren, tells the Court that the young women's behaviour was 'pretense' (Miller 1995: 205), few people in the play, including Parris, believe her. They prefer instead to cling to their false conclusions. As Malle's research shows, the explanations we offer regarding certain types of behaviour depend on our evaluations of that behaviour. But when Miller's characters categorize child's play as the work of the Devil, misguided causal explanations result from that categorical mistake.

Third, Hale begins to doubt the ethos of John and Elizabeth Proctor after questioning them in Act 2. He thinks that there are 'powers of the dark' threatening Salem, that there 'is a misty plot afoot' and that the trial is God's way of punishing Salem for its sins (Miller 1995: 185, 192, 198). That is how Hale interprets the cause of Salem's troubles at first. He will change his mind later, but in Act 2 Hale realizes that Salem is a town where neighbour accuses neighbour and where spouse accuses spouse. According to Klaus-Dieter Gross, Elizabeth Proctor was unique among Salem's victims: she 'had been accused by the girls but not her husband' (2001: 49). The young women apparently do not accuse Proctor because their leader, Abigail, loves him. Although we learn in the play that Proctor ended his adulterous relationship with Abigail eight months earlier, she is still jealous of Elizabeth. After good women like his wife are arrested for specious reasons, Proctor says, in Act 2, that 'vengeance is walking Salem' (Miller 1995: 196), and, in Act 3, that 'a whore's vengeance' might explain why Abigail accused Elizabeth of witchcraft (Miller 1995: 223). However, because 'the entire contention of the state in these trials is that the voice of Heaven is speaking through the children', as Judge Danforth states in Act 3 (Miller 1995: 204), Proctor's attempt to discredit the young women and cast doubt on their accusations proves to be futile.

Fourth, despite having no evidence to support their claims, the Putnams believe that six of their seven children did not die of natural causes but were killed by midwives like Goody Osburn. When Rebecca Nurse suggests that others are not to blame for the deaths (Miller 1995: 154), the Putnams disagree. Their one remaining child, Ruth, has, like Betty, apparently fallen ill. They blame Tituba, Parris' servant from Barbados, for this particular malady. Abigail tells Proctor in Act 1 that Ruth and Betty's behaviour has 'naught to do with witchcraft' (Miller 1995: 176), but Tituba is nevertheless forced to confess to an act she is not responsible for. Tituba is understandably confused when Parris shouts, 'You will confess yourself or I will take you out and whip you to your death' (Miller 1995: 168). Even before Tituba can reply, Thomas Putnam leaps to the conclusion that she is guilty by screaming: 'This woman must be hanged! She must be taken and hanged!' (Miller 1995: 168). Although Valerie Lowe (1998) has convincingly explained why Tituba's confession is not a confession at all, Tituba's statement is 'nearly an edited transcription of her [actual] testimony at the trial of Sarah Good' (Martin 1977: 286). Since death was the price to pay for being seen with the Devil, you could only escape the death penalty by saying you saw others with the Devil too. Such 'spectral evidence' was legitimate in the legal system at that time, and according to Neil Carson, 'The witch-hunt [only] ended when a group of church leaders in Boston declared that the unsupported evidence of witnesses was insufficient to justify the death penalty' (1982: 63). However, since 'each individual is required to tell a lie if he wants to save his life' (Bonnet 1982: 35), Act 1 ends with Tituba claiming that she was merely following the orders of Abigail and Betty round the fire the night before. This charge leads Abigail and Betty to denounce no fewer than 11 other people at the end of Act 1 in order to save themselves. Once the train of false accusations leaves the station, as it were, it becomes practically impossible to stop.

As we can see, Miller's characters behave in unexpected ways when it comes to explaining the behaviour of others. For instance, when Giles Corey says in Act 3 that Putnam is 'killing his neighbours for their land!' (Miller 1995: 211), he offers an alternative account for Salem's troubles. While it was legal to confiscate the property and goods of witches immediately upon their arrest (Martin 1977: 288), the proposition that Putnam's greed is causing Salem's problems is unreasonably simple. Putnam might have been trying to settle a score with George Jacobs, as Giles admits, but the greed of a single man cannot explain why so many people in Salem 'broke charity' with one other (i.e. turned against each other). As Jean-Marie Bonnet states, 'A whole town is involved, not simply one family whose drama might be representative of the plight of the community' (1982: 32). Salem's problems are therefore too complex to be explained simply by one man's actions alone. After all, before the Court of Oyer and Terminer in Salem shut down in October 1692, 20 people would be executed and more than 150 would be 'accused and confined to prison to await trial' (Carson 1982: 63). And while the convictions would be overturned by the General Court in 1710 (Bigsby 2005: 166), Putnam's greed or Proctor's sin are not enough to explain the sad behaviour of so many citizens in Salem. Why? Because terrible events normally prompt us to offer sophisticated explanations for those events. Unfortunately, this was not true for many of Miller's characters.

As Miller argued elsewhere (1996: 159), America's hunt for Communists circa 1950 was apparently fuelled by the belief that America had lost the ideological battle for China, and that it was losing a similar battle in Europe, especially in Italy (Miller 1996: 159). The reason given at the time for these losses? According to Miller, 'the State Department – staffed, of course, under Democratic Presidents – was full of treasonous pro-Soviet intellectuals. It was as simple as that' (1996: 159). Miller's point is that it was never 'as simple as that', neither in 1692 nor in 1952. In the play, however, there are tragic consequences when people leap to conclusions, confuse cause-and-effect relations or explain awful events in simple terms.

The Play and its Popularity

Ever since the play was first staged in 1953, *The Crucible* has remained in production somewhere in the world and has never gone out of print – a remarkable feat for a modern play. Miller might have become interested in Salem, in part, after reading Marion Starkey's 1949 book, *The Devil in Massachusetts*. Starkey called 'the story of 1692 ... an allegory of our times' (quoted in Welland 1979: 55) and Miller apparently agreed. Indeed, many critics since the play's premiere have argued that understanding *The Crucible* entails interpreting the play as a parable for the persecution of American communists. On 22 January 1953, after the play's first performance, Richard Watts wrote in the *New York Post* that some 'spectators [may] notice certain disquieting *resemblances* to present-day conditions' (1979: 73). On that same day John Chapman also wrote in the *New York Daily News* that some spectators might take the play to be a 'political *parable*' (quoted in Foulkes

1978: 302). The reviews of Chapman and Watts suggest that audiences found little 'aesthetic distance', to use Hans-Robert Jauss' famous term, between 1690s Salem and 1950s America. Although aesthetic distance 'allows us to indulge in suppressed, unadmitted, or openly frowned upon types of identification without fear' in the theatre according to Jauss (1989: 59), Watts and Chapman imply that spectators in 1953 America might have felt afraid to make explicit connections between Salem's persecution of witches in the past and America's hunt for communists in the present. That said, a decade later Henry Popkin argued that 'Miller chose an unmistakable *parallel* to current events' (1964: 140) when writing about seventeenth-century Salem, while Philip Hill commented on the play's 'obvious *parallels*' to the McCarthy era (1967: 314).

Critics in the 1970s and 1980s continued this line of reasoning. In 1977, Robert Martin called the play a 'political *allegory*' and argued that 'to many observers the *parallel* between the witchcraft trials at Salem ... in 1692 and the current Congressional hearings was the central issue of the play' (1977: 290, 279). In 1978, Peter Foulkes called the play an '*allegory*' and praised Miller for finding '*counterparts*' between 1690s Salem and 1950s America (1978: 297, 302–4). Likewise, for E. Miller Budick, *The Crucible* was 'the natural *analogue* to the McCarthy trials' in Washington DC since, by 'pretending that Salem is contemporary America', the play offered viewers an '*analogy* to a contemporary problem' (1985: 535, 548–9).

Similar remarks have been made about the play since 1990. For example, Wendy Schissel has mentioned the play's '*parallels* to McCarthy's America of 1952' (1994: 461) while Terry Otten has argued that Miller found an 'objective correlative' between the Salem trials and 'the political trials of the McCarthy era' (1996: 42). Thomas Adler has spoken of the '*analogy* at the base of Miller's political *allegory*' (1997: 93), and Joseph Valente has called the play a 'colonial *allegory*' with 'contemporary relevance' (1997: 120). In a review of Nicholas Hytner's 1997 film version of the play, Midge Decter maintained that Miller found Salem's story to be a 'useful *parallel*' (1997: paragraph 3) for America during the age of McCarthy. For Valerie Lowe, *The Crucible* 'was *intended* to draw *comparisons* between the rise of McCarthyism ... and the Salem witch hunts' (1998: 129, my italics), an opinion that, if true, would call into question the so-called intentional fallacy. More recently, Klaus-Dieter Gross has said that the play is full of 'political *parallels*' (2001: 57), and many critics would most likely agree with that assessment.

Because so many definitions of the play include terms like allegory, analogy, parallel, comparison, resemblances or counterparts, I think it is safe to call *The Crucible* a parable. Granted, 'symbol' and 'allegory' can be confusing terms (Crisp 2005), but by calling the play a parable I am following the lead of Chapman, who used that very term in his review in January 1953. According to Turner, parable is 'the projection of story' (1996: 7), which is to say that parable is a process whereby we project one story onto another and thus create new meaning as a result. In the case of *The Crucible*, many spectators conceptually project 1690s Salem onto 1950s America. While Otten has claimed that it is the play that projects 'the political realities of the 50s' (1996: 43) onto the story of Salem's witch hunt, in fact it is the other way around. Moreover, it is the human mind – not the play itself – that projects the story of Salem's witch hunt onto the story of America's hunt for communists in the 1950s.

Why does that parabolic projection occur? There may be two answers to that question. The first involves Miller himself (Popkin 1964: 140), who referred openly to America's pursuit of communists in the published version of the play, which first appeared in April 1953 (Miller 1953). Miller also said publicly that he saw an 'analogy' between the Salem trials and the Congressional hearings into Un-American Activities (Miller 1996: 162), and that he saw 'some astonishing correspondences' between the two periods when he decided to write the play (Miller 2000: 274). Comments like these encourage readers to see the play as a parable. But as Bonnet reminds us, reading the play and seeing the play are not the same thing; readers at home may encounter Miller's remarks about McCarthyism but most spectators in the theatre do not (1982: 32–3). Indeed, the play was first staged in January 1953 but was only printed three months later. Thus, theatregoers who could not have possibly read Miller's text nevertheless began interpreting the play as a parable. The reception history of the play makes this quite clear. According to Peter Foulkes, 'The spontaneous applause which greeted Proctor's question – "Is the accuser always holy now?" – was obviously prompted by the belief that the word "now" referred to 1953 at least as much as to 1692' (1978: 304).

That remark leads us to literary competence, a second potential answer to our question. Jonathan Culler famously defined literary competence as a series of rules to follow or conventions to adhere to when interpreting poetry – the first being to read the poem according to the 'rule of significance' so as to understand the poem as being about 'man's relation to the universe' (1975: 115). Obeying the rule of significance may explain why those who encounter Miller's play interpret it as a parable. Indeed, all the published interpretations of the play that I have surveyed explicitly mention McCarthyism. A critic who did not would be producing a deviant interpretation of the play since academically acceptable interpretations of the play seem to be those that display literary competence and follow the rule of significance. Even a critic like Hill, who wrote that the play 'unquestionably ... no longer depends upon such parallels' (1967: 314), nevertheless mentioned McCarthyism in his short article.

If literary competence's rule of significance may explain *why* people consistently interpret the play as a parable, Turner's theory of parable and conceptual blending may explain *how* this interpretation occurs. Conceptual blending allows us to fill fixed generic roles with new specific values and create a parable in the process. By filling roles from Miller's story of late-seventeenth-century Salem with values from mid-twentieth-century America, for example, audiences interpret the play as a parable for McCarthyism. *The Crucible* provides us with a story that contains *roles* such as judge, plaintiff and defendant. The play also provides us with specific *values* for these roles such as Danforth, Abigail and Proctor. Because similar roles exist, for example, in Bernard Shaw's *Saint Joan*, critics such as Richard Watts (1979: 73), Ronald Hayman (1972: 57) and Dennis

Welland (1979: 58) have been inspired to compare the two plays. But when a critic like Neil Carson (1982: 74) refers to the 'accused spies Julius and Ethel Rosenberg' and 'the House Committee on Un-American Activities [HUAC]', he is proposing original values for Miller's fixed roles. Despite William McGill's insistence that 'John Proctor is not Alger Hiss, Julius Rosenberg, or Owen Lattimore' (1981: 263), his denial nevertheless suggests that Proctor's role as defendant or accused can indeed be filled by other values. Lattimore, for example, was an academic expert on China who was summoned in 1952 to Washington DC before Senator Pat McCarran's Internal Security Subcommittee (on which Senator Joseph McCarthy also sat) in order to defend himself against charges of being a Soviet agent. With respect to Miller's play, we could imagine Lattimore as Proctor, McCarthy as Abigail and McCarran as Danforth. Likewise, the role of defendant could also be filled by a value such as Miller's former friend, Elia Kazan, the film director who decided to name names before HUAC in January 1952, just a few months before Miller's research trip to Salem. In short, critics like Carson and McGill, who argue over which values may fill which roles, reveal that the play does indeed inspire people to conceptually blend two stories and thus produce a parable in the process.

It is important to note that the parable is hardly provoked by anything stated overtly by Miller's characters on the stage. That is why E. Miller Budick is right to claim that '[a]nalogizing' is neither 'the major subject of the play' nor 'its major structural device' (1985: 536). Simply put, the parable is 'in' our minds, not 'in' the play. When Joseph Valente, for example, forges an analogy between Adam and Eve and Proctor and Abigail in order to examine what he sees as Miller's sexism in the play (1997: 131), that analogy is the result of his own cognition, not Miller's. To be fair to Valente, interpretation often entails speaking when a text is silent, or providing information missing from a story, but that is something we are responsible for rather than the writers we study.

This leads me to a question asked by the reviewer Robert Warshow in March 1953: 'How can he [Miller] be held responsible for what comes into my head while I watch his play?' (quoted in Foulkes 1978: 304). Warshow was referring to the parallels *he* saw between the play and the pursuit of America's Reds. Of course, Miller cannot be held responsible for the thoughts of his audience members, but writers fighting against censorship have always known that parables are the figurative products of reading minds and not the literal products of written texts. Consider, for example, Mikhail Bulgakov's 1925 novella, *The Heart of a Dog*. The Soviet secret police confiscated the manuscript in 1926, and it was never published in Russia until 1987 (BBC 2002). The story is ostensibly about a certain Professor Preobrazhenski, a urologist who takes organs from a dead worker and implants them into a stray dog. Soon the dog begins to act like a man, albeit a primitive one, and the doctor is forced to end the experiment. Although the story is very funny, Soviet officials were not amused. They no doubt saw the story as a critical parable about the 'new man' Soviet communism was meant to create (BBC 2002: paragraph 3). Since Bulgakov rarely mentions the political situation of the Soviet Union in the 1920s in his novella, that subversive parable exists in the minds of readers, not in the words of the text. But that is precisely my point: because parables are constructed in the minds of readers, rather than spoon fed to us literally by authors, political writers may use parables to comment on current events. In other words, writers count on our capacity for conceptual blending, and our adherence to the rule of significance, in the hope that their works will inspire us to produce powerful parables.

To return to Warshow's question, when watching Miller's play performed the parable is ultimately the responsibility of the audience, not the playwright. As I see it, what makes the play so popular around the world is its ability to prompt new audiences to find new stories onto which Miller's play may be projected. For instance, when Miller met Nien Cheng, author of *Life and Death in Shanghai*, she told him that when she saw *The Crucible* 'she couldn't believe a non-Chinese had written it' (Miller 2000: 293) given the similarities she found between the play and China's Cultural Revolution. According to Miller, audiences '[f]rom Argentina to Chile to Greece, Czechoslovakia, China, and a dozen other places' have all found the play to be profoundly meaningful over the years (1996: 164). Although a scholar such as Christopher Bigsby may claim that the play's eternal success is not based on 'implying contemporary analogies for past crimes' (2005: 149), when he later refers to the former Yugoslavia of the 1990s or to Stasi oppression in the former East Germany in his discussion of the play (2005: 164), he is clearly thinking analogically and imagining the play to be a parable. That said, Bigsby is right to say that 'compilers of programme notes [now] feel as great a need to explain the history of Senator McCarthy and the House Un-American Activities Committee as they do the events of seventeenth-century Salem' (2005: 159). But just as Hill said that the play 'no longer depends upon such parallels' (1967: 314) while nevertheless overtly mentioning the parallels, so too does Bigsby try to downplay the parallels while simultaneously suggesting what they might be. In short, it seems impossible for critics to discuss the play without interpreting it as a parable, and one thing that makes such interpretations possible is our capacity for conceptual blending.

Contemporary critics argue that Miller's play is no longer just about America in the early 1950s. Indeed, those like Dennis Welland claim that the play is 'not exclusively American' now (1979: 56), and the popular reception of the play in many different countries over the last few decades suggests that Welland is correct. If the play travels well in Eastern Europe or Latin America or Asia, it is because of its cognitive rhetorical nature. Audiences everywhere can (and do) interpret *The Crucible* as a parable about specific oppressive political situations. That is, they may fill old roles with new values and thus select a story from their own time or place that they imagine Miller's play, set in 1692 Salem, as honestly representing.

Conclusion

My discussion of cognitive rhetoric and *The Crucible* might seem out of place in this collection given the fact that stylistics is often defined as the linguistic analysis of literature. A linguistic analysis could address issues I have overlooked here, including Miller's prose within the printed play and his unusual dialogues, which were not written in 'historically accurate' English (Welland 1979: 62). But as cognitive rhetoric suggests, stylistics today entails more than just the linguistic analysis of literary texts. From Malle's theory of behaviour explanations to Turner's theory of parable, cognitive science clearly has more to offer literary critics than new linguistic theories. Having said that, I shall conclude here by giving Miller himself the last word. Unfortunately, Miller died on 10 February 2005; fortunately, on 26 August 2003 the BBC World Service interviewed him. Although *The Crucible* was then 50 years old, Miller predicted that it was 'not going to be overwhelmed with irrelevance [anytime] too soon' (BBC World Service 2003: paragraph 25). Only time will tell if that sad warning was right.

Note

I am grateful for the feedback I got on an earlier version of this chapter from members of the University of Fribourg English Department in Switzerland.

CHAPTER
19

The Stylistics of Drama:
The Reign of King Edward III

Beatrix Busse

The linguistic analysis of drama has on the whole been restricted to the application of speech act theory. Absurd drama, in particular, lends itself to the demonstration of implicatures, the flouting of Gricean maxims and the deliberate manipulation of conversation, to talking at cross-purposes and undermining relevant exchange.

Busse's chapter is innovative in studying a set of different features: the use of address pronouns, metaphors and foregrounding. In terms of the early modern English address pronouns *you* and *thou*, Busse concentrates on a scene in which the Countess of Salisbury's contempt for King Edward in *Edward III*, possibly co-authored by Shakespeare, is marked by her repeated use of the *thou* form. This contrasts with the more polite norm *you* and the Countess's polite use of address epithets such as *my liege lord, thrice-gentle King*, etc. The Countess's use of the more familiar form *thou* is foregrounded both qualitatively and quantitatively.

Busse links the use of address forms to metaphor and the notion of foregrounding in general. Whereas most studies of foregrounding in prose concentrate on word order, metaphor has always been treated as salient and hence foregrounded in poetry. It is therefore exciting to see the notion of foregrounding (recently given in-depth treatment by Douthwaite 2000) applied to a combination of address and metaphor. The enormity of the king's request is underlined by the double foregrounding in the Countess's speech. Moreover, theoretical analyses of foregrounding have not so far been applied to dramatic texts. It is a tempting research question to examine what can be foregrounded in dialogue, and in a theatrical setting.

The only point on which, as a literary scholar, I am perhaps sceptical is the connection established between the King's two bodies and the body as building metaphor. The Countess, after all, does not have two bodies but, like the King, a body and a soul. Looking at more plays in the Renaissance canon perhaps might deepen the analogy. It is certainly a fascinating one, particularly because it relates to the overall conception of the body as a prison enclosing the soul. Does the text indicate that the King's regal body might like to escape from his human body in the same way as the soul?

Monika Fludernik

Introduction

Investigations of drama from the viewpoint of stylistics are scarce. Reasons for this inattention may result from the fact that for a long time spoken language has not been valued as highly as written language, and analytical focus, even within stylistics, has been placed on the study of poetry and narrative fiction. In addition, earlier approaches, such as the New Criticism, have treated Shakespeare's plays, for example, almost exclusively as poetry.

In their collection of seminal essays on the stylistics of drama, Culpeper *et al.* (1998) have also stressed that drama has been relatively unexplored from a stylistics perspective. This, they say, is rather surprising because since the 1960s stylistics has been influenced by developments in linguistics – for example, Halliday's (2004) systemic functional grammar, pragmatics, conversation analysis or discourse analysis – which emphasise the social, contextual and interactive quality of language and conversation. Since the early 1990s, a number of highly influential stylistic analyses of drama or those that focus on the interactive and social features of dramatic language have appeared (Calvo 1992; Short 1996; Toolan 2000; Culpeper 2001; D. Stein 2003; Hunter 2005; B. Busse 2006; McIntyre 2006). Most recently, Short (forthcoming) is working on a book that, from the viewpoint of stylistics, also describes the equally unexplored interaction between the two communicative levels of drama – drama as texts and performance.

The neglect of stylistic investigations of drama resembles a tendency visible in historical linguistics where, as Jucker and Taavitsainen have pointed out, 'it is only recently that an interest has arisen in the historical development of pragmatic units' (2000: 67). In addition, Short (forthcoming) argues that cognitive stylisticians have not yet analysed drama frequently because dialogue is cognitively multifaceted and plays contain performance that is not so typical of novels.

In this chapter, I will present a stylistic analysis of an excerpt from the history play *The Reign of King Edward III*, which has recently been accepted as having been authored by Shakespeare, and thus included in the New Cambridge Edition (Melchiori 1998). By investigating particular (but also exemplary) pragma-linguistic items of (Shakespearean) drama – vocatives and the personal pronouns *you* and *thou* and their variants – I will show how these quantitatively and qualitatively construe as well as reflect communication, interactivity and the social situatedness of drama and the language used in plays. I will also demonstrate how the use of nominal and pronominal forms of address is *foregrounded* in *Edward III* and how it interplays with inter- and intratextual norms in Shakespeare's dramatic work or Early Modern English. In this chapter, foregrounding is not understood to be synonymous with emphasising. It should be related to the theory of foregrounding, which is crucial to stylistics and has its base in Russian formalism (see Short 1996 and especially Douthwaite 2000). Simpson defines foregrounding in the following way:

> Capable of working at any level of language, foregrounding typically involves a stylistic distortion of some sort, either through an aspect of the text which deviates from a linguistic norm or, alternatively, where an aspect of the text is brought to the fore through repetition and parallelism.
>
> (Simpson 2004: 50)

Another aspect that will be illustrated in this chapter is how vocatives and pronominal forms of address construe the feature of multi-levelled communication in drama; that is how they contribute to the meanings of drama as written text and in performance. The idea of the vocative as a grammatical metaphor is also relevant to this point of view.

Still another aspect that will be dealt with in this chapter is the ways in which the application of a cognitive stylistic approach (Stockwell 2002; Gavins and Steen 2003) to pronominal and nominal forms of address in *Edward III* shows the characters' as well as the recipients' cognitive processes at work: one of the play's preoccupations is what Munkelt and Busse (2007) describe as the tension between Edward III being a medieval king, who is portrayed on the basis of Renaissance concepts of kingship, as well as the tension between the incompatibility of being a fully fledged human being and successful monarch. The metaphor THE BODY IS A HOUSE, used by the Countess, further illustrates this tension.

Edward III – Foregrounding of Forms of Address

At one of the pivotal moments in Shakespeare's *Edward III*, the Countess of Salisbury theatrically threatens King Edward with her own suicide should he not swear to abandon his 'most unholy suit' (*Edward III*, II.ii. 183) – that is to woo the married Countess. She exclaims: 'Swear, Edward, swear,/Or I will strike and die before thee here' (*Edward III*, II.ii. 187f.).

Shapiro (2003: 35f.) has rightly pointed to the highly emotional potential of the pronominal usage of *thee* indicating the Countess's rejection of a shameful proposal from the King. Shapiro (2003: 36) links her observations about this use of pronoun to the Countess's general switching of them in preceding scenes, when the Countess addresses the King with *thou* and *you* pronouns in co-occurrence with what Shapiro defines as respectful titles. However, Shapiro (2003: 35) describes the change of pronouns as 'a puzzling anomaly'. Therewith, she implies a marked and indecorous use of pronominal forms of address, because it is often assumed that a Countess will not refer to or is not allowed to address a king with *thou*, which is often considered to be used in highly emotional situations or from superior to inferior (Taavitsainen and Jucker 2003: 13f.).

With its reference to Brown and Gilman's (1960) and Brown and Ford's (1961) 'power and solidarity paradigm' as well as to politeness theory (Brown and Levinson 1987 and Brown and Gilman 1989), Shapiro's interpretative framework represents a well-established analytical paradigm appropriated in order to explicate the use of second-person pronouns in Shakespeare. Even though the use of *nominal* forms of address – that is, for example, the use of a personal name like 'Edward' – has been more marginally treated than Shakespeare's use of second-person pronouns, recourse has been made to the power and solidarity paradigm (Brown and Gilman 1960 and Brown and Ford 1961), whenever the Shakespearean vocative is not described as 'unwieldy' (Kopytko 1993: 54). Hence, explanatory models depend upon politeness theory, and include a standard emphasis on Shakespeare's knowledge of the rigid social structure allegedly existent at his time (Breuer 1983; Stoll 1989; U. Busse 2002).

Undoubtedly, at first sight the Countess' attack on Edward is thought-provoking indeed; both in its use of nominal and pronominal forms of address. Shapiro (2003: 35f.) has even suggested that what she calls deviations from a norm give clues as to considerations of authorship, even though it has been established that Act II of *Edward III* is Shakespeare's creation: see Melchiori (1998: 36–9)). My own quantitative research confirms that a woman's use of a personal name as vocative to address a king is highly marked within the Shakespeare corpus (B. Busse 2006). But as to the Countess' usage in particular, other quantitative and qualitative findings need to be introduced alongside micro-and macro-contextual as well as inter- and intratextual parameters. These bode well for the claim that the Countess' socially provocative personal name 'Edward' as vocative is evocative of her perfect figure of womanhood, chastity, morality and natural love, which she values more highly than obedience to her King, and construes the King as torn between political and personal governance of himself and of others (Munkelt and Busse 2007). The following analysis will refer to vocatives as a concept where vocatives function as interpersonal, textual and experiential markers (B. Busse 2006). Vocatives construe identity, habitus and power relations. Warwick, the Countess' father in *Edward III*, emphasises this interpersonal and experiential potential and foregrounded meaning of vocatives for creating relationships and situational interaction when he desperately muses about the appropriate vocative that will introduce the King's suit and his role as 'an attorney from the court of hell' (*Edward III*, II.i. 381):

Warwick [Aside]	How shall I enter in this graceless arrant?
	I must not call her child, for where's the father
	That will in such a suit seduce his child?
	Then, 'wife of Salisbury,' shall I so begin?
	No, he's my friend, and where is found the friend
	That will do friendship such indamagement?

(Edward III, II.i. 373–8)

Warwick then begins his address to his daughter with the highly foregrounded vocatives: 'Neither my daughter, nor my dear friend's wife,/I'm not Warwick, as thou think'st I am' (*Edward III*, II.i. 379f.), denying his fatherhood in order to be able to perform his task.

Quantitative Observations – The Countess' and King Edward's Use of
Pronominal and Nominal Forms of Address

To begin with quantitative figures for *thou* and *you*, which I have extracted, then collected as a wordlist and built a concordance from on the basis of *The Riverside Shakespeare* (Evans 1997), there are more *thou* forms in *Edward III* than *you* forms: 277 *thou* forms occur as opposed to 210 *you* forms. These amount to a relative frequency of 1.39 for *thou* forms and 1.06 for *you* forms. Hence, in *Edward III, thou* is the unmarked and *you* the marked form. This result corresponds with U. Busse's (2002: 47f.) findings that Shakespeare's early histories feature the highest number of *thou* forms and usually (apart from *Henry IV, Part II* and *Richard III*, for example: see U. Busse (2002: 43)) contain more *thou* than *you* forms. Brainerd (1979) and Hope (1994) have also suggested that the development of pronominal usage is dependent on the correlation of the two parameters of genre and date of composition. (Although the fact that more *thou* than *you* forms occur in *Edward III* corresponds with the general pattern for the histories, the relative frequency figures do not, as they are much lower than, for example, in the three *Henry VI* plays (*Henry VI, Part I*, for example, shows a relative frequency of 2.225 for *thou* and 1.791 for *you; Richard II* shows a relative frequency of 2.094 for *thou* forms and 1.349 for *you*: see U. Busse (2002)).

The Countess' share of speech has been equally extracted as described above. Plural *you* forms were also subtracted from the general figures. Interestingly, the Countess uses 34 *thou* forms and 42 *you* forms, which amount to a high relative-frequency ratio of 2.15 for *thou* and 2.65 for *you*. This result is far above the average rate mentioned above, and (in contrast to the King) she also uses more of the marked pronominal address forms in the play in general. Therefore, deviating from the general pattern, for the Countess *thou* is the marked form and *you* is not. This result might again give food for thought about the authorship question (Melchiori 1998) given the fact that the Countess is mostly present in Act II, which identifies this as Shakespeare (Melchiori 1998: 36–9). It is also important to relate these findings to a micro-linguistic analysis, because these are crucial in their interplay with the general norm but also in their relation with a gender-specific employment of the *thou* pronoun, especially if we consider that her use of *thou* and *you* pronouns somewhat parallels Gertrude's in *Hamlet.* Gertrude uses more *thou* than *you* forms (based on Spevack's (1968–80) concordances). An additional interpretative dimension is added by the fact that, at Shakespeare's time, *thou* was the marked form opposite *you* as the norm and most frequent pronoun (Wales 1983; U. Busse 2002). Nevertheless, Shakespeare still used a strikingly high number of *thou* pronouns (U. Busse 2002: 45f.) and exploited their functional potential for his own dramatic purpose. Therefore, the Countess's use of *thou* forms may also carry idiosyncratic as well as gender-specific features of natural and uttermost emotionality.

While the use of pronominal address forms is foregrounded in *Edward III*, her use of vocatives, which amounts to 27 vocatives for the King and a relative frequency of 1.64 of 37 vocatives altogether (relative frequency of 2.34), is striking because she uses fewer vocatives than most female characters in Shakespeare's tragedies, such as Tamora in *Titus Andronicus* (rel. freq. 2.82), Gertrude in *Hamlet* (rel. freq. 3.61), Cleopatra in *Antony and Cleopatra* (rel. freq. 3.61) or Cordelia in *King Lear* (rel. freq. 4.62) (see B. Busse 2006).

The Countess' vocative usage changes from Act I to Act II. In Act I, she uses more socially compliant vocatives, such as *your highness* and *my liege*, and the position of the vocatives is finally or initially embedded in either declaratives or requests – to stress her sincerity, obedience and devoted pleading. The vocatives used in Act II belong to what I have elsewhere called conventional terms (B. Busse 2006). Their link with Early Modern social structure initially tempts one to use the interpretation model of power and solidarity. However, even a general comparative investigation illustrates that, in comparison to Act I, more vocatives appear in an amplified form, because epithets, such as 'thrice-gentle' or 'thrice-loving', are added. Furthermore, the Countess' vocative repertoire also contains forms whose semantics are immediately more emotional than those of conventional terms. As we have seen, she even uses one personal name, 'Edward', to address the King. The positions of the vocatives in the accompanying clauses move to the final place – to stress her own authority/sincerity – or appear in the middle of either declarative or clear imperatives.

The Countess' use of vocatives has to be seen in interplay with that of King Edward. King Edward shows a ratio of pronominal usage which partly corresponds with the general pattern both in quantity and quality. He has 170 *thou* forms, which amount to a relative frequency of 1.39, and only 31 *you* forms, which amount to a relative frequency of 0.24. As *thou* forms are unmarked in *Edward III*, it is impossible to apply the trapping/tempting power-paradigm (a king addresses his inferiors with *thou*) to his usage.

King Edward's vocatives for the Countess only amount to 9 and carry a relative frequency of 0.09. He uses 'lady' (*Edward III*, I.ii. 113; II.i. 197) and 'my lady' (*Edward III*, II.i. 141), 'Countess' (*Edward III*, I.ii. 125; II.i. 199; II.i. 208; II.i. 210) as well as 'fair Countess' (*Edward III*, II.i. 138), 'my dearest love' (*Edward III*, II.ii. 126) and 'my soul's playfellow' (*Edward III*, II.i. 120). These often occur in final position with imperatives to express his authority. Edward's vocatives become more foregrounded in the wooing scene than at his first meeting with the Countess, despite the fact that *lady* occurs quite frequently in Act I (though less frequently than *madam* in the corpus I have investigated elsewhere: B. Busse (2006)). There seems to be an emotional elevation involved between the switch from *Countess* to *fair Countess* and *my lady*; nevertheless, he does not directly address the Countess as often as she addresses him. Although his vocative usage underlines his kingly status, it also reminds one of Henry's cold wooing of Kate in *Henry IV, Part II*. Edward is more authoritative and cooler in his use of vocatives in Act I than in Act II. The vocatives used in Act II, when seen in comparison, also construe his assumed appropriating social and physical superiority as 'my dearest love' (*Edward III*, II.ii. 126), 'fair Countess' (*Edward III*, II.ii. 138) and 'my lady' (*Edward III*, II.ii. 141) illustrate. *Lady* only superficially alludes to the Countess's status as a mistress in a household (*OED* 1) and the King attempts, with the help of one epithet and amplified conventional terms (B. Busse 2006), to manipulate the Countess to obey him.

The Countess' Appeal to the King's 'two bodies' in Edward III – Intertextual, Intratextual, Structural and Performative Foregrounding

In *Edward III*, I.ii. 113–16, Edward brusquely returns the Countess' subservient welcome with the following directive: 'Lady, stand up. I come to bring thee peace,/However thereby I have purchased war'. She answers, compliantly at first sight, with 'No war to you, my liege: the Scots are gone'. Edward's initial conventional term *lady*, which lends additional force to the directive 'stand up', only superficially addresses the Countess as the 'lady of a household' (*OED* 1) where he is the guest. It also strongly correlates to the following two utterances in which he foreshadows his new passion for the Countess and equates it with the military fight he has begun against France, alluding to the metaphor of LOVE IS WAR. Hence, the use of the term *lady* also creates his physical passion for the beautiful Countess. In addition, the abrupt style already alludes to his personal insecurity which he tries to compensate for by his own social status.

The Countess resorts to a rather unemotional use of *you* – her unmarked form – and to one of the conventional terms, which frequently occur in the history plays of the Shakespeare corpus, *my liege*. Nevertheless, her elliptic reply immediately denies Edward's sensual allusions because she does not use the corresponding male term 'my lord' – which would have supported the double dimension of military and emotional war – but rather construes the King's social identity as a king and his military role as a soldier in war against the Scots and France.

Before the Countess' stress on moral values in Act II culminates in her 'Swear, Edward, swear,/Or I will strike and die before thee here' (*Edward III*, II.ii. 187f.), she uses an, at first sight, socially suitable repertoire of address forms, such as 'thrice-gentle king' (*Edward III*, I.ii. 201), 'my thrice-dread sovereign' (*Edward III*, II.i. 217), 'dear my liege' (*Edward III*, I.ii. 125) or 'my thrice-loving liege' (*Edward III*, II.ii. 141). Yet a closer historical inspection of this pattern reveals a foregrounded status of these vocatives when recourse is made to historical and literary sources of this play, when these are levelled against the Shakespeare corpus and also when these are compared with the Countess' vocatives in Act I. Thus, in the historical and literary sources that provide the material for the Countess scenes (Melchiori 1998: 190f.) – Froissart's *Cronycle* (1513) (Metz 1989) and Painter's collection of novels, *The Palace of Pleasure* (1567) (Bandello 1968) – the address pattern used by the Countess is less frequent and varied.

The Countess' use of vocatives is also intertextually reminiscent of the historical Richard II's vocabulary of kingship. Saul (1995: 854) argues, for example, that in contrast to the much simpler language in which earlier kings had customarily been addressed by their subjects, Richard II demanded more elaborate language and address patterns, such as *highness, prince* or *majesty* and Richard II wanted to stress the divine character of his kingship (Saul 1995: 855). Shakespeare is not faithful to the linguistic practices of the historical model Edward, but rather to that of Edward's grandson, Richard II. It may also be argued that the use of address forms for the King assumes the tone of a much more recent event: the celebration of the Spanish Armada under Elizabeth I, who once claimed that she was Richard II, and whose victory (1588) can be compared with Edward's successes in France. Melchiori (1998: 28) has illustrated that the description through French eyes of the naval battle at Sluys (1340) in the play assumes the epic tone of the defeat of the Spanish Armada. *Edward III* was collaboratively composed and performed at the time of the defeat of the Spanish fleet (Melchiori 1998: 3–9), a national victory which also reinstated the cult of Elizabeth I. In addition, from Elizabeth I's father, Henry VIII, onwards, the use of *majesty* as a form of address became more frequent (Kastan 2002: 151). Hence, the Countess' initial high evaluation of Edward in the play and her almost over-elaborate kingship vocatives may also be seen as an address to Elizabeth I. At first, Edward is the Countess' liberator from the Scots. Therefore, she pays him homage. As soon as she is sure of his moral failure in longing for her on the basis of his kingship, she initiates her didactic play and trial and is ready to die for her moral standards.

When the vocatives used by the Countess are compared with the Shakespearean corpus, it becomes obvious that her elaboration of these conventional terms by means of epithets, such as 'thrice-gentle' (*Edward III*, II.i. 201), 'thrice-loving' (*Edward III*, II.ii. 141) or 'great' (*Edward III*, II.ii. 168), are foregrounded. In B. Busse (2006) vocatives have been investigated and newly categorised within the structural potential of the nominal group. Vocatives are described as experiential, interpersonal and textual markers and the role of epithets – elements preceding the head of the noun phrase – has been highlighted as well as the lexicon of epithets used. Despite the conventional as well as socially appropriate choice of the head-vocatives, the use of epithets is foregrounded qualitatively through the use of the epithet in 'my thrice-dread sovereign' (*Edward III*, II.i. 217) and in 'my thrice-loving liege' (*Edward III*, II.ii. 141), which are rare in the corpus investigated in B. Busse (2006). In 'dear my liege' (*Edward III*, I.ii. 125) the usually occurring structural potential of the chain of deictic-epithet-thing is broken up through a change of position between deictic and epithet. Even though these forms occur in vocatives, the structure is less frequent than the deictic-epithet-head realization.

The structure of vocatives as a nominal group opens up a further meaningful potential that has to be correlated with Halliday's (2004) elaboration on grammatical metaphor. Underlying the idea of the vocative as a grammatical metaphor is not only its realisation as a nominal group but also the fact that each nominalization is, in essence or in its more congruent realization, a clause. Halliday (2004: 347–62) does not transfer this concept to vocatives. In a nominal group, things are usually construed as commodities, which take on a value and can be drawn up in lists of categories or taxonomies, so that the main source of abstract meaning seems to shift from the interpersonal to the experiential. Hence, the vocative has an experiential potential in its structural realisation and an interpersonal meaning in its communicative function in the clause and above.

How can such vocatives as 'thrice-gentle king' (*Edward III*, II.i. 201), 'my thrice-dread sovereign' (*Edward III*, II.i. 217), 'dear my liege' (*Edward III*, I.ii. 125) or 'my thrice-loving liege' (*Edward III*, II.ii. 141) be rephrased into clauses? What is the effect of or functional interplay between the realisation as a nominal group, on the one hand, and the underlying more congruent clause, on the other? How can this constructive force be ultimately transferred to unmodified vocatives realized as personal names as in 'Edward' in 'Swear, Edward, swear,/Or I will strike and die before thee here' (*Edward III*, II.ii. 187f.)?

The vocative 'thrice-gentle king' (*Edward III*, II.i. 201), for example, could be rephrased into 'thou art a thrice gentle king' or into 'thou kinged me thrice-gently' – echoing Edgar's complex word-formations in 'he childed as I fathered' (*King Lear*, III.vi. 110). Among others, *childed* and *fathered* can be seen as both conversions and derivations (Wales 1987). In the *Edward III* example, the rephrased clauses allude to Edward's position as a socially, physically and linguistically dominating king. The rephrasing of the nominal group into a clause illustrates the force of the vocative as a nominal group. The nominal group structure opens up the semogenic (meaning-creating: Halliday (2004: 272f.)) power of the vocative and its potential for taxonomizing. At the same time, this structural realisation of the vocative as a nominal group condenses the force of the vocative into a seemingly objectified, abstract and determinate 'liege' or 'sovereign'. The experiential condensation of meaning into a nominalisation is clearly experiential in outlook as it enables the speaker to give the impression he/she focuses on stable, fixed and compact reality-construing ideas, identities, concepts and positions. As such, the speaker conceals the vocative's original nature as processes. The Countess stresses that Edward is actually the king, because at the moment of utterance, the addresser uses this term in order to say something about the addressee on the experiential level and the recipient perceives it as such. The Countess is in need of this bombastic reference to the king in order to remind him of his duties. Hence, we can turn the congruent and the metaphorical poles into a productive and co-representational interdependence.

The vocatives 'great king' (*Edward III*, II.ii. 169) and 'lascivious king' (*Edward III*, II.ii. 178) contrast with one another and prepare for the Countess' didactic, experiential, textual, interpersonal and performative climax in 'Edward' (*Edward III*, II.ii. 187). 'Lascivious king' almost functions like an oxymoron, with 'lascivious' referring to 'lust, lewd, wanton' (*OED* 1) and 'king' alluding to Edward's social role and the attributes connected with kingship. The use of the personal name 'Edward' as a vocative then illustrates the importance of the personal name in general in the Shakespearean corpus. The Countess' unmodified, most demanding, almost natural 'Edward', which turns the imperative into a threat and functions like an experiential, interpersonal and textual caesura, also construes one part of what Kantorowitz (1957: 3, 9, 28) has described as the King's two bodies – the 'body politic' and the 'body natural', which need to be in perfect union. With the Countess' appeal to both the King's fleshly cravings and his sensuality as well as his role as a human being with moral standards, she shows that she values her nature, womanhood and chastity over the socially attributed role to serve the King, and she illustrates that the union between Edward's body politic and his body natural is in disruption and in need of reformation.

The performative aesthetic effect of this vocative and the Countess' appeal to the King's two bodies, which stands in correlation with the Countess threatening herself and the King with the daggers, is highly informative on the theatricality, electrifying tension and unmasking of this scene. The two communicative levels of drama, play texts in print and performed on stage, need to be seen as equal and dialectically interrelated components of vocative interpretation (for their general dependency, see, for example, Fielitz 1999). Depending on the performative choices made by the actors, one must notice the performative role of vocatives in drama as, for example, segmentation units and addresses to the audience (B. Busse 2006), and that they cannot be restricted to the function of selecting the next speaker. The Countess' vocative in 'Swear, Edward, swear,/Or I will strike and die before thee here' (*Edward III*, II.ii. 187f.) will be uttered with additional force and, in addition, because the choice of a personal name for a king is so abnormal, the audience will recognize the seriousness of the situation and the sincerity of the Countess' threat. Therefore, the Countess' address to Edward is both a subservient acknowledgement of his status as a king and a somewhat concealed reminder of his royal responsibility. In turn, the Countess' threatening potential in her use of his personal name 'Edward' contains also a reminder of Edward's personal morals and the fact that he is a married man. It can be rephrased as a relational clause 'thou art Edward' (in addition to being a king).

Cognitive Dimensions in Drama – the Metaphor of the Body as a House in Edward III

The Countess' appeal to a union between the King's 'two bodies' (Munkelt and Busse 2007) as expressed by the vocatives as grammatical metaphors and the use of *you* and *thou* is related to another central aspect in the Countess' mental life and to how well the recipient may transfer mental constructs for the meaning inference process. The complex metaphor THE BODY IS A HOUSE structures the Countess' belief system by the mapping of two different domains – the house and the body – and this is also related to more fundamental metaphorical mappings such as UNDERSTANDING IS SEEING. The Countess' body and soul are peacefully united in a moral shell of her being a loving wife. She is therefore able to see through and understand the King's moral and political failures.

In *Edward III*, II.i. 236–42, the Countess expresses her sensuality and morality through a believed union between the soul and the body. She describes the way in which her body and her soul are invariably linked and she stresses that if she were to give away her body – that is to be obedient to the King – she would lose her soul and her moral convictions:

Countess   [...] and yet my body live,

> As lend my body, palace to my soul,
> Away from her and yet retain my soul.
> My body is her bower, her court, her abbey,
> And she an angel pure, divine, unspotted.
> If I should [lend] her house, my lord, to thee,
> I kill my poor soul, and my poor soul me.
>
> (*Edward III*, II.i. 236–42)

Among others, the metaphor THE BODY IS A (the soul's) HOUSE structures the process of the Countess' identity construction. The source domain is the house and the target domain is the body. The source input domain consists of the following Renaissance attributes of house: a community or a protective building. The target domain, the body, refers to fleshly cravings, a human being, materiality, beauty. Both of these features are incorporated into one.

For the Countess, the body protects rather than displays the high and divine ambitions of morality, honour, love, womanhood and chastity. The organs of the body are connected with the inhabitants of the house; the protective shell of the body, the skin, projects onto the shielding stones of the house; the more abstract concept of the soul as part of the body projects onto the intrinsic values when owning or living in a house. Therefore, the metaphor also creates what Fludernik (1996) has described for narrative as 'experientiality,' that is the projection of consciousness and subjective experience, and what Palmer (2004) has called an 'intramental construct', in which individual cognitive functioning – that of the Countess – is described. Despite the Countess' beauty and the King's sexual cravings, the Countess appeals to the King's sense of honour and morality. The importance of the Renaissance situatedness of this metaphor becomes also visible by the fact that the Countess' understanding of sensuality is broader than that, for example, expressed in Early Modern English dictionaries where sensuality is associated with exaggerated sexual desire and lasciviousness. For example, Florio's (1598) Italian-English dictionary *A Worlde of Wordes* defines *sensualità* as 'sensualitie, licenciousnes, con tent, and pleasing of sences" (see *LEME* 2008). In the Countess' view her understanding of soul and aspects of sensuality are in a complex interplay with sense, reason, spiritual seeing and feeling.

The ever-repeated connection between the eyes and the soul, as seats of love, essence of one's being and morality, is what, for example, Gloucester describes in *King Lear* as seeing 'feelingly' (IV.vi.145). Hence, a character's eyes and touch as passion and emotion are balanced with sense and reason and the metaphor of UNDERSTANDING IS SEEING in Shakespeare. At the same time, they reflect the Renaissance world picture where passions, feeling, sense and reason are in unity. In Richard Braithwaite's *Essays upon the Five Senses* from 1620, this connection is moralized as an ideal (religious) standard which each human being needs to strive for. The Countess' clear criticism of the King's deficient morals when sexually longing for a married woman becomes obvious in the metaphor she construes. Her body governs her senses and protects the bond she has entered into with her husband and which is stored in her soul and her heart. That the

King has learned his lesson is illustrated in his vocative 'Arise true English lady, whom our isle/May better boast of than ever Roman might/of her' (*Edward III*, II.ii. 193–5). The King equates her ladyship with Englishness and morality.

Conclusions

The stylistic analysis of nominal and pronominal forms of address in *Edward III* has illustrated their foregrounded status as well as the interchange between quantitative and qualitative considerations in the meaning inference process. The concept of markedness has to be correlated with co(n)textual parameters in order to make it possible to draw microlinguistic conclusions from the Countess of Salisbury's and King Edward's address behaviour. Even the quantitative findings for pronominal and nominal forms of address question the strength of the power- and solidarity-paradigm (Brown and Gilman 1989), because, in *Edward III*, the usually occurring quantitative dominance of the personal pronoun *you* over *thou* is reversed, but correlates with a general pattern that can be discerned for the early Shakespeare history plays. While King Edward's use of personal pronouns corresponds with the common scheme in *Edward III*, the Countess' use gives preference to *you* over *thou* forms. Despite Edward's determination to take up not only a passionate war against France but also his equally ardent campaign to win the Countess, he employs few and less emotional vocatives. The Countess directly addresses the King more often than he does her. The structure and the semantics of her vocatives construe the King as a zealous ruler and as an over-adoring man.

Adding a cognitive stylistic dimension to the discussion, the interplay between inter- and intratextual norms and deviations has been demonstrated, as well as the complexity of cognitive processes at work by the recipient and the characters in drama. The metaphor of THE BODY IS A HOUSE in its affinities to the concepts of the King's two bodies has exemplified its interplay with the King's and the Countess' use of vocatives and pronominal forms of address as well as the efficiency of the cognitive approach as one convincing path for readers and viewers of drama alike.

Computer-assisted Literary Stylistics: The State of the Field

Dawn Archer

Dawn Archer presents a state-of-the-art overview of 'computational stylistics' and 'corpus stylistics'. Such an overview is timely because of the increasing number of studies that involve both stylistics and computers. Rightly, Archer first tackles the issue of what might lie behind the labels. The field is characterized by: (1) a concern with the issues considered important in mainstream stylistics (not merely authorial style but characterisation, plot development, mind style, rhetorical figures and so on); (2) the computational processing of the text through the use of a computer program; and (3) the use, whether explicit or not, of statistics. The use of (1) and (3) are certainly not new to literary stylistics. For example, Chapters 2 and 3 of Leech and Short's (1981) often cited *Style in Fiction* elaborate a quantitative approach to the analysis of style.

What is new here then is simply the mechanical advantage afforded by computers, not that that should be underestimated, as a computer can do in moments what one scholar could not in a lifetime. Text-processing (2) and statistical exploration (3) are certainly not new to fields in literary computing (e.g. 'stylometrics'), though what is missing is the broader contribution to stylistics, as most studies in this area focus solely on authorial style. As Archer points out, computational/corpus stylistics has characteristics in common with corpus linguistics, and, furthermore, it is the surge in corpus linguistics in the last couple of decades that is probably the key factor in galvanizing computational and corpus stylistics. Consider the work of Douglas Biber (e.g. 1988), who has a central concern with a quantitative methodology, computers and 'styles'.

The computational techniques and programs that Archer reviews were developed for corpus linguists. There are, however, key differences between corpus linguistic studies and computational and corpus stylistic studies. One is the role of automatic (i.e. via a computer program) analysis of linguistic features. Archer discusses the role of automation and the related topic of annotation. Another key difference, which again Archer points out, is the particular concern in computational/corpus stylistic studies with the interpretative validity of the results that are obtained by computational analysis.

Overviews such as Archer's will promote coordination of research efforts and give a sense of identity to the field. Moreover, the space she devotes to specific cutting-edge techniques will be of particular value to readers, lighting possible roads into the field.

Jonathan Culpeper

Introduction

In 'The future of computational stylistics', Bailey (1979) divided what was then an emerging subdiscipline into three generic approaches: the use of data-retrieval techniques (in particular, concordance-building), the construction of (fragments of) models and the formulation of explicit hypotheses which were then tested against empirical evidence. Bailey believed that most achievements in 1979 were representative of the first approach. However, he was concerned that they were 'merely an adjunct [...] to the real work of criticism' in the main (Bailey 1979, reprinted in 1989: 5): put simply, computational tools made 'it possible to explore an intuition that might otherwise necessitate a laborious and error-prone multiple rereading of the text' (p.6), but they were not impacting upon the field of stylistics theoretically and/or methodologically in a way that Bailey thought was possible. Bailey was also concerned by an apparent push for an autonomous 'scientific poetics' that, for him, meant disconnecting computational stylistics from its traditional humanistic roots (Bailey 1989: 9, 11; see also Martindale 1978: 276–80).

Nearly 30 years on, this chapter will present some of the most recent literature-based studies and/or developments within computational stylistics – and the related field of corpus stylistics – to show that practitioners are not only drawing meaningfully from the roots of stylistic theory and literary criticism in the twenty-first century, but are also impacting upon accepted views of (literary) language. I begin with a discussion of the close relationship between computational stylistics and corpus stylistics. I then outline two current debates within corpus and computational approaches to stylistics: namely, whether our goal should be a truly automatic stylistics tool and whether we should annotate our datasets. After introducing a number of studies that are representative of manual and automatic approaches to computer-assisted text analysis and/or utilize annotation to explore literary texts, I suggest that, if we are to further develop these stylistic subdisciplines, we must encourage even greater collaboration between stylisticians, computational analysts and literary scholars.

Is Corpus Stylistics the Same as Computational Stylistics?

'Computational stylistics' and 'corpus stylistics' are general terms for approaches that combine stylistics, computation and (in many cases) statistics (McEnery et al 2006). Within computational stylistics, for example, researchers distinguish between 'stylometry' (Binongo and Smith 1999), 'stylometrics' (Hunston 2002: 128), 'statistical stylistics' (Hoover 2001, 2002) and 'stylogenetics' (Luyckx et al

2006). Similarly, researchers within 'corpus stylistics' distinguish between a 'corpus-based' approach, which utilizes a fairly stable theoretical framework, and a 'corpus-driven' approach, which is more flexible and/or dynamic – in the sense that observations emerging from the corpus data are accommodated, where possible (see Tognini-Bonelli 2001). A notable similarity between computational stylistics and corpus stylistics is their link with corpus linguistics: both are said to be subfields of the latter. It should not surprise us to find, then, that computational stylisticians, corpus stylisticians and corpus linguists share a number of methodological concerns, such as whether to use corpora, whether one needs to build one's own corpus, whether to include markup language, the most appropriate

> computational tools [with which] to access the data within the corpora[;] whether those tools [already exist or need to be] written by the investigators themselves; and the basic design and implementation of statistical tests to determine the significance of distributional patterns.
>
> (Hardy 2003: 9)

Like corpus linguists generally, corpus-driven stylisticians and computational stylisticians are also interested in (the relationship between) meaning and form. Indeed, both Mahlberg (2007b) and Argamon et al (2007) have stressed how we might use computer-assisted/automated text analysis within stylistics as a means of identifying/gaining a better understanding of *inter alia*

> *affect* (what feeling is conveyed by the text?), *genre* (in what community of discourse does the text function?), *register* (what is the function of the text as a whole?) and *personality* (what sort of person, or who specifically, wrote the text?).
>
> Argamon et al (2007: 2)

In summary, then, whilst corpus stylistics, computational stylistics and corpus linguistics are not (nor should be regarded as) synonymous disciplines, they do overlap to a great extent – especially when their focus is the *how* of a text (i.e. *how* we say what we say). That said, it's important to note that corpus linguists tend to explore the *how* issue by focusing on 'repeated occurrences, generalisations and the description of typical patterns'. In contrast, corpus and computational stylisticians tend to be 'interested in deviations from linguistic norms that account for the artistic effects of a particular text' (Mahlberg forthcoming b).

Should our Goal be the Development of a Truly 'Automatic' Stylistics Tool?

A number of contemporary stylisticians believe (as did Bailey in 1979) that, if we are to further our understanding of *style* using corpus/computational techniques, we must build upon a firm basis of theory: stylistic, linguistic and/or literary. Where computational stylisticians tend to differ from corpus stylisticians today is in their preference for an automated approach to a theory-based stylistic analysis. Indeed, Argamon et al (2007) point out the severe limitation of studies that rely on hand-selected sets of content-independent features, be they function words, parts-of-speech/syntactic structures and/or complexity measures, which are then inputted into a generic learning algorithm (see Bailey 1979). In contrast, they have sought to find 'linguistically well-motivated features' using automatic 'text classification' to analyse 'variation in stylistic meaning' (Argamon et al 2007: 4). Starting from the theoretical premise that language may be viewed as 'a complex of choices between mutually exclusive options' (p.7), Argamon and his co-authors seek to capture variation (in style) by assessing the relative frequencies of the various options for a given language feature. More specifically, they: (1) tokenize and (part-of-speech) tag their texts, (2) extract lexical units as specified in a lexicon (or lexicons), (3) produce a 'feature vector' (by computing relative frequencies of estimated semantic attribute values for a given text) and (4) use machine learning to construct discrimination models for different stylistic text-classification tasks (i.e. authorship attribution, gender attribution, etc).

Operationally speaking, the tool devised by Argamon et al is heavily reliant on lexically based taxonomies. Indeed, the tool determines: (i) *development/expansion* within a given text via the use of conjunctions such as 'and', 'while' and 'in other words' (Matthiessen 1995: 519–28); (ii) *appraisal/orientation* (i.e. the adoption or expression of an attitude of some kind towards some target: Martin and White 2005) via a lexicon of appraisal adjectives and modifiers (including 'every' and 'sort of'); and (iii) *assessment* (i.e. the contextual qualification of the epistemic or rhetorical status of events or propositions represented in a text) via a series of modality-related criteria, including typicality ('probably', 'seldom'), necessity ('ought to'), likelihood ('likely', 'always'), objectivity ('think', 'require') and explicitness ('preferably').

Argamon and his co-authors concede that their classificatory approach is of necessity (more) simplistic because it is automated. However, they also point out that 'the system networks [they] use are the result of decades of research on textual analysis within the SFG [Systemic Functional Grammar] community, and are not *ad hoc* inventions for [their] particular purposes' (Argamon et al 2007: 8). Indeed, their *seed terms* were initially taken from example words and phrases cited in standard SFG references (i.e. Halliday 1994; Matthiessen 1995; Martin and White 2005), and candidate expansions of the various seed terms were then gleaned from online thesauri. It is also worth noting that, whilst SFGs have been applied to automatic natural language processing in several contexts since the 1960s, these studies have been mostly limited to text generation (Fawcett and Tucker 1990; Matthiessen and Bateman 1991) rather than text analysis, due to the complexity of parsing in the theory (but see O'Donnell 1993).

To Annotate, or Not to Annotate?

As Argamon et al's (2007) work reveals, a preference for automated procedures often leads to a focus on lexical, grammatical and/or semantic features. Indeed, even Luyckx et al's (2006) impressive 'stylogenetics' methodology is heavily reliant on the former. Luyckx et al define stylogenetics as 'an approach to literary analysis that groups authors [...] into family trees or closely related groups' on the basis of a stylistic genome (2006: 1). This genome becomes apparent when one: (1) combines statistical and information-theoretic methods with the 'bag of word' methodology advocated by text categorisation literature (Sebastiani 2002); (2) uses the resulting vectors of complex features (computed on a sufficiently large sample of the work of an author) as a 'signature' for the style of that author; and (3) then uses similarity-based clustering methods to develop a stylogenetic analysis of the differences and similarities between authors (and also periods, genders, etc).

It is possible to manually annotate for various features that are more functional, social and/or contextual in orientation and, as such, may not have an easily discernible linguistic form (computationally and/or linguistically speaking). A good stylistic example of this is the first monograph to be entitled *Corpus Stylistics*, i.e. Semino and Short's (2004) study of speech, thought and writing presentation, which builds upon the work of Leech and Short (1981). The latter developed their original taxonomy as a means of accounting for speech and thought presentation in fictional texts, but Semino and Short wanted to determine the model's applicability/usefulness when applied to other text types – including those representative of non-fiction. Accordingly, they have developed and annotated a dedicated corpus of different genres/text types to test out the original model (Semino and Short 2004: 4).

Semino and Short's decision to utilize an annotated corpus is not meant to imply that one cannot engage in quantitative studies of speech/thought presentation without utilising a corpus-based approach (see Cohn 1978; Fludernik 1993). Rather, they believe that their approach forces them to account for *all* data (and not just prechosen examples) and, where necessary, to adapt the original model to account for that data. Indeed, Semino and Short report that they have been led to merge some of the existing 1981 categories, add new categories and also note correlations between rhetorical functions and stylistic choices (for further detail see Semino and Short 2004).

Other manually applied annotation models which may be of interest to stylisticians include Archer and Culpeper's (2003) sociopragmatic annotation system, which captures information about the gender, age, status and role of a number of characters from plays and interactants from courtroom transcripts, and a complementary scheme, devised by Archer (2005), which captures information relating to the speech act function and interactional intent of their utterances (see also Archer et al 2008 for details of pragmatic annotation more generally).

Unfortunately, the use of annotation within corpus stylistics – and corpus linguistics more generally – has been and remains contentious. Sinclair (2004), for example, argues that annotation is not only unnecessary, but is also misleading and fundamentally flawed and advocates, instead, that we *Trust the Text*. As will become clear in subsequent sections, this may prove to be appropriate when our only interest is in linguistic *form*. However, stylistic researchers (corpus as well as computational) are also becoming increasingly interested in 'key' grammatical parts of speech and 'key' semantic classes, that is to say, those parts of speech or those semantic categories that occur *more* or *less* often in a given text, statistically speaking, than would be expected by chance in comparison to some norm (dictated by a reference corpus). Such constellations are important as they capture items that would not be identified as 'key' by themselves, and, as such, may be overlooked (Archer and Rayson 2004). Indeed, these constellations tend to be very difficult to spot from intuiting alone, especially when one is dealing with larger datasets, and they are almost impossible to deal with computationally without some sort of preprocessing (such as the development of grammatical and/or semantic lexicons against which to compare the given text).

In subsequent sections, I refer to the work of researchers who have utilized *Wordsmith Tools* to explore *keyness* in literary texts as a means of gaining a better understanding of characterisation (e.g. Culpeper 2002; see also Culpeper in Hoover et al forthcoming). I then introduce studies that have utilized the UCREL semantic annotation system (USAS) to explore characterisation (e.g. Culpeper in Hoover et al forthcoming) and the concept of *love* (Archer et al 2009) in Shakespearean plays. The latter, in particular, seeks to demonstrate how a dictionary-based content analysis tool may enhance the study of Shakespeare from the perspective of cognitive metaphor theory (Freeman 1995; Barcelona Sanchéz 1995). I also report on a projects that are seeking to determine the usefulness of USAS to the study of metaphor more generally and to the study of mind style.

Studies that Make Use of Text Analysis Tools

According to Hardy, 'central to the methodology of any computational stylistic analysis is a text analysis tool' (2003: 10). *Wordsmith Tools* (Scott 1999) is perhaps the best known within stylistics, and consists of three programs: *Keywords, Concord* and *Wordlist*. In this and subsequent sections, I will be focusing on the first of these, which allows users to conduct a statistical comparison between the frequency of words in a given text compared to a bigger reference corpus, using the classic chi-square significance test or Dunning's Log Likelihood Test. As words are characterized as 'key' if they are unusually (in)frequent (statistically speaking) in comparison with what one would expect on the basis of the larger reference list, the choice of data for the latter is extremely important. According to Scott and Tribble (2006: 58), as well as being the same type of language as the text under study, the reference list should be 'preferably many thousands of words long and possibly much more' (2006: 58). In contrast, Culpeper in Hoover et al (forthcoming) suggests that the choice of reference corpora should be determined by how specific we want our keyword results to be. Two studies involving *Romeo and Juliet* appear to lend support to both positions: Scott and Tribble (2006:

61–2) compared *Romeo and Juliet* against various reference corpora (Shakespeare's complete works, plays only, tragedies only and the British National Corpus (BNC)) and found that a 'robust core' of keywords occur whichever reference corpus is used. These include personal and place names like 'Benvolio', 'Romeo', 'Juliet' and 'Mantua' but also terms like 'banished', 'county', 'love' and 'night'. In contrast to Scott and Tribble (2006), Culpeper (2002) found that his results were more meaningful – in terms of characterisation – when using the other *Romeo and Juliet* characters (minus the target characters) as a reference corpus.

Keyword Studies of Romeo and Juliet

Culpeper's (2002) main motivation for studying the keywords of six characters in *Romeo and Juliet* was to rectify what he perceived to be a 'serious methodological deficit' shared by literary scholars and stylisticians alike: an over-reliance on short textual examples, chosen because of the foregrounded features they contain. That said, Culpeper was careful to ground his approach in established theory. Indeed, he likened keywords to what Enkvist (1964, 1973) calls 'style markers' because of their similarities in respect to frequencies, probabilities and norms (i.e. both capture words whose frequencies differ significantly from their frequencies in a norm). Moreover, Culpeper has since pointed out that the notion of keywords has an even longer history in stylometry, having been first labelled as such by Pierre Guiraud (see Hoover et al forthcoming).

Historically, keyword studies have tended to focus on the *aboutness* of texts, that is, they highlight keywords that humans would recognise/be likely to predict (Scott 1999). But Culpeper (2002) has found that many of the keywords associated with individual *Romeo and Juliet* characters are not indicative of *aboutness*. For example, Juliet is characterized by keywords which suggest she is 'the anxious target of love' (e.g. 'if', 'or' and 'yet'), whilst the Nurse is characterized by keywords that suggest she is the emotional thermometer of the play (e.g. 'warrant', 'faith', 'marry', 'ah', 'o', 'well', 'god'). In Hoover et al, Culpeper advocates that we should therefore distinguish keywords in terms of their ideational, textual and interpersonal functions, and argues that the keywords of particular characters gravitate in different directions, lending them distinct characters. He gives the examples of Romeo (whose keywords include 'beauty' and 'love') for ideational keywords, Juliet (and even more so Mercutio) for textual and the Nurse for interpersonal. Studying characterisation via a textual (or grammatical analysis) is not completely new, of course, as Toolan (1985) has linked distinct syntactic styles to distinct aspects of character when studying Faulkner.

Studies that Explore Key Domains Automatically

Culpeper (in Hoover et al forthcoming) and Archer et al (2009) also advocate exploring semantic fields as a means of furthering current thinking in respect to not only characterisation but also metaphor analysis. What makes these particular studies especially innovative is their reliance on an annotation tool – USAS – which finds semantic fields automatically (Rayson 2003). For those unfamiliar with the tool, texts are initially uploaded into *Wmatrix* (the web interface to USAS) and then grammatically and semantically annotated using two programs: CLAWS and SEMTAG. The tagset behind SEMTAG was originally based on the *Longman Lexicon of Contemporary English* (McArthur 1981) but has since been revised in the light of tagging problems met in the course of previous research dating back some 15 or so years. The present classification has a hierarchical structure with 21 top-level domains, which capture 232 semantic field tags (signalling a broadly westernized conception of the modern world). Some of these semantic field tags (i.e. 'obligation and necessity', 'comparison' and '(in)definiteness') capture similar *stylistic* features to Argamon et al's (2007) tool. However, the majority of the categories capture semantic fields that are strongly *content*-based: for example, 'medicine/medical treatment' and 'movement'. *Wmatrix* then offers users various options for considering the outputs: for example, as well as the standard corpus linguistics techniques such as frequency lists and concordances, it allows users to analyse keywords, parts-of-speech and semantic categories.

As semantic studies of characterization have been undertaken previously (Fowler 1986: 33–8; Pfister 1988: 166–70; Toolan 1988: 99–101), below I will focus on the way in which Archer et al's (2009) study has provided empirical support for the kinds of conceptual metaphor put forward by cognitive metaphor theorists when studying Shakespearean metaphors (see, for example, Freeman 1995; Barcelona Sanchéz 1995).

Using Key Domain Analysis to Further Cognitive Metaphor Theory

Archer et al's (2009) exploration of the concept of love in three Shakespearean love comedies (*Midsummer Night's Dream, As You Like It* and *Two Gentlemen of Verona*) and three Shakespearean love-tragedies (*Othello, Antony and Cleopatra* and *Romeo and Juliet*) involved identifying key domains (i.e. those semantic categories that are significantly (in)frequent in the love-comedies when compared with the love-tragedies and vice versa) and then identifying keywords within these key domains. The benefits of this as opposed to a 'pure' keyword analysis is that one can identify words that would not have been picked up by a keyword analysis (because they are not deemed to be key in and of themselves) but which nonetheless add to the aboutness and/or style of a text (because they share the same semantic space as the keywords).

As the original USAS system was designed to undertake the automatic semantic analysis of present-day English, Archer et al opted to utilize the historical version of the USAS system. The historical tagger, which is being developed by Archer and Rayson (with the help of Baron, Lancaster University), includes supplementary historical lexicons that help to account for changes in meaning over time and a preprocessing step to detect variant (i.e. non-modern) spellings (Archer and Rayson 2004). The variant detector – or VARD – currently utilizes a number of methods to search for – and replace – variants: a known word list (currently containing 45,000+ variant-to-word mappings), Soundex, Edit Distance, letter replacement heuristics and context rules. A particular strength of VARD is that it greatly facilitates the application of those standard corpus linguistic methods that are otherwise hindered by multiple variant spellings, i.e. frequency profiling, concordancing, keyword analysis, etc (see Rayson et al 2005).

There are also plans to develop a related but historically specific semantic tagset (drawing from the insights provided by other historical taxonomies/thesauri). However, the version of the historical tagger Archer et al utilize in their study makes use of the same tagset as the modern USAS tagset. One effect of this is that some of the results relating to Shakespeare contain inaccuracies. Nevertheless, they found that the historical tagger is still able to confirm existing and/or discover new conceptual metaphors. For example, *love* often collocated with the 'anatomy and physiology' semantic field in the love-comedies and, as such, appears to confirm the primary emphasis given to embodiment by cognitive linguists (Kövescses 2002: 16). Archer et al note that 'eyes'/'eye' were amongst the most frequent items within this particular semantic field, and link this finding to Barcelona Sanchéz's (1995: 679) argument that a woman's eyes were meant to be an aspect of her beauty that could capture men. That said, they disagree with her suggestion that the underlying metaphor here is EYES ARE CONTAINERS FOR SUPERFICIAL LOVE or, indeed, Lakoff and Johnson's (1980) EYES ARE CONTAINERS FOR THE EMOTIONS, as the idea of a container is not clearly articulated in the comedy data they studied. Instead, they propose their own conceptual metaphor – EYES ARE WEAPONS OF ENTRAPMENT – to capture instances like Orlando's 'Wounded it is, but with the eyes of a lady' (*As You Like It*). As USAS has been shown to provide a 'way in' to metaphorical patterns, current work now involves refining the USAS systems (modern and historical) so that analysts can distinguish more readily between metaphorical and non-metaphorical usage.

Combining Keyness and Mind Style

Together with Dan McIntyre, Archer is undertaking a second stylistics project using USAS as a means of determining whether USAS can provide a consistency meas-ure for *mind style* (see Archer and McIntyre 2005). Fowler (1977) originally coined this term to capture the world view of an author, narrator or character as constituted by the ideational structure of the text. However, although he suggested that one of the characteristics of mind style is that its effect is cumulative across a whole text, he and later researchers have not really discussed how – or indeed whether – the consistency of mind style can be measured. Instead, existing research tends to concentrate on uncovering the linguistic and paralinguistic means by which such 'unique world views' are conveyed. In practice, this has meant a (qualitative) focus on those mind styles which are noticeably odd in some way: see, for example, research reflecting the (idiosyncratic) use of (i) transitivity patterns (Bockting 1994; Hoover 1999), (ii) conceptual metaphors (Semino and Swindlehurst 1996; Semino 2002) and (iii) logical reasoning (McIntyre 2005).

Given the difficulties associated with measuring consistency of mind style, a qualitative focus on the *noticeably odd* is not surprising. Nevertheless, Archer and McIntyre's (2005) preliminary investigation suggests that it is possible to gain some measure of consistency by looking not at the number of instances of a particular indicator of mind style, but at 'the statistical significance of its occurrence within a text'. Building on McIntyre's (2005) qualitative study of deviant mind style in Alan Bennett's play *The Lady in the Van*, Archer and McIntyre have specifically concentrated on the potential for semantic domains to indicate mind style, and investigated the distribution of particular key semantic domains across the whole text of the play, using USAS. Interestingly, their work suggests that a computational semantic analysis cannot uncover features of mind style in a text in and of itself. However, an analysis of the key domains exhibited in a character's speech or in narration may indicate a *potentially* deviant mind style, which requires confirmation via close textual analysis of a qualitative nature. By way of illustration, the following table details the seven most key semantic fields of three of the *Lady in the Van* characters – Miss Shepherd (MS), the social worker (SW) and Alan Bennett the character (AB2) – and also the seven most key semantic fields of Bennett as narrator (AB1) when compared against the spoken demographic section of the BNC (please note that there were other key domains for each character, which, because of length constraints, will not be discussed here):

Notice that the domain of 'speech acts' is common to the characters and the narrator (see italicized items): linguistic items captured by this category include 'say', 'call', 'tell', 'question', 'reply' and 'shout'. Each character also seems to have at least one other domain in common with another character (see emboldened items): thus, Bennett the character and Miss Shepherd appear to share a concern for 'Movement/transport (land)', 'Music and related activities' and 'Wanting/planning/choosing'. Archer and McIntyre (2005) suggest these particular results might: (i) indicate important features of the plot such as Miss Shepherd coming to park her van in the garden of Alan Bennett the character (see Movement/transport (land)), and residing there for most of the duration of the play, and (ii) be indicative of the relationship between and/or the personality of the characters. Note, for example, that Bennett the character seems to associate music and religion with Miss Shepherd: 'Don't you like music? I thought the Virgin Mary liked music? I thought the Virgin Mary liked music … How can you dislike music? You used to play the piano.' In addition, Miss Shepherd's 'Wanting/planning/choosing' is extremely negative in comparison to Alan Bennett the narrator (i.e. 15 examples of 'I don't want …' propositions compared to 5 for the narrator). When viewed in respect to other key domains for Miss Shepherd – in particular, 'religion' and 'definiteness/modality' (key terms being 'could', 'possibly', 'may', 'might', 'probably') – these findings provide quantitative support for some of McIntyre's (2005) qualitative claims about her mind style: that Miss Shepherd is a character who is both strongly influenced by religion (in particular, a Catholic guilt) and also unwilling to commit firmly to any given proposition.

Archer and McIntyre (2005) stress that shared semantic domains can also indicate the professional function of the characters. Notice, for example, that the key domains for the social worker (SW) include 'Medicine/medical treatment',

Table 20.1 Key semantic domains in the speech of four characters (taken from Archer and McIntyre 2005)

Character	Seven most key semantic fields (compared against the BNC spoken demographic)						
MS	Religion/super-natural	Definiteness (modality)	*Speech acts*	**Music and related activities**	**Movement/transport (land)**	**Ability: success**	**Wanting/planning/choosing**
SW	*Speech acts*	Medicine/medical treatment	lack of approach-ability/friendliness	Social actions/states/processes	Helping	**Ability: success**	Personal names
AB1	*Speech acts*	**Movement/transport (land)**	**Music and related activities**	**Life and living things**	**Lack of life and living things**	**Wanting/planning/choosing**	Residence
AB2	People (female)	Grammar bin	Sensory (smell)	General appearance/physical properties	**Life and living things**	**Lack of life and living things**	*Speech acts*

'Social actions/states/processes' and 'Helping'. Notice, also, that the social worker is the only character to have a 'lack of approachability/friendliness' in her seven most frequent domains. On consulting the play text, Archer and McIntyre found that this particular result can be explained (in part) by the social worker's sense of Miss Shepherd's hostility towards her: 'I'm getting a bit of hostility here ... I'm sensing that hostility again'.

As well as discussing the relevance of their findings in respect to specific characters and/or events, they were able to show that the elements that contribute to a unique mind style for Miss Shepherd are consistent (i.e. statistically significant) throughout the whole play text. The real strength of the USAS system, then, appears to be that it allows researchers to investigate differences between characters empirically/systematically using automated techniques in a way that means they no longer have to rely on intuition alone when seeking to determine mind style (and the extent to which it remains consistent across a given play or novel). This has been a deficiency of qualitative studies of mind style, according to Leech and Short (1981). Leech and Short are also critical of studies which have ignored the possibility that mind style exists on a cline (with normal linguistic behaviour at one end and deviant linguistic behaviour at the other), but further work is required to determine whether USAS offers a means of 'positioning' novels and plays along such a cline.

Other Computer-assisted Stylistic Studies Worthy of Attention

Due to length constraints, I have only been able to discuss a small proportion of the many computer-assisted stylistic studies that are worthy of attention (see Popping et al 2000 and Pommel 2004 for detailed overviews). In particular, my focus on literary-based studies has meant that I have not discussed work in respect of: authorship attribution and profiling (Burrows 1987; McEnery and Oakes 2000); genre-based text analysis, classification and retrieval (Biber 1988; Karlgren 2000; Finn et al 2002); sentiment analysis (Turney 2002); spam/scam filtering (Patrick 2004), criminal and national security forensics (McMenamin 2002); the mining of customer feedback (McKinney et al 2002); and aiding humanities scholarship (Hoover 2002), including the creation of text-mining software for the humanities.

Of course, any distinction between literary-based and non-literary-based work is an artificial one, in practice. Note, for example, that Biber's (1988) multi-dimensional analysis model has been used by him to investigate both scientific texts and also eighteenth-century authors (Biber and Finegan 1994). Biber utilizes bipolar factor scores (based on the co-occurrence of a number of linguistic features) as a means of situating texts along particular situational or functional parameters (i.e. formal/informal, interactive/non-interactive, literary/colloquial, restricted/elaborated). Interestingly, because of the need to engage with complex algorithms when extracting certain grammatical features from a given corpus, Biber's approach tends to demand more of its users than, for example, keyword analysis (see Xiao and McEnery 2005: 77 for details of a comparative study of the multidimensional approach and keyword analysis). As Culpeper (in Hoover et al forthcoming) highlights, a multidimensional analysis can also prove problematic in the sense that the *a priori* decisions about what to count may lead to instances where an important lexical feature such as interjections is omitted from an analysis: by way of illustration, interjections would not have been accounted for when analysing the Nurse's speech in *Romeo and Juliet* using Biber's approach, even though they are an important means of creating her colloquial style.

Concluding Comments

My aims, in this chapter, have been multiple: first, to demonstrate that stylistics is not being steered towards an autonomous 'scientific poetics', as Bailey (1979) feared, and to signal that many corpus computational researchers who investigate *style* today do so in a way that signals their engagement with or desire to further existing theory (literary, linguistic and stylistic).

Second, I have sought to show that the tools they utilize are designed to *aid the interpretative endeavour* (i.e. human interpretation is still crucial): for the tokens captured by a *keyness* list have to be (in)validated not only with respect to their occurrence, but also with respect to the researcher(s)'s specific research questions and/or the extent to which they further one's understanding of a specific text or theory (Baker 2004: 348: see also Culpeper 2002; Archer and McIntyre 2005; Mahlberg forthcoming b). Similarly, automated tools that utilize statistical and probabilistic measures to determine gender/authorship attribution, etc., are always reliant on human interpretation in the final instance.

Third, I hope that this chapter encourages more researchers to begin engaging with tools like *WordSmith* and USAS when investigating *style* – especially given that the keyword approach is regarded as being both extremely efficient and also relatively undemanding of its user – at least computationally speaking (Xiao and McEnery 2005: 76–7).

Finally, I would encourage those who are already part of the corpus stylistic and computational stylistic communities to foster closer ties with each other and, in turn, with literary scholars, so that we can continue to develop existing tools and create new tools that address our *style* issues more effectively and efficiently.

References

Aarseth. E. J. (1994) 'Nonlinearity and literary theory', in G. P. Landow (ed.) *Hyper/Text/Theory*. Baltimore: Johns Hopkins University Press, pp. 53–86.

Acorn, M. (1975) *The Island Means Minago*. Toronto: NC Press.

Acorn, M. (1983) *Dig Up My Heart: Selected Poems 1952–1983*. Toronto: McClelland and Stewart.

Acorn, M. (1988) *Hundred Proof Earth*. Toronto: Aya Press.

Adler, T. (1997) 'Conscience and community in *An Enemy of the People* and *The Crucible*', in C. Bigsby (ed.) *The Cambridge Companion to Arthur Miller*, Cambridge: Cambridge University Press, pp. 86–100.

Adolphs, S. (2006) *Introducing Electronic Text Analysis: A Practical Guide for Language and Literary Studies*. London: Routledge.

Adolphs, S. and Carter, R. (2002) 'Point of view and semantic prosodies in Virginia Woolf's *To the Lighthouse*', *Poetica* 58: 7–20.

Anderson, A. S. (1995) 'Gendered pleasure, gendered plot: defloration as climax in *Clarissa* and *Memoirs of a Woman of Pleasure*', *Journal of Narrative Technique* 28(2): 108–38.

Anderson, M. (1998) 'Folklore, folklife and other bootstrapping traditions', in R. Kevelson (ed.) *Hi-Fives: A Trip to Semiotics*. New York: Peter Lang.

Andringa, E. (1996) 'Effects of "narrative distance" on reader's emotional involvement and response', *Poetics* 23: 431–52.

Angus, I. (1997) *A Border Within: National Identity, Cultural Plurality, and Wilderness*. Montreal: McGill-Queen's University Press.

Archer, D. (2005) *Questions and Answers in the English Courtroom (1640–1760): A Sociopragmatic Analysis*. Amsterdam: John Benjamins.

Archer, D. (forthcoming 2007) 'Verbal aggression in the courtroom: *sanctioned* but not necessarily *impolite?*', in D. Bousfield and M. Locher (eds) *Impoliteness in Language*. Berlin: Mouton de Gruyter.

Archer, D. and Culpeper, J. (2003) 'Sociopragmatic annotation: new directions and possibilities in historical corpus linguistics', in A. Wilson, P. Rayson and A. M. McEnery (eds) *Corpus Linguistics by the Lune*. Frankfurt/Main: Peter Lang, pp. 37–58.

Archer, D. and McIntyre, D. (2005) 'A computational approach to mind style', paper given at the 25th Conference of the Poetics and Linguistics Association, University of Huddersfield.

Archer, D. and Rayson, P. (2004) 'Using an historical semantic tagger as a diagnostic tool for variation in spelling', paper presented at the 13th International Conference on English Historical Linguistics (ICEHL 13), University of Vienna.

Archer, D., Culpeper, J. and Davies, M. (2008) Pragmatic annotation, in A. Lüdeling and M. Kytö (eds) *Corpus Linguistics: An International Handbook.* Mouton de Gruyter, pp. 613–641.

Archer, D., Culpeper, J. and Rayson, P. (2009) 'Love – "a familiar or a devil"? An exploration of key domains in Shakespeare's comedies and tragedies', in D. Archer (ed.) *What's in a Word-List? Investigating Word Frequency and Keyword Extraction.* London: Ashgate, pp.137–158.

Argamon, S., Whitelaw, C., Chase, P., Raj Hota, S., Garg, N. and Levitan, S. (2007) 'Stylistic text classification using functional lexical features', *Journal of the American Society for Information Science and Technology* 58(6): 802–22.

Aristotle (1954) *Rhetoric* (trans. W. Rhys Roberts). New York: Random.

Aristotle (1959) *The Art of Rhetoric* (trans. J. H. Freese). Cambridge, MA: Harvard University Press.

Ashbery, J. (1971) 'Introduction', in D. Allen (ed.) *The Collected Poems of Frank O'Hara.* Berkeley: University of California Press, pp. ii–ix.

Ashline, W. L. (1995) 'The problem of impossible fictions', *Style* 29(2): 215–34.

Atwood, M. (1996) *Survival: A Thematic Guide to Canadian Literature* [original 1972]. Toronto: McClelland and Stewart.

Auster, P. (1988) *The New York Trilogy.* London: Faber and Faber.

Bailey, R. W. (1979) 'The future of computational stylistics', *ALLC Bulletin* 7(1): 4–11. Reprinted in Potter, R. G. (ed.) (1989) *Literary Computing and Literary Criticism.* Philadelphia: University of Pennsylvania Press, pp. 3–12.

Bainbridge, B. (2001) 'Bainbridge denounces Chick Lit as "froth"', *The Guardian Unlimited.* http://books.guardian.co.uk/bookerprize2001/story/0,,541335,00.html

Baker, P. (2004) 'Querying keywords: questions of difference, frequency and sense in keywords analysis', *Journal of English Linguistics* 32(4): 346–59.

Bakhtin, M. (1984) 'Appendix: towards a reworking of the Dostoevsky book', in *Problems of Dostoevsky's Poetics* (ed. and trans. C. Emerson). Manchester: Manchester University Press, pp. 283–302 [original 1961].

Bal, M. (1999) 'Close reading today: from narratology to cultural analysis', in W. Grünzweig and A. Solbach (eds) *Transcending Boundaries: Narratology in Context.* Tübingen: Gunter Narr Verlag, pp. 19–40.

Bally, C. (1912) 'Le style indirect libre en français moderne I', *Germanische-Romanische Monatsschrift* 4: 549–56.

Bamberg, M. (2005) 'Positioning', in D. Herman, M. Jahn and M.-L. Ryan (eds) *The Routledge Encyclopedia of Narrative Theory.* London: Routledge, pp. 445–6.

Bamberg, M. (ed.) (1997) *Journal of Narrative and Life History, Special Issue: Oral Versions of Personal Experience: Three Decades of Narrative Analysis* 7: 1–4.

Bandello, Matteo (1968) 'The Forty-Sixth Nouell', (trans William Painter) *The Palace of Pleasure, 1567,* 4th edition Joseph Jacobs. Hildesheim: Olms, pp. 334–63 [original 1890, London: David Nutt].

Banfield, A. (1982) *Unspeakable Sentences*. London: Routledge.

Banfield, A. (2003) 'Time passes: Virginia Woolf, post-impressionism, and Cambridge time', *Poetics Today* 24(3): 471–516.

Barcelona Sanchéz, A. (1995) 'Metaphorical models of romantic love in *Romeo and Juliet*', *Journal of Pragmatics* 24: 667–88.

Barcroft, J. (2002) 'Semantic and structural elaboration in L2 lexical acquisition', *Language Learning* 52(2): 323–63.

Bateson, G. (1979) *Mind and Nature: A Necessary Unity*. Cresskill, NJ: Hampton Press.

BBC (2002) 'Mikhail Bulgakov: satirist and playwright', 19 December 2002. URL: http://www.bbc.co.uk/dna/h2g2/A868278#footnote2

BBC World Service (2003) 'Playwright Miller hears Crucible echo', 23 August 2003. URL: http://news.bbc.co.uk/2/hi/entertainment/3182451.stm

Beckett, S. L. (ed.) (1999) *Transcending Boundaries: Writing for a Dual Audience of Children and Adults*. New York: Garland.

Bell, A. (2006) 'The possible worlds of hypertext fiction', unpublished PhD thesis, University of Sheffield.

Benigni, R. (1997) *La Vita è Bella*. Rome: Melampo Cinematograpica/Miramax.

Benton, M. (2000) *Studies in the Spectator Role: Literature, Painting and Pedagogy*. London: Routledge.

Berry-Dee, C. (2003) *Talking with Serial Killers: The Most Evil People in the World Tell Their Own Stories*. London: John Blake.

Berry-Dee, C. (2005) *Talking with Serial Killers 2: The Most Evil People in the World Tell Their Own Stories*. London: John Blake.

Bertens, H. and D'haen, T. (2001) *Contemporary American Crime Fiction*. New York: Palgrave.

Biber, D. (1988) *Variation across Speech and Writing*. Cambridge: Cambridge University Press.

Biber, D. and Finegan, E. (1994) 'Multi-dimensional analyses of authors' style: some case studies from the eighteenth century', in D. Ross and D. Brink (eds) *Research in Humanities Computing 3*. Oxford: Oxford University Press, pp. 3–17.

Bigsby, C. (2005) *Arthur Miller: A Critical Study*. Cambridge: Cambridge University Press.

Binongo, J. and Smith, M. (1999) 'A bridge between statistics and literature: the graphs of Oscar Wilde's literary genres', *Journal of Applied Linguistics* 26(7): 781–7.

Binyan, T. J. (1989) *Murder Will Out: The Detective in Fiction*. Oxford: Oxford University Press.

Birch, D. (1989) *Language, Literature and Critical Practice*. London: Routledge.

Birch, D. and O'Toole, M. (1988) 'The power of functional stylistics', in D. Birch and M. O'Toole (eds) *Functions of Style*, London: Pinter, pp. 1–11.

Birch, D. and O'Toole, M. (eds) (1988) *Functions of Style*, London: Pinter.

Blasing, M. K. (1995) *Politics and Form in Postmodern Poetry: O'Hara, Bishop, Ashbery, and Merrill*. Cambridge: Cambridge University Press.

Bockting, I. (1994) 'Mind style as an interdisciplinary approach to characterisation in Faulkner', *Language and Literature* 3(3): 157–74.

Bolter, J. D. (2001) *Writing Space: Computers, Writing and the Remediation of Print* (second edition). New Jersey: Lawrence Erlbaum.

Bonnet, J.-M. (1982) 'Society vs. the individual in Arthur Miller's *The Crucible*', *English Studies* 63(1): 32–6.

Bortolussi, M. and Dixon, P. (2003) *Psychonarratology: Foundations for the Empirical Study of Literary Response.* Cambridge: Cambridge University Press.

Bousfield, D. (2007a) 'Impoliteness, preference organization and conductivity', *Multilingua* 26(1/2): 1–33.

Bousfield, D. (2007b) 'Beginnings, middles and ends: a biopsy of the dynamics of impolite exchanges', *Journal of Pragmatics.*

Bousfield, D. (2007c) 'Power and impoliteness', in D. Bousfield and M. Locher (eds) *Impoliteness in Language.* Berlin: Mouton de Gruyter.

Bousfield, D. and Locher, M. (eds) (2007) *Impoliteness in Language.* Berlin: Mouton de Gruyter.

Bowers, B. K. and Brothers, B. (1990) *Reading and Writing Women's Lives: A Study of the Novel of Manners.* Ann Arbor, MI: UMI Research Press.

Brainerd, B. (1979) 'Pronouns and genre in Shakespeare's drama', *Computer and the Humanities* 13: 3–16.

Braithwaite, R. (1620), *Essays vpon the fiue Senses, with a pithie one vpon detraction. Continued vvith sundry Christian resolues, full of passion and deuotion, purposely composed for the zealously-disposed.* London: Printed by E. G[riffin]: for Richard Whittaker, and are to be sold at his shop at the kings head in Paules Churchyard. *Early English Books Online* http://eebo.chadwyck.com/search

Bråten, S. (1992) 'The virtual other in infants' minds and social feelings', in A. H. Wold (ed.) *The Dialogical Alternative,* Oslo: Scandinavian University Press, pp. 77–97.

Breuer, H. (1983) 'Titel und Anreden bei Shakespeare und in der Shakespearezeit', *Anglia* 101: 49–77.

Brook, G. L. (1970) *The Language of Dickens.* London: André Deutsch.

Brooks, P. (1984) *Reading for the Plot: Design and Intention in Narrative.* Oxford: Clarendon.

Brown, P. and Levinson, S. C. (1987) *Politeness. Some Universals in Language Usage.* Cambridge: Cambridge University Press.

Brown, R. W. and Gilman, A. (1958) 'Who says "tu" to whom?', *A Review of General Semantics* 15: 169–174.

Brown, R. W. and Gilman, A. (1960) 'The pronouns of power and solidarity', in T. Sebeok (ed.) *Style in Language,* Cambridge, MA: MIT Press, pp. 253–76 [reprinted 1972 in J. Laver and S. Hutcheson (eds) *Communication in Face to Face Interaction,* Harmondsworth: Penguin, pp. 103–27].

Brown, R. W. and Gilman, A. (1989) 'Politeness theory and Shakespeare's four major tragedies', *Language in Society* 18: 159–212.

Brown, W. and Ford, M. (1961) 'Address in American English', *Journal of Abnormal and Social Psychology* 62: 375–85 [reprinted 1964 in D. Hymes (ed.) *Language in Culture and Society.* New York: Harper and Row, pp. 234–44].

Brumfit, C. and Carter, R. (eds) (1986) *Literature and Language Teaching.* Oxford: Oxford University Press.

Bruner, J. (1990) *Acts of Meaning.* Cambridge, MA: Harvard University Press.

Bruner, J. (1997) 'Labov and Waletzky thirty years on', *Journal of Narrative and Life History* 7(1–4): 61–8.

Bruner, J. (2003) *Making Stories: Law, Literature and Life.* London: Harvard University Press.

Bryson, V. (1999) *Feminist Debates: Issues of Theory and Political Practice.* Basingstoke: Macmillan.

Bucholtz, M. (2003) 'Theories of discourse as theories of gender', in J. Holmes and M. Meyerhoff (eds) *The Handbook of Language and Gender.* Blackwell: Oxford, pp. 43–68.

Bucholtz, M, and Hall, K. (2005) 'Identity and interaction: a sociocultural linguistic approach', *Discourse Processes* 7: 585–614.

Budick, E. M. (1985) 'History and other spectres in Arthur Miller's *The Crucible*', *Modern Drama* 28: 535–52.

Bühler, K. (1982) 'The deictic field of language and deictic worlds', in R. J. Jarvella and W. Klein (eds) *Speech, Place and Action: Studies in Deixis and Related Topics.* Chichester: John Wiley, pp. 9–30 [original 1934].

Bulgakov, Mikhail (1968) *The Heart of a Dog* (trans. Michael Glenny). London: Harvill Press [original 1925].

Burke, K. (1945) *A Grammar of Motives.* New York: Prentice Hall.

Burke, M. (2005) 'How cognition can augment stylistic analysis', *European Journal of English Studies* 9(2): 185–95.

Burney, F. (1972) *Camilla; or, A Picture of Youth* (eds E. A. Bloom and L. D. Bloom). Oxford: Oxford University Press [original 1796].

Burrows, J. F. (1987) *Computation into Criticism: A Study of Jane Austen's Novels and an Experiment in Method.* Oxford: Clarendon Press.

Burton, D. (1996) 'Through glass darkly: through dark glasses', in J. J. Weber (ed.) *The Stylistics Reader: From Roman Jakobson to the Present.* London: Edward Arnold, pp. 224–40.

Busse, B. (2006) *Vocative Constructions in the Language of Shakespeare.* Amsterdam: John Benjamins.

Busse, U. (2002) *The Function of Linguistic Variation in the Shakespeare Corpus: A Corpus-Based Study of the Morpho-Syntactic Variability of the Address Pronouns and their SocioHistorical and Pragmatic Implication.* Amsterdam: John Benjamins.

Calvo, C. (1992) 'Pronouns of address and social negotiation in *As You Like It*', *Language and Literature* 1: 5–27.

Cameron, D. (1995) *Verbal Hygiene.* London: Routledge.

Cameron, D. and Fraser, E. (1987) *The Lust To Kill: A Feminist Investigation of Sexual Murder.* New York: New York University Press.

Caputi, J. (1987) *The Age of Sex Crime.* Bowling Green: Bowling Green State University Popular Press.

Carpenter, H. and Prichard, M. (1984) *The Oxford Companion to Children's Literature*. Oxford: Oxford University Press.

Carson, N. (1982) *Arthur Miller*. New York: Grove Press.

Carter, R. (1998) *Vocabulary*. London: Routledge.

Carter, R. and Nash, W. (1990) *Seeing through Language: A Guide to Styles in English Writing*. Oxford: Blackwell.

Chambers, A. (1973) *Introducing Books to Children*. London: Heinemann Educational.

Chapman, R. (1973) *Linguistics and Literature: An Introduction to Literary Stylistics*. Edinburgh: Edward Arnold.

Chatman, S. (1990) *Coming to Terms: The Rhetoric of Narrative in Fiction and Film*. Ithaca, NY: Cornell University Press.

Cheng, Nien (1986) *Life and Death in Shanghai*. London: Graftan.

Ciccoricco, D. (2007) *Reading Network Fiction*. Tuscaloosa: University of Alabama Press.

Clark, A. and Chalmers, D. J. (1998) 'The extended mind', *Analysis* 58: 7–19.

Clausen, C. (1982) 'Home and away in children's fiction', *Children's Literature* 10: 141–52.

Cobley, P. (2001) *Narrative*. London: Routledge.

Coe, J. (2002) *The Rotters' Club*. London: Penguin.

Cohn, D. (1978) *Transparent Minds: Narrative Modes for Presenting Consciousness in Fiction*. Princeton, NJ: Princeton University Press.

Colgan, J. (1999) *Amanda's Wedding*. London: Harper Collins.

Cook, G. (1994) *Discourse and Literature*. Oxford: Oxford University Press.

Cool-reads (2007) URL: http://cool-reads.co.uk

Corbett, E. P. J. and Connors, R. J. (1999) *Classical Rhetoric for the Modern Student* (fourth edition). Oxford: Oxford University Press.

Corse, S. M. (1997) *Nationalism and Literature: The Politics of Culture in Canada and the United States*. New York: Cambridge University Press.

Crago, H. (1999) 'Can stories heal?', in P. Hunt (ed.) *Understanding Children's Literature*. London: Routledge, pp. 163–73.

Crisp, P. (2005) 'Allegory and symbol – a fundamental opposition?', *Language and Literature* 14: 323–38.

Culler, J. (1975) *Structuralist Poetics*. Ithaca, NY: Cornell University Press.

Culler, J. (1981) 'The poetics of the lyric', in *The Pursuit of Signs: Semiotics, Literature, Deconstruction*. Ithaca, NY: Cornell University Press, pp. 161–88.

Culler, J. (1997) *Literary Theory*. Oxford: Oxford University Press.

Culpeper, J. (1996) 'Towards an anatomy of impoliteness', *Journal of Pragmatics* 25: 349–67.

Culpeper, J. (1998) '(Im)politeness in drama', in P. Verdonk, M. Short and J. Culpeper (eds) *Exploring the Language of Drama: From Text to Context*. London: Routledge.

Culpeper, J. (2001) *Language and Characterisation. People in Plays and Other Texts*. Harlow: Longman.

Culpeper, J. (2002) 'Computers, language and characterisation: an analysis of six characters in *Romeo and Juliet*', in U. Melander-Marttala, C. Östman and M. Kytö (eds) *Conversation in Life and in Literature*. Uppsala, Sweden: Universitetstryckeriet.

Culpeper, J. (2005) 'Impoliteness and entertainment in the television quiz show: The Weakest Link', *Journal of Politeness Research* 1: 35–72.

Culpeper, J., Bousfield, D. and Wichmann, A. (2003) 'Impoliteness revisited: with special reference to dynamic and prosodic aspects', *Journal of Pragmatics* 35: 1545–79.

Culpeper, J., Short, M. and Verdonk P. (eds) (1998) *Exploring the Language of Drama: From Text to Context*. London: Routledge.

cummings, e.e. (1923) *Tulips & Chimneys*. New York: Liveright.

cummings, e.e. (1944) *1 X 1*. New York: Henry Holt.

Cupchik, G. C., Leonard, G., Axelrad, E. and Kalin, J. D. (1998) 'The landscape of emotion in literary encounters', *Cognition and Emotion* 12(6): 825–47.

D'Cruz, G. (1994) 'Representing the serial killer: "postmodern" pedagogy in performance studies', *Southern Review* 27(3): 323–32.

Daly, N., Holmes, J., Newton, J. and Stubbe, M. (2004) 'Expletives as solidarity signals in FTAs on the factory floor', *Journal of Pragmatics* 36: 945–64.

Damasio, A. (1994) *Descartes' Error: Emotion, Reason, and the Human Brain*. New York: Grosset-Putnam.

Damasio, A. (2000) *The Feeling of What Happens: Body, Emotion and the Making of Consciousness*. London: Heinemann.

Da Silva, N. T. (1990) *Modernism and Virginia Woolf*. Windsor: Windsor Publications.

de Beaugrande, R. (1987) 'Schemas for literary communication', in L. Hàlàsz (ed.) *Literary Discourse: Aspects of Cognitive and Social Psychological Approaches*. Berlin: de Gruyter, pp. 49–99.

de Saussure, F. (1916) *Course in General Linguistics*. La Salle: Open Court.

Decter, M. (1997) 'Review of *The Crucible*, dir. Nicholas Hytner', *Commentary* 103(3) (March 1997): 54–7.

Dennett, D. (1987) *The Intentional Stance*. Cambridge, MA: MIT Press.

Dennis, R. and Howells, C. A. (1996) 'Geography, gender and identity in Canadian literature: some introductory comments', *The London Journal of Canadian Studies* 12: 1–5.

Dickens, C. (1967) *Little Dorrit* (ed. J. Holloway). Harmondsworth: Penguin [original 1867].

Doležel, L. (1998a) *Heterocosmica: Fiction and Possible Worlds*. Baltimore, MD: Johns Hopkins University Press.

Doležel, L. (1998b) 'Possible worlds of fiction and history', *New Literary History* 29(4): 785–809.

Doležel, L. (1989) 'Possible worlds and literary fictions', in S. Allen (ed.) *Possible Worlds in Humanities, Arts and Sciences*. New York: de Gruyter, pp. 221–42.

Douglas, J. Y. (1992) 'What hypertexts can do that print narratives cannot', *Reader* 28: 1–22.

Douglas, J. Y. (1994) ' "How do I stop this thing?" closure and indeterminacy in interactive narratives', in G. P. Landow (ed.) *Hyper/Text/Theory*. Baltimore: Johns Hopkins University Press, pp. 159–88.

Douthwaite, J. (2000) *Towards a Linguistic Theory of Foregrounding*. Turin: Edizioni dell'Orso.

Downes, W. (1993) 'Reading the language itself: some methodological problems in D.C. Freeman's "According to my bond": King Lear and re-cognition', *Language and Literature* 2(2): 121–8.

Doyle, A. C. (2001) *The Hound of the Baskervilles*. Harmondsworth: Penguin [original 1901].

Duchan, J. F., Bruder, G. A. and Hewitt, L. E. (eds) (1995) *Deixis in Narrative: A Cognitive Science Perspective*. Hillsdale, NY: Lawrence Erlbaum.

Duffy, C. A. (2003) 'Review of *The Curious Case of the Dog in the Night-time*'. Accessed May 2007, URL: www.arts.telegraph.co.uk/arts/main.jhtml?xml+/arts/2003

Duffy, D. (1971) 'In defense of North America: the past in the poetry of Alfred Purdy', *Journal of Canadian Studies* 6(2): 17–27.

Edward-Jones, I. (2000) *My Canapé Hell*. London: Flame.

Edwards, D. (1997) *Discourse and Cognition*. London: Sage.

Edwards, D. and Potter, J. (1992) *Discursive Psychology*. London: Sage.

Eggins, S. and Slade, D. (1997) *Analysing Casual Conversation*. London: Cassell.

Eikhenbaum, B. M. (1926) 'The theory of the formal method', in L. Matejka and K. Pomorska (eds) *Readings in Russian Poetics*. Ann Arbor, MI: Michigan University Press [original 1878].

EMEDD 2003, *The Early Modern English Dictionaries Database* 2003. Accessed 22 October 2006, URL: http://www.chass.utoronto/ca/english/emed/emedd.html

Emmott, C. (1997) *Narrative Comprehension: A Discourse Perspective*. Oxford: Oxford University Press.

Encarta World English Dictionary (1999) Microsoft Corporation Bloomsbury Publishing.

Enkvist, N. E. (1964) 'On defining style', in N. E. Enkvist, J. Spencer and M. Gregory (eds) *Linguistics and Style*. Oxford: Oxford University Press, pp. 1–56.

Enkvist, N. E. (1973) *Linguistic Stylistics*. The Hague: Mouton.

Ensslin, A. (2007) *Canonising Hypertext: Explorations and Constructions*. London: Continuum.

Evans, G. B. (ed.) (1997) *The Riverside Shakespeare* (second edition with J. J. M. Tobin). Boston: Houghton Mifflin.

Fabb, N., Attridge, D., Durant, A. and MacCabe, C. (eds) (1987) *The Linguistics of Writing: Arguments between Language and Literature*. Manchester: Manchester University Press.

Fairclough, N. (1995) *Media Discourse*. London: Edward Arnold.

Faulks, S. (1999) *Charlotte Gray*. London: Vintage.

Faulks, S. (2006) *Human Traces*. London: Vintage Books.

Fawcett, R. P. and Tucker, G. H. (1990) 'Demonstration of GENESYS: a very large, semantically based systemic function grammar', Proceedings of the 13th

International Conference on Computational Linguistics (COLING-90). Helsinki: University of Helsinki Press, pp. 47–9.

Ferguson, R. (1999) *Memory of My Feelings: Frank O'Hara and American Art.* Berkeley: University of California Press.

Ferris, S. and Young, M. (2006) *Chick Lit. The New Woman's Fiction.* London: Routledge.

Field, T. (1990) *Infancy.* Cambridge, MA: Harvard University Press.

Fielding, H. (1996) *Bridget Jones's Diary.* London: Picador.

Fielitz, S. (1999) *Drama: Text and Theater: Anglistik-Amerikanistik.* Berlin: Cornelsen.

Finn, A., Kushmerick, N. and Smyth, B. (2002) 'Genre classification and domain transfer for information filtering', in F. Crestani, M. Girolami and C. J. van Rijsbergen (eds) *Proceedings of ECIR–02 24th European Colloquium on Information Retrieval Research.* Heidelberg: Springer Verlag.

Fish, S. (1980) *Is There a Text in This Class?* Harvard: Harvard University Press.

Fiske, S. and Taylor, S. E. (1991) *Social Cognition* (second edition). New York: McGraw-Hill.

Florio, J. (1598) *A Worlde of Wordes.* Hildesheim and New York: Olms [reprinted 1972 in *Anglistica and Americana* 114].

Flower, L. (1979) 'Writer-based prose: a cognitive basis for problems in writing', *College English* 41(1): 19–37.

Flower, L. (1989) 'Cognition, context, and theory building', *College Composition and Communication* 40(3): 282–311.

Flower, L. (1993) 'Cognitive rhetoric: an inquiry into the art of inquiry', in T. Enos and S. Brown (eds) *Defining the New Rhetorics, vol. 7.* Newbury Park: Sage, pp. 171–90.

Fludernik, M. (1993) *The Fictions of Language and the Languages of Fiction: The Linguistic Representation of Speech and Consciousness.* London: Routledge.

Fludernik, M. (1995) 'The linguistic illusion of alterity: the free indirect as paradigm of discourse representation', *Diacritics* 25(4): 89–115.

Fludernik, M. (1996) *Towards a 'Natural' Narratology.* London: Routledge.

Foakes, Richard (ed.) (1997) *King Lear* (The Arden Shakespeare, third series). Walton-on-Thames: Nelson and Sons.

Forrest-Thomson, V. (1978) *Poetic Artifice: A Theory of Twentieth-Century Poetry.* Manchester: Manchester University Press.

Foulkes, A. P. (1978) 'Arthur Miller's *The Crucible*', in E. Lohner and R. Haas (eds) *Theater und Drama in Amerika: Aspekte und Interpretationen,* Berlin: Erich Schmidt Verlag, pp. 295–309.

Fowler, R. (1977) *Linguistics and the Novel.* London: Methuen.

Fowler, R. (1986) *Linguistic Criticism.* Oxford: Oxford University Press.

Fowler, R. (1997) *Linguistics and the Novel* (second edition). London: Methuen.

Freeman, D. C. (1993) 'Read "reading the language itself" itself', *Language and Literature* 2(2): 129–33.

Freeman, D. C. (1995) '"Catch[ing] the nearest way": *Macbeth* and cognitive metaphor', *Journal of Pragmatics* 24: 689–708.

Freeman, D. C. (ed.) (1981) *Essays in Modern Stylistics.* London and New York: Methuen.

Freeman, W. J. (2000), *How Brains Make Up Their Minds.* New York: Columbia University Press.

Frye. N. (1971) *The Bush Garden: Essays on the Canadian Imagination.* Toronto: Anansi.

Gaggi, S. (1997) *From Text to Hypertext: Decentering the Subject in Fiction, Film, the Visual Arts and Electronic Media.* Philadelphia: University of Pennsylvania Press.

Galbraith, M. (1995) 'Deictic shift theory and the poetics of involvement in narrative', in J. F. Duchan, G. A. Bruder and L. E. Hewitt (eds) *Deixis in Narrative: A Cognitive Science Perspective,* Hillsdale, NY: Lawrence Erlbaum, pp. 19–59.

Gallese, V. and Goldman, A. (1998) 'Mirror neurons and the simulation theory of mind-reading', *Trends in Cognitive Science* 2(2): 493–501.

Garrett-Petts, W. F. (1988) 'Exploring an interpretive community: reader response to Canadian prairie literature', *College English* 50(8): 920–6.

Gavins, J. (2001) 'Text World Theory: a critical exposition and development in relation to Absurd prose fiction', unpublished PhD thesis, Sheffield Hallam University.

Gavins, J. (2005) '(Re)thinking modality: a text-world perspective', *Journal of Literary Semantics* 34(2): 79–93.

Gavins, J. (2007) *Text World Theory: An Introduction.* Edinburgh: Edinburgh University Press.

Gavins, J. and Steen, G. (eds) (2003) *Cognitive Poetics in Practice.* London: Routledge.

Gerrig, R. (1993) *Experiencing Narrative Worlds: On the Psychological Activities of Reading.* New Haven, CT: Yale University Press.

Gibbs, R. W. (1994) *The Poetics of Mind: Figurative Thought, Language, and Understanding.* Cambridge: Cambridge University Press.

Gibson, J. J. (1979) *The Ecological Approach to Visual Perception.* Hillsdale, NJ: Lawrence Erlbaum.

Gilbert, R. (2005) 'Watching the detectives: Mark Haddon's *The Curious Incident of the Dog in the Night-Time* and Kevin Brooks' *Martyn Pig*', *Children's Literature in Education* 26(3): 241–53.

Glickman, S. (1998) *The Picturesque and the Sublime: A Poetics of the Canadian Landscape.* Montreal: McGill-Queen's University Press.

Goffman, E. (1967) *Interactional Ritual.* Chicago: Aldine.

Goffman, E. (1981) *Forms of Talk.* Philadelphia: University of Pennsylvania Press.

Green, K. (1992) 'Deixis and the poetic persona', *Language and Literature* 1(2): 121–34.

Green, K. (ed.) (1995) *New Essays in Deixis: Discourse, Narrative, Literature.* Amsterdam: Rodopi.

Gregoriou, C. (2002) 'Behaving badly: a cognitive stylistics of the criminal mind', *Nottingham Linguistic Circular* 17: 61–73.

Gregoriou, C. (2003a) 'Demystifying the criminal mind: linguistic, social and generic deviance in contemporary American crime fiction', *Working With English* 1. Accessed May 2007 at: www.nottingham.ac.uk/english/working_with_english

Gregoriou, C. (2003b) 'Criminally minded: the stylistics of justification in contemporary American crime fiction', *Style* 37(2): 144–59.

Gregoriou, C. (2007) *Deviance in Contemporary Crime Fiction*. London: Palgrave.

Griswold, C. L. (1999) *Adam Smith and the Virtues of Enlightenment*. Cambridge: Cambridge University Press.

Gross, K.-D. (2001) '*The Crucible* as drama and as opera', *Zeitschrift für Anglistik und Amerikanistik* 49(1): 44–58.

Guns, B. (dir) (2004) *The Mysterious Naked Man*. Video recording. Morningtide Films in association with CBC Atlantic.

Gutenberg, A. (2000) *Mögliche Welten: Plot und Sinnstiftung im englischen Frauenroman*. Heidelberg: C. Winter.

Habermas, J. (1984) *The Theory of Communicative Action* (trans. T. McCarthy). Boston: Beacon.

Haddon, M. (2003) *The Curious Incident of the Dog in the Night-time*. London: Jonathan Cape (adult imprint), Oxford: David Fickling Books (children's imprint).

Hall, G. (2005) *Literature in Language Education* London: Palgrave Macmillan.

Hall, G. and Gavins, J. (2004) 'The year's work in stylistics 2003', *Language and Literature* 13(4): 349–64.

Halliday, M. A. K. (1994) *An Introduction to Functional Grammar* (second edition). London: Arnold.

Halliday, M. A. K. (2004) *An Introduction to Functional Grammar* (third edition, with C. Mattiessen). London: Arnold.

Hamilton, C. (2003) 'Genetic roulette: on the cognitive rhetoric of biorisk', in R. Dirven, R. Frank and M. Pütz (eds) *Cognitive Models in Language and Thought*. Berlin: Mouton de Gruyter, pp. 353–93.

Hamilton, C. (2004) 'Towards a cognitive rhetoric of Imagism', *Style* 38(4): 468–90.

Hamilton, C. (2005) 'A cognitive rhetoric of poetry and Emily Dickinson', *Language and Literature* 14: 279–94.

Hamilton, C. (2006) 'Stylistics or cognitive stylistics?', *Bulletin de la Société de Stylistique Anglaise* 27.

Hanson, C. (2004) 'Fiction, feminism and femininity from the '80s to the noughties', in E. Parker (ed.) *Contemporary British Women Writers*. Cambridge: D. S. Brewer, pp. 16–27.

Hardy, D. E. (2003) *Narrating Knowledge in Flannery O'Connor's Fiction*. Columbia: University of South Carolina Press.

Harré, R. and Gillett, G. (1994) *The Discursive Mind*. London: Sage.

Hayman, R. (1972) *Arthur Miller*. New York: Frederick Ungar.

Heaney, S. (1990) *New Selected Poems, 1966–1987*. London: Faber and Faber.

Heath, S. (1998) 'Education – academia: the value of literature', *Critical Quarterly* 41(1): 132–8.

Hegel, G. W. F. (1993) *Introductory Lectures on Aesthetics* (trans. B. Bosanquet, ed. M. Inwood). London: Penguin [original 1886].

Heider, F. (1958) *The Psychology of Interpersonal Relations.* New York: Wiley.

Herman, D. (2001) *Story Logic.* Nebraska: University of Nebraska Press.

Herman, D. (2002) 'Quantitative methods in narratology: a corpus-based study of motion events in stories', in J.-C. Meister (ed.) *Narratology Beyond Literary Criticism.* Berlin: de Gruyter, pp. 125–49.

Hess, N. (2003) 'Real language through poetry: a formula for meaning making', *ELT Journal* 51(1): 19–25.

Hidalgo Downing, L. (2000) *Negation, Text Worlds and Discourse: The Pragmatics of Fiction.* Stanford, CT: Ablex.

Hill, P. (1967) '*The Crucible*: a structural view', *Modern Drama* (1967): 312–17.

Hintikka, J. (1967) 'Individuals, possible worlds, and epistemic logic', *Nous* 1: 33–62.

Hoey, M. (2001) *Textual Interaction: An Introduction to Written Discourse Analysis.* London: Routledge.

Hollindale, P. (1997) *Signs of Childness in Children's Books.* Stroud: Thimble Press.

Holt, E. and Clift, R. (eds) (2006) *Voicing: Reported Speech and Footing in Conversation.* Cambridge: Cambridge University Press.

Hoover, D. (1999) *Language and Style in* The Inheritors. Lanham, MD: University Press of America.

Hoover, D. (2001) 'Statistical stylistics and authorship attribution: an empirical investigation', *Literary and Linguistic Computing* 16(4): 421–44.

Hoover, D. (2002) 'Frequent word sequences and statistical stylistics', *Literary and Linguistic Computing* 17(2): 157–80.

Hoover, D., Culpeper, J. and Louw, W. (forthcoming) *Approaches to Corpus Stylistics.* London: Routledge.

Hope, J. (1994) *The Authorship of Shakespeare's Plays: A Socio-Linguistic Study.* Cambridge: Cambridge University Press.

Hori, M. (2004) *Investigating Dicken's Style. A Collocational Analysis.* Basingstoke: Palgrave Macmillan.

Howe, S. (1980) 'White foolscap' from *The Liberties.* Chicago: Loon Press, p. 88 [reprinted 1983 within *The Defenestration of Prague*, New York: Kulchur Foundation].

Hulstijn, J. H. and Laufer, B. (2001) 'Some empirical evidence for the involvement load hypothesis in vocabulary acquisition', *Language Learning* 51(3): 539–58.

Humphrey, A. R. (ed.) (1960) *The First Part of King Henry IV* (The Arden Shakespeare). London: Methuen.

Humphrey, A. R. (ed.) (1965) *The Second Part of King Henry IV* (The Arden Shakespeare). London: Methuen.

Hunston, S. (2002) *Corpora in Applied Linguistics.* Cambridge: Cambridge University Press.

Hunt, P. (1991) *Criticism, Theory and Children's Literature.* Oxford: Blackwell.

Hunt, P. (ed.) (1999) *Understanding Children's Literature*. London: Routledge, pp. 138–50.

Hunter, L. (2005) 'Echolocation, figuration and tellings: rhetorical strategies in *Romeo and Juliet*', *Language and Literature* 14(3): 259–78.

Hutcheon, L. (1980) *Narcissistic Narrative: The Metafictional Paradox*. New York: Methuen.

Hutcheon, L. (1988) *A Poetics of Postmodernism: History Theory Fiction*. London: Routledge.

Hutcheon, L. (1989) *The Politics of Postmodernism*. London: Routledge.

Hutchins, E. (1995) *Cognition in the Wild*. Cambridge, MA: MIT Press.

Hutto, D. (2002) 'The world is not enough: shared emotions and other minds,' in P. Goldie (ed.) *Understanding Emotions*. London: Ashgate, pp. 37–53.

Hymes, D. (1996) *Ethnography, Linguistics, Narrative Inequality: Towards an Understanding of Voice*. London: Taylor and Francis.

Iverson, J. M. and Thelen, E. (1999) 'Hand, mouth and brain: the dynamic emergence of speech and gesture', in R. Nunez and W. J. Freeman (eds) *Reclaiming Cognition: The Primacy of Action, Intention and Emotion*. Thorverton: Imprint Academic, pp. 79–93.

Jackson, S. (1993) 'Love and romance as objects of feminist knowledge', in M. Kennedy, C. Lubelska and V. Walsh (eds) *Making Connections: Women's Studies, Women's Movements, Women's Lives*. London: Taylor and Francis, pp. 39–50.

Jakobson, R. (1960) 'Closing statement: linguistics and poetics', in A. Jaworski and N. Coupland (eds) (1998) *The Discourse Reader*. London: Routledge, pp. 54–62.

Jauss, H. R. (1989) *Question and Answer: Forms of Dialogic Understanding* (trans. M. Hays). Minneapolis: University of Minnesota Press.

Jaworski, A. and Coupland, N. (eds) (1998) *The Discourse Reader*. London: Routledge.

Jeffries, L. (2000) 'Point of view and the reader in the poetry of Carol Ann Duffy', in L. Jeffries and P. Sansom (eds) *Contemporary Poems: Some Critical Approaches*. Huddersfield: Smith/Doorstop, pp. 54–68.

Jeffries, L. (2003) 'Analogy and multi-modal exploration in the teaching of language theory', *Style* 37(1): 67–85.

Jenkins, P. (1994) *Using Murder: The Social Construction of Serial Homicide*. New York: de Gruyter.

Johnson, M. (1987) *The Body in the Mind*. Chicago: University of Chicago Press.

Jones, D. G. (1970) *Butterfly on Rock: Images in Canadian Literature*. Toronto: University of Toronto Press.

Jones, E. E., Kannouse, D. E., Kelley, H. H., Nisbett, R. E., Valins, S. and Weiner, B. (eds) (1972) *Attribution: Perceiving the Causes of Behaviour*. Morristown, NJ: General Learning Press.

Joyce, M. (1987) *afternoon, a story*, CD-ROM. Massachusetts: Eastgate Systems.

Jucker, A. H. and Taavitsainen, I. (2000) 'Diachronic speech act analysis. Insults from flyting to flaming', *Journal of Historical Pragmatics* 1: 67–95.

Kantorowitz, E. (1957) *The King's Two Bodies. A Study in Medieval Political Theology*. Princeton, NJ: Princeton University Press.

Karlgren, J. (2000) 'Stylistic experiments for Information Retrieval', unpublished doctoral dissertation, Swedish Institute of Computer Science, Kista, Stockholm.

Kastan, D. S. (ed.) (2002) *King Henry IV Part I* (The Arden Shakespeare, third series). London: Thomson.

Kavka, M. (2001) 'Introduction', in E. Bronfen and M. Kavka (eds) *Feminist Consequences: Theory for the New Century*. New York: Columbia University Press, pp. ix–xxvi.

Keen, S. (2006) 'A theory of narrative empathy', *Narrative* 14(3): 207–36.

Keith, W. J. (1985) *Canadian Literature in English*. London: Longman.

Kellaway, K. (2003) 'Autistic differences', *Observer*, 27 April.

Kelley, H. H. (1973) 'The process of causal attribution', *American Psychologist*, February: 107–28.

Kennedy, R. S. (1996), 'Introduction', in e.e. cummings *Tulips and Chimneys*. New York: Liveright, pp. xiii–xix.

Kenward, H. (2005) 'The Challenge of Crossover: An investigation into the existence and implications of crossover fiction', unpublished MA dissertation, Sheffield University.

Kernan, K. T. (1977) 'Semantic and expressive elaboration in children's narratives', in S. Ervin-Tripp (ed.) *Child Discourse*. New York: Academic Press, pp. 91–102.

Keyes, M. (2004) *The Other Side of the Story*. London: Michael Joseph.

Kinsella, S. (2003) *Can You Keep a Secret?* London: Black Swan.

Kopytko, R. (1993) *Polite Discourse in Shakespeare's English*. Poznan: Adam Mickiewicza University Press.

Koskimaa, R. (2000) 'Digital literature: from text to hypertext and beyond', unpublished PhD thesis, University of Jyväskylä. URL: www.cc.jyu.fi/~koskimaa/thesis

Kövescses, Z. (2002) *Metaphor: A Practical Introduction*. New York: Oxford University Press.

Kress, G. (1988) 'Textual matters: the social effectiveness of style', in D. Birch and M. O'Toole (eds) *Functions of Style*. London: Pinter, pp. 126–41.

Kripke, S. (1972) *Naming and Necessity*. Oxford: Blackwell.

Kristeva, J. (1997) 'Women's time' (trans. A. Jardine and H. Blake), in R. Warhol and D. P. Herndl (eds) *Feminisms: An Anthology of Literary Theory and Criticism*. New York: Rutgers University Press, pp. 443–62.

Kuiken, D., Miall, D. S. and Sikora, S. (2004) 'Forms of self-implication in literary reading', *Poetics Today* 25(2): 171–203.

Kuno, S. (1987) *Functional Syntax: Anaphora, Discourse and Empathy*. Chicago: Chicago University Press.

Labov, W. (1972) *Language in the Inner City: Studies in the Black English Vernacular*. Philadelphia: University of Pennsylvania Press.

Labov, W. (1997) 'Further steps in narrative analysis', *Journal of Narrative and Life History* 7(1–4): 395–415.

Labov, W. and Waletzky, J. (1967) 'Narrative analysis: oral versions of personal experience', in J. Holm (ed.) *Essays on the Verbal and Visual Arts*. Seattle: University of Washington Press, pp. 12–44.

Lachenicht, L. G. (1980) 'Aggravating language: a study of abusive and insulting language', *International Journal of Human Communication* 13(4): 607–87.

Lahey, E. (2005) 'Text-world landscapes and English-Canadian national identity in the poetry of Al Purdy, Milton Acorn and Alden Nowlan', unpublished PhD thesis, University of Nottingham.

Lahey, E. (2006) '(Re)thinking world-building: locating the text-worlds of Canadian lyric poetry', *Journal of Literary Semantics* 35(2): 145–64.

Lakoff, G. and Johnson, M. (1980) *Metaphors We Live By*. Chicago: University of Chicago Press.

Lakoff, G. and Turner, M. (1989) *More than Cool Reason: A Field Guide to Poetic Metaphor*. Chicago: Chicago University Press.

Lakoff, R. (1995), 'Cries and whispers: the shattering of the silence', in K. Hall and M. Bucholtz (eds) *Gender Articulated*. London: Routledge, pp. 25–50.

Lambrou, M. (2003) 'Collaborative oral narratives of general experience: when an interview becomes a conversation', *Language and Literature* 12(2): 153–74.

Lambrou, M. (2005) 'Story patterns in oral narratives: a variationist critique of Labov and Waletzky's model of narrative schemas', unpublished PhD thesis, Middlesex University, London.

Land, E. (1977) 'The retinex theory of color vision', *Scientific American* 237: 108–28.

Landow, G. P. (1994) 'What's a critic to do? critical theory in the age of hypertext', in G. P. Landow (ed.) *Hyper/Text/Theory*. Baltimore: Johns Hopkins University Press, pp. 1–48.

Landow, G. P. (1997) *Hypertext 2.0: The Convergence of Contemporary Critical Theory and Technology* (revised edition). Baltimore: Johns Hopkins University Press.

Landow, G. P. and Delany, P. (1991) *Hypermedia and Literary Studies*. Massachusetts: MIT Press.

Lanser, S. (1986) 'Towards a feminist narratology', *Style*, 20(3): 341–63.

Lanser, S. (1995) 'Sexing the narrative: propriety, desire and the engendering of narratology', *Narrative* 3: 85–94.

László, J. (1986) 'Same story with different points of view', *SPIEL* 5: 1–22.

Laufer, B. and Paribakht, T. S. (1998) 'The relationship between passive and active vocabularies: effects of language learning contexts', *Language Learning* 48(3): 365–91.

Le Doux, J. (1999) *The Emotional Brain*. London: Orion.

Lee, D. (1992) *Competing Discourses: Perspective and Ideology in Language*. Harlow: Longman.

Leech, G. (1969) *A Linguistic Guide to English Poetry*. London: Longman.

Leech, G. (1983) *Principles of Pragmatics*. London: Longman.

Leech, G. (1985) 'Stylistics', in T. A. van Dijk (ed.) *Discourse and Literature. New Approaches to the Analysis of Literary Genres*. Amsterdam: John Benjamins, pp. 39–57.

Leech, G. (1987) 'Stylistics and functionalism', in N. Fabb, D. Attridge, A. Durant and C. MacCabe (eds) *The Linguistics of Writing: Arguments between Language and Literature.* Manchester: Manchester University Press, pp. 76–88.

Leech, G. and Short, M. (1981) *Style in Fiction. A Linguistic Introduction to English Fictional Prose.* Harlow: Longman.

LEME (2008), *Lexicons of Early Modern English.* Accessed 30 March 2009, URL: http://leme.library.utoronto.ca/

Leonard, M. (2001) 'Old wine in new bottles? Women working inside and outside the household', *Women's Studies International Forum* 24(1): 67–78.

Levinson, S. (1983) *Pragmatics.* Cambridge: Cambridge University Press.

Lewis, D. (1973) *Counterfactuals.* Oxford: Blackwell.

Libby, A. (1976) 'O'Hara on the Silver Range', *Contemporary Literature* 17(2): 240–62.

Lim, D. (2003) 'Review of *The Curious Case of the Dog in the Night-Time*'. Accessed May 2007, URL: http://www.villagevoice.com/issues/0330/lim.php

Lipps, T. (1900) 'Aesthetische Einfühlung', *Zeitschrift für Psychologie* 22: 415–50.

Livia, A. (2003) '"One man in two is a woman": linguistic approaches to gender in literary texts', in J. Holmes and M. Meyerhoff (eds) *The Handbook of Language and Gender.* Blackwell: Oxford, pp. 142–58.

Louw, W. (1993) 'Irony in the text or insincerity in the writer? The diagnostic potential of semantic prosodies', in M. Baker *et al.* (eds) *Text and Technology.* Amsterdam: John Benjamins.

Louw, W. (2006) 'Literary worlds as collocation', in G. Watson and S. Zyngier (eds) *Literature and Stylistics for Language Learners: Theory and Practice.* London: Palgrave.

Lowe, V. (1998) '"Unhappy" confessions in *The Crucible*: a pragmatic explanation', in J. Culpeper, M. Short and P. Verdonk (eds) *Exploring the Language of Drama: From Text to Context.* London: Routledge, pp. 128–41.

Ludwig, H. W. and Faulstich, W. (1985) *Erzählperspektive Empirisch.* Tübingen: Gunter Narr.

Luyckx, K., Daelemans, W. and Vanhoutte, E. (2006) 'Stylogenetics: clustering-based stylistic analysis of literary corpora', *Proceedings of LREC 2006 5th International Conference on Language Resources and Evaluation.* Genoa: Istituto di Linguistica Computazionale, pp. 30–5.

McArthur, T. (1981) *The Longman Lexicon of Contemporary English.* London: Longman.

McCallum, R. (1999) 'Very advanced texts: metafictions and experimental work', in P. Hunt (ed.) *Understanding Children's Literature.* London: Routledge, pp. 138–50.

McCann, C. D. and Higgins, T. (1990) 'Social cognition and communication', in H. Giles and W. P. Robinson (eds) *Handbook of Social Psychology.* Chichester: John Wiley, pp. 13–32.

MacDonald, S. P. (2002) 'Prose styles, genres, and levels of analysis', *Style* 36(4): 618–39.

McEnery, T. and Oakes, M. (2000) 'Authorship studies/textual statistics', in R. Dale, H. Moisl and H. Somers (eds) *Handbook of Natural Language Processing.* New York: Marcel Dekker.

McEnery, T., Xiao, R. and Tono, Y. (2006) *Corpus-Based Language Studies: An Advanced Resource Book.* London: Routledge.

McGill, W. (1981) 'The crucible of history: Arthur Miller's John Proctor', *The New England Quarterly* 54(2) (June): 258–64.

McHale, B. (1978), 'Free indirect discourse: a survey of recent accounts', *Poetics and Theory of Literature* 3: 249–87.

McHale, B. (1987) *Postmodernist Fiction.* London: Methuen.

McHale, B. (1992) *Constructing Postmodernism.* London: Routledge.

McHale, B. (2005) 'Free indirect discourse', in D. Herman, M. Jahn and M.-L. Ryan (eds) *Routledge Encyclopedia of Narrative Theory.* London: Routledge, p. 189.

McIntyre, D. (2003) 'Using foregrounding theory as a teaching methodology in a stylistics course', *Style* 37(1): 1–13.

McIntyre, D. (2004) 'Point of view in drama: a socio-pragmatic analysis of Dennis Potter's *Brimstone and Treacle*', *Language and Literature* 13(2): 139–60.

McIntyre, D. (2005) 'Logic, reality and mind style in Alan Bennett's *The Lady in the Van*', *Journal of Literary Semantics* 34(1): 21–40.

McIntyre, D. (2006) *Point of View in Plays: A Cognitive Stylistic Approach to Viewpoint in Drama and Other Text-types.* Amsterdam: John Benjamins.

Mackay, R. (1992) 'Lexicide and goblin-spotting in the language/literature classroom', *ELT Journal* 46(2): 63–74.

McKinney, V., Yoon, K. and Zahedi, F. M. (2002) 'The measurement of web-customer satisfaction: an expectation and disconfirmation approach', *Information Systems Research* 13(3): 296–315.

McMenamin, G. (2002) *Forensic Linguistics: Advances in Forensic Stylistics.* London: CRC Press.

McNeillie, A. (1994) *The Essays of Virginia Woolf, Vol. IV, 1925–1928.* London: Hogarth Press.

McRobbie, A. (2004) 'Post-feminism and popular culture', *Feminist Media Studies* 4(3): 255–64.

Mahlberg, M. (2005a) *English General Nouns: A Corpus Theoretical Approach.* Amsterdam: John Benjamins.

Mahlberg, M. (2005b) 'The evidence: corpus design and the words in a dictionary', in F. F. M. Dolezal (ed.) *Lexicographica. Internationales Jahrbuch fuer Lexikographie* (guest editors W. Teubert and M. Mahlberg) 20: 114–29.

Mahlberg, M. (2007a) 'Clusters, key clusters and local textual functions in Dickens', *Corpora.* Vol 2(1), 1–31.

Mahlberg, M. (2007b) 'Corpus stylistics: bridging the gap between linguistic and literary studies', in M. Hoey, M. Mahlberg, M. Stubbs and W. Teubert (eds) *Texts, Discourse and Corpora. Theory and Analysis* London: Continuum. 219–46.

Mahlberg, M. (forthcoming c) 'Corpora and translation studies: textual functions of lexis in *Bleak House* and in a translation of the novel into German', in V. Intonti, G. Todisco and M. Gatto (eds), *La Traduzione: La Stato dell' Arte/ Translation: The State of the Art.* Ravenna: Longo. 115–35.

Malle, B. F. (2004) *How the Mind Explains Behavior: Folk Explanations, Meaning, and Social Interaction.* Cambridge, MA: MIT Press.

Marsh, K. (2004) 'Contextualizing Bridget Jones', *College Literature* 31(1): 52–72.

Marshall, T. (1979) *Harsh and Lovely Land: The Major Canadian Poets and the Making of a Canadian Tradition.* Vancouver: University of British Columbia Press.

Martin, J. R. and P. R. R. White (2005) *The Language of Evaluation: Appraisal in English.* London: Palgrave.

Martin, R. (1977) 'Arthur Miller's *The Crucible*: background and sources', *Modern Drama* 20: 279–92.

Martindale, C. (1978) 'Sit with statisticians and commit a social science: inter-disciplinary aspects of poetics', *Poetics* 7: 272–82.

Matthiessen, C. M. I. M. (1995) *Lexicogrammatical Cartography: English Systems.* Tokyo: International Language Sciences Publishers.

Matthiessen, C. M. I. M. and J. A. Bateman (1991) *Text Generation and Systemic-Functional Linguistics: Experiences from English and Japanese.* London: Frances Pinter and St Martin's Press.

Meehan, B. (1994) 'Son of Cain or son of Sam? The monster as serial killer in Beowulf', *Connecticut Review* 16(2) (Fall): 1–7.

Meek, M. (1988) *How Texts Teach What Readers Learn.* Stroud: Thimble Press.

Melchiori, G. (ed.) (1998) *King Edward III* (The New Cambridge Shakespeare). Cambridge: Cambridge University Press.

Mele, A. R. (ed.) (1997) *The Philosophy of Action.* Oxford: Oxford University Press.

Metz, G. H. (ed.) (1989) *Sources of Four Plays Ascribed to Shakespeare.* Columbia: University of Missouri Press.

Mey, J. (1998) *When Voices Clash. A Study in Literary Pragmatics.* Berlin: Mouton de Gruyter.

Miles, A. (2003) 'There's no need to bite the breast', *Journal of Digital Information* 3(3), URL: http://jodi.ecs.soton.ac.uk/Articles/v03/i03/Miles/breast.html

Mill, J. S. (1965) 'What is poetry?', in J. B. Schneewind (ed.) *Mill's Essays on Literature and Society.* New York: Collier Books, p. 113 [original 1833].

Miller, A. (1953) *The Crucible: A Play in Four Acts.* New York: Viking.

Miller, A. (1995) '*The Crucible*' in *The Portable Arthur Miller* (ed. C. Bigsby). New York: Penguin, pp. 132–258.

Miller, A. (1996) 'Why I wrote *The Crucible*: an artist's answer to politics', *The New Yorker* (21 October 1996), pp. 158–64.

Miller, A. (2000) '*The Crucible* in history', in *Echoes down the Corridor: Collected Essays, 1944–2000* (ed. S. Centola). New York: Viking, pp. 274–95.

Miller, J. (1971) 'Interpretation in *Bleak House*', in *Victorian Subjects.* Durham, CA: Duke University Press, pp. 179–99 [reprinted in 1991].

Mills, S. (1995) *Feminist Stylistics.* London: Routledge.

Mills, S. (1998) 'Post-feminist text analysis', *Language and Literature* 7(3): 235–53.

Mills, S. (2003) *Gender and Politeness.* Cambridge: Cambridge University Press.

Mills, S. (2005) 'Gender and impoliteness', *Journal of Politeness Research: Language, Behaviour, Culture* 1(1): 263–80.

Mills, S. (2006) 'Feminist stylistics', in K. Brown (ed.) *Encyclopedia of Language and Linguistics, vol. 12* (second edition). London: Elsevier, pp. 221–3.

Modleski, T. (1982) *Loving with a Vengeance: Mass-Produced Fantasies for Women*. Hamden, CT: Archon Books.

Modleski, T. (1984) *Loving with a Vengeance*. London: Methuen.

Montoro, R. (2003) ' "Shall we meet for lunch, darling?" or the evaluation of contemporary fiction from a socio-stylistic perspective', in S. Csabi. and J. Zerkowitz (eds) *Textual Secrets: The Message of the Medium*. Budapest: Budapest University Press, pp. 468–77.

Moore, A. and Campbell, E. (2004) *From Hell*. Marietta: Top Shelf Productions.

Morgan, E. (1997) ' "Bewitched" review of *The Crucible* (film), dir. Nicholas Hytner and *The Crucible Screenplay*, by Arthur Miller (New York: Penguin, 1997)', *New York Review of Books* 44 (9 January 1997): 4–6.

Morrison, J. (1978) 'Awake', in *An American Prayer*. New York: Electra Entertainment Group.

Munkelt, M. and Busse, B. (2007) 'Aspects of governance in Shakespeare's *Edward III*: the quest for personal and political identity', in S. Fielitz (ed) *Literature as History. History as Literature*. Frankfurt: Peter Lang.

Murray, J. H. (1997) *Hamlet on the Holodeck: The Future of Narrative in Cyberspace*. New York: Free Press.

Murray, L. and Trevarthen, C. (1985) 'Emotion regulation of interaction between two months old and their mothers', in T. Field and N. Fox (eds) *Social Perceptions in Infants*. Norwood, NJ: Ablex, pp. 137–54.

Murray, S. (2006) 'Autism, contemporary sentimental fiction and the narrative fascination of the present', *Literature and Medicine* 25(1): 24–36.

Nation, I. S. P. (1990) *Teaching and Learning Vocabulary*. New York: Newbury House.

Nellis, M. (2002) 'Prose and cons: offender auto/biographies, penal reform and probation training', *The Howard Journal* 41(5) (Dec.): 434–68.

New, W. H. (1997) *Land Sliding: Imagining Space, Presence and Power in Canadian Writing*. Toronto: University of Toronto Press.

Newitz, A. (1995) 'Serial killers, true crime, and economic performance anxiety', *Cine-Action* 38 (Sept.): 38–46.

Newsom, R. (1999) 'Style of Dickens', in P. Schlicke (ed.) *Oxford Reader's Companion to Dickens*. Oxford: Oxford University Press, 540–5.

Niedenthal, P. M., Rohmann, A. and Dalle, N. (2003) 'What is primed by emotion concepts and emotion words?', in J. Musch and K. C. Klauer (eds) *The Psychology of Evaluation: Affective Processes in Cognition and Emotion*. Mahwah, NJ: Lawrence Erlbaum.

Nietzsche, F. (1973) *Beyond Good and Evil*. Harmondsworth: Penguin [original 1886].

Nodelman, P. and Reimer, M. (2003) *The Pleasures of Children's Literature* (third edition). New York: Allyn and Bacon.

Norcliffe, G. and Simpson–Housley, P. (eds) (1992) *A Few Acres of Snow: Literary and Artistic Images of Canada*. Toronto: Dundurn Press.

Nowlan, A. (1967) *Bread, Wine and Salt*. Toronto: Clarke, Irwin.

Nowlan, A. (1971) *Between Tears and Laughter*. Toronto: Clarke, Irwin.

Nowlan, A. (1977) *Smoked Glass.* Toronto: Clarke, Irwin.

Nowlan, A. (1978) *Double Exposure.* Fredericton, NB: Brunswick Press.

Nowlan, A. (1996) *Alden Nowlan: Selected Poems* (eds P. Lane and L. Crozier). Toronto: Anansi.

Oatley, K. (1994) 'A taxonomy of the emotions of literary response and a theory of identification in fictional narrative', *Poetics* 23: 53–74.

O'Donnell, M. (1993) 'Reducing complexity in a systematic parser', in *Proceedings of the Third International Workshop on Parsing Technologies,* Tilburg, the Netherlands, 10–13 August.

O'Hara, F. (1964) 'The day lady died', in *Lunch Poems.* New York: City Lights, p.27.

O'Hara, F. (1971) 'Personism: a manifesto', in D. Allen (ed.) *The Collected Poems of Frank O'Hara.* Berkeley: University of California Press, pp. 498–9.

Oliver, M. B. (1991) *Alden Nowlan and His Works: Alden Nowlan 1933–83.* Toronto: ECW Press.

Olson, C. (1951) 'Projective verse', in R. Creeley (ed.) *Charles Olson: Selected Writings.* New York: New Directions, pp. 15–30.

Oltean, S. (1993) 'A survey of the pragmatic and referential functions of free indirect discourse', *Poetics Today* 14(4): 691–714.

Otten, T. (1996) 'Historical drama and the dimensions of tragedy: *A Man for All Seasons* and *The Crucible*', *American Drama* 6(1) (Fall): 42–60.

Oyama, S. (1985) *The Ontogeny of Information: Developmental Systems and Evolution* (second edition). Durham: Duke University Press.

Page, R. E. (2006) *Literary and Linguistic Approaches to Feminist Narratology.* Basingstoke: Palgrave.

Palmer, A. (2002) 'The construction of fictional minds', *Narrative* 10(1): 28–46.

Palmer, A. (2004) *Fictional Minds.* Lincoln: University of Nebraska Press.

Palmer, A. (2006) 'Intermental thought in the novel: the Middlemarch mind', *Style* 39(4): 427–39.

Paribakht, T. S. (2005) 'The influence of first language lexicalization on second language lexical inferencing: a study of Farsi-speaking learners of English as a foreign language', *Language Learning* 55(4): 701–48.

Parks, A. (2001) *Game Over.* London: Penguin.

Patrick, J. (2004) 'The scamseek project: text mining for financial scams on the internet', in S. Simoff and G. Williams (eds) *Proceedings of the 3rd Australasian Data Mining Conference.* Cairns, pp. 33–8.

Pavel, T. G. (1986) *Fictional Worlds.* London: Harvard University Press.

Peirce, C. S. (1955) 'The principles of phenomenology', in *Philosophical Writings of Peirce.* New York: Dover.

Peirce, C. S. (1990) 'A guess at the riddle', in N. Houser and C. Kloesel (eds) *The Essential Peirce.* Bloomington: Indiana University Press, pp. 245–79.

Pennington, D. C. (2000) *Social Cognition.* London: Routledge.

Perloff, M. (1977) *Frank O'Hara: Poet among Painters.* Chicago: University of Chicago Press.

Perloff, M. (2001) 'Watchman, spy and deadman: Jasper Johns, Frank O'Hara,

John Cage and the "Aesthetic of indifference" ', *Modernism and Modernity* 8(2): 197–223.

Peters, E. (1980) *Monk's Hood*. London: Macmillan.

Pfister, M. (1988) *The Theory and Analysis of Drama*. Cambridge: Cambridge University Press.

Plantinga, A. (1974) *The Nature of Necessity*. Oxford: Clarendon Press.

Plum, G. A. (1988) 'Text and contextual conditioning in spoken English: a genre-based approach', PhD thesis, University of Sydney.

Pommel, T. (2004) 'Literasy studies' in S. Schreibman, R. Siemens and J. Unsworth (eds) *A Companion to Digital Humanities*. Malden, MA/Oxford/Carlton, Victoria: Blackwell Publishing, pp. 88–96.

Popkin, H. (1964) 'Arthur Miller's *The Crucible*', *College English* 26(2): 139–46.

Popping, R., Quah, S. R. and A. Sales (2000) *Computer-assisted Text Analysis*. London: Sage.

Pratt, M. L. (1981) 'Literary cooperation and implicature', in D. C. Freeman (ed.) *Essays in Modern Stylistics*. London: Methuen, pp. 377–412.

Priestman, M. (1998) *Crime Fiction: From Poe to the Present*. Plymouth: Northcote House.

Project Gutenberg (2003–06) URL: http://www.gutenberg.org/

Punday, P. (1997) 'Meaning in postmodern words: the case of *The French Lieutenant's Woman*', *Semiotica* 115(3/4): 313–43.

Purdy, A. (1967) *North of Summer: Poems from Baffin Island*. Toronto: McClelland and Stewart.

Purdy, A. (1970) *Love in a Burning Building*. Toronto: McClelland and Stewart.

Purdy, A. (1973) *Poems for All the Annettes*. Toronto: Anansi [original 1962].

Purdy, A. (1976) *Sundance at Dusk*. Toronto: McClelland and Stewart.

Purdy, A. (2000) *Beyond Remembering: The Collected Poems of Al Purdy* (eds A. Purdy and S. Solecki). Madeira Park: Harbour.

Pynchon, T. (1996) *The Crying of Lot 49*. London: Vintage [original 1966].

Qian, D. D. (2002) 'Investigating the relationship between vocabulary knowledge and academic reading performance: an assessment perspective', *Language Learning* 52(3): 513–36.

Quirk, R. (1961) 'Some observations on the language of Dickens', *A Review of English Literature* 2(3): 19–28.

Radzikhovskii, L. A. (1991) 'Dialogue as a unit of analysis of consciousness', *Soviet Psychology* 29: 8–21.

Random House (2003), interview with Mark Haddon (2003), URL: www.randomhouse.co.uk/readersgroup/qanda0309.htm

Rayson, P. (2003) 'Matrix: a statistical method and software tool for linguistic analysis through corpus comparison', PhD thesis, Lancaster University.

Rayson, P., Archer, D. and Smith, N. (2005) 'VARD versus Word: a comparison of the UCREL variant detector and modern spell checkers on English historical corpora', *Proceedings of the Corpus Linguistics Conference Series On-Line E-Journal* 1: 1.

Rescher, N. (1975) *A Theory of Possibility*. Pittsburgh: Pittsburgh University Press.

Richardson, B. (2000) 'Linearity and its discontents: rethinking narrative form and ideological valence', *College English* 62(6): 685–95.

Ronen, R. (1994) *Possible Worlds in Literary Theory*. Cambridge: Cambridge University Press.

Rosenblatt, L. (1995) *Literature as Exploration* (fifth edition). New York: MLA [original 1938].

Rothery, J. and Stenglin, M. (2000) 'Interpreting literature: the role of APPRAISAL', in L. Unsworth (ed.) *Researching Language in Schools and Functional Linguistic Perspectives*. London: Cassell.

Rudanko, J. (2006) 'Aggravated impoliteness and two types of speaker intention in an episode in Shakespeare's *Timon of Athens*', *Journal of Pragmatics* 38: 829–41.

Russell, P. (ed.) (1966) *Nationalism in Canada*. Toronto: McGraw-Hill.

Ryan, M. L. (1991) *Possible Worlds, Artificial Intelligence and Narrative Theory*. Bloomington: Indiana University Press.

Ryan, M. L. (1992) 'Possible worlds in recent literary theory', *Style* 26(4): 528–52.

Ryan, M. L. (1998) 'The text as world versus the text as game: possible worlds semantics and postmodern theory', *Journal of Literary Semantics* 27(3): 137–63.

Saul, N. E. (1995) '*Richard II* and the vocabulary of kingship', *English Historical Review* 110: 854–77.

Schafer, D. P. (1995) *Canadian Culture: Key to Canada's Future Development*. Markham: World Culture Project.

Schank, R. C. (1982) *Dynamic Memory: A Theory of Reminding and Learning in Computers and People*. Cambridge: Cambridge University Press.

Schank, R. C. (1984) *The Cognitive Computer*. Reading: Addison-Wesley.

Schank, R. C. (1986) *Explanation Patterns*. Hillsdale, NJ: Lawrence Erlbaum.

Schank, R. C. and Abelson, R. (1977) *Scripts, Plans, Goals and Understanding*. Hillsdale, NJ: Lawrence Erlbaum.

Schegloff, E. A. (1997) 'Narrative analysis thirty years later', *Journal of Narrative and Life History* 7(1–4): 97–106.

Schiffrin, D. (1994) *Approaches to Discourse*. Oxford: Blackwell.

Schissel, W. (1994) 'Re(dis)covering the witches in Arthur Miller's *The Crucible*: a feminist reading', *Modern Drama* 37: 461–73.

Schmitt, N. (1998) 'Tracking the incremental acquisition of second language vocabulary: a longitudinal study', *Language Learning* 48(2): 281–317.

Scott, M. (1999) *Wordsmith Tools Users Help File*. Oxford: Oxford University Press.

Scott, M. (2004) *WordSmith Tools. Version 4.0*. Oxford: Oxford University Press.

Scott, M. and Tribble, C. (2006) *Textual Patterns. Key Words and Corpus Analysis in Language Education*. Amsterdam: John Benjamins.

Searle, J. R. (1992) *The Rediscovery of the Mind*. Cambridge, MA: MIT Press.

Sebastiani, F. (2002) 'Machine learning in automated text categorization', *ACM Computing Surveys* 34(1): 1–47.

Segal, E. M. (1995) 'Narrative comprehension and the role of deictic shift theory', in J. F. Duchan, G. A. Bruder and L. E. Hewitt (eds) *Deixis in Narrative: A Cognitive Science Perspective*. Hillsdale, NJ: Lawrence Erlbaum, pp. 3–17.

Seltzer, M. (1998) *Serial Killers: Death and Life in America's Wound Culture.* New York: Routledge.

Semino, E. (1992) 'Building on Keith Green's "Deixis and the poetic persona": further reflections on deixis in poetry', *Language and Literature* 1(2): 135–40.

Semino, E. (1995) 'Schema theory and the analysis of text-worlds in poetry', *Language and Literature* 4(2): 79–108.

Semino, E. (1997) *Language and World Creation in Poems and Other Texts.* London: Longman.

Semino, E. (2002) 'A cognitive stylistic approach to mind style in narrative fiction', in E. Semino and J. Culpeper (eds) *Cognitive Stylistics: Language and Cognition in Text Analysis.* Amsterdam: John Benjamins, pp. 95–122.

Semino, E. (2003) 'Possible worlds and mental spaces in Hemingway's "A Very Short Story"', in J. Gavins and G. Steen (eds) *Cognitive Poetics in Practice.* London: Routledge, pp. 107–15.

Semino, E. (2006), 'Blending and characters' mental functioning in Virginia Woolf's "Lappin and Lapinova"', *Language and Literature* 15(1): 55–72.

Semino, E. (2007) 'Mind style 25 years on', *Style* 41.

Semino, E. and Culpeper, J. (eds) (2002) *Cognitive Stylistics: Language and Cognition in Text Analysis.* Amsterdam: John Benjamins.

Semino, E. and Short, M. (2004) *Corpus Stylistics: Speech, Writing and Thought Presentation in a Corpus of English Writing.* London: Routledge.

Semino, E. and Swindlehurst, K. (1996) 'Metaphor and mind style in Ken Kesey's *One Flew over The Cuckoo's Nest*', *Style* 30(1): 143–66.

Semino, E., Short, M. and Culpeper, J. (1997) 'Using a corpus to test a model of speech and thought presentation', *Poetics* 25(1): 17–43.

Sendak, M. (1971) *Where the Wild Things Are.* Harmondsworth: Penguin [original 1967].

Shapiro, I. A. (2003) 'The text of the Raigne of Edward III', *Notes and Queries* 50(1): 35–6.

Shelley, P. B. (1991) 'A defence of poetry', in C. Kaplan and W. Anderson (eds) *Criticism: The Major Statements* (third edition). New York: St Martin's [original 1819].

Shen, D. (2005a) 'What narratology and stylistics can do for each other', in J. Phelan and P. Rabinowitz (eds) *A Companion to Narrative Theory.* Oxford: Blackwell, pp. 136–49.

Shen, D. (2005b) 'Why contextual and formal narratologies need each other', *Journal of Narrative Technique* 35(2): 141–71.

Short, M. (1996) *Exploring the Language of Poems, Plays and Prose.* London: Longman.

Short, M. (forthcoming) *Exploring the Language of Drama and Film.* London: Longman.

Silcox, D. P. (2003) *The Group of Seven and Tom Thompson.* Toronto: Firefly Books.

Simpson, P. (1993) *Language, Ideology and Point of View.* London: Routledge.

Simpson, P. (1997) *Language through Literature.* London: Routledge.

Simpson, P. (2004) *Stylistics: A Resource Book for Students.* London: Routledge.

Simpson, P. L. (2000) *Psychopaths: Tracking the Serial Killer through Contemporary American Film and Fiction.* Carbondale: Southern Illinois University Press.

Sinclair, J. M. (2004) *Trust the Text. Language, Corpus and Discourse.* London: Routledge.

Skarda, C. (1999) 'The perceptual form of life', in R. Nunez and W. J. Freeman (eds) *Reclaiming Cognition: The Primacy of Action, Intention, and Emotion.* Thorverton, Devon: Imprint Academic, pp. 79–93.

Smith, A. (1976), *The Theory of Moral Sentiments* (eds D. D. Raphael and A. L. Macfie). Oxford: Clarendon Press [original 1759 and 1790].

Smith, H. (2000) *Hyperscapes in the Poetry of Frank O'Hara.* Liverpool: Liverpool University Press.

Sotirova, V. (2004) 'Connectives in free indirect style: continuity or shift?', *Language and Literature* 13(3): 216–34.

Sperber, D. (1975) 'Rudiments de rhétorique cognitive', *Poétique* 6: 389–415.

Sperber, D. and Wilson, D. (1986) *Relevance: Communication and Cognition.* Oxford: Blackwell.

Spevack, M. (1968–80) *A Complete and Systematic Concordance to the Works of Shakespeare* (9 vols). Hildesheim, Germany: Georg Ohms.

Spielberg, S. (2005) *War of the Worlds.* Paramount Pictures/DreamWorks SKG/Amblin Entertainment/Cruise/Wagner Productions.

Spufford, F. (2002) *The Child that Books Built.* London: Faber.

Starcke, B. (2006) 'The phraseology of Jane Austen's *Persuasion*: phraseological units as carriers of meaning', *ICAME Journal* 30: 87–104.

Starkey, Marion (1949) *The Devil in Massachusetts: A Modern Enquiry into the Salem Witch Trials.* New York: Anchor Books.

Stein, D. (2003) 'Pronominal usage in Shakespeare: between sociolinguistics and conversational analysis', in I. Taavitsainen and A. H. Jucker (eds) *Diachronic Perspectives on Address Term Systems.* Amsterdam: John Benjamins, pp. 251–307.

Stein, K. (1996) *Private Poets, Worldly Acts: Public and Private History in Contemporary American Poetry.* Athens: Ohio University Press.

Stephens, J. (1992) *Language and Ideology in Children's Fiction.* Harlow: Longman.

Stevens, W. (1957) 'Adagia', in M. J. Bates (ed.) *Opus Posthumous: Poems, Plays, Prose.* New York: Vintage Books.

Stevenson, R. L. (1994) *Treasure Island.* Harmondsworth: Puffin [original 1883].

Stockwell, P. (2002) *Cognitive Poetics: An Introduction.* London: Routledge.

Stockwell, P. (2003) 'Schema poetics and speculative cosmology', *Language and Literature* 12(3): 252–71.

Stoll, R. (1989) *Die Nicht-Pronominale Anrede bei Shakespeare.* Frankfurt: Peter Lang.

Stubbs, M. (2005) 'Conrad in the computer: examples of quantitative stylistic methods', *Language and Literature* 14(1): 5–24.

Styles, M. and Arizpe, E. (2001) 'A Gorilla with "Grandpa's eyes". How children interpret visual texts – a case study of Arthur Browne's "Zoo"', *Children's Literature in Education* 32(4): 26–81.

Swales, M. (2000) 'Introduction', in W. Chernaik, M. Swales and R. Vilain (eds) *The Art of Detective Fiction.* New York: St Martin's Press, pp. xi–xv.

Taavitsainen, I. and Jucker, A. H. (eds) (2003) *Diachronic Perspectives on Address Term Systems.* Berlin: John Benjamins.

Tabata, T. (2002) 'Investigating stylistic variation in Dickens through correspondence analysis of word-class distribution', in T. Saito, J. Nakamura, S. Yamazaki (eds) *English Corpus Linguistics in Japan.* Amsterdam: Rodopi, pp. 165–82.

Tan, E. S.-H. (1994) 'Film-induced affect as a witness emotion', *Poetics* 23: 7–32.

Tapia, E. (2006) 'Beyond a comparison of two distinct things; or, what students of literature gain from a cognitive linguistics approach to metaphor', *College Literature* 33(2): 135–53.

Thomas, T. (1587) *Dictionarium Linguae Latinae et Anglicanae.* Canterbury: R. Boyle.

Tiffany, D. (2001) 'Lyric substance: on riddles, materialism, and poetic obscurity', *Critical Inquiry* 29: 72–98.

Tinker, J. (2003) 'Vagrant sympathies: from stylistic analysis to a pedagogy of style', *Style* 37(1): 86–100.

Tithecott, R. (1997) *Of Men and Monsters: Jeffrey Dahmer and the Construction of the Serial Killer.* Madison: University of Wisconsin Press.

Tognini-Bonelli, E. (2001) *Corpus Linguistics at Work.* Amsterdam: Benjamins.

Toner, P. (2000) *If I Could Turn and Meet Myself: The Life of Alden Nowlan.* Fredericton: Goose Lane.

Toolan, M. (1985) 'Syntactical styles as a means of characterization in narrative', *Style* 19: 78–93.

Toolan, M. (1988) *Narrative: A Critical Linguistic Introduction.* London: Routledge.

Toolan, M. (2000) ' "What makes you think you exist?" A speech more schematic and its application to Harold Pinter's *The Birthday Party*', *Journal of Pragmatics* 32: 171–201.

Toolan, M. (2001) *Narrative, A Critical Linguistic Introduction.* London: Routledge.

Townsend, J. R. (1990) *Written for Children.* London: Bodley Head.

Townsend, S. (2003) *The Secret Diary of Adrian Mole, aged 13 & 3/4.* New York: Harper Tempest [original 1982].

Turner, M. (1987) *Death is the Mother of Beauty.* Chicago: University of Chicago Press.

Turner, M. (1991) *Reading Minds.* Princeton: Princeton University Press.

Turner, M. (1996) *The Literary Mind.* New York: Oxford University Press.

Turner, M. (2002) 'The cognitive study of art, language, and literature', *Poetics Today* 23: 9–20.

Turney, P. D. (2002) 'Thumbs up or thumbs down? Semantic orientation applied to unsupervised classification of reviews', *Proceedings 40th Annual Meeting of the ACL (2002).* Philadelphia: University of Pennsylvania, pp. 417–24.

Ungerer, F. and Schmid, H. J. (1996) *An Introduction to Cognitive Linguistics.* Harlow: Longman.

Unsworth, L. (ed.) (2000) *Researching Language in Schools and Functional Linguistic Perspectives.* London: Cassell.

Valente, J. (1997) 'Rehearsing the witch trials: gender injustice in *The Crucible*', *New Formations* 32: 120–34.

van Dijk, T. A. (1976) 'Philosophy of action and theory of narrative', *Poetics* 5: 287–338.

van Dijk, T. A. (1987) *Communicating Racism: Ethnic Prejudice in Thought and Talk*. Newbury Park, CA: Sage.

van Dijk, T. A. (1988) 'Social cognition, social power and social discourse', *Text* 8(1–2): 129–57.

van Peer, W. and Pander Maat, H. (1996) 'Perspectivation and sympathy: effects of narrative point of view', in R. J. Kreuz and M. S. MacNealy (eds) *Empirical Approaches to Literature and Aesthetics*. Norwood, NJ: Ablex, pp. 143–54.

Varela, F., Thompson, E. and Rosch, E. (1991) *The Embodied Mind: Cognitive Science and Human Experience*. Cambridge, MA: MIT Press.

Vendler, H. (1980) *Part of Nature, Part of Us: Modern American Poets*, Cambridge, MA: Harvard University Press.

Verdonk, P. (2002) *Stylistics*. Oxford: Oxford University Press.

Vigotsky, L. (1986) *Thought and Language* (trans. A. Kozulin). Cambridge, MA: MIT Press.

Vološinov, V. N. (1986) *Marxism and the Philosophy of Language* (trans. L. Matejka and I. R. Titunik). Cambridge, MA: Harvard University Press.

Wales, K. (1983) '*Thou* and *you* in Early Modern English: Brown and Gilman re-appraised', *Studia Linguistica* 37: 107–25.

Wales, K. (1987) 'An aspect of Shakespeare's dynamic language: a note on the interpretation of *King Lear* III.VII.113: "He childed as I father'd!"', in V. Salmon and E. Burness (eds) *A Reader in the Language of Shakespearean Drama*. Berlin: John Benjamins, pp. 181–90.

Walker, F. (2000) *Lucy Talk*. London: Hodder and Stoughton.

Walker, J. (1999) 'Piecing together and tearing apart: finding the story in *after-noon*', *Proceedings of the Tenth ACM Conference on Hypertext and Hypermedia*, 21–5 February 1999. Darmstadt: ACM Press, pp. 111–17.

Wallace, H. M. (2000) 'Desire and the female protagonist: a critique of feminist narrative theory', *Style* 34(2): 176–87.

Walsh, C. (2001) *Gender and Discourse: Language and Power in Politics, the Church and Other Organisations*. Harlow: Longman.

Walsh, J. P. (1975) 'Seeing green', in E. Blishen (ed.) *The Thorny Paradise*. Harmondsworth: Kestrel Books, pp. 58–61.

Ward, J. (1984) 'Check out your sexism', *Women and Language* 7: 41–3.

Warhol, R. (2002) 'Queering the marriage plot: how serial form works in Maupin's *Tales of the City*', in B. Richardson (ed.) *Narrative Dynamics: Essays on Time, Plot, Closure and Frames*. Columbus: Ohio State University Press, pp. 229–48.

Warhol, R. (2003) *Having a Good Cry: Effeminate Feelings and Pop-Culture Forms*. Columbus: Ohio State University Press.

Watts, R. (1979) '*The Crucible*: Mr. Miller looks at witch-hunting', *New York Post* 23 January 1953 [reprinted in *Critical Essays on Arthur Miller* (ed. J. Martine), Boston: G. K. Hall, pp. 7–74].

Watts, R. J. (2003) *Politeness*. Cambridge: Cambridge University Press.

Waugh, D. (2002) *The New You Survival Kit*. London: HarperCollins.

Waugh, E. (1996) *Vile Bodies*. Harmondsworth: Penguin [original 1930].

Waugh, P. (1984) *Metafiction: The Theory and Practice of Self-Conscious Fiction*. London: Methuen.

Weber, J. J. (1992) *Critical Analysis of Fiction*. Amsterdam: Rodopi.

Weil, H. and Weil, J. (eds) (1997) *The First Part of King Henry IV* (The New Cambridge Shakespeare). Cambridge: Cambridge University Press.

Welch, D. (2003) 'The curiously irresistible literary debut of Mark Haddon'. URL: www.powells.com/authors/haddon.html

Welland, D. (1979) *Arthur Miller: A Study of His Plays*. London: Methuen.

Werth, P. (1997) 'Remote worlds: the conceptual representation of linguistic *would*', in J. Nuyts and E. Pedersen (eds) *Language and Conceptualization*. Cambridge: Cambridge University Press, pp. 84–115.

Werth, P. (1999) *Text Worlds: Representing Conceptual Space in Discourse*. London: Longman.

Wertsch, J. V. (1991) *Voices of the Mind: A Sociocultural Approach to Mediated Action*. Cambridge, MA: Harvard University Press.

Weston, A. (1996) 'Picking holes: cloze procedures in prose', in R. Carter and J. McRae (eds) *Language, Literature and the Learner: Creative Classroom Practice*. Longman: London.

Whelehan, I. (2000) *Overloaded. Popular Culture and the Future of Feminism*. London: Women's Press.

Whelehan, I. (2004) 'Sex and the single girl: Helen Fielding, Erica Jong and Helen Gurley Brown', in E. Parker (ed.) *Contemporary British Women Writers*. Cambridge: D. S. Brewer, pp. 28–40.

Whelehan, I. (2005) *The Feminist Bestseller*. Basingstoke: Palgrave.

Whipple, M. (2003) '*The Curious Incident of the Dog in the Night-Time*'. URL: www.mostlyfiction.com/contemp/haddon.htm

Whitehead, A. N. (1978) *Process and Reality*. New York: Free Press.

Wilkie, C. (1999) 'Relating texts: intertextuality', in P. Hunt (ed.) *Understanding Children's Literature*. London: Routledge, pp. 130–7.

Wilson, T. (2002) *Strangers to Ourselves: Discovering the Adaptive Unconscious*. Cambridge, MA: Harvard University Press.

Winkler, D. (dir.) (1988) *Al Purdy: A Sensitive Man*. Video recording. Montreal: National Film Board of Canada.

Winnett, S. (1990) 'Coming unstrung: women, men, narrative and principles of pleasure', *PMLA* 105(3): 505–18.

Winton, W. M. (1990) 'Language and emotion', in H. Giles and W. P. Robinson (eds) *Handbook of Language and Social Psychology*. Chichester: John Wiley.

Wittgenstein, L. (1958) *Philosophical Investigations*. Oxford: Blackwell.

Wolfe, T. (2004) *I Am Charlotte Simmons*. London: Vintage.

Woolf, V. (1977) *To the Lighthouse*. London: Grafton Books [original 1927].

Xiao, Z. and McEnery, A. (2005) 'Two approaches to genre analysis: three genres in modern American English', *Journal of English Linguistics* 33(1): 62–82.

Zarillo, J. and Cox, C. (1992) 'Efferent and aesthetic teaching', in J. Many and C. Cox (eds) *Reader Stance and Literary Understanding*. Norwood, NJ: Ablex, pp. 235–49.

Zillmann, D. (1994) 'Mechanisms of emotional involvement with drama', *Poetics* 23: 33–51.

Zunshine, L. (2003) 'Theory of mind and experimental representations of fictional consciousness', *Narrative* 11(3): 270–91.

Zunshine, L. (2006) *Why We Read Fiction: Theory of Mind and the Novel.* Columbus: Ohio State University Press.

Zyngier, S. and Shepherd, T. M. G. (2003) 'What is literature, really? A corpus-driven study of students' statements', *Style* 37(1): 14–26.

Index

'A Boy Named Sue' 185–6
accretion 108
Acorn, Milton 156–7, 159–64
addressivity 8, 24, 48–51, 123–4, 140, 160–5, 179, 199, 232–43
affect 17–18, 60–5, 79, 108–9, 114, 152–3, 246
afternoon, a story 43–55
agency 37–8, 87–90, 100–4, 114, 119, 142–3, 173, 197, 206
allegory 156, 226–7
ambiguity 53–4, 133–43, 168, 172, 178, 185, 192, or 218
anaphora 13–14, 141
animism 26
annotation 244–5, 248–51
anthropological stylistics 157
appraisal 150–1, 207–8, 247
assertion 216–17
attribution theory 81–92
'Awake' 187–91

banter 209–20
Bennett, Alan 253–4
blending theory 221–2, 228–31
Bridget Jones's Diary 72–8, 93, 105
British National Corpus 21, 250–4
Burney, Frances 60–7

Camilla 60–7
Can You Keep a Secret? 72–80
cappuccino fiction 68–80
Cash, Johnny 185–7
character 7–18, 24–31, 36, 47–9, 51–5, 57–67, 70–80, 81–92, 100–4, 109, 113–17, 121–6, 159–67, 209–20, 223–6, 242–3, 248–55
children's literature 106–17
coda 199–200, 203
Coe, Jonathan 119–20
cognitive poetics 68–80, 81–92, 106–17, 118–30, 133–43, 144–55, 156–67, 168–79, 221–31
communicative action 87–8
complicating action 199–203, 206–8
conceptual metaphor 36–42, 146–7, 152–5, 156–67, 230–1, 241–3

consciousness 7–18, 32–42, 56–67, 81–92, 118–30, 156–67, 168–79, 242
construal 222
corpus stylistics 19–31, 180, 202, 232–43, 244–56
crime fiction 32–42, 115
critical stylistics 93, 95, 105
crossover fiction 106–17
culture 7, 17, 35–6, 69–70, 77, 85, 89–90, 94–5, 99, 106, 133–4, 137, 143, 146, 153, 156–60, 166–7, 168, 196, 201
cummings, e.e. 144–55
cue reason words 85

deictic shift theory 118, 123–30
deixis 12–13, 118–30, 133, 138–9, 164–9, 176
deviation 20–1, 108, 122, 145, 147–53, 184–6, 235, 243, 246
dialogism 7–18
dialogue 7–18, 21–6, 30–1, 49, 52, 56–67, 122, 195–208, 213–17
Dickens, Charles 19–31, 81–92, 98
discourse analysis 195–208, 221, 233
discourse world 125, 128–9, 133–43, 158–67

Edward-Jones, Imogen 72–3
ellipsis 62–3, 149
embeddedness 10, 12, 15, 33, 52, 59, 68, 106, 125, 140, 152, 170–9, 237
embodiment 134, 147, 152–4, 163, 165, 169, 170–9, 252
empathy 7, 17–18, 56–67, 71, 109, 114, 123–4
enactors 133, 138–43
evaluation 13, 21, 41, 48–9, 57–8, 74, 79, 82, 98–102, 114, 126, 128, 199–207
events 33–4, 44–7, 50–1, 56, 84, 89, 91, 98, 106–7, 113–14, 119–21, 124–9, 137–8, 141, 170, 174, 196–205, 221, 223–7, 230, 247, 255

face 209–20
feminism 35, 68–80, 93–105
Fielding, Helen 72, 77, 93–105
figurative language 32–42, 48–9, 112, 150, 168–79, 223

film 59–60, 69, 95, 97–8, 110, 119, 125, 137, 227, 229
flashback 98, 125, 141–3, 158
focalisation 7–18, 29–31, 56–67, 95, 118–30, 139–43
free indirect discourse 56–67
frequency 19, 22–31, 51, 180, 189, 236–9, 247, 249–52
From Hell 122
function-advancers 138–9, 158–67

Game Over 72–3
gender 75–6, 93–105, 196, 201, 236, 247, 248, 256
genre 21, 33–5, 44, 45, 61, 68–80, 94, 100–4, 109–10, 113, 119, 169, 172, 176, 179, 183–4, 186, 195, 196, 198, 200–8, 236, 246, 248, 255
goal 71–2, 91, 93, 99–103, 154, 164, 206
graphology 52, 112, 115, 122, 146, 149–50
Great Expectations 19–31
Group of Seven 165–6

Haddon, Mark 106–17
Harry Potter 108
Heaney, Seamus 126–9
Henry IV, part I 209–20
hermeneutics 43, 47, 50, 54
His Dark Materials 108
Howe, Susan 177–9
hyperfiction 43–55

I Am Charlotte Simmons 60–7
identification 57–64, 69, 97, 106
ideology 32, 34, 68, 74–5, 79, 93, 95–8, 103, 120, 153, 172, 183, 226
image schema 146–7, 154
implicature 58, 212, 232
impoliteness 209–20
intermentality 9, 81–92
intersubjectivity 15–18, 87, 134, 144, 156, 181, 197
intertextuality 106–10, 112, 238–41
intratextuality 186, 233, 235, 238–43
intuition 21, 31, 38, 147, 170, 171, 245, 249, 255
irony 16, 36, 41–2, 49, 50, 57–9, 68–9, 80, 90, 103, 213, 223

Joyce, Michael 43–54

Keywords 22, 249–56
Kinsella, Sophie 72–80

landscape 45–55, 139, 143, 156–67, 184
language teaching 180–92

lexis 3, 14, 20–5, 29–31, 32, 35, 42, 43, 62, 69, 95, 121, 126, 146, 151–2, 173, 180, 191, 239, 247, 248–9, 251, 256
linearity 44, 49, 52, 54–5, 93–4, 96–9, 109, 154
literariness 56, 108, 110, 116–17, 140, 180, 182, 186, 192, 228
Little Dorrit 25, 28, 81–92
local textual functions 20–31
logic 46–7, 50
Lucy Talk 72–80
lyric 138, 166, 168–79, 185

megametaphor 156–67
metafiction 45, 110, 112, 116
metaphor 32–42, 46, 48, 54, 88, 96, 98, 104, 112, 115, 120, 123–4, 146–7, 149–55, 156–7, 171, 188, 190, 232, 234, 238–43, 249–52
Miller, Arthur 221–31
mind-style 32–42
modal world 46, 139–43
modality 20, 38, 46, 62, 110, 118, 120, 122, 139–43
modernism 7–18, 168, 172
Monk's Hood 125–6
monologue 12, 57–8, 62, 195
Moore, Alan 122
Morrison, Jim 187–91
'Mossbawn' 127
Mrs Dalloway 10
My Canapé Hell 72–80

narrative 7–18, 43–55, 68–80, 93–105, 195–208
narratology 8–10, 47, 57, 81, 93–105, 195–208
narrator 7–8, 15–16, 22, 24, 31, 32, 43, 48–54, 57–66, 81–4, 87–92, 110–14, 119–26, 129, 185, 197–208, 252–3
negation 20, 48, 101, 126, 140–1, 153–5
New York poets 134
node 44–55
Nowlan, Alden 156–67

O'Hara, Frank 133–43
obscurity 168, 171–4, 177–9
omniscience 8, 16, 32, 36, 50–1, 66, 121
ontology 43–55, 57, 139, 146, 173
oral narrative 195–208

parable 221–31
parallelism 15–16, 29, 59, 145, 150–3, 168, 172, 234
Parks, Adele 72–80
participant 9, 17, 56, 120, 136–43, 158–67, 195, 199

Peters, Ellis 125–6
plot 28–31, 81–3, 93, 95–104, 112–13, 158, 217–19, 244, 253
poetic persona 138–42, 159–67, 169
point of view 21, 31, 52, 60, 62, 69, 82, 98, 111, 113–14, 118–30, 146, 186, 234
possible worlds theory 43–55
postmodernism 34, 44–6, 69, 87, 95, 105, 172, 178
pragmastylistics 209–20
pragmatics 12, 21, 49, 56, 58, 146, 209–20, 221–2, 233, 248
presupposition 10, 16–17, 57, 170, 216
Project Gutenberg 19, 22
pronouns 12, 24, 26–7, 48–9, 51, 58–9, 93, 111, 123, 129, 138, 142, 149, 153, 163, 232–41, 243
prosody 21, 174–7
Pullman, Philip 108–9
Purdy, Al 156–67
Pynchon, Thomas 81–82

reality 16–18, 33, 36, 43, 46, 51, 54, 57, 145, 176, 197, 227, 240
recount 98, 195–208
reflector 121, 126
rhetoric 90, 144–55, 182, 187, 192, 200, 221–31, 244, 247–8
Rowling, J.K. 108

sarcasm 212–13
schema theory 33, 35, 42, 68–80, 99, 102, 106–17, 121, 147, 172
scripts 86, 107
semantics 12, 14, 21, 58, 128, 142, 146, 149–52, 169, 173, 177, 180, 186–90, 196, 237, 243, 247–54
Shakespeare, William 209–20, 232–43, 249–52
simile 36, 39, 112
social cognition 70–4
social constructivism 35
sociolinguistics 95–6, 144, 195, 198

speech 7–18, 21–6, 30–1, 49, 52, 56–67, 84, 89, 122–3, 140, 146, 195–208, 213–17, 218–19, 232–43, 248, 253–6
subjectivity 8, 10, 13–18, 27, 31, 57, 87, 90, 134, 141, 144, 147, 156, 168–79, 181, 197, 242
sympathy 38, 59–65, 71, 76, 106
syntax 11–12, 95–6, 103, 111, 113, 119, 146, 149–52, 172, 179, 183, 247, 250

Talking with Serial Killers 32–42
teleological action 85, 96, 98
text world theory 46, 81, 113, 124–9, 133–43, 156–67
The Crucible 221–31
The Crying of Lot 49 81–92
The Curious Incident of the Dog in the Night-Time 106–17
'The Day Lady Died' 133–43
The Lady in the Van 253
The Reign of King Edward III 232–43
The Rotters' Club 119–21
thought 7–18, 21, 29–31, 32–42, 56–67, 81–92, 121–2, 126, 140–3, 146, 163, 248
thought-action continuum 81, 85
To the Lighthouse 7–18, 21
translation 107, 175–7, 187
Trouble 206–8
Tulips & Chimneys 147–9

vernacular 198
vocabulary 113, 180–92, 238
voice 7, 35, 57–67, 86, 88, 93, 95–6, 122, 139, 154, 169, 173, 176

Walker, Fiona 72–80
'White Foolscap' 177–9
Wolfe, Tom 60–1
Woolf, Virginia 7–18, 21
Wordsmith 19, 22, 25, 249, 256
world switch 140–3, 158
world-builders 55, 138
worlds 20, 43–55, 82, 118, 123, 126, 133–43, 156–67